CAN WE TRUST CHINA?

Pascal
Coppens

CAN WE TRUST CHINA?

A Different View on a Country in Transition

CAN WE TRUST CHINA?
A Different View on a Country in Transition
by Pascal Coppens
1. POL011000 2. POL011010 3. POL054000
ISBN: 979-8-88636-005-9 (paperback)
979-8-88636-006-6 (ebook)

Cover design and graphic design by Inge Van Damme
Drawings: Stefaan van Biesen
Artistic assistance drawings: Annemie Mestdagh
Drawings based on pictures by Alex Plavevski (pg 61), Richard Ellis (pg 149), Diego Azubel (pg. 179), Martin Lindsey (pg. 215), Chi Nguyen Thi Van (pg. 249) , Stefaan Van Biesen (pg. 311)
Original Publication (Dutch): *Kunnen we China vertrouwen? Een andere blik op een land in transitie* (Pelckmans/Van Duuren Feb 2022)

Printed in the United States of America

Authority Publishing
11230 Gold Express Dr. #310-413
Gold River, CA 95670
800-877-1097
www.AuthorityPublishing.com

You don't need to agree with everything in this book to still find it very interesting. Pascal Coppens manages to put himself in the minds of the Chinese, both the man on the street and the government official. In recent years, as a result of the coronavirus crisis, China has become more introverted (journalists can no longer enter the country) and that's why I consider this book a valuable resource. Only by trying to understand each other do we get closer to each other. As a reader, you ultimately have to decide for yourself whether we can actually trust China, but Pascal already provides us with some useful tools. It is up to the reader to develop a more critical view of what we are being presented with from various different directions.

Tom Van de Weghe
Journalist and former China correspondent for VRT (the Flemish public broadcast), author of *Beestig China* (Beastly China)

Whether China is a friend or enemy, or something in between, the Chinese think differently. See the world differently. It is interesting to understand this, to broaden our own thinking. This is a very informative book. China is a real mystery to most of us. With its fascinating history and current economic success. But the country is also frightening, with its political model and its unpredictable behavior on the global stage. With his years spent living in the country and his razor-sharp analysis, Pascal Coppens is the best person to guide us through China's logic. An absolute must-read to gain a better understanding of the world today.

Thierry Geerts
Director of Google Belgium, author of *Digitalis* and *Homo Digitalis*

Pascal Coppens is a regular teacher of our General Management Program in Fontainebleau. During this program we provide senior executives from all over the world with insights into, among other things, the complex geo-eco-political environment we are living and working in. These insights are then translated into the business strategies of companies like L'Oréal, Brystol Myers Squibb, LVMH, and Tata Steel. Drawing on his twenty-year experience in China and his roots in Ghent, Pascal shares his story, which is essentially based on building mutual trust between China and the rest of the world, a story of "circles" that resonates both with our participants from China and executives from the Western world. This new book is therefore a wonderful reflection of his many years of experience in China, the very thorough research that followed, and the interactions during his keynotes.

Wim Wuyts
Program Director of CEDEP (Fontainebleau) and CEO WTS Global (Rotterdam)

The perception of "the Yellow Peril" is being fueled in the West. Like it or not, China has once again become a global power, and will continue to become more assertive on the global stage. This book is a journey through eight universal circles of trust. A must-read for any policymakers needing to develop a China strategy to achieve a win-win. This book can act as a counterbalance to the increasing polarization.

Carl Decaluwé
Governor of West Flanders

Based on his many years of experience with and in China, Pascal Coppens gives us a clear picture of what drives this superpower. For anyone willing to understand both the Western and the Chinese side of the story. An open mind is essential!

Hans Borghouts
Former Senior Partner at PwC

Contents

Chapter 2. Family and friends

Chapter 3. Company and team

Chapter 4. Network and tribes

Chapter 5. System and the CPC

Chapter 6. Nation and people

In loving memory of my father,
Claude Coppens

My biggest thanks go to my wife and daughter for putting up with my reclusive author's lifestyle. You have always been my rock.

Thank you also to all the close friends who have helped me produce this book.

Thank you, Temperance Shen (Meng), for discussing and adding to the new sections of my book every week for a year. You were often my anchor in these very polarizing times. Thank you, Luc de Cleir, for also editing my second book as I was writing chapter by chapter. The trust you place in me as an author has been a constant source of motivation. Thank you so much to Stefaan van Biesen for creating a wonderful illustration for each chapter. I wish I had your talent for drawing. Thanks also to your wife, Annemie Mestdagh, for her artistic help. Thank you to Thomas De Boever for always being prepared to reflect my words in beautiful images.

A huge thank you to Delphine Desmedt for your diligence, efficiency, and flexibility that gave me the space and tranquility to write this book. We make a fantastic team!

Thank you to Heather Sills for translating the book from Dutch to English. You truly understood my mind and I could not have wished for a better translation. Thanks to my best childhood friend Henri De Cannière for thoroughly proofreading Heather's translations.

I would especially like to thank my very good friend David G. Brooks once again for the diligent and meticulous manner of proofreading my second book. The book improved substantially in both content and language thanks to your work.

Thanks to Frank Willems, Rob de Wijk and Tom Van de Weghe for your extremely valuable insights. I would also like to thank Katelijn Verstraete, Fred Sengers, Albert-Jan Shi, and Nancy Rademaker for their crucial feedback.

Thanks to Authority Publishing. In particular I would like to thank Stephanie Chandler and Chela Hardy. I would also like to thank Inge Van Damme for once again creating a wonderful book design.

Thank you to everyone who has provided me with a platform and voice to make this book a success. Thanks in particular to Dimitri Stuer for making that voice more powerful. Finally, I would like to thank everyone from the nexxworks team. In particular Peter Hinssen, Steven Van Belleghem, Rik Vera, Julie Vens-De Vos, Laurence Van Elegem, and Matthias De Clercq. You are my favorite eccentric people.

感

huò

Meaning: **confused, puzzled, bewildered, or have lost direction.** This character is built up of one symbol for **perhaps, maybe, probably** and one for **heart**. Something is going on in your heart (or mind), but you're not exactly sure what. You seek clarity. Is China trustworthy or not?

Foreword

On the last day of 2019, I made a New Year's resolution to write another book in 2020. The working title was *China's New Normal 2.0*, which would be a follow-up to my first book, *China's New Normal*, published seven months earlier. I would write about how China might take the next step in its innovation leadership. I would describe how, in this fourth industrial revolution, China intended to make the same types of investments as the United States (US) had done in the past. In the previous two industrial revolutions since the mid-nineteenth century, the US took the lead globally by developing the most advanced infrastructure for transport, telecommunications, internet, energy, and financial and knowledge institutions. This turned the US into the world's strongest magnet, attracting talent, investors, policymakers, and entrepreneurs. It is China's master plan to follow that same investment plan by building the most connected, advanced, reliable, and smart infrastructure in the world today. With this strategy, China will help realize the real relaunch of what has been called the Asian Century. And as the protagonist of this new story, China will become the de facto magnet for the emerging world of knowledge and entrepreneurship beyond the West, from Indonesia to Mexico. However, for that to happen, China needs the Western intellectual elite to be involved. Can it win them over? This may be difficult, because this is linked to the factor of trust, and whether people can trust a country like China.

Perhaps our Western pride will blind us from taking part in this emerging opportunity in the best way we can. After years spent trying to decouple from China and imposing protectionist measures, it is highly unlikely we'll have a well-thought-out plan for this new reality. A new world is coming, where 200 million Western Europeans and 330 million US inhabitants will no longer be able to dominate the other seven billion people on this planet, for many of whom China's success over the past four decades represents an extremely attractive alternative. It will be a rude awakening for the West when we suddenly realize that it is us—and not the rest of the world or China—that has to change. That blind spot exists today because in the West we are too focused on the ruler of the superpower that is China—Xi Jinping and his Communist Party—and are not paying nearly enough attention to the real driving force of the country—1.4 billion patriotic citizens, around 800 million hopeful employees, eighty million passionate entrepreneurs, and more than eight million hard-working civil servants.[1] I strongly believe that the greatest challenge facing the West should not be seen as the ideology of China's Communist Party, but rather the emerging economic competition within a new world order led by a strongly meritocratic, efficient, and successful system of governance in China. At the time, I thought *China's New Normal 2.0* would outline an inspiring story of how we in the West can learn from the very simple, pragmatic steps China is taking to maintain its momentum and share knowledge with the world, and how we in the West can best prepare for this new world order by investing in the future, instead of clinging to our past.

A DIFFERENT BOOK

During the first lockdown in Belgium in the spring of 2020, I suddenly had plenty of time to write my new book, *China's New Normal 2.0*. All my speaking engagements had been put on hold, innovation tours to China became impossible, and many of my clients had not yet made the switch to online webinars. I threw myself into my writing, but it was extremely difficult to make progress. I thought the lockdown had given me writer's block, but the problem lay elsewhere. I continued to do my daily blog or vlog post about China. It would normally take me an hour a day to put the post online and respond to questions and comments. But during the lockdown it suddenly required four to five hours each day. Now that everyone was online, I received a lot more responses. The biggest difference from 2019, however, was that the comments were now much more loaded and destructive. Regardless of whether I was talking about China's 5G, new sustainability policies, or self-driving cars, it seemed people weren't really interested in China's technological evolution anymore.

In my naive ambition to open up the debate, I continued to respond to all of the incoming comments, including negative ones for around eight weeks. I thought I could learn something about the Western perspective on China, but most of all what I learned was that people were angry. Where was this anger coming from? China's own attitude and ambitions in 2020 weren't that different from 2019, were they? Was it the media now portraying China as the bad guy? Was this the start of a geopolitical cold war? Did we need a scapegoat for the misery the "China virus" was causing us? So many questions, but I had no answers. What was very clear to me after eight weeks was that fewer and fewer people were interested in another story about China's New Normal. If my goal was to further inspire companies in the West, then simply showcasing China's latest innovations, successful business models, or social progress might now completely miss the mark.

Then suddenly I thought it might be better to write a book about China and trust, with the title "Can We Trust China?" I shared this idea with my closest friends to gauge their response. Without knowing what the others had said, each friend reacted in exactly the same way: deeply concerned, they asked me if China would ever let me back in if I gave a book that title. "You don't want to get on the wrong side of China," I was told. I found this unanimous reaction very telling. The intuitive response of my closest Western friends, who follow my China stories with an open mind, and some of whom lived in China themselves, was to warn me that we can't really trust China. This only convinced me to address the subject of trust head-on. I would risk my own future as a China expert to make a point; how exciting!

My point is that you can trust China if you have a better understanding of its context. The West needs a much better understanding of China in order to trust China, and China certainly needs better communication if it wants to be trusted by the West. That's what this book is about. I'm not worried that the Chinese won't be able to read beyond the title, because in their world, context is more important than the words. My aim with this new book is therefore not to give a conclusive answer, but to provide more context. I am truly convinced that we can only learn from those we trust. So, if we want to learn from China and the Chinese people, we must first learn to trust them. But do we need to learn from China? As I wrote in my book *China's New Normal*, companies, academics, and policy makers can no longer afford not to have China on their radar, as China is slowly but surely setting the standard for innovation. But also simply because, by 2030, China will likely become the largest economic and political power in the world and represent the single greatest challenge and opportunity for the West. We are frequently warned about this new world order, yet people too often think we will defeat the Chinese dragon by distrusting it. This doesn't seem logical to me. Why not take a look under the hood and really see how that Chinese engine keeps running at full speed?

How is it that, on January 1, 2021, China was …?
- the only major economy with a positive growth in gross domestic income (GDP): 2.3 percent?
- the most connected country in the world with 5G in more than 300 cities?
- free of extreme poverty—850 million fewer extreme poor people than in 1980?
- the largest producer of (non-mRNA) coronavirus vaccines in the world, with twice as many in phase 3 testing than in America?
- the country with the biggest middle class (almost 500 million people) in the world?
- on course to become the biggest economy (in GDP) in the world by 2030?

Did these achievements happen because the Chinese government is able to push all Chinese people in the same direction? Does China's five-thousand-year-old civilization have something to do with it? Is their collective society simply more decisive? Does China have the wealthy West to thank for this? Maybe the Chinese just don't play by the rules? Is it a bubble that's about to burst?

All these questions almost always imply bias, an opinion that would be either positive or negative, but rarely neutral. Just the word "China" often evokes an emotional reaction and predetermined image. I hope this book will stir up other emotions and fresh images. In this book, my aim is to present my version of a trusted China through a double lens—a Western and a Chinese one. Similar to sunglasses, I will try to apply a Polaroid filter to our Western lens so we are better protected against the currently prevalent overdose of negative exposure about the China of today, and to give more visibility and clarity about the China of tomorrow.

Introduction

WUHAN

New Year's Eve – I had, just like anybody else, no idea the world was about to change forever. On December 31, 2019, China reported to the World Health Organization (WHO) the outbreak of a new virus that had been identified in twenty-seven patients; an outbreak that supposedly took place in a market in a place called Wuhan—despite its eleven million people, it was a city that few of us had ever heard of. The name Wuhan is special to me because it was the last stop on my first trip to China in 1990, when the city had only three million inhabitants. Wuhan was where the river boats would end their Yangzi (or Yangtse) River cruises. Heading upstream, the five-day boat trip leads toward the Himalayas to Chongqing, the least known, yet most-populated agglomeration in the world with its current thirty-one million inhabitants. The ferry cruised through the breathtaking three-gorge mountain flanks where the world's most powerful, expensive, and controversial dam was to be opened in 2012. Beyond China, this so-called prestige project by the Chinese government was seen as a disaster for nature, farmers, and villages, putting them at risk of landslides and earthquakes. For the Chinese government, the dam was crucial, not only to produce clean electricity for millions of Chinese, but mainly to protect the downstream city of Wuhan from the floods that ravage China every year. China tends to tackle big problems with big infrastructure solutions.

I took the boat in the other direction, a forty-eight-hour journey downstream to Shanghai. As this was the end of my very long journey across China, I was running out of cash, so I paid 20 CNY ($4) for a bed in a fourth-class cabin with sixteen bunk beds. Memories of Wuhan have always stayed with me, because on that boat ride I met a couple from Wuhan who kept me entertained for two days with the most fantastic stories about their lives, plans, and dreams. During that trip I understood for the very first time how important friendship, trust, and progress are for the Chinese. Over two days, they gave me a crash course in Chinese culture. After traveling across China for two whole months, I had more questions than answers. Why don't you see any fat Chinese people? Why do men often walk hand in hand? Why can't I take photos of bridges? My new friends from Wuhan immediately gave me the answers. In order: "The Chinese still largely live in poverty, Chinese masculinity is less defined than in the West, and bridges are a state secret." They also took the time to provide commentary and context to my travel experience.

It was like reliving my entire trip, but this time with subtitles. Despite studying Chinese at university for two years and being able to rattle off facts about China's five-thousand-year history, I really hadn't understood China at all. Layer by layer, like an onion, I got closer to the core and essence of the real China. In less than forty-eight hours, with their openness and honesty, they had completely won my trust—like true friends do. When we were just a few hours from Shanghai, the man asked me a completely unexpected yet extremely sincere and direct question. He asked me if I wanted to marry his wife. They were deadly serious and argued this proposal rationally: "It was a win-win; as a poor Belgian student I would get a lot of money, and my knowledge of China and Chinese would greatly improve." She would get a Belgian passport and, after an eventual divorce from me, the reunited couple could have several children, all of whom would study abroad. That was their biggest wish. I have to admit, I considered it for a moment, but then I suddenly thought, how would I explain this to my mother? I politely declined their offer and parted on good terms with my new friends from Wuhan.

LOCKDOWN

Today, the name Wuhan has taken on a completely different meaning for the whole world. Since early 2020, the coronavirus has dominated our lives. As a China expert with a front-row seat, I looked on in surprise at how the world watched China tackle this new SARS-type virus as if through a dystopian window on the future. Every day there was another story in the news about how the Chinese government forcefully shut down the market in Wuhan on January 1, shut down Wuhan itself with its eleven million inhabitants (equal to the Belgian population), and shortly afterwards put the entire Hubei province of sixty million people (the size of France) into lockdown. On Valentine's Day, 2020, China closed off and imposed a semi-lockdown on all residential neighborhoods in forty-eight cities, home to around five hundred million people (equivalent to the entire EU). In China, every Chinese person fully understood how serious the crisis was. At the time, what surprised me the most was that the Western media reports focused on China's ruthless approach of lockdown and quarantine methods as outdated, ineffective, and above all inhumane. Images from Wuhan were ingrained in our minds. Images of empty streets, overcrowded hospitals, hundreds of hospital beds in a large sports hall, the military being deployed, thousands of volunteers in protective white suits, community workers spraying disinfectant, and two gigantic new hospitals being built in ten days. Through these images, reporters all over the world were giving weight to the storyline of how dystopian, autocratic, and chaotic China is. The underlying message was that this kind of authoritarian approach could, thankfully, never happen in the democratic West. Today, we realize that China's lockdowns and other measures are certainly not unique to any one regime or ideology. In retrospect, it was mainly island nations which quickly imposed strict bans on entry that were spared the worst of the pandemic. Many of China's neighboring countries that had been hit by SARS in 2004 also dealt with the new virus quickly and effectively.

The question on my mind at the time was why China's harsh, rapid actions didn't prompt the West to also act more quickly? Instead of preparing our countries for the worst scenarios, the focus seemed to be on blaming China. We all know the many allegations that were made: China had manufactured the virus, wanted to cover everything up, wasn't being transparent, and had made lots of mistakes. This finger-pointing cost us a lot of valuable time. China formally denied each accusation as fake news, but that only created more mistrust in the West. Perhaps we should not look to China's timeline but rather to our own Western timeline to draw conclusions about how quickly China reacted?

On January 11, China provided the genetic material of the coronavirus to the WHO. This enabled Moderna to finalize the mRNA-1273 sequence and start clinical trials by January 13.[2] China was largely locked down ten days later, but it was another two months before Belgium—my home country—went into lockdown, and we were very unprepared.

I fear that the mistakes many countries made in preparing for the pandemic, and the main reason we lost so much time is a direct result of our distrust of China. I think that many tend to see China's solutions as unique to that country because the political system is so different, and therefore often find them worthless and irrelevant. Worse still, when China had the impact of the coronavirus completely under control by the spring of 2020, the disinterest in learning from China's experience even turned into a systemic distrust of China and its leaders. In July 2020, Mike Pompeo, the Secretary of State under President Trump, even compared China's Communist Party to "Frankenstein", inciting Washington to use a Soviet-era Cold War slogan, "distrust and verify", as a basic strategy in the negotiations with Beijing.

THE TRUTH IS NOT BINARY

As a China expert, I watched from the front row as the debates about China in 2020 became more aggressive and polarized. "Nothing good can come from China, or China is wonderful: I or 0." This black-and-white thinking paralyzes our society. To build trust, the central theme of this book, we must bridge our differences to find common solution. Given the scale of the global problems we now face, such as the environment, healthcare, or privacy, collaboration is a must.

At the same time, today's social environment expects us to have an opinion about everything. The coronavirus crisis forced us to become experts in fields we had never even heard of: from epidemiology to constitutional rights. Despite the mass of complex and ambiguous information we absorb every day, few of us dare to answer these increasingly cryptic questions with: "we don't know." These honest words would allow us to listen, learn, and find new solutions. But we're just waking up from a world dominated by Trump and COVID-19, where stress, fear, and anxiety became the new normal, and the truth was less important than believing you're right. We were forced to believe what we heard or read most. We lack the time and energy to collect, analyze, and question facts. That's why in 2020 and 2021, we increasingly formed our opinions based on feeling. We took more of an emotionally binary position on "the truth", which sharpened the polarization in our world. A lie told often enough becomes the truth.

THE CHINESE PARADOX

Part of the answer lies hidden in how people in the West primarily think in a binary way, while the Chinese think more in terms of harmony. **Western |** thinking versus **Chinese O** thinking. By this I don't mean, as in binary code, that the West is "true" and China is therefore "false". No; Westerners simply tend to think along a fixed **LINE (I)**, while more Chinese people think within a **CIRCLE (O)**. In the West, the focus is on **|**: simplicity, ego, individual, straightforward, sincerity, specific, purposeful, dialectic, demarcation, settlement. In China, people much prefer to move within a circle **O**: contextual, sensing, holistic, collective, circumventing, defensive, controlling, timeless, rotational, respectful, faithful.

We think more in terms of **"OR",** while the Chinese think more in **"AND",** The roots of this dual perspective come from Christianity, where something is either good or bad. Later, in eighteenth-century Europe, the Enlightenment would show us the importance of science and reason. That tradition resulted in a society that thought in a more binary way. In science, something is either exact or not. Westerners therefore think more in reason, facts, and deductions, while the Chinese think more in terms of context and induction. The difference becomes really clear when we compare Western and Chinese medicine, language, business, and communication. The difference in communication, for example, makes the Chinese very bad at public relations, which only fuels the mistrust of the West. The Chinese tend to speak in circles and metaphors in order to scan the full range of options before making a decision. As a result, they can live much more comfortably in a reality that to outsiders seems contradictory. If we look at China through our Western lens, it seems to be full of paradoxes that we can't get our heads around: a "communist" party promoting extreme entrepreneurship; a "dictatorship" that lifted more than fifty percent of its population out of extreme poverty in just a few decades; 140 million Chinese people who travel abroad every year and all return to China's "unfree, repressive" regime of their own free will. This doesn't make sense to us, but it does to the nearly 1.4 billion Chinese.

When we hear loaded words about China like "unfree", "police state", "repressive", "communism", "forced labor", "concentration camps", or "dictator", we are hit by strong emotions that translate directly into hostility. To increase trust in China, we must try to let go of the emotional impressions and open our minds to a more nuanced and colorful world. This certainly doesn't mean we should let go of our values. We neither can nor want to do that. We just need to be aware that between 0 and 1 there is a whole wealth of realities. I am not writing this book to claim that 0 is better than 1 or vice versa, but to reduce the tension between the two by giving more options, more alternative visions, and more context to different topics.

A QUBIT FRAME OF MIND

To understand China, we can try to think more **AND** instead of **OR**. With its roots in Taoism and Confucianism, China's social system strives for harmony through self-sacrifice. This harmony combines the drive for individual success **AND** the need for recognition through individual contribution to the community. The tension between strictly following social norms and at the same time expressing a strong sense of individualism is precisely where China gets its energy from. While this might seem like a massive contradiction to outsiders, these two motivations are not mutually exclusive, rather each one reinforces the other. This gives China a cultural advantage over the West in that they can better deal with uncertainty and change, as we saw during the pandemic.

In 2020, every government on earth had to make tough choices, but no large country beat the virus as well as China. The choices we made definitely did not give us the result we wanted. We were forced to choose: economics or public health, privacy or tracking, mental or physical health. Western governments had to defend a position supported by data, experts, and opinion leaders. They needed wide-reaching buy-in from both the population and their supporters to make decisions that were usually extremely late, unpopular, and painful. In China, on the other hand, I saw a very different dynamic during the outbreak. Very tough measures were simultaneously imposed and explained as a necessity to keep the entire population safe: wearing masks, closing borders, imposing quarantines, large-scale testing, relying on peer pressure, getting community workers to help, using a combination of Western and Chinese medicine, converting companies into medical equipment manufacturers, deploying new 5G and AI technology to keep everything in check, getting furloughed workers to carry out home deliveries, etc. Put simply, Chinese governments, companies, and citizens quickly made lots of tough choices in order to support each other. In the West, we made choices that were more balanced, but where one choice sometimes weakened or even put the other at risk because it was seen as unfair to a particular section of society.

To build better relationships with China and the Chinese, we can try to create a different atmosphere or frame of mind by changing from the previously binary train of thought to a **qubit** mindset or **AND** thinking. By accepting all options between I and 0 as possibilities or potential truths, **q**ubit thinking is mainly questioning, in flux, volatile, complex, ambiguous, uncertain, fleeting, empathetic, diverse, inclusive. This is the mindset that most start-up founders and eccentrics like Elon Musk or Jack Ma have in common: a strong, intrinsic, long-term vision, but the path to it today may be completely different tomorrow. The possibilities are endless, and each day they question the future and their truths. Imagine our brain as a quantum computer not limited to two unique states, but a frame of mind that can store information in **q**uantum bits, or qubits, in the form of **I** and **0**. Instead of thinking more about China, we should give free rein to our minds. This will give us the space and allow us to break free from our binary thoughts about China so that we can then try to make the right connections.

CHINESE TUNNEL VISION

We sometimes hear that because of their level of social control and propaganda, the Chinese cannot be open-minded, creative, or critical. There is certainly some truth in that. The Chinese live in echo chambers as much as we do, but I wouldn't call them narrow-minded because they are also the most inquisitive people on the planet. I have always been amazed at how much the average Chinese person knows. An example: I could jump into a taxi in the city of Tianjin and the driver would be able to tell me at least five things about Belgium. Usually this would include the soccer team (the Red Devils), Brussels, beer or chocolate, good social security, and Hercules Poirot. Do you know five things about the city of Tianjin (which has more inhabitants than Paris or London)?

Along with Beijing, Shanghai, and Chongqing, Tianjin is one of the four cities that is also classed as a province in China. After the Second Opium War in 1860, Tianjin was the first treaty port for Europe in northern China. As a result of the colonial ambitions of King Leopold II, in 1902 Belgium had a concession in the city of Tianjin, where the first Sino-Belgian Bank was set up. In 1904, Belgium built the city's tram and electric street lighting, and was allowed to run them for a further fifty years. The port of Tianjin is bigger than Rotterdam, and was a co-host city for the 2008 Beijing Olympic Games, in the run-up to which it built a rail connection to Beijing, the first high-speed train in China. And yes, Belgian international soccer player Axel Witsel played for Tianjin Quanjian FC for three and a half seasons.

Is this information important to be able to understand China? Not really. But that taxi driver from Tianjin is an example of my frequent surprise at how the Chinese suffer less from tunnel vision than we do. After more than thirty years of immersion in China, I have personally come to the conclusion that China's modesty, inquisitiveness, and curiosity outweigh the lack of access to information. There is also very little useful information that really can't get around the great firewall of China. On the other hand, I fear that—because of our Western pride, ignorance, and general disinterest in the non-Western world, and despite a flood of information—we certainly don't know more about the world than the Chinese do. We are able to know more, but we rarely do. If we want to fight this, and view China from a broader, different perspective, in addition to our binary view of China, there are two other aspects that are crucial to adjust our view of China:

A TOO-STATIC VIEW OF CHINA

When we describe China, experts will often look at China's structural deficits on the basis of a snapshot, linear trends, and previous results or approaches in China. On that basis, we decide that China will not deliver on its commitments such as the EU-China or Paris Agreements; that the entire population and businesses will be increasingly controlled by the Chinese Communist Party; or that national debt, the obsession with investment, the real estate bubble, social inequality, and stagnating productivity will cause the country to implode. From a causal, linear train of thought, this is logical. The flaw in this form of argument is that it is static, while China is extremely dynamic.

China's greatest strength is its ability to self-evaluate and self-correct, a result of its circular thinking. Western cultures, led by the US, are active in a highly linear way, while countries such as China or Japan are extremely reactive.[3] The former are constantly striving for disruptive change in order to survive; and creative individuals achieve this with a clear goal supported by a large base. Highly reactive countries see change as gradual and unnecessary if the system works; individuals maintain this social harmony by making continuous assessments and reflecting on previous precedents without being disruptive. Put simply, the US seeks disruption in order to make the leap toward a better future, while China sees disruption as a danger to its future. Whereas we look at major linear trends, the Chinese see small cracks that need to be repaired. This is what makes China more dynamic.

While change is the only constant in China, every change China makes aims at maintaining everything unchanged. China never stands still and is anything but linear. China is cyclical, empowering, and timeless. To put it in software terms, the West aims to write the perfect code that can regulate our society, while China is using an AI algorithm to optimize society by feeding it more data and then fine-tuning the algorithm based on the latest results. We're fighting a war, while the Chinese are fighting thousands of battles. And every battle they fight is an opportunity to learn from their mistakes. This is why China is very self-regulating. Chinese employees take part in self-evaluation, civil servants in self-criticism, and teachers in self-reflection.

A TOO-MONOLITHIC VIEW OF CHINA

There is no "the Chinese". There are 1.41 billion Chinese people, and the differences between them are huge. It is a fact that ninety-four percent of the population are Han Chinese; that they all learn Mandarin and the same culture in school; and that Beijing drives forward megaprojects like the world's largest dam, the one-child policy, or the Belt and Road Initiative. As goals like these would meet a lot of resistance in the West, we conclude that the Chinese are just following what the one-party state decides on their behalf. Therefore, all Chinese people are obedient and uniform. The Chinese are... and then comes another generalization. I have to admit, in this book I am guilty of this too. There is a difference, however, between thinking from a prejudiced viewpoint and generalizing to perpetuate the differences, and thinking from a perspective of diversity and generalizing in order to bridge the differences. But even though we all do this subconsciously, it is important to know that in fact Chinese society is enormously diverse, opinionated, and restless. Probably more so than we are.

The reality of China is much more complex than it seems. China has fifty-six ethnic groups, a third of the population who speak a dialect that differs from Mandarin to the same degree that German does from English, and six hundred million people who live on less than $150 a month (and almost as many belong to a middle class comparable to those in Western Europe). Despite China being officially atheist, 21.5 percent believe in a folk religion, 18.2 percent are Buddhists, 5.1 percent are Christians, 1.8 percent are Muslims, and 1 percent identify with another religion.[4]

More than three hundred million internet accounts in China use a VPN to bypass the great firewall of China, and rest assured they do read the negative reports about their country. There is a Chinese proverb that says, "Heaven is high and the emperor is far away." What this really means is that local governments of larger cities have just as much power as Beijing—and they all think very differently. To get everyone on the same page, Beijing needs the support of different levels of local governments, local Communist Party leaders, state-owned companies, and even the military. But Beijing has a weapon the others don't: more money and influence. Just like in the US, where money and influence strongly determine the political agenda, Beijing's money is able to determine the local political agenda in China. But claiming Beijing is supreme and that the rest of the country simply follows the center is like claiming Washington is a puppet of Walmart, Rupert Murdoch, and Jeff Bezos. If you live in China, it doesn't take long to notice the diversity of the country. An employee from northern Harbin is very different from one in Shanghai, Shenzhen, or Chengdu in the West. You also quickly learn to take into account which government official makes the decisions, the ambitions and reach of each local official, their relationship network and reputation, personal policy style and level of corruption, and much more. There is a continuous internal power struggle going on, not only locally and in Beijing, but also between the two.

A major bottleneck to trusting China without having lived there is that we don't realize enough that behind every decision there are Chinese people who also have dreams and a moral compass; that direction from Beijing sometimes says more about their internal struggles than how the world sees it. This is one of the reasons I never really believed the Belt and Road Initiative was a Chinese Marshall Plan. Xi Jinping wants this, but many Chinese people are questioning on social media why all that money is going to faraway countries and state-owned companies, while China has so many other problems that need solving first. By taking a too-monolithic view of China, we often read too much of a powerplay into Beijing's bold initiatives and not enough into the indirect changes that any ambitious decision may provide in the long term. One example of long-term benefits is the Chinese vaccine that the country put out into the world. The Western world saw this as soft-power diplomacy from Beijing and was very suspicious about the effectiveness and safety of the Chinese vaccine. The fact that it could save millions of lives around the world wasn't even worth an open discussion. Apparently, we were willing to pay for our mistrust in China with human lives. The West does not trust China, while the rest of the world is now starting to think very differently. China's soft power really does work, not because Beijing is bribing the world, but mainly because—in times of crisis—Beijing doesn't seem to abandon the world as much as America and Europe do.

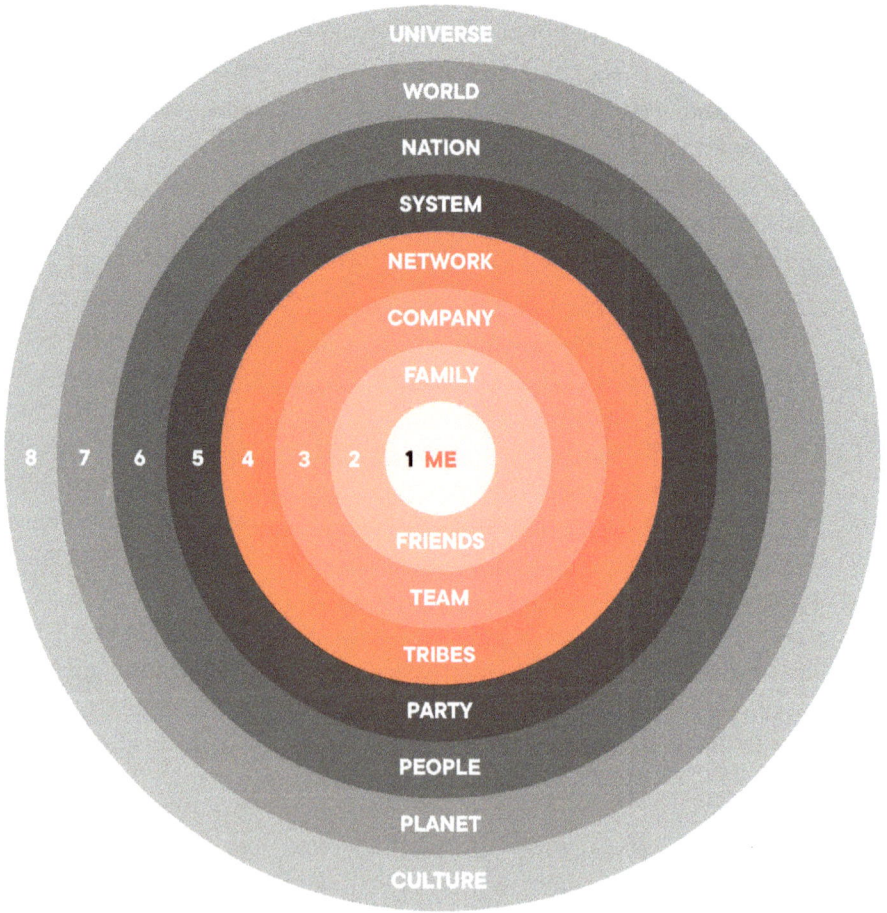

EIGHT CIRCLES OF TRUST

This book aims to answer the question of whether we can trust China or not. The question, of course, needs context. Is this trust in reference to Chinese citizens, companies, China's government, or the powerful man Xi Jinping himself? Is it about China's ambitions, actions, agreements, or statements? Is this about China's culture, ideology, system, or increasing power? And isn't trust something China should earn, not get? And does China trust us? Infinite perspectives and conditions that can fuel an infinite debate. My answer to the central question of this book can of course only be personal. I'm going to tell my own story and give my own interpretation of how I understand China through my Chinese lens.

When I am asked whether we can trust the Chinese, I answer that this is not the right question. The right question is: How can Chinese people trust each other? How can Chinese society function if there is no trust? Why did Confucius put the word "trust" (**xìn** 信), at the center of his moral teachings? Why is there always talk about the need to build *guanxi* (relationships) with the Chinese in order to gain trust? Why is trust between strangers in China so low, while Chinese trust their government and companies much more than Westerners do? To answer all these questions and many more, I've divided this book into eight circles of trust that start from the smallest circle—the individual—and extend to the largest circle—the universe. This is not a Chinese philosophical idea, but a universal way of organizing the entities we know as a unit.

These eight circles are as follows:

I deliberately chose these eight circles of trust because each of these contexts plays a fundamental role in how the Chinese trust each other and the world around them. The bigger the circle, the more complex the environment, and therefore the harder it is to have that trust in China and the Chinese. So, the challenge for China is to work from the inside out in order to better trust itself, but also for the world to trust China.

- The **individual and family** circles are strongly influenced by China's past and culture.
- The **company and network** circles seek anchorage and purpose for all Chinese people.
- The **system and nation** circles outline the rapid change taking place in China and the future for the Chinese people.
- The **world and universe** circles describe China's search for the balance between dream and reality.

1 →

The individual

Trust me. Why do the Chinese lie? Do they have the same work ethic as us? Why aren't they very transparent? Do they trust each other? Do Chinese people think as collectivists and Westerners more as individualists? Does their culture or the regime play a role in this crisis of confidence with China? How do they deal with lies, and what can we still believe?

2 →

Family and friends

Blind faith. What are the Chinese Confucian virtues? How traditional are Chinese people today? What is the position of women in the Chinese family and in society? Why do the closest relatives in the world's oldest family culture live apart from each other? Do the Chinese trust each other on social media? Why is WeChat your best friend?

3 →

Company and team

Trust each other. Can Chinese bosses be trusted? Why aren't Chinese workers loyal? Do you always have to make friends first before you can do business in China? Which do the Chinese trust more—people or technology? Is China's top-down hierarchy holding back their innovation and cre-ativity? Why are Chinese customers so demanding?

4 →

Network and tribes

Collective trust. Why doesn't China seem to trust minorities and nonconformists? Are the Chinese actually hospitable or is this just for show? Does the opinion of Chinese people really count? How can the Chinese bring about change if they're not allowed to protest openly? Do the Chinese have role models they trust? How authentic and self-aware are the Chinese?

5 →

System and Party

Trust the system. What does freedom mean to the Chinese? Do the Chinese trust the Communist Party? Is the Party a danger to the Chinese and the world? Why don't the Chinese want more freedom and democracy? Do all Chinese people live in fear and in a dystopian reality? Is China a Big Brother state and Xi Jinping a dictator?

6 →

Nation and people

Trust China. Why should we trust a regime that violates human rights? Isn't Hong Kong proof that China can't be trusted? Is China going back to being more nationalistic, totalitarian, and closed? Is the Communist Party restricting private businesses again? Does Beijing want to knock the US dollar off its throne?

7 →

World and planet

Crisis of confidence. Is China building a new world order? How should we deal with an assertive and aggressive China? Is China a danger to the planet, the world, and our freedom? What is China's master plan for the new Silk Road? What does China think about international rules and agreements? Can we still decouple ourselves from China?

8 →

Universe and culture

Trust the future. Do the Chinese themselves believe the propaganda about a perfect and harmonious future for all? Will China ever catch up with the West in terms of technology? Is Xi Jinping the new all-powerful emperor of a new Chinese empire? Is Beijing redistributing the wealth of the super-rich? Do the Chinese feel superior?

Trust is not just a Chinese challenge. The whole world today is experiencing a crisis of confidence. Who or what can we still believe? This book therefore doesn't just aim to be a guide to how we can trust China better, but above all to how the Chinese are solving their own crisis of confidence differently than we are. Which technologies does China use to give its citizens and consumers more confidence? Which business and leadership models provide companies and organizations with more strength and resilience? How can the relationship between government and business make both more sustainable? Can China's dream give the world new hope?

As I wrote at the beginning of this chapter, this is not an OR, but an AND story. Not everything that comes out of China is good or bad, useful or inappropriate, reliable or insecure, true or false. We need to select, adapt, and improve the right Chinese solutions to our needs and situation. Most of all, I hope that this book can provide new ideas and inspiration on how to tackle our challenges. The question I was asked the most in 2020 was how China made such a quick V-shaped recovery and came back stronger. My answer has always been that they trusted they would get through it together quickly; they trusted their system, leaders, and community; but above all, they trusted that this was their moment in history to be proud to be Chinese.

A dual perspective

Can we trust China? Can we take China at its word? By using the word "we" in the title of my book, I'm actually already guilty of binary thinking. Because "we" is in direct contrast to "they", which is polarizing. Why not call it: *How to Trust China?* And who do I mean by "we" anyway? I decided to leave the title unchanged because I want to start from a polarizing position and the reality of today's society. It is precisely this "us" versus "them" narrative that I want to address and break through in order to extract the arguments from our own echo chambers. So, who we and they are doesn't actually matter. "We" is anyone who is more likely to mistrust, reject, or condemn the actions and intentions of China and the Chinese. So "we" can also be Chinese people, and "they" can also be Westerners. In the book I sometimes use "Westerners" or "West" to mean "we" and vice versa. The intention of this is not to set the West up against China, but to represent the dominant opinion of the West as different from the general opinion in China. Here, "the West" corresponds to the average opinion of a resident of the European Union or of a region with a significant presence of European migrants since the fifteenth century, from North America to Australia. "Westerners" doesn't refer to any ethnic group. And beyond the West and China, there are still over five billion people whose trust in China and the West can't be generalized at all.

When I published *China's New Normal* in 2019, the most positive comments I received were about how the book was an eye-opener for under-standing China's capacity and ambition for innovation. The few skeptical or criticizing notes that came in related to China's sensitive topics, such as human rights. As these fit better into the topic of trust, I'd like to address them in this second book. To answer the question "Can we trust China?" I suggest keeping all options open. My goal with this book is to share my qubit mindset about China and to introduce you to my own view of a wonderful, ambiguous China. So, let's dive straight in by sharing nine important reasons why people (no longer) trust China. While I would also like to share my own point of view, the aim is certainly not to persuade, but rather to depolarize the too-often binary debate about China. I want to add more color to the discussion. I will give more context to these arguments throughout the book, but I want to present them here as binary statements to highlight the current state of polarization of the debate. By focusing on these contrasts, I hope to provide a more critical look at the criticism about China. By placing nine colored opinions of the West and of China next to (and opposite) each other, I aim to show how black and white our opinions have become.

The Chinese steal, copy, and spy

President Trump accused China of theft of American intellectual property, costing the United States between $225 and $600 billion a year.[5] In addition, eighty percent of all economic espionage lawsuits involve China. China mainly steals our Western technology through espionage or forced technology transfers in exchange for access to the Chinese market. The Chinese don't play by the rules![6] The strong underlying message is that China steals because it can't innovate like Silicon Valley. How can a country that has no freedom of expression ever be completely free to innovate? Although the Chinese get the best grades on PISA tests at the age of fifteen, and are also the best students at the top American universities, China only has a handful of Nobel Prize winners in the sciences.[7] The most common argument is that Chinese academic programs are known for teaching methods that put the focus on learning by committing to memory and self-censorship around sensitive political topics, rather than creative, critical, or conceptual problem-solving. This is why the Chinese steal our technology!

When it comes to business, you hear again and again that the Chinese are ruthless business people who have no problem bribing policymakers, manipulating partners, or even reporting their competitors to the government. Western companies in China often find that their trademark or intellectual property rights have been violated, or that they can't get a license or patent, while local companies can. Another of China's tricks is to make it compulsory for Western companies to set up a joint venture and transfer their technology in order to gain access to the Chinese market. Worse still, Chinese companies encourage Western business partners to set up a joint venture in China, only to then go and create a complete copy of the company on the other side of town, but without the Western partner. China being open for business is a myth. The Chinese think they can get away with anything! They're thieves!

The West has China in a straitjacket

If we go very far back in time, Chinese inventions such as paper, printing, gunpowder, or the compass do in fact show that the Chinese can innovate, and the Europeans were happy to adopt all those inventions. In the last 150 years, almost all developing countries, even the United States in the beginning, have stolen from more-developed Western industrialized countries. China is no different from Japan or South Korea when it comes to copying technology from the West. The Chinese like to mention that, after the opening-up of China in 1978, the West abused the Western intellectual property system in order to keep China in its grip. In a country like China, with a communist government, creations that serve the people should be partly common property or open source. Those Chinese people who, by stealing from or spying on the West, have freed their country from the straitjacket of the West are sometimes seen as a Chinese Houdini or Robin Hood.

Today we also see American internet companies openly copying WeChat or TikTok.[8] China is even leading the way when it comes to the more-advanced technology like 5G, artificial intelligence, or quantum computers. The protection of intellectual property (IP) is now also a priority for the Chinese government, among other reasons, in order to protect Chinese companies from each other. This trend shows how China's capacity to innovate is much greater than its foreign dependence. It is also overly one-sided to label all technology "acquisitions" by China as theft. In reality, China already has more than enough financial means to buy or license completely legal intellectual property, or to develop intellectual property together with foreign universities or experts.

The Chinese see the allegations of intellectual property theft against China as a sign of Western overconfidence and "not invented here" syndrome, so that we simply can't imagine that the Chinese can actually innovate. Today, China's property protection, jurisdiction, patents, trademarks, and copyright are no longer all that different from the European equivalents.[9] Almost all sectors that are not a national security risk to China are now open to Western investment without a local partner. The Western allegations are reopening old wounds rather than celebrating the success of China's intellectual property transformation.

The Chinese don't keep agreements

Already more than once this century, Western companies and governments have expressed their dissatisfaction that China isn't keeping to its agreements. Numerous Western companies have signed contracts with the Chinese only to later discover that they aren't really abiding by the terms. The Chinese see a contract as a first step in a negotiation, and not as a water-tight agreement. Personal relationships are more important than any legal agreements. But that's no way to do business, is it? There are many Western investors whose money has been used by their Chinese partner for some-thing completely different than what was agreed. For the last two decades, the European Commission has accused China of making false promises when it joined the World Trade Organization (WTO) in 2001: not to demand forced technology transfer, to better protect property rights, not to dump products with subsidies in Europe, to be impartial about the country of origin in govern-ment procurement, to open their financial and telecoms markets to Europe, and not to develop their own standards that would show favoritism toward China.[10] China hasn't honored its agreements with Australia, the European Union, America, with the United Kingdom over Hong Kong, with multiple coun-tries in Africa, in the South China Sea, with Lithuania... enough examples to not just take China at its word. In almost all cases it seems at first glance that China was mainly pursuing its own self-interests and economic benefits. Why then should we trust that China will keep to the Paris environmental agreement, or respect the new agreements with Europe on banning forced labor, or reduce the debt trap with Africa, or continue to respect its border with India?

The conclusion is: China simply doesn't follow international rules. We also see China creating its own rules, standards, and new international institutions in order not to have to meet international regulations. But if Western compa-nies don't comply with Chinese agreements, then they just get pushed away or boycotted. China even uses its economic power against companies from coun-tries that don't respect China politically. Paradoxically, China presents itself as a champion of liberal globalization and even as being against protectionism. This apparently very hypocritical attitude is confirmation for many that China in general, and the Communist Party in particular, is not only untrustworthy, but perhaps even malicious. This is also often the destructive assumption of those who really condemn China.

The West wants to control China

So why is China doing all of this? We think: the West has placed the trust of the free world in China, and China has played us. But China feels exactly the same, just in reverse. For example, a lot of Chinese people think that they have opened up the Chinese market to the West and that the West has treated them unfairly. These international agreements were drawn up in the previous century without China's involvement. International patents, universal agreements, and the financial anchoring of the dollar in trade made it almost impossible for Chinese companies and the Chinese government to develop their own strong industry. As the factory of the world, China became the slave of the West, of the powerful Western multinationals. If China wanted products from the West, it usually paid a very high price. Many Western companies have made a lot of money in China. This is why the attitude of the Chinese is often that the West was the first to start playing the game unfairly. A game according to the rules of pure profit maximization, without any consideration for how poor China was at the time. A world trade system that didn't want to contribute to the improvement of the living standards of the entire Chinese population. The sale of Western medicines at prices that the average Chinese person couldn't afford was labeled as unfair practices. So, when asked why it hasn't kept to its agreements, China will answer that, unless you want to lose, the only option in an unfair game is to not play by the rules. That's Chinese pragmatism for you.

The goal of the United States under Bill Clinton when accepting China into the World Trade Organization after fifteen years of applying for a membership was a strategic attempt to replace the communist regime with a market economy and ultimately make liberal democracy triumph in China. But that didn't happen because it was exactly the same Communist Party protecting its people from the West. The ultimate goal of China in joining the World Trade Organization was however achieved: to eradicate extreme poverty and become the world's second largest economy.

Since 2020, China has opened up the financial, telecommunications, tourism, education, and cultural sectors to foreign investors. In 2021, Beijing created a lot of Western-inspired laws that they are also now enforcing more strictly. In the future, the Chinese will be keeping more to the agreements they've made, since from now on playing by the international rules will mainly work in China's favor.[11]

The Yellow Peril

"The Yellow Peril" is a metaphor so ingrained in the Western imagination that we forget that it doesn't refer directly to China or the Chinese, but to the fear of the anonymous, foreign, barbaric, nameless masses of "yellow people" from Asia. This described a terror that spread across the Western world at the end of the nineteenth century when white Americans were scared of losing their jobs to the Chinese labor. It also began in China during the anti-colonial Boxer Rebellion of 1900, and reached its peak with the Japanese attack on Pearl Harbor at the end of 1941. After World War II, this phrase was focused on the Chinese communists.

Although today Western rhetoric strongly rejects all expressions of racial discrimination, the reality is that, more than a hundred years later, the struggle over these ideas is still very much alive. Today, the threat is seen in the context of strategic competition and as a historic development that leads to war when an emerging power challenges the established powers; or a cultural rhetoric in which the DNA of the Chinese is described as very predatory and shrewd, making world domination inherent to the Chinese.[12] But given that China will soon become the world's largest economy, there are fears that the "yellow nation" will want to expand its global position of power on a political, military, and ideological level. The question of whether China is imperialist or not has become a very lively topic of debate in the geopolitical think tanks. What is China doing in Africa? What lies behind the new Silk Road (Belt and Road Initiative, or BRI for short)? Why is China militarizing the South China Sea? Why is Australia being blackmailed by China in response to allegations about the origins of COVID-19? Is China reviving its ancient tribute system,[13] which strictly regulated ritual exchanges between the mighty imperial palace and the leaders of other Asian societies, with countries such as Sri Lanka? These actions seem to indicate that China does in fact want to control the world.

The phrase "Yellow Peril" reminds us of the European powers during the colonial period. It reminds us of World War II, when one nation—the Germans—rose above other cultures and with the aim to either subjugate other countries, or exterminate them. China and Chinese people also feel superior, about their culture, their economy, and soon perhaps even about their military. The Chinese don't care about the working conditions of the people in Africa or Eastern Europe, they play Western countries off against each other, or fire a hypersonic missile over the Pacific Ocean. The Yellow Peril points to China as a new enemy, an evil government, and an untrustworthy country. Surely then it's only logical that the West forms a united front against China!

Western imperialism

The suspicion that China is working on a secret master plan to control the West has puzzled the Chinese. Their response is often that the biggest mistake foreigners make is in seeing China as they see themselves. Just because history has shown that the English colonized and evangelized, the Germans started two world wars, and the Americans destroyed many Arab countries with their bombs, doesn't mean that China will do the same, does it? Western historical facts are no guarantee for predictions about China. The Chinese stress that they really aren't expansionist by pointing out that, despite having the strongest navy in the world, the Chinese Empire has never conquered any other countries. Regions such as Tibet, Inner Mongolia, or Xinjiang were annexed during the Yuan and Qing dynasties, when China itself was under foreign rule, namely the Mongols and the Manchus. At the time, China also had little need for expansion, given that the country had its own supply of raw materials and fertile land. Things are of course different today, and many initiatives on the New Silk Road and in Africa show that China is looking far into the future to meet its own needs.

What the Chinese don't often say in public is that they, like many Westerners, still consider many of the New Silk Road countries to be dangerous areas home to mainly poor, lazy people. The Chinese don't want to make the same mistake as the Westerners have in the past by taking on other people's problems. They will never forget the hundred years of humiliation from the West, Russia, and Japan after the Opium War in 1839. This is the shared national hangover that still deters them from getting another lecture from the West. China therefore avoids getting involved in the politics of other countries in order to avoid the same happening to them. Many of China's expansionist initiatives are less the result of a master plan and more the result of China's risk management plan to protect itself from Western intervention. Understanding which of China's actions is the chicken or the egg is an endless debate preoccupying geopolitical strategists.

No country today is the absolute center to which other states are subordinate; we live in a so-called multipolar world order. The fact that China wants to play an increasingly bigger role in this is only logical given its current economic status. A power shift in favor of China and Asia is inevitable. The West will have to choose between continuing to wage a political war against China, and coming to terms with this reality, learning to coexist, manage risk better, and intensify the competition through self-improvement. Continuing with aggressive confrontation will not work. As long as China isn't threatened or held back by the West, China is definitely not a "Yellow Peril".

Everything from China is junk

For forty years now, "Made in China" has been associated with poor quality and cheap products. This is also true: no country in the world makes as much junk as China. If you're ever in Shanghai, I really recommend taking the high-speed train to the city of Yiwu, one hour away. The city is the world's largest wholesale market for light industry commodities, with more than a hundred thousand stores. Each store is owned by one of the factories in the province that spew out junk like plastic Christmas trees, Trump election flags, and PPE (Personal Protective Equipment) for coronavirus, of course. If you can't find it in Yiwu, you won't find it anywhere. The city is an hour and a half drive from Alibaba's head office, where you can order your Christmas presents through AliExpress at prices you won't find anywhere else. We've all bought something "Made in China" that barely lasted a week. The image this creates is that products from China can't really be trusted. In recent years, we've seen more and more Chinese brands in our stores, from smartphones and drones to refrigerators that are being promoted for their quality, not just their price. But somewhere in the back of our minds, a little voice still tells us to be careful with Chinese brands.

And it's not just about poor-quality consumer products. Apartment blocks or public infrastructure built in China over the past four decades now and then collapse or have to be blown up because they are unsafe. A major earthquake in Sichuan in 2008 led to cracks in the walls or roof of many skyscrapers in Shanghai 1,200 miles away. Rapid construction allowed China to fill cities across the country with high-rise buildings, but the finish of both the exteriors and interiors has failed to live up to expectations. Each year over the last few decades, China has built the equivalent of a new city the size of London. The plumbing and electricity in a new apartment building sometimes already need to be replaced after just ten years. The pressure to constantly build cheaper really hasn't done China's buildings any good. If you live in China, you'll notice how owners renovate their apartments in the cheapest possible way, like real slumlords. The Chinese try to make everything as cheap as possible and then sell or rent it out for as much as they possibly can.

You get what you pay for

Almost all products we buy today, from Western brands like Apple to Prada, are manufactured in China. But even the cheapest IKEA furniture or private-labeled Walmart products are also made in China. The quality therefore doesn't depend on where it is produced, but on what the end customer is willing to pay. The Chinese see this junk made for export as a symbol of the greed of large Western companies that just want to make a profit and don't care about quality. By putting the "Made in China" label on products, Western brands can easily shift the blame for every problem or safety concern onto the Chinese factories. This hasn't helped the reputation of Chinese quality. In 1990, a factory worker in China earned twenty times less per month than the same worker in Hong Kong, Taiwan, or South Korea. Fast forward: now China has had thirty-five years of experience in Western quality manufacturing, gaining all the knowledge, experience, and technology needed to make the best quality products in the world, and still at the best price. China isn't a country of bad quality, rather of all quality—the full range from dirt-cheap toys to the most-advanced electric cars.

Furthermore, the Chinese middle class has become the largest in the world. Half a billion consumers who used to trust Western products and are now challenging Chinese brands to level up. As a result, and for several years now, the Chinese have had as much confidence in their local brands as they do in foreign ones. These new consumers are now also making higher demands when it comes to the quality of their homes. They have traveled the world and adapted their frame of reference. They also want to live in harmony with nature and have all the comforts available to them. New apartment blocks in China are often greener than in the West, have the latest in-built digital and security gadgets, are much better insulated, more sustainably built, and have sports facilities plus much more. Over the past decade, the Chinese government has dramatically increased the safety, environmental, energy, and quality standards of buildings, with public tenders no longer being decided purely on the best price, but on a whole range of factors. The only question now is when the West will make the mental leap that Chinese quality can actually be trusted if you pay the same price as you do for your "Made in Germany" stuff. The Chinese are increasingly paying that extra price for top-quality Chinese brands.

China is not transparent

In 2020, China was repeatedly accused of not being transparent about COVID-19. During the outbreak in Wuhan: China silenced all whistleblowers; the number of reported deaths was lower than the number of funerary urns that had been prepared in March; China ignored demands for an independent international investigation into the origins of the virus. The West was unanimous: China wasn't being transparent, fueling suspicions that it was trying to hide something, perhaps information that might show that the pandemic could have been avoided? After all, China is known for not being transparent when it comes to data. The annual growth of China's gross domestic product has been questioned for some time; history is sometimes rewritten, such as with the Cultural Revolution or the 1989 student protests in Tiananmen Square, and American stock exchanges have considered delisting Chinese companies for not following disclosure rules. On top of that, if you see Chinese politicians at work, you get the impression of a highly orchestrated piece of theater. Every year, hundreds of them stand in the Great Hall of the People in Beijing, neatly dressed like robots in matching gray suits. During the session, they simply formalize what has already been agreed on long in advance, showing zero emotions. How can you trust China if they don't reveal their human side? Is it all just for show?

Western companies often have a hard time vetting a Chinese company before investing in it. The accounts are often incorrect. With its $300 billion of debt in 2021, the property developer Evergrande was almost bankrupt, but the books told a different story. Many of their real estate projects and sites had turned out to be worthless, but they hadn't been written off in the accounts. New US legislation requires American companies operating in Xinjiang to demonstrate that their suppliers in the region are not using forced labor. But China rarely allows any kind of full-fledged audit in the region. They are very wary that the Western media, under the pretext of external audits, wants to fabricate false evidence of forced labor against China. But in doing so, China indirectly prevents Western companies from achieving what they need. What are we supposed to believe if there's no transparency? The West's mistrust in China is being fueled by a lack of transparency.

The West likes to put everything on display

What people don't see, or forget, is that a lot of internal discussions do take place before a decision is made and the show is put on. Millions of Chinese follow the open TV debate where the prime minister speaks to journalists. The fact that this all seems very rehearsed has little to do with transparency and much more to do with Chinese Confucian culture. Hierarchy and formality are the best ways to gain the respect and trust of the people. Western bankers and professors take the same approach. It isn't odd, it's just that in China it has been the norm for two thousand five hundred years. Chinese dignitaries do not show their emotions in public. But even work colleagues don't talk to each other about their personal lives. In China, emotions remain within the relational context. This is different in the West. When the prime minister of New Zealand gave birth and broadcast it to the media, the Chinese found this very strange. When American politicians add "in God we trust" to the end of a speech, a lot of Chinese atheists don't feel that this is very genuine. In the West, those "formal" and "emotionless" Chinese who don't show their feelings come across as propaganda figures. In China, however, it is the "transparent" and "humane" Westerners, who display all their emotions at every given opportunity, who make it sound more like self-promotion or propaganda. Business and political leaders in China need to lead by example, so when a political scandal or rumor becomes public, the natural response of Chinese leaders is to communicate as little as possible. For the Chinese, this has as much to do with self-control as with a lack of transparency.

The challenge that we have when it comes to reading the Chinese, the Chinese also have among themselves. Since the first emperor, officials in China have been elected or chosen on the basis of a meritocratic political model. China's current political system also strives to promote leaders on the basis of their exceptional qualities. Strict exams and crystal-clear objectives are evidence of this. Of course, this quickly leads to data falsification, as failure to meet growth targets, investment quotas, or social objectives can put the job or career of the leader at risk. So, it's not surprising that, under such immense pressure, Chinese leaders and companies have sometimes falsified the numbers—and in doing so confirmed the mistrust of the world. But China itself is even more upset about this than we are, which is why in 2012 Xi Jinping launched a drastic anti-corruption campaign demanding greater transparency. Xi Jinping is now waging war against the "tigers and flies"—corrupt senior figures and local officials. This has meant that, as a control state, China has reached a completely different level with a trend for too much control rather than a lack of transparency. The large-scale introduction of technologies such as blockchain to make everything more transparent and controllable are the best proof of this.

WESTERN LENS

China is a control state without any freedom

The Communist Party has complete control over China. There is no freedom of expression in China. The Chinese are censored on social media and the Social Credit System, where every Chinese person gets a citizen "trust score". It seems like a dystopian nightmare.

Since Xi Jinping has been in power, the level of control over people's lives seems to keep increasing every day. Western companies operating in China confirm that they are less free today than they were a few years ago. They are forced to hire a Communist Party member who constantly keeps an eye on everything. Is China going back to the Cultural Revolution, where anyone who thinks differently can be randomly detained and sent to the countryside or a camp to be re-educated? It's gotten worse since 2021. Children are barely allowed to play games online, influencers need to behave in a dignified way, professional soccer players have to hide their tattoos, and the very wealthy are better off keeping a low profile. For years, China has been at the forefront of the digitalization of a national surveillance apparatus. With artificial intelligence, digital social security passports, digital currency, smart cities, and much more, China has become the world's largest laboratory for an authoritarian surveillance state.

Connected to central databases, more than five hundred million cameras, often with facial recognition capability, continuously monitor every citizen in the smart cities that are being implemented across China. In 2020, nine hundred million people in three hundred Chinese cities were required to share their daily movements with the government through QR code-based health applications on their smartphones. China is said to have collected DNA samples from seventy million men.[14] The news media is state-owned and more than two hundred thousand journalists have already passed the entrance exam, which makes them the perfect mouthpiece for the Party.[15] Overly critical journalists, freedom fighters, and activists are quickly arrested and sometimes imprisoned after a controversial "fair" trial. Beijing's crackdown using a new security law to simply silence a million demonstrators in Hong Kong has shattered the city's hopes of any return to its previous freedoms. There seems to be no doubt that China is building an Orwellian Big Brother security state so it can continue to oppress and control its citizens. No wonder that people are taking to the streets in Hong Kong and that the West is concerned this model could gradually mean the end of privacy worldwide.

The Chinese feel just as free as Westerners

And yet most Chinese people aren't that worried. In fact, they often feel that there aren't enough cameras in China and that the government isn't keeping enough of a close eye on everyone. They demand more security, not just more privacy. Have the Chinese all been brainwashed? Every year in my hometown of Ghent, there's a ten-day street festival that attracts a million people. In 1991 there was a big debate about whether the police should be allowed to install six cameras to catch people peeing in public, disturbing the peace, pick-pocketing, and being violent. When in the same year a camera helped find a little girl that had gotten lost in the crowd, that was the end of the debate. And now nobody worries about it anymore. Per inhabitant, London has more cameras than Beijing.[16] You just need to think of Chinese cities as if there's a festival going on every day. There are around a hundred Chinese cities that have over a million Chinese inhabitants.

Before 2017, you certainly didn't feel that too much control was the problem in China. The problem of trust in China was not about government control, but about too many fake products, rich people breaking the rules, a rise in the number of scammers and their victims, increasing inequality between the middle class and the poor, and too little protection for the most vulnerable citizens and consumers. The average Chinese person wanted better regulation and more controls to protect them.

Since 2018, Xi Jinping has responded to this, and greatly increased control in the country. Is he now going too much in this direction? Policymakers and citizens are constantly testing that very delicate balance between government control and civil liberties. The power and control of the Party are significant, but certainly not unlimited. The Party also fears social unrest among the people. That's why citizens are censored and controlled, but not too much, otherwise it could lead to revolution. The biggest difference compared to the West is that in China, the bounds within which something is allowed are smaller. Those bounds are China's norm. We have a different Western norm. In both cases, that level of freedom seems to be quite acceptable for more than ninety-nine percent of the population. When considering China's control state from a Western perspective, it might help not to look at the one percent, but rather at the other ninety-nine percent of Chinese people who don't really feel restricted in their freedoms. During the pandemic, most of us in the West agreed with the restrictions on our freedom, but this certainly wasn't the case for everyone. It is no different for the Chinese. Meanwhile, the Chinese feel that the West is constantly criticizing China's restrictions on freedom, but has no problem pushing its own principles to one side. How can we find it acceptable for all social media to block Trump? Why are the Hong Kong protesters portrayed as freedom fighters and the Capitol stormers as criminals and terrorists? Why would Catalonian independence from Spain threaten European unity, while it's a different story in Hong Kong? China accuses the West of double standards, of using one rule for China and another for the West. When it comes to national security, the whole world seems to have double standards on freedom, according to the Chinese.

The new dictator Xi Jinping

It's not Trump, Biden, or Putin, but Xi Jinping who is now the most powerful man on earth. Hundreds of books and articles have been written about this mysterious man, who is often referred to as the new Chinese emperor. A real cult of personality has emerged around him. In addition to the absolute power he seems to have consolidated over the military, Communist Party, security services, and government, Xi Jinping has immortalized himself like Mao through his lifetime appointment and by having his "Thought on Socialism with Chinese Characteristics for a New Era" written into the Communist Party constitution.

Dictatorships are always oppressive and inefficient at home and dangerous abroad. Dictators are usually a danger to their people and sometimes the world. Strong communist regimes have almost always had a dictator in power. They don't tolerate opposition, contradiction, elections, free media, or the independent rule of law. They govern based on terror, absolute control, and repression. Dictatorships rarely lead to more stability, prosperity, or peace in the long run. Xi Jinping seems to fit the profile of well-known dictators who increasingly take control, and so the world can expect more international conflicts with China as well as growing nationalism within China.

Xi Jinping's "Thought on Socialism with Chinese Characteristics for a New Era" marks the beginning of the third era of China's return to its golden age and rightful place in the world. Mao Zedong united China, Deng Xiaoping made China economically strong, and now Xi Jinping will realize the Chinese dream. Like Mao, Xi is also increasing the level of control; strengthening the power of the Party and state enterprises; rooting out the corrupt, the opposition, and nonconformists; increasing censorship and propaganda; and isn't scared of a power struggle with anything beyond China. A lot of prominent Western politicians and thinkers warn of the danger of this dictator to the future of our Western democracy, economy, and freedoms. "The free world must triumph over this new tyranny," US Secretary of State Mike Pompeo said in 2020.

The right leader for China

Is China a dictatorship? Yes. Since 1949, China has, according to its constitution, been a "people's democratic dictatorship" (**rénmín mínzhǔ zhuānzhèng** 人民民主专政). Another qubit concept that, in the eyes of the West, cannot co-exist: democracy and dictatorship. Despite the Communist Party's authoritarian power, it can only justify its existence by constantly seeking feedback from its citizens and using these insights to adjust its policies. The Chinese believe that China is the most self-regulating political order in the world. China may be called a dictatorship, but this dictatorship is heavily built on the advancement of the Chinese people. Xi Jinping has therefore been referred to within the Party as the "people's leader". Despite his so-called unlimited power, most Westerners still mispronounce his name: "Xi" is pronounced like "she". Xi's priorities are to increase the inclusion of the poor and the elderly, bring universal healthcare and prosperity to all Chinese people, provide stability for the entire country, protect consumers, support small- and medium-sized businesses, and much more—not the typical goals of a dictator or a dictatorship.

Is Xi like Mao? Absolutely not. They couldn't be more different. Mao governed by creating more chaos and by fighting bureaucracy. Obsessed with order, Xi is reviving that bureaucracy. Mao grew up in the countryside and forced everyone, friends and enemies alike, to follow his communist ideology strictly. As a privileged "princeling", Xi saw his own father thrown out of Mao's regime, and is therefore no faithful follower of China's father figure or dogmatic believer in egalitarian communism, but focuses on restoring the culture, people, and nation of China to the former glory of the Middle Kingdom within a fair socialist model. Mao lived in a poor, humiliated, weak, and oppressed country that needed a strong revolutionary leader to restore its self-esteem. Xi rules a rich, proud, united, hopeful country that is more corrupt, dishonest, and unequal. Both leaders want to put China's values back on the map. Mao was a revolutionary, Xi is a nationalist. Mao had to overthrow a system with ideology, Xi has to make the system sustainable with nationalism—even against Western rivalry. One thing they both pursued is the socialist ideal, and this is what also unites them in history in their aspirations for China.

China's ideology isn't compatible with ours

When President Trump came to power, America's tone about China changed. There was already tension about power, the economy, and diplomatic priorities, but in 2016 the White House spoke of an existential confrontation between liberal democracy and authoritarian communism. This was the start of a new cold war. America had won the last one against the Soviet Union in 1991, after forty-five years of proxy wars around the world, from Cuba to Vietnam. In the 1970s, China was even a secret ally of the United States in the fight against the communist Soviet Union. Despite the world witnessing the Tiananmen repression by an authoritarian regime in June 1989, the West remained convinced that the Communist Party of China would give in to pressure from all the Chinese people who would increasingly crave our Western freedoms. If the West allowed China to enter the world economy and institutions like the World Trade Organization, the country would become richer and the Chinese would long for democratic freedoms, rights, and the rule of law. The West lost the bet. During the 2020 US presidency campaign, the only thing the Democrats and Republicans agreed on was that the Chinese Communist Party was the biggest threat to the world as well as to its own people. For the Chinese Communist Party, there is no CCP without China, and no China without the CCP, while the West portrays China and the CCP as independent entities. This is even reflected by the acronym CCP (Chinese Communist Party) that is commonly used in the West, instead of the official acronym, CPC: the Communist Party of China.

Of the forty-six countries[17] in the world that were once communist, today only five are led by a communist party. So, it makes sense that twenty years ago the West was convinced that communism would continue to decline. Relations with the United States vary greatly, from Vietnam as economic ally to the North Korean enemy, with Laos, China, and Cuba somewhere in-between, depending on who is in the White House. The Communist Party of China is today's biggest threat to global stability and peace. It is not China that's the problem, rather the CPC. The CPC doesn't hesitate to show its military aggression in the South China Sea, and it undermines global norms and values. The CPC influences Western academic establishments, institutions, media, and smaller countries to spread China's propaganda around the world. China has no problem putting pressure on countries, companies, and people who attack the CPC or do not see it as a legitimate governing party. The CPC takes advantage of the open, free economy of the West, but cuts itself off from the world. Have we been naive about the real purpose of the CPC? It keeps the Marxist-Leninist regime and totalitarian ideology alive. Both the West and the CPC see each other as ideologically too different to be compatible.

The West doesn't own the patent on democracy

For fifty years, America was successful at managing and dealing with the ideological difference of opinion with China. Clinton may have been too cooperative, Trump too confrontational, and Biden too strategic. If there's one thing we can thank Trump for, it is that he has made the world wake up and realize that China is a major challenge that needs to be tackled differently. What the Trump years have also proven is that China doesn't give in, even under pressure from the United States, and certainly won't change. The problem is not that China rejects the democratic model, rather that it is worried about the West using its model of "democracy" as a verbal weapon to impose its influence on other countries. In 2020, Mike Pompeo urged the 1.4 billion oppressed, controlled, and fearful citizens to join the "international community" in building a new democratic alliance to fight the Chinese Communist Party.[18] As a result, the mainlanders' suspicion against the pro-democracy fighters in Hong Kong took on a completely different meaning. The Chinese suspected that the United States and its allies secretly sponsored the protests in Hong Kong, which led to violent attacks. According to the Chinese, the greatest danger to China isn't Beijing, but Washington: a regime that, under the pretense of protecting human rights, uses violence to interfere with the interests of other countries.

At the end of 2021, Joe Biden invited 111 countries to his democracy summit,[19] including thirty-three countries that are certainly not considered "free" democracies by the United States, but that are geopolitically very important allies of the United States—among other things as a counterweight to an emerging China. What most Chinese people really hate is that you can only be a friend of the United States if you do what they say. Europeans sometimes feel the same way. Will China ever become a democracy? Perhaps, but with strong Chinese characteristics—more for the people, less by the people. It took the United States over a century to give women and black people the right to vote, so from a historic perspective, China still has quite a bit of time to introduce democracy. But the start of this decade has given Beijing the chance to study all the weaknesses and problems of Western democracy in great detail, from the response to the pandemic to the Black Lives Matter movement to the storming of the Capitol. The first conclusion is that today European social democracy is viewed more positively than liberal American democracy. The other conclusion is that, in times of crisis, China's democratic model works much more efficiently than the West's. China doesn't see its ideology as the main driving force of its future. But the West does. Meanwhile, China sees Western democracy failing more and more. The Chinese therefore believe that we certainly have no right to challenge China's ideology.

China violates human rights

For the "international community", it is an acknowledged fact that China violates human rights. The number of violations is significant. Journalists, dissidents, human rights activists, and political opponents sometimes end up being detained for long periods without a fair trial. Despite what the constitution says about all Chinese citizens being equal regardless of gender, religion, or ethnic background, the oppression of LGBTQ, religious leaders, and minorities such as the Tibetans, Mongols, or Uyghurs cannot be denied. And let's not forget the repression in Hong Kong. In recent years, more and more alarming media reports have also emerged about the more than a million Uyghurs that have been imprisoned in detention camps, where they are being indoctrinated, tortured, sterilized, and often subjected to forced labor.

Each of these violations is worrying and deserves an appropriate amount of attention, but the most controversial reports are about the Uyghurs in Xinjiang. It all started when German anthropologist Adrian Zenz claimed in 2019 that there was a cultural genocide going on inside re-education camps. China's response to the allegations remains unchanged: that this is a purely domestic matter—with measures being taken in line with Chinese law—and a response to the threat of terrorism and extremism in the region, precisely to guarantee the human rights of all ethnic groups in Xinjiang. But where there's smoke, there's usually fire.

According to Amnesty International, the human rights situation across China is deteriorating. The Chinese government continues to implement far-reaching policies under the guise of a national security campaign against "terrorism" in a systemic manner that severely restricted the freedoms for millions of Uyghurs, Kazaks and predominantly Muslim ethnic minorities in Xinjiang. End of 2021, a United Kingdom tribunal had concluded that China had committed genocide by the imposition of measures to destroy a significant part of Uyghurs in Xinjiang. As China has been mostly prohibiting the international community to conduct independent investigations, more than forty members of the Unites Nations have now condemned China's human rights violations in Xinjiang. The national parliaments of eight liberal democracies even called the violations in Xinjiang a cultural genocide.

Under pressure from the "international community," at the end of 2020 China released a white paper showing that from 2014 to 2019 China provided 1.3 million vocational trainings a year to workers in Xinjiang. They were taught the Chinese language and labor skills in order to tackle the extreme poverty in the region.[20] We can therefore assume that China has indeed made a large-scale attempt to convert Uyghurs to a more pro-China mindset. Given that there haven't been any terrorist attacks in the region since 2017, it must have been a success. A success that came at a high price for humanity.

The West violates human rights

Three documentaries on China's Global TV network[21] that are well worth watching show how hundreds of terrorist attacks against China and the police have taken place in Xinjiang since 1990. China compares this to the 9/11 attacks, which led America to see the war on terror as the greatest threat to the world. China realized this too and dealt with it in its own way in Xinjiang. Surveillance was increased in the region's cities, both with smart cameras and through the many police checkpoints. Were these centers horrific detention camps or an integration course on steroids? For many Uyghurs it appeared to be short courses of a single day, but certainly for those who had not yet mastered Mandarin, those lessons were forced. This detention of Uyghurs is described in the West as a violation of human rights, but for the Chinese it feels like the only possible way to learn the Chinese language quickly. The controversial training centers were even formally shut down by the government at the end of 2019, because the Uyghurs had successfully completed their training.[22] They now understand the Chinese language and culture and have the skills they need. China continues to insist that the information the West reads is fabricated and false—taking down Adrian Zenz and organizations like ASPI as far-right military think tanks sponsored by the United States.[23]

At the heart of the problem is also the fact that China thinks much more collectively than individualistically about human rights. The pandemic is the best example of this. Almost all Chinese people thought it was perfectly normal that they were locked up by the government during the outbreak, because this was about more than each individual. The Chinese expect their government to decide this for them. In order to protect the collective, the individual must temporarily give up their freedom. If the collective isn't safe, then from the Chinese perspective, you're not free. So, it is not always about imprisoning minorities or taking away freedoms. In the event of a pandemic, terrorism, or unrest, the Chinese are expected to obey the government, like a good child, and the Chinese government is expected to take care of its children, like a good father. It's a family. The individual having to give way to the collective is normal and the Chinese will follow that authority.

The Chinese believe that individual freedom and collective security are both human rights. They are both important, but we give priority to the first, China to the second. The Chinese take it a step further by pointing out how the West's incorrect handling of the coronavirus has violated human rights on an unprecedented scale.

DO WE EVEN WANT TO TRUST CHINA?

I fear that the answer to this question is usually that we don't. The answer is also hidden in these nine polarizing statements. I would be very surprised if, when reading them, you agreed with both the Western and the Chinese perspectives. Do you lean more toward the Western or the Chinese claims? And did you read the other with that little bit higher level of mistrust? The title of this book is: Can **We** Trust China? My assumption is that most readers will agree more with the Western point of view than the Chinese perspective.

You may wonder what perspective I have. I haven't described the nine conflicting statements about China based on my personal perspective, rather those of my YouTube followers. Every week since I started writing this book, I've posted a video about China. The nine conflicting statements were therefore a compilation of more than twenty-five thousand comments on my videos. This is the opinion of fifty thousand followers, from the most passionate pro-China supporters to fanatical China and CCP haters, but mainly of those who shared a different insider's perspective. Less than twenty percent of the followers appear to be Chinese. So, my own YouTube channel became part of my source of research for this book. I also spoke to a lot of friends. The most common feedback I get from my Chinese friends is that I am being naive to think that the West still wants to trust China. Most are convinced that after two hundred years of Western global domination, the West will do whatever it takes to prevent China from becoming the dominant nation in the world. My Western friends, on the other hand, warn me that I am being naive to have faith in China. They are more convinced that China, and certainly the Party, has only one goal—to become a control state that determines the world order. I refuse to start from either point of view.

My perspective in this book is not that the West no longer wants to trust China, nor that China has given up its trust in the West. However, you will notice in this book that I often talk more positively about China than the West. I sometimes use superlatives about China and worry more about the West. This has less to do with any position I want to take, and more to do with the fact that over the last thirty years I have had a front-row seat from which to watch China evolve into a more hopeful, energetic, and structured society, while in the West I've only seen these positive attributes fade away. I am therefore generally quite positive and optimistic about China. Not because I want to minimize China's problems and dangers, but because I trust that China doesn't sidestep its challenges as much as we do in the West. In a world where we hear so much negative information about China, a different, more positive view of course raises many questions. I hope that my cautious optimism about China is not limiting, but above all liberating and hopeful. I hope that new insights about China's way of thinking, culture, and system will not only provide answers but also raise new questions and discussions about China and the Chinese.

劳

láo

Meaning: **work hard, labor, bother someone, tired, merit.** The original ancient character is built up of one symbol for **fire** and one for **heart**. Together they mean that your heart is on fire and it hurts; but you have to keep working hard to win. You have to trust in your own efforts.

1.

Trust me. Why do the Chinese lie? Do they have the same work ethic as us? Why aren't they very transparent? Do they trust each other? Do Chinese people think as collectivists and Westerners more as individualists? Does their culture or the regime play a role in this crisis of confidence with China? How do they deal with lies, and what can we still believe?

The Individual

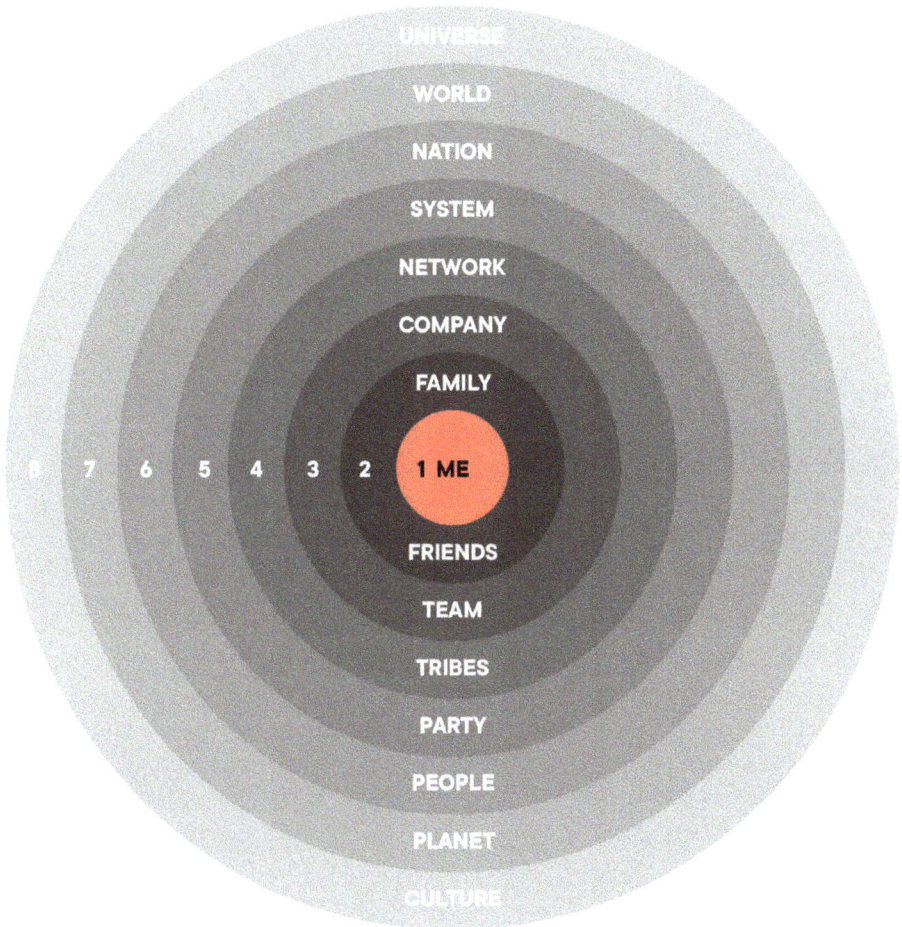

UNIVERSE
WORLD
NATION
SYSTEM
NETWORK
COMPANY
FAMILY
1 ME
FRIENDS
TEAM
TRIBES
PARTY
PEOPLE
PLANET
CULTURE

8   7   6   5   4   3   2   1 ME

WANG FANGCHAO

In the summer of 1996, I left for Beijing as a recently graduated sinologist to study Chinese at university for a year. I had already visited the Chinese capital as a tourist in 1991 and 1993, and I had fallen in love with it. On both trips I had visited over a hundred different cities and traveled 20,000 km by train. Beijing stole my heart: cycling through the narrow backstreets, chatting with old folks in the park, or just quietly reading a book in one of the tea houses gave me a calm yet vibrant feeling that I didn't experience anywhere else in China. The city radiated an incredible sense of peace, wealth, and depth. I was sold: this is where I would study Chinese.

My lessons were at a university of economics, but I would stay at the art college nearby. Each ten-square-meter room accommodated two students. So, I would spend three hundred days with a South Korean who couldn't speak a word of English or Chinese. With a deafening silence between us, Beijing suddenly seemed much less attractive. Fortunately, I barely saw my new Korean acquaintance as he was always out with other Koreans during the day.

With a grant from the Belgian state for just eight hundred francs a month ($22), I was not left with much to spend on enjoying the city. But I was in China to study Chinese, so I thought I would start to exchange English for Chinese lessons. That's how I met my first Chinese friend: Wang Fangchao. He was studying Fine Arts and was extremely eager to discover more about the world. Our teaching material consisted of old *National Geographic* and *Vogue* magazines that he'd bought at the book market. So, I would learn less about China than he would about the West, but I didn't realize that at the time; he'd been pretty smart about that. I was just happy to have made my first Chinese friend. We often sat together in my room for hours talking about Madonna, Princess Diana, or African rhinoceroses. It would be a very enriching year for both of us.

After a few weeks, he took me to *his* room, and that was when I realized why he liked being in my room so much. His own room was as big as mine, but it slept six students in three bunk beds, and everyone sat on the bottom bunk to study at the two tables in the middle. So, for four years, privacy was a luxury he couldn't really afford.

DO YOU HAVE SOMETHING TO HIDE?

"There's no privacy in China!" is the statement I hear most often about China. This then tends to be followed by the usual complaint about how the Chinese are super naive with their data and how the government is listening in everywhere, thereby fundamentally violating human rights. When you ask a Chinese person if they care about privacy, you usually get the immediate response: "What privacy?" Right. So, no privacy then.

The question is really whether we have correctly understood the answer. In Chinese families, whether they live in Beijing, Taipei, or San Francisco, privacy within the family is thought about differently. Chinese children are often raised with the idea that privacy conflicts with the traditional Confucian values of showing respect for your parents. Why would you need to hide something from your parents? The Chinese word for privacy (**sī** 私) also means "secret." As a teenager, you're not allowed to close your bedroom door, and you're expected to be very open toward your parents. Chinese children often grow up with little sense of privacy or personal space, and in turn raise their own children in the same way. The tradition is passed on.

Therefore, for the average Chinese there is often more privacy outside the home than within it, especially if you live in one room with your parents or fellow students. But beyond the home, for example in an elevator, bus, or subway, the Chinese still look to us like sardines in a can. This is not just because there are so many of them. The Chinese sense their personal space as slightly smaller and less confidential. So long as there's no physical touching, how close strangers are really doesn't bother them. They are much less sensitive to the stress and annoyance that we as outsiders experience when someone invades "our space." Intrusions by strangers who stare, make noise, or produce all kinds of bodily sounds and smells are stimuli that hardly seem to cause them any stress. The Chinese seem to go through life thick-skinned, which comes across to many Westerners as uncivilized and rude. But that's not the case at all. In my experience, their need for personal space is simply smaller than ours.

Even more unusual is when a complete stranger on the street suddenly tells you to dress a little warmer, asks you why you bought so many vegetables, or says you paid too much for them. And while this really annoys newcomers to China, often causing them to make it perfectly clear that it's none of their business, you soon learn that these Chinese people are actually trying to show some sort of parental concern or care. Isn't this all very suffocating? That really depends on your answer. If you see their intentions as positive, which is actually the case, then a non-committal reply is the best way to respond. So, if you live in China, when you're outside of the home, you need to be able to put your individual privacy bubble to one side, otherwise China really isn't for you.

But the universal concept of privacy is about being free to be who we want to be, not to have to justify everything, not letting our thoughts be controlled. It is therefore a matter of trusting people as human beings. We need that psychological and physical boundary, and China is no different. While Westerners see privacy as a sign of trust in the individual, the Chinese see privacy more as a sign of distrust in others. And that's why they often answer with a question: What privacy? What secret am I supposed to have? This is certainly true within the family, especially toward your father, and if you extend the circle much wider: the fatherland, the state, or the Communist Party. What would the government not be allowed to know about me? I really have nothing to hide, you often hear. While in a more individualistic society we see privacy as a basic human right, in China people place more importance on the value of a collective, open camaraderie than on privacy.

This is why the Chinese do not always distinguish between the individual and collective dimensions of privacy. Just like many Europeans, they consider the right to privacy a personal necessity. "I have nothing to hide, so what's the problem?" is the most common response you hear when the privacy concerns arising from surveillance capitalism are put on the table. However, privacy should be a collective right aimed at safeguarding the fundamental freedoms of a society. Rights like freedom of movement within and beyond borders, and freedom of opinion and religion can come under a lot of pressure due to privacy concerns. It is in this light that the debate should be conducted, in the EU as well as in the US and in China, but unfortunately this is certainly not always the case. So, we are very similar in that respect. On an individual level, however, we are radically different. But in our society, not everyone can be trusted, which is why privacy rules also exist to protect people against wrongdoers who can manipulate our data in increasingly clever ways. So Chinese people who, often unconsciously, are in general less careful with their own personal data, have become very vulnerable in recent years. An awareness of the risks has grown over the last few years, with eighty-five percent of Chinese citizens already experiencing data breaches, according to a survey by the *Financial Times*. On social media, consumers aren't hiding their anger at companies and people who have misused their data, and the Chinese government is certainly not insensitive to that. More on this in Chapter 6.

CHINESE CURIOUSNESS

Let's briefly go back to my best friend Wang Fangchao. There was another reason for his daily visits, in addition to our language lessons. He was completely in love with a girl in his class—Liu Di. He saw her every day, but making his intentions clear was unthinkable for him. Not only did I become his personal dating coach, but my room also became neutral ground for them to meet. This is what really opened my eyes to how little informed the Chinese were about "real" life at that time. But that innocence was inversely proportional to the curiosity he showed for finding out about anything and everything. The Chinese are the most inquisitive people on the planet. And because few questions are considered "private," they soak up everything like a sponge. I'd given my friend Wang Fangchao dozens of crash courses in life that would earn me a lot of money in today's online age. So, you can imagine what the arrival of the internet in China meant to the hundreds of millions of Chinese who all had the same questions as my Chinese friend. In this way, one of the apparently least free internet zones became the most liberating platform on the planet. It is that same internet which helped all Chinese people to discover and accept themselves. And as American drag queen RuPaul says: "If you can't love yourself, how the hell are you going to love somebody else?" It was the daily conversations I had with Wang Fangchao that strengthened our trust in each other.

WHAT IS MY GOAL IN LIFE?

With the pandemic that broke out in China at the end of December 2019, like everywhere else in the world, another normal has arrived in the country, with everyone's priorities being rearranged.[24] In the first half of 2020, more than half of all Chinese people saw both their income and savings disappear, causing many to suddenly stop and think about the real meaning of life. For thirty years I have been telling my Chinese and other friends that China's biggest challenge is not the government or the regime, not the copycats or poor business ethics, nor lack of creativity or the ability to think critically; no, the real challenge for China is that most Chinese haven't really experienced a crisis since 1977. Before COVID-19, the vast majority of the Chinese were living in a world that only knew one direction: onward and upward. A Chinese bubble. As a manager in China since 2000, it was a real achievement to retain good employees each January. Just before they would go back to their hometown to celebrate Chinese New Year with their families, I would promise a fifteen to twenty percent salary increase, a more important position and title, but above all more responsibilities. All too often, I would even pay their return flight just to make sure they would actually return to Shanghai. For the past twenty years, China has been a country so full of confidence and optimism that their only comfort zone has been the Chinese rat race. Or put another way, we all felt—expats included—like we were driving on a Formula 1 track.

January 25, 2020, was the start of the year of the rat in the Chinese calendar, but suddenly the Chinese rat race was over. The world stood still and the race car was suddenly out of action. A hundred million Chinese sat at home under lockdowns for at least two months, which gave them the psychological and emotional space to reflect on life and to do some self-discovery. Time stood still for the whole world, but the way that reflection time was used by the middle classes in China and in the West seemed diametrically opposed. If you were to take Maslow's 1943 hierarchy of needs (figure 1), it would be like everyone in the West suddenly catapulted down the pyramid.

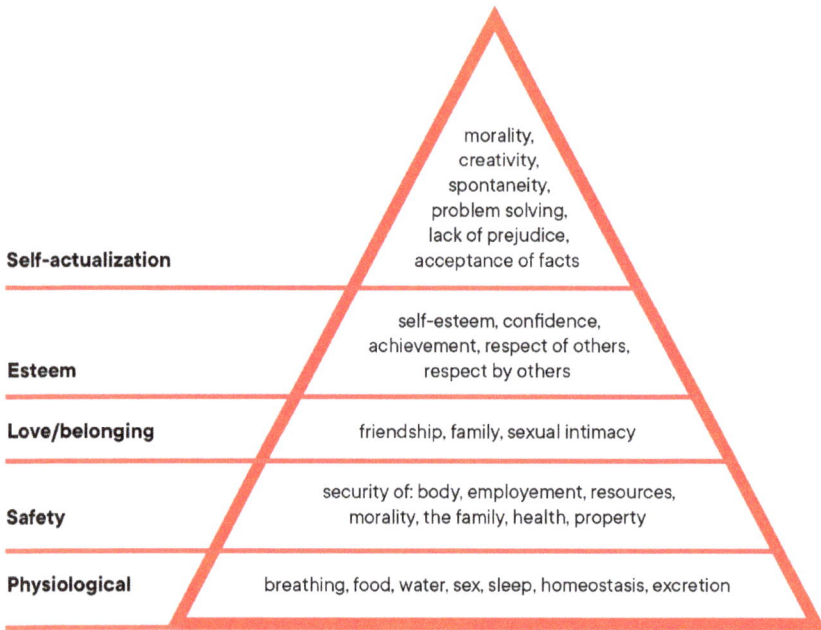

Figure 1 / Maslow's hierarchy of needs pyramid

In the West, we were no longer occupied by self-actualization or recognition, and the quarantine made social contact impossible. The main motivation became the preservation of our security needs: physical safety, order, stability, and health, but even our basic physical needs were suddenly under discussion: food, sleep, exercise, relaxation, and yes, even breathing. In terms of Maslow's hierarchy of needs, we have fallen from the Tower of Babel and need to build a new tower.

In China, on the other hand, it seems the opposite happened. If you look at China from a Western perspective, you could say that over the last forty years most Chinese have worked their way up Maslow's pyramid, and today in China there are hundreds of millions of people who have reached the highest level of self-fulfillment. What we forget is that Maslow's theory of human development is a Western concept, based on a highly individualistic society: China is different. China has three cornerstones that give the half a billion Chinese who are still striving for more basic needs room for self-actualization: Taoism, Confucianism, and the Communist Party. In Taoism, the wise man is he who, in addition to intellectual knowledge, also reflects on the meaning of life, and works on himself to become one with the universe. In Confucianism, the wise man is he who, through self-cultivation, always acts correctly to maintain harmony in the world. The Communist Party, which serves as the father of Chinese society, gives a sense of safety to its subjects. So, the Chinese model of self-fulfillment seems much more of a binding goal for each individual within the collective than Maslow's rather descriptive evolutionary model for each individual.

In contrast to the way many in the West viewed the coronavirus tsunami as an impoverishment and a crisis, for many Chinese it was opportunity for enrichment and respite. I certainly don't want to downplay how awful it was for the millions of Chinese people who lost their jobs or the companies that went bankrupt, but there is a clear trend toward higher self-actualization and self-reflection. You could almost call it a reboot of Chinese society, with more attention being paid to the top of Maslow's pyramid: being able to be yourself, studying, creativity, ethics, being open-minded, and self-awareness. The house arrest imposed on the Chinese people pushed the pause button for a while, and perhaps this was also really needed after decades of always being in overdrive. In China, people are now talking more and more about what Alibaba calls the Double-H strategy: Happiness and Health. The Chinese are buying pets, cooking more at home, studying more online, doing more fitness and wellness activities, buying more healthcare products, and using telemedicine. In 2019, Chinese consumers were already the most demanding customers in the world in terms of convenience and digitalization, known as "new retail," but since 2020 the trend has only intensified. Chinese consumers are now looking for public benefit objectives, the corporate values behind the brands they buy, and the quality assurance and ecological-properties of products.

DELIVERING AT THE SPEED OF LIGHT

If you walk around Shanghai or other Chinese cities, you'll struggle to find a street without a JD.com tricycle, moped, or cart. When we talk about e-commerce in China, we automatically think of the giant Alibaba, but the biggest online retailer inside China is actually JD.com (JinDong). While from day one, Alibaba was an internet company with no stock and few assets, JD started out as a retailer selling electronic products. In 2004, after the SARS outbreak, owner Richard Liu decided to close his store and turn JD into an online platform, building a delivery empire, like Amazon, in China. When I visited their headquarters in Beijing in 2019, the history of their logistics service was explained on one slide. My colleague Steven Van Belleghem and I were in awe. In 2010, they were talking about twenty-four-hour deliveries; in 2013, two to three hours; in 2015, one hour; in 2016, thirty minutes; and in 2018, deliveries within minutes or at the "speed of light." This can only be achieved by a combination of being able to predict what the consumer wants and an extremely efficient distribution system. In both cases, China is unbeatable. Further on in this chapter we will talk more about predicting needs by discovering each individual's habits (Ant

Group). In terms of deliveries, JD's logistics service today covers ninety-nine percent of the country, delivering fifty-seven percent of parcels within twelve hours and ninety-two percent the same day, even if the products come from abroad. Thanks to 700 warehouses, drones, robots, and fully automated sorting centers, they now achieve a customer satisfaction rate of 98.4 percent among 380 million active customers, and only one complaint per million orders.[25] Many retailers in the West would happily sign up for that.

But how do you keep online customers happy in a country that makes the biggest number of counterfeit products in the world? We don't trust China for many reasons, but the main one is usually that the country is branded as a producer of low-quality or fake products, which e-commerce makes easier to trade and more difficult to control. All global e-commerce companies have been struggling with this for years, but what is not so well known is that both Alibaba and JD.com have a zero-tolerance policy when it comes to counterfeit products. If you get caught once, you're out. You are immediately blacklisted. JD is relentless when it comes to protecting trademarks on its platform with a focus on quality. This is not exactly the image many have of Chinese companies, but integrity in business is the driving force that has enabled JD to grow healthily into a reputable brand in China. Although the whole world is wary of Chinese counterfeiters, Chinese consumers are even more unforgiving of internet platforms that allow such practices. Therefore, like Amazon (and unlike Alibaba), companies such as JD don't want to hand over the entire supply chain, and instead purchase all products themselves in order to ensure a quality guarantee.[26] So you can trust JD, because if you are not satisfied, you get your money back. Their cost of product purchasing is on average a bit higher and slightly more premium compared to their competitors, but JD's growth shows that more and more Chinese consumers are choosing quality over price and that China's middle class is growing at speed. Chinese people trust those who can prove they are trustworthy.

YOUR NEW BEST FRIEND

How did JD get so fast and so big? During our visit, above the workplace, we saw this slogan hanging on a large banner in preparation for the annual e-commerce shopping festival in China on November 11 read: "Double 11, double hard work, double speed, double satisfaction!" The 996 rule, from 9:00 a.m. to 9:00 p.m., six days a week, was the standard at JD. An army of 220,000 employees, many of whom make deliveries all over China, have one goal: to make their deliveries as quickly and as smoothly as possible. But this is also what sets JD apart, because since 2017 door-to-door deliveries have always been done by the same delivery person within their own neighborhood, like how mail is delivered.

This quickly establishes a direct relationship with the delivery person so that dissatisfaction can be spotted fast, new orders taken, and unwanted packages returned. And of course we see an aspect of Chinese technology innovation here too. The delivery person has limited time but optimizes this by—after a few deliveries—asking a familiar face to add them on WeChat, an app similar to WhatsApp or Facebook Messenger. The delivery person then creates a group with everyone from the same apartment building or neighborhood they serve. In this online group, they'll tell you when they're coming, when your delivery is on its way, and also happily share JD discount coupons. Interestingly enough, this is exactly where we see how nuanced the privacy discussion is becoming in China. After all, for the newly elevated middle class, this way of doing things represents an invasion of their private lives. They don't want their neighbors, who they see as strangers, to know what they're buying, or even know who their neighbors are. They don't give the delivery people access to their WeChat "Moments," similar to Facebook News Feed, because they don't see them as friends. More often than not, they are and remain just a name in their WeChat list rather a real social contact. It is almost paradoxical that it is not the West making China aware of the importance of privacy, but that awareness is growing due to the increasing interaction between two classes of Chinese society.

HOW CAN WE TRUST WITHOUT TRANSPARENCY?

We read everywhere that China needs to become more transparent, because this is damaging the confidence of the West toward China. We don't trust the data. We don't trust a country that censors. We don't trust copycat companies. We don't trust a government without checks and balances. We have more than enough reasons not to trust the Chinese.

Since 2018, I have accompanied hundreds of Western business leaders on nexxworks innovation trips to China. In the space of one week, we visit about twenty innovative companies together, from start-ups to Alibaba. The reaction to the last day is always the same: with a sense of renewed humility, I am told that the speed, scale, determination, and resilience of the Chinese is astonishing. However, what always strikes me the most is their amazement at how transparent our Chinese hosts are in sharing information, data, and ideas. I often hear that in Europe we would never publicly share what the Chinese are showing us. The CEO or founder of billion-dollar start-up companies like iCarbonX, Tencent Trusted Doctors, or UBTech showed how they cleverly raised hundreds of millions of dollars from Tencent (the Facebook of China). Strategic questions were answered very openly, although they were still in full scale-up mode. We were also able to visit the control room of major players like CTRIP (the booking.com of China) and the state-owned energy company State Grid, where questions were also not avoided. On a visit to TikTok, we were amazed that the manager explained to us in great detail how their management was still years behind companies like Facebook. Why were their weaknesses and challenges being shared so publicly? One of the reasons was that we, as executives of successful Western companies, were shown the full respect of our humble host. By being open and sharing, they hoped to learn and build valuable relationships. This basic principle is quite universal in China.

One of the biggest misunderstandings is to think that the Chinese are not transparent at all. Follow this logic for a moment: When a population places less importance on privacy, isn't it just being more transparent? If we think it's a violation of privacy for Chinese people's names and faces to appear on a big screen when they get caught on camera jaywalking in Shenzhen, we can't argue that it isn't transparent. If you choose to share with friends your own credit score from FinTech company Ant Group, which shows your purchasing behavior and creditworthiness, then you're being transparent, aren't you?

The question we should be asking ourselves is whether China's main problem is with privacy or with transparency? For several years now it has become clear that the Chinese government wants to protect its citizens from third-party privacy breaches, meanwhile citizens are urging the government to increase transparency, mainly to fight corruption.

At the end of 2019, Xi Jinping unexpectedly announced that China would become the global leader in blockchain. Blockchain is the underlying technology of cryptocurrencies such as Bitcoin, the mining and trading of which are banned in China. The reason for the ban is Beijing's fear that the wealthy could be using cryptocurrencies to move illegally acquired money from China abroad, under the radar. Cryptocurrencies are anonymous, not controlled by any central authority, and aren't limited by country borders. They are therefore ideal as a means of payment for money laundering, extortion, drug trafficking, gambling, and terrorism. Another reason for the government's cryptocurrencies ban is that the Chinese like to gamble and take risks. The volatility of the value of cryptocurrencies means that many Chinese would be going all in with their savings for a coin that could suddenly be worth nothing. That could then lead to a social revolution like the one they experienced in 2018 with lots of fraudulent peer-to-peer lending. Beijing doesn't want to take that risk. But paradoxically, blockchain is also China's trusted technology of choice. What interests China is the power of a technology like blockchain to trace the origin and path of products. The technology makes it possible to guarantee that the information, products, and all links in the production chain are authentic. This provides the ideal trusted technology for China to ensure food safety, brand authenticity, logistics traceability, or the achievement of environmental goals.

The cause of fake or bad quality products or data is usually the result of human intervention. To migrate from an environment where people are verifying every step of the supply chain to a fully automated process, billions of sensors have to be embedded along the global supply chain. The sensors can then feed correct data automatically into the blockchain. As China is the world's largest producer of sensors, it can create a ubiquitous IoT (Internet-of-Things) network. And with China now implementing an IoT and blockchain platform on a massive scale, it is at the forefront to create the world's most trustworthy logistics network, which is made even more effective by its 5G network. Imagine you're Chinese and you have a smart Haier washing machine connected to the internet. By doing your laundry during State Grid's off-peak hours, for example, you can get discounts on your electricity bill. This means State Grid can improve its energy capacity, you get to pay less, and Beijing can reduce CO_2 emissions. A win-win-win for the consumer, the producer, and the country by combining blockchain and IoT.

Since President Xi's announcement, China has become the global forerunner in blockchain. China has built the largest "Blockchain Service Network" in the world, almost forcing suppliers, importers, and retailers to hook up to China's massive, open-source blockchain infrastructure in order to be trusted by consumers. For a country like China where a previous lack of transparency has led to massive abuses and damaged the entire country's reputation, blockchain technology has become the answer to making China more transparent and credible. It sounds utopian, but in the years to come blockchain has the potential to make China the most trusted country in the world. For the 1.4 billion Chinese, this is music to their ears.

DO YOU TRUST ME?

My opinion is therefore that China is rapidly fixing its previous lack of transparency. The biggest challenge for the Chinese is not to give trust, but to gain it. For 2,500 years trust was based on relational agreements and obligations, with the transparency of intentions based on each person's reputation. More than thirty years ago, that suddenly changed. In 1988 you could suddenly raise private capital, start a company, or invest. But how do you do that if your friends are no longer your guarantor, and you now need to give collateral that you don't yet have as a guarantee? For the majority of the Chinese, this was a problem as prior the late 1970s everything belonged to the state, and before 1949 to the landowners or the emperor. In the new era, a bank would decide whether or not you would get a loan, and—like everywhere—banks would rather lend to someone with capital or property. A bank prefers to lend to someone who doesn't need it. The same lending model you see in the West was also found in

China, the difference being that the Chinese had built up even fewer assets. Chinese banks therefore lent mainly to state-owned or larger companies. The average Chinese person was left out in the cold.

But with the digital revolution that China has seen since 2014, FinTech companies like Ant Group have broken that curse by offering loans and microloans based on data and customer insights instead of asking for collateral. Suddenly, based on their buying, repayment, and spending habits, everyone can share data to show that they are in fact a reliable customer or prospect. This may seem trivial, but this is how a company like Ant Group has been replacing the global institution of the bank—which has built up the trust to manage and trade customers' money—with an algorithm that calculates how much you can be trusted based on your lifestyle habits. In China's almost cashless society, Ant Group and its payment application Alipay can track daily when and what you pay for, and decide at any moment and in the blink of an eye whether you'll be able to repay a loan, afford an investment, and still have enough money to get through the month. Based on your lifestyle, Ant can advise you how much of a risk you can take. And so the company becomes your partner in life, one that knows more about you than your own life partner, parents, or children. This of course raises questions about privacy, the myths and stories about which we will later debunk as we cover them in more detail.

Another example of the benefits of sharing your data with technology companies can be seen in the sharing of smartphone power banks in most restaurants in China. To take the portable charger to your table, you need to pay a deposit of one hundred yuan ($15), but if you have a good enough credit score, no payment is needed. With a good score you can decrease your hospital waiting times, take advantage of a fast-track procedure to get a visa for Singapore, or rent a car or bicycle without a deposit.[27] Of course, this also has its downside, because someone with a bad credit score would lose certain rights. The questions we can ask are how a company like Alibaba uses the data, and what safety net there is for the weaker or sicker people if Alibaba's main goal is to make a profit. We will come back to this later.

Because Chinese tech companies can track consumer lifestyle habits so closely, in the future a company like JD will be able to deliver within minutes, and a company like DiDi (the Chinese Uber) will know you need a ride before you even leave the building. The loan for that car of your dreams will already be set up by the time you walk into the Volvo dealership. While in the West we still often see this as the distant future, it's all becoming the reality in China today. When the iPhone 8 was launched in 2017, within five minutes JD had made home deliveries to those who had preordered the smartphone. The average delivery time for new phone orders via JD was 1.65 days, while it took one to two weeks for them to arrive at Apple Stores in China. Using its predictions,

JD had built up enough stock and already given it to the delivery people on the day of the launch. And this was the "slowness" of five years ago. The main reason this is possible is because we humans are creatures of habit, and we are actually very predictable. We take the same route to work each day, get up at the same time, mostly eat the same thing, etc. And when a service company like JD makes mistakes in that predictability, it only helps refine the algorithm. The question of whether the Chinese can be trusted is therefore perhaps something we won't be asking as much in ten years' time, because companies like Ant, JD, or DiDi will—thanks to blockchain and their algorithms—be able to answer this with the greatest precision. The majority of honest Chinese citizens will be happy to show their "trust credit" to third parties if it gets them more or better services, as long as the government guarantees the security of their personal data.

At the same time, Chinese netizens have become increasingly vocal about companies that violate data security. In September 2020, acclaimed AI investor Lee Kai-Fu came under fire when he claimed at a technology forum that one of his portfolio companies, Megvii, had been given facial photos by Ant Group and Meituan to fine-tune their algorithm. The Chinese Twitter, Weibo, went crazy over this.[28] Both companies immediately responded that they do not share user data with third parties, and Megvii added that they do not collect or store users' facial data. Lee Kai-Fu apologized for what he had said and the damage it caused the three companies. The Chinese are really no less concerned about the misuse of their data than Westerners. In fact, they are probably even more concerned given that their personal data has been made available by tech companies in China more often.

As a conclusion so far, let's remember that: in China, transparency, data breaches, and privacy are very sensitive topics that get a lot of attention. Privacy, in its collective application as a basic right for everyone, is much less of a debate.

ALL LIES

How often do you hear that Chinese people don't shy away from lying? I often got puzzled about this during my first years in China. We think the Chinese want to scam foreigners, but this is incorrect. They lie just as much to each other. Back then, every day you would see a police officer stopping a moped rider because they'd run a red light. The immediate reaction: no, it was green. Everyone saw that it was red, yet the moped rider kept claiming it was green. Why do so many Chinese people do that, even to someone with authority like a police officer? We often think that the Chinese all live in fear of the power of the law, but nothing could be further from the truth. They have no shame in lying to a police officer, and there are many reasons for this. I would like to expand on the four main ones I observed in my time in China:

- Chinese culture
- China's visible wound
- The new materialistic society
- Financial reasons

CHINESE CULTURE

In the West, our self-image and self-promotion is often more important than modesty or the harmony of our social environment. In China, it's the other way around. Growing up in the West, most children are strongly encouraged to recognize our good deeds and achievements for ourselves and others. Lying is immoral, but overconfidence is fine. To the Chinese, on the other hand, this too much confidence comes across as a lie, even if it's the truth. If you're overconfident, you probably have something to hide, and that's why you're lying. The Chinese worldview is much more focused on a collective idea that puts the group above the individual and therefore aims to maintain group harmony. Revealing information that can damage the cohesion of the group can harm the tranquility of the group. So modesty is needed, and a white lie to avoid the humiliation of others in the group is acceptable. The Chinese are much more practical about this than we are. Very often in negotiations I've heard a non-Chinese person say that the price was way too high, and that this was a showstopper. The interpreter would then translate this as: "The price will be difficult for him to explain to his shareholders" or "The price is an important discussion that we certainly still need to have." Everyone nodded in satisfaction, and the negotiations continued. The interpreter had lied, and in some cases the Chinese boss had even understood the English, but also the purpose of the lie.[29]

The Chinese are more concerned with self-preservation or the status of others, if necessary through a lie, than they are with blaming someone who lies. Let's take another example. Bart is asked by another foreigner, Alex, to introduce him to a Chinese person called Pang. Bart is good friends with Pang, and Alex wants to do business with Pang. So, Bart introduces Alex to Pang. They all go out for dinner and sing karaoke together, and Pang says he is so happy to have met Alex and that they will definitely do business together. Alex and Bart are super happy, but Pang doesn't want to do business with Alex at all. Then why is Pang lying? Why did he agree to meet up with Alex? The reason is simple: Pang thinks maintaining his relationship with Bart is so important that he puts on a whole act to keep him happy. He doesn't feel guilty, because he's done Bart a favor, and in doing so gained Bart's respect, without bringing any shame on himself.

In Western, Christian-influenced societies, we are more concerned with guilt and punishment than shame and honor. In the past, we would go to confession every week to free ourselves of our sins, while the Chinese are judged for their lies depending on whether they've been able to maintain harmony or not. In China, lies are not seen as better or worse than anywhere else, but we are judged differently for lying. If the Chinese are not caught lying, the harmony is not disturbed. There is a stupid Chinese joke where an American walks into a McDonald's in New York. When the server says they're no longer doing breakfast, the man pulls out a gun and demands they serve him, because that is his right. If the McDonald's server had been Chinese, he would simply have said they were out of eggs. The modern Western response is: you're guilty of a lie. We define guilt from the perspective of another individual. For the Chinese, the question of guilt is much more one of context, aligning themselves with Immanuel Kant's categorical imperative. It is the intention that is the deciding factor: do you act to protect society overall or to protect yourself, driven by selfish pride?

CHINA'S VISIBLE WOUND[30]

China's deeply traumatic past, most notably the Cultural Revolution (1966-1976), plays a continuing role in why the Chinese sometimes have no shame in lying. During this period, everyone was encouraged to inform on relatives, friends, neighbors, and colleagues, in order to show allegiance to the Party. Spurred on by the Maoist ideology during the Cultural Revolution, the behavior of conspiring against others affected the general level of trust in China. This chaotic semi-anarchist class struggle was orchestrated by the central government but fought from below by the people. This represented the greatest social change for the country, shaking the values and certainties of each class. Everyone lost their frame of reference. What you could trust had disappeared, and with it went the trust between people. Everyone from the "bad" class—landowners, rich farmers, or intellectuals—suddenly became the new enemy or possible spy. It was precisely this elite who had previously operated the local governments, security, and legal framework throughout the entire country. They were often humiliated, imprisoned, or tortured, as well as robbed of their property. Historical items, ancient customs, and writings were all destroyed. Everything became unpredictable. Nothing had any value anymore; no one could be trusted.

In ten short years, centuries-old traditions of trust were turned on their head for the generations that would follow. Regardless of whether you were a Red Guard fighter or victim during this turbulent period, you stood a very good chance of becoming hardened and above all, suspicious. It is the children of this red revolution who are running the country today from Beijing. This may explain why they rarely show their cards. It may also explain the gap in trust between people who live in cities, and the immigrants, workers, or farmers. A much deeper wound is the fact that this decade of chaos seriously damaged the fundamental values of Chinese society. Too many Chinese people still fail to see that lying no longer has a place in modern China. Particularly in what were the most revolutionary hotbeds of China during the Cultural Revolution, many, especially slightly older people, are still without their moral compass. Shame is one of the main reasons that Chinese don't like to talk about the Cultural Revolution, while the West usually claims the reason is because the Communist Party wants to cover up its mistakes. For years, Xi Jinping has been successfully restoring that moral compass within the Party and the wider population by turning back to some aspects of the core values of ancient Confucian China.

THE NEW MATERIALISTIC SOCIETY

In 1979, China woke up after thirty years under Mao's rule and also a hundred years of shame before that, when imperialist foreign invaders from England to Japan stripped the country of its riches and held back its progress. Deng Xiaoping's famous statement, "poverty is not socialism, to be rich is glorious," gave everyone in China the green light to get rich. With his Open-Door Policy to the West, the very short-statured Deng Xiaoping opened the floodgates that had been closed for 130 years. As Chinese became more and more wealthy, with a continuous annual salary growth of ten percent, this obsession of the Chinese resulted in China's new materialistic culture of consumption.

But it was more than the Open-Door Policy that made China ultra-materialistic. We've all heard some pretty shocking stories. Like seventeen-year-old Wang Shangkun who sold his kidney for over $2000 to buy an iPhone and iPad. When the news broke, his response was that he only needed one kidney but an iPhone would give him respect (face) with his friends.[31] This dark deed shows how poor Chinese people like Wang Shangkun are driven by ultra-materialism to create a new, better identity that will provide them with a future. The illegal surgeons were caught and the family received over $200,000 in compensation. Another example is the many crypto scams in China, where the benefits are greatly outweighed by the costs and dangers involved for the Chinese scammers.

These illegal acts must therefore be framed by the urge to survive and become successful in China's extremely competitive society. The economic floodgates have been thrown wide open and every fish is scared they're going to close again, right in front of their eyes—which has some truth if you look at the inequality or Gini index that almost doubled from 1980 to 2008. "Every man for himself, and the Party for us all." People sometimes forget that twenty years ago only two percent of the Chinese (thirty-nine million people) belonged to the middle class. Today this is forty percent, or 550 million people. So almost half of all Chinese people today don't need to worry about ending up on the wrong side of the dam of wealth. The Gini inequality index in China has fallen since 2008 to a level comparable to the unequal distribution of wealth in America today. Hopefully, both materialism and the lies people told to get rich can now slowly trickle away.

FINANCIAL REASONS

When it comes to this, I see little difference from the rest of the world. No one likes paying a traffic fine, and a white lie is socially acceptable as long as you get away with it. Especially at a time when China's legal framework wasn't quite ready yet and before there were cameras at every intersection. But it often went further than that. You regularly saw someone lying in the street in front of a car that had hit them. In reality, that person had simply jumped on the hood of a car waiting at the traffic lights, in order to stage an accident. Insurance fraud is also not uncommon among the Chinese. Anyone who saw it usually didn't want to come forward for fear of getting caught up in a web of lies. What we too often forget here is that these scammers mostly came from the poorest regions, and this one desperate act meant they could earn a whole year's salary, send their child to college, or pay the hospital bills for a parent. This is actually not that different from petty crime in big cities in the West. I am not saying this is acceptable, but I like to highlight the difference between the actual responsibility, "you did this", and the moral responsibility, "now you deserve a punishment as a way to cause you harm".

The pragmatic solution in China: in 2013, every car owner bought a camera for the front of their car, and several cameras were added to each intersection by the local government to help the police verify events. China is a society without lethal weapons, and physical violence is rare. But in a country with 1.4 billion inhabitants, there are of course a lot of criminals, from copycats to cyber criminals. My own software company in Shanghai was brazenly copied five times in ten years: three times by Europeans and twice by Chinese. I learned the hard way that in the business world, lying is not a Chinese concept, but unfortunately a universal phenomenon. In China, especially if you had the right connections, you just got away with it faster; especially when legislation and implementation of the law were still falling behind, or no regulatory body even existed. This is very different today.

Lying is universal. But the Chinese have become really smart at it, driven by their particular economic, social, historical, or cultural circumstances. The mistake is therefore assuming that the Chinese can't be trusted. The challenge for foreigners is not to see this as a moral injustice, but as the result of a period in history that has defined society, and that they themselves all want to leave behind. My advice is to try and find out what is motivating the Chinese in a given situation, and see if it is economics, society, history, or culture driving their desire for progress. The Chinese have their own built-in trust radar. The question is, how can you get access to it? The best advice I can give is to find a Chinese friend who is not connected to your business and use their radar. Another piece of advice that really helps me is to invest more time in your Chinese contacts' closest friends than your contacts themselves. They will be quicker to speak their mind or give you tips. Taking into account the four motives for Chinese people to lie above, it is a case of, during each interaction, interpreting which goal your Chinese partner wants to achieve the most. Is it money? Is it status? Is it security? Is it a passion? Is it power? To discover the sincerity of their objective, pay special attention to values such as openness, empathy, respect for others, reciprocity, and directness when talking to your contact. Actually, this is all universally human, but we usually forget to do our homework because we too are blinded by our own goals, which are usually money or growth. The Chinese are very aware of this and the pitfall that for-eigners fall into again and again. We assume our objectives are the same as our counterpart's—which is often not the case in China. We also quickly forget that the Chinese themselves experience far more fraud, lies, and theft from their fellow citizens than we do.

Now that more than half of the Chinese have achieved a good standard of living, they too strive for a society that is fairer and more trustworthy. This change is quite rapid and is being driven by three main phenomena:
- The Chinese traveling beyond the country and being inspired by other cultures.
- A growing middle class who want to live in a society of trust.
- The internet that allows hundreds of millions of young people to report abuses.

Ultimately, China goes back to the roots of the ancient Chinese culture once taught by the great teacher Confucius, where trust is the cornerstone of all human relationships: *"I wouldn't know what to do with someone whose word cannot be trusted. How would you drive a wagon without a yoke or a chariot without a crossbar?"*

WHO CAN I STILL BELIEVE?

In today's hyperconnected digital world, it is even more difficult to trust anyone or anything online. We live in an era of fake news, deep fakes, and online information disorder. Fake websites, profiles, and internet accounts pollute the internet with rumors, conspiracy theories, lies, or half-truths taken out of context. Every day during the 2020 pandemic, there were an enormous amount of news reports about China that mainly served to discredit the country. Many of the reports were well-researched, written by professional journalists from reputable publications, and were even backed up by scientific evidence, intelligence reports, or political policy statements. Because most of us in 2020 found ourselves in a period of uncertainty or fear, but also wanted to help each other, more and more misleading information was shared, without people being critical or thinking about it carefully.

In the spring of 2020, for example, I received dozens of news items daily from friends who wanted to warn me about what was really going on in China. I mistakenly thought that they wanted to hear my opinion on whether these reports were genuine or not. But no. The reports were reliable because the source was well known and they had been shared a hundred thousand times. When I pointed out the errors, incorrect data, or inconsistent context in the reports, I often opened a Pandora's box, and this would haunt me for days. Using data from the Chinese media to support my case backfired. The general assumption is that the Chinese media is state-owned or state-influenced and therefore fundamentally unreliable. When these Chinese media channels pointed out the fact that there was no evidence whatsoever for the allegations, and it could even show they were simply lies, few were interested. In 2020, China was presumed guilty until proven innocent. How dare I argue with a universal Western truth? After all, China is a country that doesn't avoid propaganda, restricts foreign journalists, and is certainly not against censorship. Why should it be any different now? It was at that point that I came to the shocking realization that it is what we hear often that is accepted as true, and that we are quicker to believe stories that are familiar more than stories that are unknown or unpopular. As far as China is concerned, the West collectively suffers increasingly from confirmation bias: we look for facts to prove what we already believe, that the Chinese can't be trusted.

A NEW CULTURAL REVOLUTION

The Cultural Revolution (1966-1976) in China remains etched in our collective memory. That period of massive anarchy has largely defined global distrust in China. However, the Chinese would rather forget that period. The Cultural Revolution was started by Mao Zedong to promote a pure form of socialism, starting with the cultural and ideological values and extending to all aspects of society. At the same time, it aided to protect his own position as the undisputed supreme leader of China. This revolution came after the failure of the Great Leap Forward (1958-1962) where Chairman Mao tried to too quickly transform China from an agricultural into an industrial society, leading to a famine that resulted in millions of deaths. Mao then began to lose the confidence of the Communist Party, but mainly feared that the government had been infiltrated by people who wanted to restore capitalism, and that a new elite would cause China to fall back to deep inequality. This resulted in a ban on the consumption of "hedonistic goods" and everyone being urged to demonstrate their "revolutionary background" and "loyalty" to Mao over individual consumption.

Everything suspected of being bourgeois or feudal had to go; universities and high schools were closed and millions of smart young people were sent to the countryside to learn from the farmers and to promote greater respect and equality between the classes. The basic idea of social equality came about even before the Cultural Revolution with the "iron rice bowl", a promise from Mao that all Chinese people would have work: respect for the poor, improved healthcare, good literacy, and nutrition, but this was mainly at the expense of the people in the cities. Gender equality was also heavily promoted, with Mao's famous statement: "Women hold up half the sky." Women even acted out violence as Red Guards, which was also an indirect attack on the feudal rulers who usually had a negative impact on women's lives. So, the Confucian patriarchal society was suddenly replaced by a more gender-equal society that banned forced marriages and concubines, allowed divorce, and—within the land reforms—extended property rights to the benefit of women. For the first time, women debated their role in society and balance in the household. I am not doing justice to condense this complicated part of history into just one paragraph, but these few insights are critical to understand how Chinese individuals have evolved since and as a result of Mao coming to power in 1949.

Most people are familiar with the propaganda posters of female Red Guards in military uniforms with a red armbands, holding up the "little red book" during the Cultural Revolution. Since the start of China's Open-Door Policy in 1978, consumer habits have changed a lot, gradually becoming more similar to those of Western capitalism. But the internal drive of consumption is still very different from the West, influenced by both Mao's Cultural Revolution and more than two thousand years of Confucian patriarchal society. Millions of Chinese, mainly women, today find themselves in a psychological triangular relationship between age-old hierarchical family values, Maoist ideas about social equality, and Western individualistic values and lifestyles.

In addition, the Chinese economy has developed so rapidly in recent decades that the differences in lifestyle between the largest and smallest cities have become even bigger. For several years now, the Chinese consumer market has therefore been at the start of a new cultural revolution: the "lifestyle upgrade" or "consumer upgrade" revolution. This trend has been particularly visible since 2018, with consumers spending less and less on food and housing, and more on premium products like cosmetics or quality brands from clothes to electronics. This new Chinese cultural consumption revolution toward greater quality and sustainability today replaces the Chinese consumers' previous forty-year-old preference for abundance and the transient. People living in Chinese cities are becoming more conscious and sophisticated in what they buy, placing more importance on the environment, healthy food, or the impact on society. The reason this trend is extremely strong is less about individual consciousness, like in the West, and more about a tight collective consciousness among friends and families of a new middle class in China's major cities.

THE COLLECTIVE CHINESE

Just imagine listening to someone glorifying China's system or saying they've lost faith in the Western system. Would that person also say that the main difference between China and the West is that China is a collectivist society and the West is much more individualistic? They might also argue that China, with its long-term vision and one-party state, is able to make important, top-down decisions that the Chinese are also very happy to collectively follow. For many, the combination of top-down directives in the context of China's more collective society explains why China can deliver enormous change at exceptional speed and on such a large scale. These pro-China or anti-Western thinkers sometimes indicate that China's system could be the answer to the many problems of the West. They go on to explain that the bottom-up democratically elected Western politicians do so much short-term thinking because, if they didn't, it'd be hard to get re-elected. They have to please the individualistic citizen who insists on their freedom and rights, but they also have to fight the opposition, which leads to the delay, dilution, fragmentation, or breakdown of decisions and initiatives. So, we often end up in a deadlock. However, China's system is not the solution to our challenges.

We are quick to jump to the wrong conclusion that China is a top-down system with a collective society, in contrast to the West, which has a bottom-up system and is far more individualistic. Let me be very clear: China is just as individualistic as the West. China is also just as collective as the West. The Chinese are also very individualistic. Just think how materialistic they are, how impatiently they sneak to the front of the line, or how they put themselves in the limelight on the Chinese TikTok. The West is as collective as China. Just think how easily we collectively take to the streets to protest against any collective social injustice, how many non-governmental or charitable organizations we have to help communities, or how decent and fair the general healthcare or education is in many Western European countries. Why then do we think that China is collective and the West is individualistic?

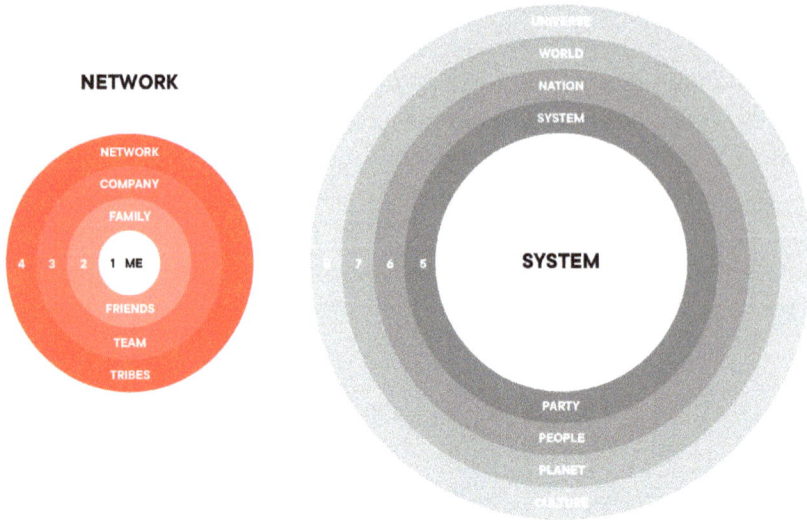

Figure 2 / The circles of trust, the innermost network circles, and outermost system circles

The four innermost network circles of trust (the individual, family/friends, company/leaders, network/tribes), where you know someone personally, or have a relationship or direct connection with them as an individual, are very strongly embedded in China's relationship culture. It is this culture that, through the centuries, has taken care of the collective, including the safety of individuals within the group and provided the needed social structure. In the West, the Enlightenment put the individual more at the center, which meant acquaintances and those involved in your network would support and encourage you as an individual to achieve your progress, goals, prosperity, and purpose.

In their close relationship circles, the Chinese think much more protectively, a safe-haven, while Westerners treat these same networks more as base for personal progress. The Chinese think more collectively within their networks; we more as individualists.

The outermost circles of trust (system/party, nation/people, world/planet, universe/culture) play less of a protective role in China's past but form a path to the future. The main reason is that in the past, China was largely closed off from the rest of the world politically, culturally, and socially, and therefore had much less need to build structures and systems to defend the country and its people from outsiders. China did have a lot of economic ties to the world, but these were more of a benefit than a threat to the system. After having focused on running the country for two thousand years, the administrative apparatus is fully able to provide ample structure for the country and protect the system from civilian chaos or farmer revolts, and is less concerned with threats from outside China.

For more than seventy years under the rule of the Communist Party, citizens received even more attention from the local and central governments; their goal being progress rather than stability this time. The great leap forward (here I'm not referring to the 1958 campaign that caused great famine and many millions of deaths) that Mao wanted to make was intended to take hundreds of millions of often illiterate, poor farmers with little land and future out of the agricultural economy and toward an industrial, prosperous society. As Mao set the country back several times after 1958, he obviously failed to achieve the goal of common prosperity for all Chinese in his lifetime. Under Deng Xiaoping's reforms starting in 1978, all citizens were given the opportunity to achieve prosperity. In the eyes of many Chinese, Mao and Deng helped Chinese citizens as human beings and liberated every Chinese person from lasting poverty. They gave every Chinese person another chance at more progress, prosperity, and purpose in life.

China's system circles of trust are more related to and concerned with the individual than with the collective. Or rather, the Chinese expect the government to partly fulfill their individual expectations and future. We shouldn't see this as a collective objective, but as an individual expectation of each citizen. The Chinese think in an individualistic way in the sense that they expect the system, leaders, and the world to advance them personally.

In the West, we think much more collectively about the system circles. In the Western concept of nation states—in contrast to China, which acts more as a culture or civilization state—Western countries have placed much more trust in the system to protect the collective with more structure, agreements, and rules. When we act collectively, it is usually against the system or the leaders. If the Chinese act collectively, it is more against individuals who abuse the system than against the system itself. The system itself is strongly defended by citizens and leaders, not just out of self-protection by the Party, but also because it gives the best guarantee to each person for their individual progress. In their outer system circles, the Chinese think much more in terms of progress, while Westerners approach their outer system much more to protect all people.

The Chinese system and its leaders must advance the Chinese; while Chinese relationships and networks should keep China stable. The Western system must keep the West stable; while the networks in the West are there to move each Westerner forward. This basic idea is the common thread running through this book.

For example, it can help us to know why China is taking a more forceful approach to the pandemic, environmental issues, or the repression of Uyghurs. We see these images as the result of a collective society that strictly follows, or must follow, orders from Beijing; but it is the collective support of China's close relationship society that is more a driving force here. The close collective fabric and the sustainability of Chinese culture are central to this, much more so than the individual or progress.

For example, it can help us to understand why it seems that the Chinese are sometimes less careful with intellectual property, working conditions, or international agreements. We see those examples as acts of individual pragmatism or greed on the part of the Chinese; while the Chinese system and administration has long allowed these malpractices precisely to provide for a better future for all Chinese people; and to then truly tackle them again today because the vacuum of rules would otherwise harm more than benefit Chinese citizens.

The individual, as well as the change and future of the citizen are central here, and are accelerated by the Party and the system; they are much less driven by Party power retention or protectionism as is often said. **As individuals, many Chinese people trust that their system and China will help them progress.** For them, it is therefore a matter of riding the wave of Chinese growth, priorities, and the budgets of the government. That is why Chinese seldom swim against the current, or the guidance of the Communist Party. **In contrast, as a collective, the Chinese trust that their networks will protect them.** So, for them it is a case of building relationships with Chinese people with the right reputation, power, and wisdom.

If we could turn the image of China as a top-down government with collective obedience into one of a bottom-up collective citizen network that, through local governments, enables the central government to support the progress of all citizens, then we would look at China very differently. Of course, historically, culturally, and politically, everything is much more complex, but this **individual-collective inversion** can be a simple way to see China in a different light. The many examples and stories in the following chapters will show a different perspective on China. If you like, you can use that inversion as a way to reflect on this.

親

qīn

Meaning: **parent, relative, marriage, (emotional) relationship, people from the same home or town.** One ancient character is built up of one symbol for **relationships** and one for **seeing**; the character for relationships shows a symbol of a man close to a tree. If you see each other often, you have a very trusting relationship.

2.

Blind faith. What are the Chinese Confucian virtues? How traditional are Chinese people today? What is the position of women in the Chinese family and in society? Why do the closest relatives in the world's oldest family culture live apart from each other? Do the Chinese trust each other on social media? Why is WeChat your best friend?

Family and friends

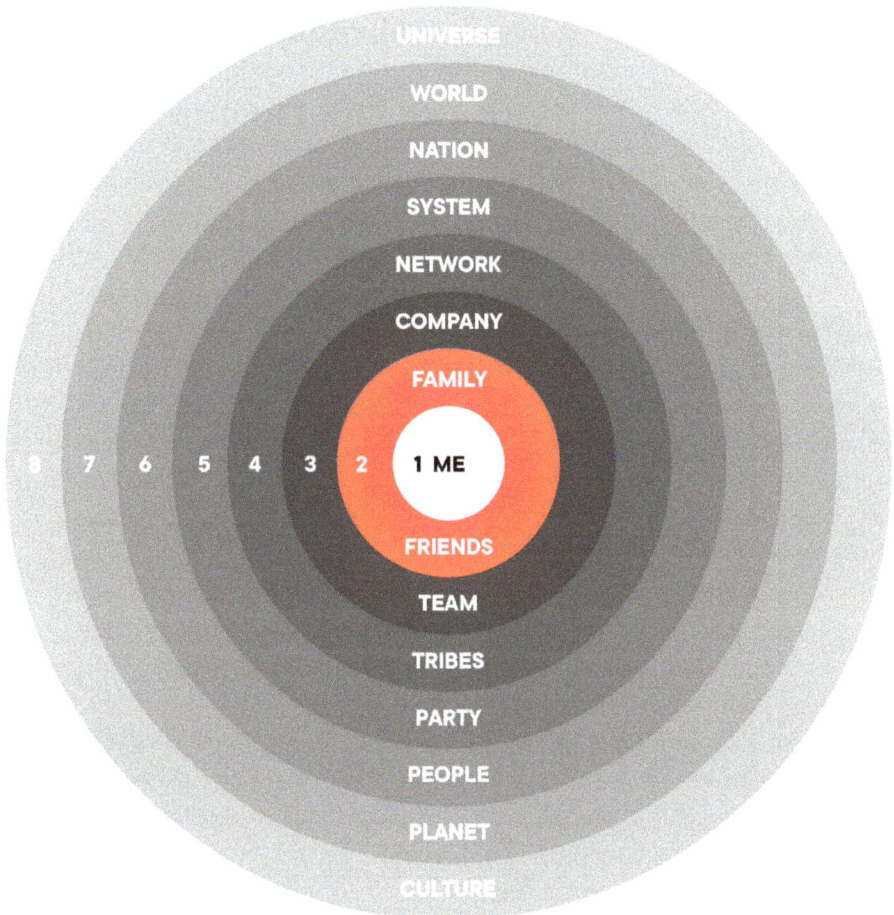

UNIVERSE
WORLD
NATION
SYSTEM
NETWORK
COMPANY
FAMILY
1 ME
FRIENDS
TEAM
TRIBES
PARTY
PEOPLE
PLANET
CULTURE

8 7 6 5 4 3 2

A FAMILY AFFAIR

I started my university studies in Ghent (Belgium) in 1988. The Sinology department was known as the best in Europe for the study of Buddhism. My main interest was in modern China and its past as the basis for today's society and culture. As a result, philosophical Confucianism was much more fascinating to me than Buddhism or Taoism, given its greater influence on Chinese culture. Confucianism has been the driving force behind Chinese virtues and moral and ethical thinking for 2,500 years. In the West, we are mainly familiar with Confucius from the many quotes popular on social media. This philosopher, called Kong Zi in Chinese (551-479 BC), has had the same great impact on Chinese culture as his contemporaries Socrates and Plato have had on our Western culture. It was no coincidence that all three of them lived in a period of change and chaos that led to doubt in the divine and a new search for more humanistic ideas. Ancient China and Greece were very different in many ways, but both cultures had a strict hierarchical and patriarchal structure that strongly influences us to this day.

These three philosophers (Confucius, Socrates, and Plato) placed great importance on the social structure of an ordered society, in which a ruling class is distinguished from the wider population. To achieve this goal, Confucius describes a strict hierarchical relationship system in which the subject obeys the leader; the son, the father; the wife, her husband; and the younger brother, the older. The subordinate is loyal to the dominant role, while the latter must be kindhearted to his subject. According to Confucius, clear social relationships keep the harmony of society intact—and that is still how most Chinese people think 2,500 years later. Above all, it was the importance of maintaining family harmony that became the basis of a healthy Chinese society and good governance of the country. The family's interests come before the individual's. Not keeping the family together is seen as failure, which of course puts a lot of pressure on children—even today.

This sounds very rigid, but in stark contrast to the ancient Greeks, Confucius does encourage social mobility. In fact, Chinese children are almost duty-bound to climb the social ladder through study, hard work, or talent. The most important word here is **xiào** (孝), or filial piety, which is a combination of the characters **lăo** (老) and **zi** (子), meaning parent and child, with parent above the child. The child does not rebel, shows respect, fulfills the wishes of the father, and takes care of the parents in later life. The parents have to be kind to their children and give them the best opportunities. The individual decisions and actions of the Chinese are therefore heavily influenced by the family context—the continued presence of both family pressure and a support structure from the family are the backbone to achieve individual aspirations.

In the West, people often refer to China as a collectivist society, in contrast to the Western model of an individualist society. I believe it is actually better to call China a relational society vs. a collective society; that way it's not defined as being the opposite of individualism. This also better explains why the Chinese can sometimes be very individualistic and selfish, as long as the value of their own social circle is maintained in the process. The feeling this sometimes creates outside of China is that they are dishonest, not being true to themselves, or putting on a mask—a land of two-faced Januses. The Chinese do often appear to have two faces, and it is the social context that determines which face they put on. This is because the success and advantages of the group are more important than those of the individual; not because the Chinese strive for the collective interest of all Chinese, but because for them the success of the individual is strongly determined by the success of the group. The fact that ties are tight among close relatives is not just a Chinese trait. In other cultures, direct blood relatives are also central to a person's life. All over the world, mutual respect and love form the basis of close and trusting family relationships. It's no different in China. Yet I was often surprised by the scope of commitments that Chinese people are prepared to make to strengthen or maintain their family bonds, even these days.

It is impossible to understand or trust China unless you understand China's culture based on the family. This is the basis of the relational society that keeps China strong. China is primarily a human-centered society in which people and the individual, not nature, take a central position. This is why the individual is central to the first circle of trust. In a Confucian context, the essence of being human is to examine everything in order to gain more knowledge and insights with the aim of becoming as sincere as possible. This is the reason the Chinese are naturally very inquisitive and questioning. Confucius stated that if a man is sincere, his mind is free to be civilized. This is the foundation of the civilized form of society that Confucius envisioned for China. If the individual is cultivated, there can be order in society. That order is defined and held in place by the second circle—the family. As a foundational element, the family represents hierarchy and order. Therefore, I believe China will never become a country of complete equality, because Chinese culture is based on hierarchical relationships of power and responsibility, respect and obedience. So, forget the idea that China will one day become an ideal communist egalitarian society. China values inequality, but not dishonesty. Compare China with a mythical largest company in the world, where everyone knows their place and role in the organization and respects their superiors; where you don't hit any glass ceiling if you work hard; and where business leaders have to develop all their employees to maintain and improve their own position. In the same way, the family culture of China is a culture of well-defined relationships between people. Within the family, these are based on the Confucian hierarchical relationships, such as the four described above. Confucius also describes relationships among friends, which is the only bond of equals in his model of society. Although even this bond isn't always equal because of how real friends gain each other's trust: reciprocity (人情 **rénqíng**). There is never an absolutely equal balance of debits and credits. You always owe your friend a favor, or they owe you one. This cultural concept of reciprocity is like playing the stock market, except every day you invest in your friends, and they invest in you. Sometimes you want to make a long-term investment, sometimes a short-term one. As long as you remain sincere and invest in friends who are sincere with you, your stock in life will always continue to rise. If you don't follow the rules, and instead misuse, manipulate, or cheat on your friends, then your environment will give you a slap on the wrist: your boss, your network, the system, the Party, the people, or the universe. In Confucian thought, the intent was not only to regulate the family within a well-defined ethical system, but to use the well-ordered family as the cornerstone to regulate the government of the entire country. Only when family values are in balance can the state be well governed and everything under the sun can be at peace and in harmony. Based on this, Confucius promotes eight virtues that form the backbone of Chinese society: justice (义 **yì**), benevolence (仁 **rén**), courtesy (礼 **lǐ**), wisdom (智 **zhì**), trust (信 **xìn**), loyalty (忠 **zhōng**), filial piety (孝 **xiào**), and moral integrity (节 **jié**). In addition, elements such as honesty, kindness, forgiveness, respect, courage, frugality, and shame further highlight the eight Chinese virtues. We would have to delve too far into Chinese philosophy to explain each of these terms in detail, but even a brief exploration clearly shows how Chinese family values are centered on the backbone of a 2,500-year-old moral code. This moral code and relational order of behavior is still practiced within Chinese families to this day and continues to radiate through all of the larger circles of trust. In my mind, Chinese culture is actually Chinese family culture applied at a national level.

If we don't trust China, it may be because we forget to tell a story about China starting from its foundation in family values. This goes beyond the difference between a relational or individualistic society. It is also better not to compare this too much to examples of close family ties in other societies. In China, it is less about the strong bond between blood relatives than it is about order and morality within the Chinese family. I would like to use a story to illustrate the "magnet and propeller" effect of the family on Chinese people. Imagine a twenty-two-year-old Chinese girl named Angela. She is from the port city of Ningbo, 120 miles south of Shanghai. Her parents put everything into getting her through the university entrance exam, and four years later she has just graduated as a chemical engineer from the highly prestigious Fudan University in Shanghai. She owes everything to her parents, and according to Confucian morality she now has to obey and support them. Ideally, later on she will be able to support her parents financially and care for them in their old age.

Her neatly mapped-out path in life is clear: a good job in a chemical company, an apartment in Ningbo, and a successful husband with whom to raise a son together. Her father is very well connected with the Ningbo government and of course wants to help his daughter via his connections. But Angela wants to stay in the metropolis of Shanghai and not return to Ningbo. A conflict arises: her father makes it clear that Angela needs to know her place in the family, and that she cannot just deny her father's wishes. But Angela stands her ground. She decides to stay in Shanghai anyway, without a job, and lives in a tiny apartment a long way from the city center. Her father isn't happy, but with a heavy heart, decides to support his daughter. He puts money in her bank account every month and calls all his business associates in Shanghai to ask if they can help his daughter find a job. Meanwhile, her mother tries to find her a suitable husband from Ningbo. But Angela is a lesbian, and eventually decides one day to tell her father in order to put an end to all those blind dates her mother has been organizing for her. They didn't see this latest twist in the tale coming and they don't know how to deal with it, but they accept it. The father continues to support Angela financially and now even pays an advance for her to buy an apartment in Shanghai. By now, Angela has found a job, as a junior communications manager in an advertising agency. She works as much overtime as possible so that her father no longer has to send her money. In a few years she works her way up to marketing director and now lives with a friend. She can now buy an apartment for her parents in the same neighborhood in Shanghai so she can take care of them after they retire.

This story of Angela is a composite of the real stories of two good Chinese friends of mine. It illustrates that family values in China are not a matter of a rigid, formal contract between parent and child, but rather grounded on understanding, humane, and relaxed relationships. It demonstrates a moral order based on many basic values such as respect, loyalty, justice, humanity, wisdom, forgiveness, reciprocity, and sacrifice, which come extremely naturally, and above all ensures you're really not a burden, but rather a help and support for your parents or for your child depending on your role. As a father myself, I lived in Shanghai with my wife and daughter for fifteen years. The whole neighborhood knew us as the two Belgians with a Chinese daughter. We adopted Amelie when she was nine months old. But when my wife and I walked down the street without our daughter, people would ask us if Amelie was in Belgium. Our Chinese neighbors naturally expected us to leave our daughter with her grandparents in Belgium, where in their eyes at least, education, healthcare, and life in general were better. Belgium would give our daughter the best opportunities for her future, while we could earn a lot of money for her in Shanghai and then travel back once or twice a year to see her. We couldn't imagine for a moment our child living so far away from us. And how do we reconcile the questions we faced with the idea that the Chinese consider family ties so important? To me, this just shows to what extent Chinese parents are willing to put themselves last, and even tolerate physical distance from their only child, if it means improving their child's future. More on this later. The cultural impact of 2,500-year-old Confucian family values on the Chinese people and China today is certainly not to be underestimated.

THE "LEFTOVER" WOMEN

And now we turn to **gender stereotypes**, where the roles of a woman and her husband were clearly defined by the wise man Confucius 2,500 years ago. In traditional Chinese culture, the wife's role is at home, supporting her husband and protecting the family. Once married, she follows her husband, whom she sometimes even had to share with a concubine. For a woman, divorce was very shameful, and even illegal during many periods of Chinese history. Remarrying was extremely difficult, especially if she was widowed or not childless (i.e., unchaste). These "leftover" women were mostly doomed to continue serving their in-laws, and some were celebrated because they honorably committed suicide. Although Confucius never approved of the practice, we're also familiar with the stories of the tiny lotus feet imposed on women as a beauty ideal from the time of the Song dynasty (960-1279 AD). Foot binding made the woman even less mobile and transformed her from being a person into a desirable object or possession.[32] In the Tang dynasty (618-907 AD), characterized by its high culture and art, including the well-known porcelain vases and horses, Chinese women had a much higher status than in the other dynasties. The Song and Tang dynasties are associated with seven golden centuries for China in terms of prosperity and technological progress, with inventions such as printing, gunpowder, clocks, the compass, paper money, and something we can't live without today: toilet paper. At the time, China was the richest, most powerful, and most advanced country in the world, but the Tang and Song were very different in terms of freedoms for women.

During the Tang, women were given the opportunity to study and serve in political and military roles. They lived in social harmony, had a more independent status, many were even well-educated, and were allowed to manage social and business activities. At that time, China was noticeably ahead of the West in this respect. Chinese women of the Tang period were fortunate to live in an era characterized by openness and what we now call liberal ideas. Fast-forward to this century, can China once again reach its peak as a harmonious society like it did during the Tang dynasty? And will the relatively liberal Tang thoughts and openness also return to Chinese society? Or with Xi Jinping will there be a return to the Confucian bureaucratic society of the Song dynasty?

Although these ancient feudal societies no longer exist in China, it is obvious that strongly traditional patriarchal thinking is still deeply rooted in Chinese society of today. For example, the bride price (**cǎilǐ** 彩礼), where the groom's family gives money to the bride's family, has existed in China since 1046 BC. This concept was created as a gift to balance out the dowry, but it became more and more a custom practice over the centuries. Bride price symbolizes and enforces the ancient traditions of treating women as a commodity to be transacted with the husband's family. After marriage, the wife would traditionally live with the husband's family and take care of his parents. The bride price was equal to the loss of labor for the woman's family. The strange thing about China today is that both the obligatory bride price and the optional dowry, which—as in India—is given by the woman's family, continue to exist. Although bride price was banned during the communist Mao era, this ancient custom has reappeared in modern China. The bride price that the groom's family has to pay can be up to $13,500 (four years of average annual income in the cities and twelve years in the countryside).[33] That bride price is important for a bride to maintain economic security, since it is still the husband who is expected to provide the income. The bride price therefore also contributes to reinforcing traditional gender roles. Because men, or their parents, cannot always afford this, many women are left out in the cold. But it is above all the psychological gender inequality, with the bride price as its symbol, that really holds back modern, literate, self-confident, self-assured, and career-minded Chinese women. Regardless of the preserved custom of the bride price in the countryside, modern Chinese urban women today remain single more out of choice, and decide to marry later on in life, or even not at all. And why there are so many "leftover" women—known by the derogatory term **shèngnǚ** (剩女)—a name to describe unmarried women over the age of thirty. In this chapter, we'll see how this has created a whole new generation of successful single women in China.

The seriousness of the Shengnu situation becomes clear when you see "rent-a-boyfriend" adverts appearing on some Chinese e-commerce sites like Alibaba's Taobao. On these sites you'll find plenty of guys who are happy to spend, for example, the Chinese or Western Valentine's Day with single women, for a fee. These services get even more popular during Chinese New Year. Weeks in advance, the "leftover" women really start to worry how they'll answer annoying questions from their parents and other relatives about their boyfriends and marriage plans. With such a large online offering of "stand-in boyfriends," there's a good chance you can hire someone who comes from the same province or city as where your parents live; a guy of the right age and with a promising future. Good looks are a bonus, but not required. For around $200 you can hire a guy to go home with you to your family and play your partner for the day. This is a perfectly normal transaction in China, and given the prudish nature of Chinese culture, there is no need to kiss or hug in front of your parents.

Family pressure is often so great that they prefer to hire a partner to take home for Chinese New Year. For many, keeping up appearances is less painful than having to face disappointed parents year after year. This shows how great the social pressure is for many women, as they sometimes practice for two weeks to ensure this family gathering runs smoothly. Here again, we come across the important lesson from the previous chapter: rather than intended to hurt someone, lies are quite normal if they can make someone happy and maintain harmony.

These ancient traditions live on, despite two factors that should have had the opposite effect. First, China's one-child policy (1979-2015) that created an excess of men; and second, the government's commitment to promote gender equality. The latter goes back to Mao Zedong who, as I already mentioned, once said that "women hold up half the sky," and who in 1954 had written into the constitution that women had equal rights in politics, economics, culture, and social and domestic life. To make this a reality, many laws were created that resulted in semi-equal rights between men and women. And progress has been made. Twenty-eight of the sixty-seven self-made female billionaires in the world are Chinese;[34] Chinese women make up forty-one percent of China's gross domestic product (GDP); eighty percent of technology companies in China have a woman in a position of leadership, and for most of these companies more than forty percent of the workforce is made up of women; nearly fifty percent of all engineers in China are women.[35]

This gives China much greater "girl power" than many other countries. Yet the feminist struggle of women in China for true equality remains a work in progress. It is a struggle that hinges on the big discrepancy between the many opportunities that women have today in China to independently follow their own path and climb the corporate ladder; and at the same time the family expectations to ensure financial security by marrying well. The conflict between highly successful female role models in China and legal framework of equal opportunity on the one hand, and marriage and very well-sustained Confucian traditions on the other, still makes it a challenge for many Chinese women to choose between their own personal development and family obligations, especially in rural areas or in labor-intensive industries.[36]

CHINA'S WOMEN WARRIORS

For many Chinese mothers, this is still a huge source of tension in their daily lives. On the one hand, these modern Chinese women grew up exposed to a much more liberal Western lifestyle in terms of their upbringing, education, and nutrition; but on the other hand, their own parents always overprotected them as an only child and made all their big life choices for them. Many women are therefore totally unprepared to be mothers and are caught between the freedoms of the new China and the expectations and traditions of parental obedience. They want to keep going out, be fashionably dressed, and get a job outside the home, but in the eyes of their parents they are mainly expected to fulfill their role as mothers. Because in China it is the four grandparents who often take full care of their only grandchild during the first few years, it is too tempting for the mothers to refuse this help as it allows them to continue their glamorous social lives. Many women live in the twilight zone between two roles: mother and independent woman—practical-minded and full of dreams. They represent the ideal targets for brands promising to empower them with new products, and this group is the biggest driver of social e-commerce, which we'll cover later in this chapter.

You could say that this consumer group is trying to break down the barrier between family tradition and the modern individual with the help of brand names. This reminds me of advertising images in America from the 1950s. During World War II, American women went out to work in the factories, and then when their husbands returned after the war, they were expected to carry on with their traditional roles as housewives and mothers, symbolizing American family values during the Cold War. Although it was still a man's world, the world of advertising was already beginning to portray both the emerging independence and influence of women consumers. Back then, the advertising world was well aware that American women were the influencers of their era and the key to changing the buying behavior of their friends and families.[37] Through consumption, the American women of the 1950s had the power to change their identities and potentially their lives. That was the beginning of the feminist movement in America. China is now experiencing a similar feminist trend, only much more quickly due to the role of social media. Today, the compromise between Chinese mothers and their parents is achieved by keeping some of the traditional domestic roles but taking on a different identity for themselves and their child beyond the home.

We all know the story of Mulan that was made into a Disney cartoon and later movie. Hua Mulan was a Chinese warrior 2,500 years ago who didn't want her sick father to serve in the military. With the approval of her parents, she dressed as a boy and took her father's place in the army. After twelve years of fighting, she returns to her family and once again dresses as a woman. Only then do her fellow soldiers discover she is female. Fictional or not, this story has been an inspiration to women and shows that women can go against tradition and fulfill the traditionally male roles as well, or even better than men. I too had the opportunity to work with a real version of Mulan—Florence, who was the employee I respected the most over my years in China. Florence was incredibly self-reliant and a top salesperson, but she was much less fortunate in love.

She did however teach me the biggest secret to sales in China, which I am sharing with you: in China, the big boss always decides on the important purchases, so you have to talk directly to the boss. But these bosses always have an army of foot soldiers who block you with lies and useless questions or have nothing better to do than just give you the runaround. This corporate spider web exists to protect the boss from rejections that would cause them to lose face, but above all not to miss any opportunities. Florence knew the secret ingredient to getting through these barriers. You just have to show those foot soldiers an incredible opportunity, one where they can't give you an answer themselves, and so they are forced to involve their boss. For Florence, this was an imaginary distributor in Belgium she described who wanted to distribute their Chinese products in Europe. Only the big boss could make this kind of strategic decision. Thanks to Florence, in just two years I personally spoke to the bosses of more than a hundred of China's largest companies. At first, I found it really difficult and was very nervous at every meeting. My reputation and integrity were at stake. But Florence convinced me again and again that if I declined the appointment she had set up with the big boss, her own face was at stake. I could always go back to Belgium, but it wouldn't be so easy for her to leave China. She won me over. I quickly noticed, however, that I never needed to mention the name of that imaginary distributor in Europe, and we were never accused of anything underhanded. It was a see-through trick, and the Chinese bosses soon realized it, but that didn't get in the way of negotiations. The Chinese like to do business with commercially-minded partners. It was as if this were a competition to see who was the smartest. Instead of falling into disgrace, sometimes I even gained more respect. In my experience, Florence had never lied or misled me. One day she suddenly told me she wanted to leave the company to go back to Fujian and help her parents, and she asked me if I could write her a letter of recommendation for a new job there. Even though I was very disappointed to lose her, I agreed. Anticipating my reaction, she immediately conjured up the letter out of nowhere—all I had to do was sign it. The next day, Florence was gone.

It was not until many years later that I found out that after she left my company, she got married the same week, and shortly afterwards she moved to America to study at a university there. I didn't understand it at all because she had always told me everything. I assumed she had no boyfriend and that is why she threw herself so enthusiastically into her work. Ten years later, she came back to China and confessed everything to me. Back then, her parents had found her a very smart guy who had been accepted to do a doctorate program in America, and by getting married to him she could go to the prom-ised land. After she got a green card, the divorce was quickly set in motion and she returned to her roots. Perhaps like all over the world, most Chinese people from poorer families hardly ever miss a chance at a better life. Florence trusted me blindly, but apparently not blindly enough to put her own future or family at risk. In China, friends are friends and family is family. Florence was my example of a Chinese woman who stepped out of the straitjacket to grab her "once in a lifetime" opportunity with both hands. Like with everything, some things are universal, not just "Chinese".

FAMILIES LIVING APART

Florence is a typical example of how many Chinese people live apart from their families. One of the reasons for this is the entrance examination system for Chinese universities, known as the **gāokǎo** (高考). From June 7-9 each year, eleven million Chinese teenagers sit for one of the world's most difficult entrance exams, often with multiple attempts, as those three days determine the future of every child. Parents spend a small fortune on tutoring to prepare for this one exam and the kids spend years studying as hard as they can. While this meritocratic system aims to give everyone equal opportunities, the pressure on migrants and children from the countryside is much greater because they don't have the resources to properly prepare; but also because middle-class children from the big cities now have other ways to work their way up the career ladder, even without a university degree. In 2021, the government suddenly banned all commercial activity for online tutoring to prepare for the gāokǎo in order to increase the chances of success for the poorer children. In China, as elsewhere, companies still look at which university you studied at before offering you your first job.

As a boss, I've been guilty of this too. Having hired dozens of graduates from top universities, I can confirm that perseverance is not something you need to teach them. However, in large countries like the US or China, if students are accepted into a good university, this is rarely in the province where their parents live. As part of the Chinese Gaokao rules, there are three levels of university, and depending on the grade you think you can achieve, you have to indicate your preference of university per level. If you choose the best universities, but in the end don't make the grade required for that university subject, you drop a level or two—and quickly end up a long way from home. As a result, many smart children live apart from their parents from the age of eighteen. They start their lives in an unknown, anonymous city in September, and the result for most of them is loneliness. They look for a second family, which they find in their classes or in their shared college room. These bonds bring university students together intimately close for five years and then follow them into their careers.

The best students in China go to work for Alibaba, Huawei, or Microsoft, or do a PhD abroad. Those who climb the corporate ladder recommend people they studied with as team members to their managers. After a few years, the most courageous of them are brave enough to set up their own business, and their first step is always to involve their friends from university days. This is all about the personal trust and knowledge that is so critical when setting up a start-up in China because as a founder, you want to surround yourself with people with the right expertise, talent, mentality, and confidence. If you don't, things quickly go wrong in China. In fact, it's not unheard of for companies like Alibaba or Tencent to invest in your venture even if you've taken a whole team away from them. These powerful companies are also very aware that personal connections increase your chances of success. How different is that from many Western companies who aim to impose as many non-compete clauses on their managers as possible?

Most Chinese people who move to the larger cities do so to get a better paycheck. They often work in construction, production, hospitality, or become taxi drivers or deliverymen. Often, they find work because of one of their friends from their village, or through a family member who has already made the move to the big city. These networks of acquaintances were the anchor and guide needed for the hundreds of millions of rural migrants that took the big step into the anonymous concrete jungles of China. As a construction or factory worker in 1990 in Shenzhen, you could earn an hourly wage of almost $1, which was the daily wage in the countryside. Back then, the difference in the cost of living in the cities compared to the countryside was not so big, because the employer covered the largest costs—housing and meals. Basic food and daily necessities were very cheap at the time. A bank clerk or teacher, who worked fewer hours than a migrant worker, would even have to make do with the same daily wage. In 1980, twenty percent of the Chinese population lived in cities, but by 2020 that had already increased to sixty-three percent, as nearly seven hundred million people moved to the cities over the last forty years.[38] That's more than double the total population of America, which took over a hundred years to achieve the same degree of urbanization, and almost as much as all of Europe, where the process took two hundred years.

In the early days of the Open-Door Policy, if you lived in the countryside and wanted a better life, your best choice was to go and work as a migrant in the cities. From 1980 to 2010, the rural working age population fled en-masse to the cities, while elderly grandparents were left with the grandchildren, better known as the "left-behind children." This created a worrying situation that impacted at least sixty-nine million children, or thirty percent of all rural children, according to UNICEF.[39] Many of these left-behind children suffered emotional neglect and even malnutrition, leaving them intellectually and even physically affected for life. Often, they were denied access to better education and were still growing up in desperate poverty, despite China's growing economy. The tragic situation is that their parents, who chose hard work and a tough life far from home in order to give their children a better future, often achieved precisely the opposite result. The absence of the parents meant that many left-behind children were given more household tasks and also had to help their grandparents work the land, which in turn meant they abandoned their studies earlier. Under the one-child policy that ended in 2016, parents in the rural areas were permitted a second child if their first child was a girl. Many rural grandparents had never known the importance of education for a better future, so often girls living in the countryside give up their studies to work within the home; potentially even to give their little brother more opportunities for an education. This created a downward spiral of poverty and despair that the family and children could not easily escape. Despite their better economic situation, these very vulnerable families were unable to really take advantage of China's economic miracle. Their version of the Chinese dream often became a lasting nightmare. Many of these parents today regret having left their children behind to give them a better future.[40]

But times are changing. Nowadays, the minimum monthly base salary for an employee in the most expensive city in China (Shanghai) is $385, while it is only half that in the most remote villages in China where life is much cheaper. A house on the outskirts of Shanghai costs around $700 per square foot, so a migrant couple earning more than the bare minimum still has to work hard for at least forty years to afford a small, one-bedroom apartment of five hundred square feet. The average salary in Shanghai is $1,500 a month, which really is the minimum needed to make ends meet. This new reality has forced many migrants to decide to return to their families in the countryside or the smaller towns. This process is now being accelerated by other phenomena. It's not just the people returning to the countryside, but now more and more companies are moving there too. Costs in the major cities have simply risen too high, and more and more old industries are being banned from the cities and surrounding areas by new environmental legislation. The government is incentivizing them to move with new suburbanization policies and subsidies, but also by modernizing more and more locations. Migrants can easily get grants or a loan of up to $20,000 to return to the countryside. But returning to a place with less work, fewer customers, and lower quality social facilities such as hospitals and schools isn't easy. The government has made a promise to returning migrants that it will improve this infrastructure. And so it is based on these plans and other factors that the outflow of migrants from the major cities has increased since 2018.[41] Later in the book I will also describe how the government is putting a lot of effort into integrating all these migrants into China's smaller and medium-sized cities.

Companies like Alibaba have been aware of this trend for some time and have also played their part in this relocation. The strong presence of e-commerce in China has really shaken up the entire retail and manufacturing sector, to the advantage of small-scale self-employed business owners. E-commerce means that location plays less of a role for both sellers and consumers, who sell and buy online. In China, e-commerce already represents twenty-five percent, or $1.5 trillion, of all retail sales.[42] Did you know that three Chinese companies make up forty-two percent of all e-commerce in the world: Alibaba, twenty-nine percent; JD.com, nine percent; and Pinduoduo, four percent? By comparison, Amazon accounts for thirteen percent and eBay three percent.[43]

So today, the returning migrant or local family of farmers in a remote village can easily start their own online Alibaba store. In the West, retailers blame large online stores for destroying local traders. The hard-working small business owner has been squeezed out by the large online retailers and shopping malls. By contrast, in a country like China, where hundreds of millions of people are still poor, this trend has been much more inclusive than exclusive. Of the 6.8 million independent family-owned convenience stores, Alibaba has already given more than a million of them a digital makeover.[44] With real-time inventory and price management, as well as Alibaba branding, these store owners get access to a wider range of products, services, and financing. Given that most of these stores are run by a single family, this keeps the family together.

For migrants still living in the city while their families are in the countryside, Alibaba can also provide a means of reunification. This is how the "Taobao villages" came about. Taobao is Alibaba's online platform where Chinese sellers offer their products in their own online "stores." City migrants and local entrepreneurs suddenly saw an opportunity to set up a Taobao shop in their home villages. In 2013, there were about twenty rural Chinese villages that were all called Taobao villages because many entrepreneurs from those villages employed local families to sell their products only through Taobao. By 2020, there were already more than five thousand Taobao villages in China, generating more than a $100 billion in revenue and creating more than seven million new jobs in the countryside every year.[45] In these villages, ninety percent of the inhabitants often work in online business as owners or employees because the average salary per family is three times higher than in the other rural villages, and matches the typical $500 monthly income per migrant employee in the cities.

Why would anyone still move to the city and be separated from their family when the whole family can now work together at the same Taobao company in their village? They sell all kinds of products, from fruit, to clothes, to fishing equipment...you name it, they'll sell it. Sometimes they work from home or in a small building to keep their costs down. Distribution and promotion are done through Alibaba. To eradicate extreme poverty, the government invested in local infrastructure and services in the most remote areas to enable this online transformation. Not only does this trend increase employment, but it also keeps families together and improves education and healthcare in the village. By 2030, the government predicts there will be twenty thousand Taobao villages that could attract twenty million young people to return to the countryside. It seems that over time, rural China is regaining the importance it had before 1978, but this time without the poverty and other social and mobility restrictions.

THE SILVER GENERATION

Dave Wei was my best friend, first employee, and right-hand man in my start-up in Shanghai. My wife gave him the nickname "Teddy Bear" because he looked like a strong yet cuddly panda bear. He came from the far north of China, near the Siberian border, where temperatures can drop to forty degrees below zero in winter. The extreme cold, Manchurian genes, and a hearty carbohydrate-rich diet meant traditionally that people from the north of China were on average almost four inches taller than the rice-eaters from the south. Today, the Chinese diet is much more homogeneous across the entire country. According to his Chinese grandparents, Dave had the ideal build because his belly made him look just like the "laughing Buddha." They had fattened him up from childhood, partly because "fat" in China symbolizes "rich." You can't blame his grandparents: fifty years ago they were often starving, and they had even seen friends starve to death. Hunger and conflict, or what the Chinese call a "bitter" life, is the trauma that has scarred many Chinese grandparents. They saved a lot and worked hard, and passed on those habits to their children, albeit in a period of great economic growth and plentiful opportunities. It is their grandchildren, or little princes and princesses, who have been spoiled by the older generations. Today, however, more than fourteen percent of the Chinese are overweight[46] and 116 million Chinese people suffer from type 2 diabetes, which represents five times more sufferers than twenty years ago.[47] Better healthcare and less junk food is crucial, but the real cause of this evolution are the grandparents who cannot let go of the troubles and traditions of their past. Fortunately, though, and just like in the West, the Chinese for several years now haven't considered being overweight as a healthy sign of good fortune, rather as a sign of poor health. The fitness and sports industry in China is currently booming.

After eight years of very close friendship, one day Dave invited me to his home. I didn't think too much of it, but this was very important to Dave as I would be meeting his mother. Seven years earlier, Dave had bought a tiny apartment in a suburb of Shanghai, and he lived there with his mother who took care of him. Being a good son, Dave had bought the apartment for his parents' old age. His mother had lived with Dave for four years, separated from her own husband, who continued to live in the family home 1,200 miles away. She did this to give Dave every opportunity in life. Twice a year, they would all be reunited for a week at the family home in the north of China, once during the national holiday in early October and again for the cold winter days of Chinese New Year. For the rest of the year, the parents put themselves second in order to give every opportunity to Dave, and every day Dave slaved away to honor them, and also to create more opportunities for himself. The circle was as round as our panda bear-shaped friend. Family circles like Dave's are so tightly bound together that sometimes you get the impression that every Chinese person is working their fingers to the bone for someone else: their child, their parents, or their in-laws. As a result, almost all older people in China now enjoy a much more comfortable life once they retire. The difference in their comfort level mainly depends on the success of their working children.

We mustn't forget that in the last century, most Chinese people opted for security, not the new market economy. The safest option back then was to work for a state company, bank, or on the land. This is known as the "iron rice bowl", as a state company would guarantee you food for life. The worry about not having enough food is so deeply rooted in China's past and psyche that even today the government is constantly trying to reassure the population there is enough to go around in the event of an epidemic, price hike, or trade war. The second generation of "iron rice bowl" adults were not that different from their parents—the silver generation today. But in the 1980s and 1990s, many moved from the safety of working for state-owned companies to the export factories of Shenzhen, set up a business, or—if they got lucky—went to work for a multinational. Their parents benefited from this too. By 2030, this group of older people will be made up of roughly two hundred million relatively wealthy retirees living in the cities,[48] where they're happy to spend their money. Since this generation of Chinese saved thirty to fifty percent of their wages over their whole lives, they have sometimes savings of over $100,000; and if they invested in the purchase of an apartment in the last century, they are at least as wealthy as the average retired European or American. The fundamental difference between China and the West is that the younger a person is, the richer they often are. This is because the country's free market economy has only existed for forty years. Salaries and house prices have skyrocketed faster than China's growth, and business opportunities have grown from zero to above those in the West today.

To take full advantage of this enormous growth, these silver generations' hard-earned savings were often used to make a down payment on a purchase of one or more apartments in the city. This meant the children of the silver generation, the next generation of young parents, were not only bound by tradition, but also by their parents' money. These well-off silver generations prefer to live near their children and only grandchild, but no longer under the same roof, like before. What has also changed is that these middle-class older people want to take care of themselves rather than be a burden to their children. While teenagers and young adults in China look for ways to escape their parents' traditions, often their parents do not want to leave behind their own parents' traditions. However, it is also very difficult for the grandchild to escape the traditions of the grandparents. Everyone wants to help the silver generation. They want the best for them, especially when it comes to healthcare or outpatient care at home. The silver generation has a lot of time, and especially the younger seniors are becoming increasingly prosperous and open to new experiences and consumption. This is the most interesting consumer group for comparing the effect of digitalization in China with the rest of the world.

Up until the coronavirus pandemic, their children often helped them to shop online, but this has now completely changed. On Singles Day in 2021 (held on November 11, this is China's largest e-commerce festival, similar to Black Friday), Alibaba traded $84.5 billion on its platforms. This figure, which is more than the annual GDP of Luxembourg, is often shown as an example of how e-commerce in China is simply years ahead of the West. What is not mentioned is that most purchases are family purchases that are made for the whole or at least half of the year. This is when the working generation buy in bulk for themselves, their child, and their parents—the silver generation. Weeks in advance, the silver generation are asked what they need for the coming year, and then the entire list is bought by their children on November 11. So, it's important to apply the family context to these numbers to fully understand this digital revolution.

Since 2020, seniors across China have become a lot more familiar with the digital world. Across all cities of the country, there are now 110 million seniors who own a smartphone, including fifty-seven percent of elder women, who spend an average of 4.5 hours a day searching for information and products on social media, e-commerce, and video sites.[49] They are mainly interested in knowledge, courses, and news, but they also have no problem using e-commerce applications. Each month, these consumers spend an average of $140 online on clothes, food, electronics, healthcare products, or online education. To my mind, this is the most invisible yet promising consumer group in China. Chinese seniors today are very proud of their age and achievements. They are brimming with confidence and personality. Some have even become famous online and have millions of followers.[50]

The digital world in China is bridging the generations and reducing the generation gap. The lifelong learning that we so often talk about in the West is becoming a reality in China due to rapid digitalization. Many Chinese people are taking the expression that you are never too old to learn seriously.

At the same time, the Chinese tech giants are helping to bridge the digital generation gap by making all their apps available with larger fonts, one-click services, and simpler user interfaces. At the end of 2020, the Chinese government launched a national program to make 115 government websites and the forty-three best-known private applications such as WeChat, Alipay, JD, Douyin (TikTok), and Ctrip user-friendly and accessible to the older generation. The companies' motivation to follow the government recommendations is not just for the greater good. Since 2018, there has been a huge growth in the older generation's use of online services such as e-commerce, food delivery, leisure, healthcare, and education. This also means many more transactions and therefore profit for these technology platforms. Education in particular is on the rise, ranging from training sessions to learning to use smartphones to the creation of universities for seniors.[51]

STAYING IN TOUCH

How do spread-out Chinese families stay in touch with each other? The answer to this was provided in 1999 by Tencent's QQ internet application, China's first social network. Back then, smartphones didn't exist, and not many Chinese people had a computer. But a genius named Pony Ma, the founder of Tencent, thought of using the internet to let people send text and voice messages to a "pager". Pagers were sort of an upgrade from the walkie-talkies of the 1980s and 90s. You could send a signal or text message between them. When the entire Western world started buying mobile phones and similar devices at the end of the last century, the Chinese preferred the much cheaper one- or two-way pagers. I still remember as if it were yesterday the constant beeping of Motorola pagers clipped onto the fake Dunhill belts that every Chinese person wore. Tencent was founded in 1999 with a portfolio featuring its pager software and an ICQ computer application. You would find a QQ ID number on every business card in China. Within two years, Tencent had more than a hundred million Chinese users, connecting all Chinese families, friends, and business partners.[52] QQ would become the training ground for Tencent's super app WeChat, which was created in 2011.

By 2007, Tencent's "QQ-group" application was already more extensive in terms of features than the current WhatsApp application, which itself was only launched in 2009. We need to view this success through the lens of a time when the Chinese were looking for answers to questions amid a world of internet censorship, questionable search engines, and fraudulent companies. The internet in China evolved very differently than in the West, and that has created a different dynamic. The hunger for information and new services was so much greater than ours, which was determined much more by culture than censorship. You could say that before the advent of the internet, most young Chinese people still lived in a very closed world of family and school, which really didn't prepare them for modern life. Then suddenly the internet was unlocked, and the Chinese were happily drowning in information and new experiences. It was like letting a child run wild at Disneyland. They weren't looking for specific information, products, or services like we did outside China through Google or Amazon, but they wanted to try out all the new gadgets and share those experiences with their friends and families everywhere. They consumed, but also created and shared in an intense frenzy of discovery. For us, the internet arrived in the form of a new tool, but for the Chinese it was a door to a new way of life: a new life online where almost anything was possible, and allowed. The difficulty was that you couldn't trust everything on the internet. So, they found safety in the closed online communities or QQ-groups that gave them more confidence in the authenticity of the information and online services.

WECHAT IS YOUR BEST FRIEND

Similar to WhatsApp, these groups on QQ and later on WeChat are the ideal way to keep in touch and share things with your friends, family, or colleagues. The biggest difference between WeChat and Facebook (now called Meta) products is that WeChat combines all the functionality of Facebook, WhatsApp, and Instagram, plus much more in one single application. WeChat is known as the super app that you can use to manage your whole life—both online and offline.

As a smartphone user outside China, you may be able to live without Facebook or WhatsApp, but not one of the billion daily Chinese smartphone users can survive without WeChat. As well as its social media and chat services, WeChat gives you a complete collection of applications that a person needs in their daily life: for payments, transportation, financial services, healthcare, e-commerce, deliveries, networking, dating, education, government services, utilities, telecoms, donations, and more. In addition, WeChat connects almost four million mini-programs,[53] which is more than the total number of apps in all app stores in China. All these applications are similar to websites and apps that we download from brands, games, news, mobility, and other services, but the WeChat mini-programs have unparalleled advantages: you scan a QR code and the mini-program is ready in your WeChat without you having to download the app. So, they only take up memory on your cellphone if you use them regularly, they often do something super simple, you can pay immediately without leaving WeChat, and it is very efficient to share information or discounts with friends. While iOS or Android apps are normally more user-friendly for more complex or extensive applications, the WeChat mini-programs are ideal for the super-fast, efficient, and user-friendly world of China: instant access, payment, and sharing among friends.[54]

For me, what makes WeChat so powerful is not mainly the access to millions of apps, but the fact that all the functionality is in the same super app, and you never need to leave it. WeChat is an integral part of every Chinese person's life, from morning to night, anywhere, and anytime. WeChat is very user-friendly; in fact, it's your best friend. But can you trust it?

In terms of information flows, WeChat Moments work like Facebook's News Feed, where you can scroll through photos, news, and personal updates shared by friends. But WeChat also has a Twitter-like search function that allows you to follow trends, articles, and official accounts. If you want to share information online, you don't just share it on your timeline, but usually also in the relevant WeChat groups. It is not uncommon for Chinese people to be in hundreds of groups on WeChat. On my own WeChat account I'm in more than a hundred groups, even though I now live in Belgium. Dozens are about Chinese innovation, trends, and entrepreneurship in China; I have a separate group for every discussion, visit, meeting, or project that involved several people; a group for finding apartments and second-hand items in Shanghai; ten groups for my favorite stores in Shanghai. Children in China are in groups for doing school activities together or talking to the teacher; parents have their own parent groups with and without the teachers. It is similar to WhatsApp but when there is something that needs to be discussed, the first reflex in China is always to create a WeChat group, regardless of the age of the participants. The most active form of communication on WeChat is not the public Moments, as with the News Feed from Facebook, but the individual and group chats, which compares more to Facebook Messenger or WhatsApp. They are the ideal virtual spaces in a culture where a lot of importance is placed on private conversations; but at the same time in a country where everyone is constantly on the move and where business and leisure go hand in hand. But are those small WeChat private groups helping get rid of misinformation?[55]

To a great extent, WeChat censors all messages that are false or considered "inappropriate" by the government, but often this information remains in the restricted groups or echo chambers. Despite the fact that messages in China more often come from people you trust, such as family and friends, the information is not more correct, objective, or qualitative. Within the WeChat groups, members will spread rumors, conspiracy theories, and false messages as quickly as they do on Facebook. This is how scams and fake news in China very easily find their way to the silver generation, who sometimes put pressure on their children in the WeChat groups to believe the fake news or to join them in buying a service or product. This amplification effect within the circles of family and friends spreads fake news and scams even faster than elsewhere. Seniors in particular are more likely to spread false information; and within the family group it is difficult for children or grandchildren to argue against their elders. And the elders don't like to admit they're wrong because that means losing face. As a result, they often force immediate family members to buy a questionable service or product, or to do, or not do something. This problem is so rooted in society that wrongdoers almost always target the silver generation first, so that young people are extremely concerned about fake news. It is not government censorship or propaganda, but the combination of private and social applications in China that makes the Chinese internet unreliable and young consumers more alert. If a fake news story claims that 5G masts caused the coronavirus, or that you have to buy a certain oil to lose weight, the Chinese are quick to believe it because the circulation within closed groups is very intense.

The family WeChat groups are the gateway to fake news in China. It is especially the more political news items about the US or how the West tackled COVID-19 that are spreading like wildfire within these groups. You might think that the Chinese government is behind fake news, but the source is often, just as it is for us, scammers, extremists, and people with a certain agenda. The Chinese government is actually annoyed by these rumors, as they could lead to social unrest.[56] It is always more difficult to manage someone else's rumors. That's why in China many anti-rumor journalists, so-called fact-checkers, have emerged, who mainly help young people to protect themselves against the bias of their parents or grandparents. Tencent itself also has an anti-rumor department that detects false information and answers all kinds of questions about it online.[57]

The problem can also come from outside your circle of friends. When you receive a home delivery from JD, the courier will ask you to add them to your WeChat so they can let you know the next time they're on their way, or so they can send you JD discounts. This is all very innocent and super convenient, but this is how the Chinese quickly and subconsciously share fake news from someone outside their "circle of friends." News takes on a life of its own in the close-knit trust groups. But behind every scan of a QR code that connects you to a person or brand, there can also be a different intention. The best-known misinterpretation is the photos that have popped up of beggars walking around the streets with a QR code to receive money. The story then went global that China had become a completely cashless society: "In China, even the beggars need a QR code because nobody has any cash in their pockets." The real story was that there was a company giving each beggar 1 RMB ($0.20) per scan, because people thought it was fun to scan the beggar's QR code, but rarely did they give them any money. Once you had scanned the QR code, you were actually connected to someone who would cheat you out of money another way. It is therefore no surprise that, since the growth of the internet at the end of the last century, and especially since the mobile 3G network appeared in

2008, the Chinese have increasingly relied on the trust of family and friends to find their way within the minefield that is the untrustworthy online world.

EXAMPLE – More fun and better deals together

Pinduoduo (PDD) is the best example of how a newcomer has challenged the original e-commerce giants Alibaba and JD.com within a short period of five years. In addition to **product innovation**, which is a more well-known form of innovation, PDD is mainly a master of three other forms of innovation: **service innovation**, **market innovation**, and **business model innovation**. When PDD launched its business in 2015, there was little room in China for a new e-commerce player. JD.com and Alibaba had a firm grip on the market in China, just like Amazon did in America. Yet, within five years, PDD has grown from nothing to become the largest e-commerce company in China with 788 million annual users, which is more than Alibaba,[58] and a valuation of more than $100 billion. In 2020, they became profitable and grew five times faster than Facebook, Amazon, or TikTok in their first five years. The founder Colin Huang is the genius behind this machine. In 2015, he wondered why WeChat had a billion users, but only five hundred million people bought online from Alibaba or its competitor JD.com. Where were the other five hundred million and why weren't they buying online? They have money for a smartphone, but not for e-commerce. He noted that those people lived in 180 cities of less than three million inhabitants, and not in the fifty biggest cities in China.[59] What do these people want, he asked. Mostly, a very good price. But how can you get goods at a lower price than Alibaba or JD?

Colin's insight was the same as the topic of this chapter: family and friends. If more people buy together, the price gets significantly lower. Group buying, in other words. Group buying, similar to the Groupon business model, had already been popular in China for some time, but Pinduoduo's innovative **business model** meant it was up to the consumer to set up a group to get big discounts: **team purchases**. If a user wants to make a team purchase, they can either join an existing team or create their own. The customer then has twenty-four hours to form a team to get that order confirmed at a much lower price. The innovative thing about this model is that you give the buyer the initiative to make a deal, and not the seller, as Groupon does. So, the consumer has to convince others, and in China this of course leads to WeChat groups, where all their social ties between friends and family have already been developed.

The 2016 investment of the owner of WeChat, Tencent, in 16.9 percent of Pinduoduo's shares was therefore no coincidence. PDD has built its success on China's trust model, where consumers rely heavily on recommendations from family and friends before they buy. Through WeChat groups, PDD solves the lack of trust that still haunts Alibaba and others. And thanks to all those recommendations between friends and family that PDD now also knows about, the platform can make much more personalized offers to its users.

Instead of competing with China's e-commerce giants that had become nearly unbeatable in efficiency, conversion, and purchasing power, Pinduoduo would return to the playful and interactive nature of going shopping together. How often do we go shopping together with friends or family in a shopping mall or shopping street? So why not turn e-commerce into a social event that's fun and entertaining? Colin Huang found that people who stay longer in a shopping mall also buy more, which is why you will find a supermarket, movie theater, or Starbucks in every Chinese mall. Why not bring that idea online, and give users a reason to stay longer on PDD? Colin Huang himself set up two e-commerce start-ups and a web-based gaming studio before he founded PDD, and with that experience created a new and innovative service model for the e-commerce world. Through playful interactive games and big discounts, the PDD platform would offer a personalized experience. The best-known features of this are the daily check-ins to get loyalty vouchers, encouraging users to open the app at least once a day. The other feature that is super popular is the "price cut." If someone wants to make a certain purchase on PDD, you as a user can get a discount if you share the promotion link with enough people. Your friends don't even have to buy it, just as long as they click on the link. If you share it enough times, you can even get it for free, but the more you do this, the harder it gets—just like in a game. But it's the PDD mini-games that make the experience really fun. The simplest is the Duo Duo Orchard. You have to create and take care of a virtual orchard, and if you do that consistently well, you'll get real fruit sent to you for free by PDD. If you buy more on the platform, you can make the virtual orchard grow faster. Eleven million Chinese people are addicted to this simple game, but PDD has a whole collection of similar games. Now that games have become a worldwide phenomenon among young people, this model will no doubt be introduced in the West.

Finally, PDD has also introduced a new market innovation, or rather created a new market. Instead of offering products that are available on other e-commerce sites, PDD focuses on consumables that people need every day. Consumers can receive discounts on products that they will always need, like food, toilet paper, or cleaning products. Fruit and vegetables in particular were heavily promoted because there was little competition for PDD there, and because it involved very regular purchases. It is therefore no surprise that PDD was particularly successful in the smaller cities. By allowing sellers of these products all over China to sell their goods on the PDD platform, PDD has opened up three new markets in one go: the five hundred million WeChat users who weren't buying online; the farmers or producers who could now sell everywhere via PDD; and the factories that could now produce on the basis of actual orders placed, rather than expected orders. The latter is called the consumer-driven (C2M) production model, in which traditional production evolves from "Research and Development" and marketing-driven processes into a consumer-driven process.[60] This new model allows manufacturers to understand customer needs and preferences in order to drive the production process faster and more efficiently. It allows them to offer better quality at lower prices.

Today, PDD's model is called the social e-commerce model, but through his genius innovations, Colin Huang has actually completely redesigned four industries in just five years: e-commerce, manufacturing, wholesale, and distribution. Before PDD existed, in these four sectors, both in China and worldwide, it was mainly the big brands that had the upper hand. Nowadays, it is consumers, producers, and platforms together that are in control. And that trend is now also establishing itself outside of China.

同

tóng

Meaning: **same, similar, together, in common, with, and.** The character shows **commonality** and solidarity. It symbolizes people thinking alike, acting together, sharing the same feelings, and being on the same path. If you work as one team, you can trust in the direction.

3.

Trust each other. Can Chinese bosses be trusted? Why aren't Chinese workers loyal? Do you always have to make friends first before you can do business in China? Which do the Chinese trust more— people or technology? Is China's top-down hierarchy holding back their innovation and creativity? Why are Chinese customers so demanding?

Company
and team

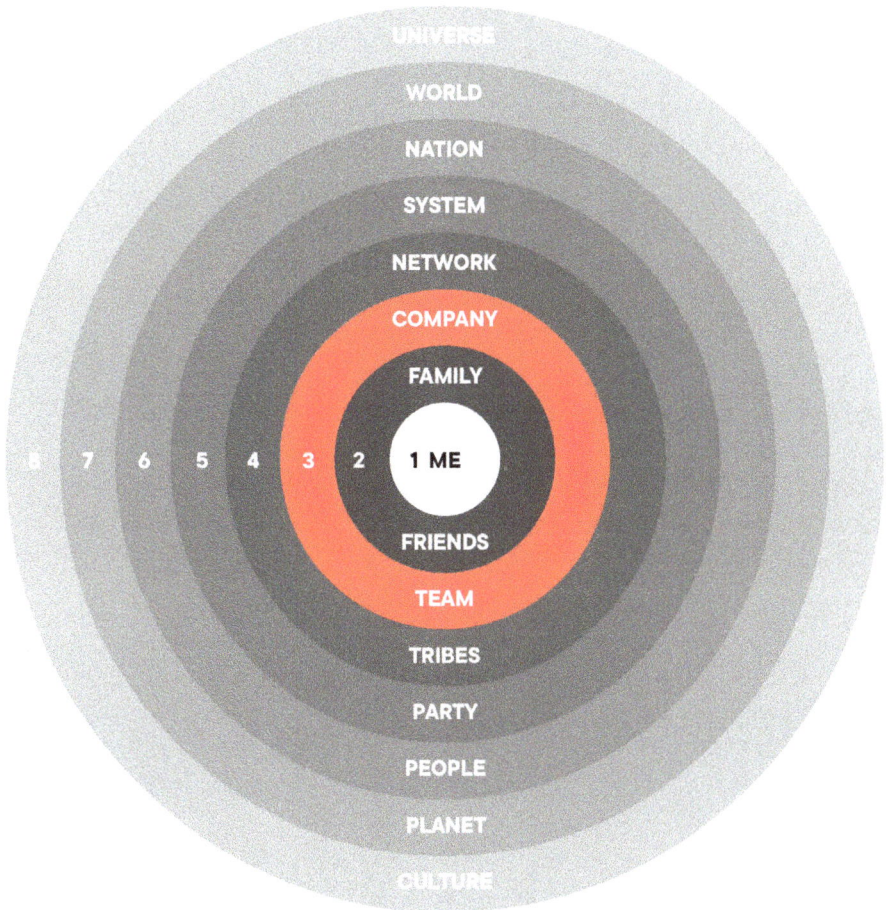

UNIVERSE
WORLD
NATION
SYSTEM
NETWORK
COMPANY
FAMILY
1 ME
FRIENDS
TEAM
TRIBES
PARTY
PEOPLE
PLANET
CULTURE

8 7 6 5 4 3 2 1 ME

In 2000 I met my best friend "Teddy Bear" Dave Wei; we worked together every day for six months. We were both in the sales and marketing department of Shanghai Bell, Alcatel's joint venture in China. We traveled all over the country together, promoting and selling Alcatel's telecom networks. For each trip, our Chinese manager gave us a fixed daily budget for accommodation, taxis, and food. Although the budget was tight, it was doable. But to save money, we stayed in the cheapest Chinese hotels (which I'd rather not describe here), shared a room, ate noodles three times a day, and took public transport, never taxis. Some of our colleagues boasted about saving money by spending the night in the even cheaper public saunas. They were open until five a.m., which meant you could also go to your client meeting feeling refreshed. Others would book a single hotel room for five people. Fake receipts to prove your inflated expenses could simply be bought on the street or at the front desk of the hotel for three percent of the total amount. This meant salespeople who were on the road a lot could easily double their monthly income without the manager or the tax bureau noticing.

At the time, my Chinese colleagues didn't see this as dishonest or corrupt practice, but as fair compensation for all the overtime the company wasn't paying. Since Shanghai Bell wanted to match Alcatel's international HR standards, there was no obligation to work overtime, which seemed to be different compared to our main competitor Huawei. But nobody worked the normal eight hours a day, so you didn't either, as there were at least ten applicants waiting in line to do your job with that little bit more conviction. Jack Ma once called this China's unspoken "9-9-6" work rule. You are expected to work from 9 a.m. to 9 p.m., 6 days a week. He wasn't popular when he said that in 2019;[61] but twenty years earlier this was already the norm at private companies in China. And not just for Chinese companies; many foreign companies also adopted this custom. If you wanted to make money, you didn't have a lot of choice. My wife's best friend in Shanghai at the time was a Dutch sinologist who worked for a foreign company. Every evening around seven p.m., as she was getting ready to go home after a ten-hour day at the office, her Western supervisor in Shanghai would sarcastically wish her a good afternoon.

However, it is mainly devotion to work that has made companies like Huawei and Alibaba big and successful, much more so than any direct pressure that forces staff to work against their will. If you aren't really committed to working hard, then go and work for a Chinese state-owned company; this is how many people think in China. In the West, they would be quick to send in the unions, go on strike, or make collective demands. This also happens in China today, because striking is not illegal, but complaining on social media is often a more successful approach. The impact of this is much greater and more effective than in the West. We can definitely learn a thing or two here from the Chinese about achieving change without putting our jobs at risk. Consumer power in China is much greater than the power of employees or trade unions. In China, under the law any employee can join or form a union if there are more than twenty-five employees. Each union does, however, need to join the government-run ACFTU (All-China Federation of Trade Unions), which all together has more than 300 million members. The role of the trade union in China is much more about negotiating with management than protecting employee rights. In 2020, netizens complained about the overworked staff at the delivery companies Meituan and Ele.me. These employees had become slaves to a demanding AI algorithm that forced all their couriers to commit traffic violations in order to make every customer delivery within the promised thirty minutes.[62] In less than two weeks, both companies had responded by adding twenty percent to the delivery time in order to reduce the workload. In the past, overtime was rarely compensated, whereas today in China it is required by law.

Because overtime was the norm at the time, we solved this problem individually and creatively by claiming more traveling expenses than we actually incurred. Everyone was happy and the company continued to grow. I couldn't blame my colleagues, and in fact I picked up the same bad habit myself. Meanwhile, the managers felt that growth opportunities for employees in a well-managed multinational like Alcatel compensated enough for this. Compared with Belgian employees at Alcatel, my Chinese colleagues with the same responsibility and job title in China were indeed at least five years younger. And that job title in China is extremely important because it reflects status and authority. Many Chinese colleagues desired a higher management title even more than a pay raise, as this gave them more power in the hierarchical business world. Power is influence and that leads to opportunities that are sooner or later converted into money.

As the founder of a start-up in China, I was always amazed at how, whenever I promoted someone to manager, their behavior towards previous colleagues on the same level quickly changed, as if they were a different person. They suddenly became bossier, less understanding and, above all, began to give themselves a lot more privileges than the people below them. Managers believe that they provide employees with lots of opportunities, and that they must perform and deliver first. For many Chinese bosses, this means that employees are to be put under a lot of pressure, because the managers themselves are also under pressure from their own supervisor. This pressure comes in the form not so much of an order given from above, but rather competition from the marketplace. If you can't get the job done, someone else will. You therefore have to continuously show your motivation in front of your manager. This creates a kind of waterfall model of upward expectations and downward pressure. The top Chinese executive, usually the company founder, almost always embodies the company culture in China. In the past, when employees mostly just carried out simple tasks, there were a lot of bosses who liked to tell nice empty stories in order to satisfy their employees' hunger for advancement and in doing so make themselves rich or meet objectives for the investors. In Chinese this is called "**huàbǐng chōngjī** (画饼充饥)", which means "draw a pancake to satisfy hunger." Instead of giving employees real compensation, they made empty, often unachievable promises to motivate their employees. This damaged the reputation of Chinese bosses and is something they carry around with them even today. And this is just one reason why there isn't a lot of trust between Chinese employees and their bosses, in either direction.

Who can be trusted more then: employees or management? Between the layers of the hierarchy, or within the same group, it is a different environment. Within their own circle, among employees and among managers, there was an extremely strong peer relationship at Shanghai Bell, comparable to start-ups in the West. In the trenches together, we had to fight the competition to survive. This was the new family you were quickly welcomed into at every new employer. Your colleagues on the same level as you soon become your new friends. You often have to depend on each other. You could also deduce that the Chinese corporate hierarchy is determined by culture, just like France is more hierarchical than the Netherlands. The Chinese, however, sometimes claim that the real origin of this linear top-down leadership style isn't China, but the multinationals that imported the Western culture of profit maximization into China at the end of the last century, along with a climate of strong distrust of their Chinese employees. It's an interesting thought, because during the last century China was seen by almost all foreign companies firstly as a cheap factory, and only later as a sales market. Let's be honest: in many industries the Chinese were simply cheaper than Westerner employees or robots at carrying out repetitive work efficiently. But I do believe the often-Western hierarchical style of exploitation established itself well in China precisely because the country had already been cultivating a clearly defined superior-subordinate leadership style for millennia. Isn't it double standards that the West today is so vocal in accusing China of violating human rights, while we made good use of China's bad labor practices when it suited us? What amazes me is that today, we in the West make loud allegations, founded or unfounded, about the bad working conditions of the minorities, but for forty years very few Western companies cared, even though there was plenty of proof.[63] In today's China, more and more employees are aware of and won't accept unfair treatment by their bosses. If the gap between reality and the "*huabing*" dream becomes too large, employees quickly change employers, to which they then quickly become loyal again.

IS THE WESTERN MANAGEMENT MODEL BETTER?

In today's Western corporate culture, a lot of importance is placed on efficient leadership. In the past it was a lot simpler: leaders were transactional, transformational, or charismatic. Today there is a whole range of Western leadership styles. Since the pandemic, some have become more popular than ever, such as the coach, laissez-faire, or servant leader. These days, we are expected to treat employees as human beings, not as machines with brains (the role of Chief Happiness Officer is a good example of this). We are now moving from hard, performance-oriented styles to soft, inclusive leadership styles where social skills, collaboration, and consensus are increasingly important. Humans have never been so key to achieving economic added value.

In contrast, we correctly perceive China's highly pragmatic leadership approach as autocratic, bureaucratic, and highly transactional. Westerners who have worked for a Chinese company will agree that in China the boss decides, the hierarchy always wins, and that your Chinese employees are not really team players. A Western management model that leaves more room for employees to take their own initiative and for self-development often doesn't seem to work in China.

In addition, employees in China job hop all the time, so the general consensus among many Western managers in China is that Chinese employees aren't loyal or trustworthy. Western business leaders are therefore rarely interested in learning from or applying the Chinese management style. With the exception of companies like Haier or Ping An, the latter with the help of McKinsey, who have completely transformed their organization to a model that seems very Western, Chinese management practices aren't really on the radar of Western business schools. In fact, many business schools readily conclude that China has no GE, Google, or Toyota that will conquer the world with a radically new management model. I don't know if it's ignorance, wishful thinking, or Western centric thinking, but the belief that Western management models are better than Chinese ones is false and even a dangerous blind spot for the future competitiveness of Western companies. In less than twenty years, and in nearly all industries, China has created the largest companies in the world, and these firms are now making it very difficult for their Western or North Asian competitors. We have to ask ourselves whether we are blinded by our past successes, or if it is because we simply don't know how to incorporate these Chinese management styles? Or maybe we're just misunderstanding it, or not yet seeing this style of leadership in its full global context?

We're making three fundamentally incorrect assumptions:

- Chinese employees follow orders because of their conformist nature
- The Chinese management style is a command hierarchy
- China's large market requires a management style that only works with a lot of staff

CHINESE EMPLOYEES FOLLOW ORDERS BECAUSE OF THEIR CONFORMIST NATURE

The typical image of Chinese employees is that they are oppressed because they have no real choice. This is inferred from the Confucian paternalistic culture where subjects expect strict guidelines and then follow these without question, even if the supervisor is wrong. At school, the teacher has already taught the students rules, and later on, in the workplace, every manager will therefore also give clear instructions. Otherwise, you can assume the task won't get done. In the West, we not only see such a hierarchical structure as inefficient and not helpful for showing initiative and innovation, but also very slow. How is it possible then that the Chinese are so fast, highly efficient, and increasingly innovative? The mistake we make with this reasoning is our seeing all Chinese employees as subordinate. Today, Chinese millennials between the ages of twenty-six and forty are typically the managers in China. They are taking on more and more important roles and need more and more recognition as both employees and managers. They have more disposable income, have traveled and discovered the world, want to work more flexibly, enjoy working in teams, and they are looking for space for personal development. They don't just follow their managers' orders, they are very opinionated, and they prefer flatter organizations, open communication, and teamwork.[64]

The days of migrant workers without any experience heading en masse to factories in the South to do any kind of work are clearly numbered. The image of the poor factory worker in a sewing workshop or overworked staff member at Alibaba or Foxconn are ingrained in our minds. Many think that Chinese bosses exploit their workers to make cheap products for the rich West. We do feel somewhat guilty about the impact of our overconsumption but prefer to blame China and Western brands for these labor malpractices. The reality is that violations are still going on all over the world, and a country like China, where there are still six hundred million people on a low income, still has some way to go to get all these factory bosses to follow the stricter national labor regulations. But the idea that hundreds of millions of Chinese employees have to work themselves to the bone because they really have no choice is simply false and Western self-deception. Even today, many Chinese willingly move to the other side of China to work twelve hours a day, six days a week because they want to earn more money, learn new skills, or gain knowledge. For most Chinese people, it's not because they don't have a choice that they work so hard, but because it increases their chances of a better life. Their ambitions outweigh their conformist behavior. They may look like the worker ants of the Chinese dream, but they each have their own dream. We shouldn't see these Chinese people as a tool to make a product, but as individuals who consider very carefully how long they need to work to take the next step, to save enough money to get married, buy a house, or pay for their child's education.

This is also why Chinese people do so much job hopping. You often hear foreign companies in China complaining that Chinese employees aren't loyal to the company and therefore can't be trusted: once you've trained them, they're gone. If an employee stays with a company longer than two years, then you can call them loyal. I disagree with those statements. My own experience is that Chinese employees are just as loyal and trustworthy as foreign ones, but they are much quicker to consider whether staying at a company will help them achieve their own dreams or not. They are loyal to their own dream for the future. I remember asking an employee in 2014 if she was willing to work weekend overtime for a Nike event. Her answer has stayed with me ever since: "You pay for my time, so if you want to pay, then I'll give a tiny bit more of my life to the company." I felt bad about it all day, but then it became really clear to me that despite all my inspiring stories about how our start-up would change the world and how we were an incredible team, in her eyes I was actually a pure transactional manager. She mainly respected me because I kept my commitments to paying her on time, treated her like an individual, and had a very strong dream of my own. What I then realized is that I was not only making my dream come true, but mainly her dream. Because of me, she could change her life, and as long as I continued to fulfill her wish, she would stay with us. Executives in China must take this individual social mobility into account, otherwise the employee will be gone.

Perhaps the reason we misjudge Chinese employees is because in the West we have partly given up on our social upward mobility. We can't imagine that Chinese employees are willing to suffer and follow orders, and that many of them are in fact totally fine with it. This isn't a new thought. It is just as difficult to imagine that four thousand years ago the pyramids were built not by slaves, but by laborers loyal to the pharaohs. When we read in the media that Chinese factories are subjecting people to forced labor, we will never believe Chinese government claims that people are getting better wages. If we were to transport the current Uyghur "forced labor" storyline circulating in the West to the 1990s, China should have built a labor camp of more than a hundred million slaves to produce for our Western consumption. But when you talk to those former so-called "slaves" today, they often have a much better life than the average northern American and they are buying the products that we can only dream of. I agree that in China and even in Africa there are certainly still a lot of Chinese factory bosses treating their employees badly, but our ignorance about how Chinese employees really feel and why they do this work shows, above all, how far removed our world is from the real ambition of the Chinese. Many Chinese people are disturbed by the West's judgments, which show little understanding of the real-life situation in which millions of Chinese people still find themselves: too many poor and elderly, inequality, and health problems. It is their view that the Chinese government is generally doing much more about these problems than most governments in the world.

THE CHINESE MANAGEMENT STYLE IS A COMMAND HIERARCHY

If we want to better understand how so many Chinese companies are affecting and even disrupting our Western market, businesses, and industries, we need to delve deep into the mindset that comes from China's past. Over its history, China was known for its hundred schools of philosophy. Today, there are three major ones that define China, its society, and business culture: Confucianism, Legalism, and Taoism. We must move away from the idea that Chinese leadership is a purely monolithic, top-down, master-subject system; and instead, appreciate the rich influences within Chinese organizations that are made up of a mix of the three major Chinese tendencies plus Western influences:[65]

- the Confucian mindset;
- the Legalistic tradition;
- Taoist philosophy.

THE CONFUCIAN MINDSET

The Confucian mindset, which is paternalistic and pursues harmony, mutual respect, and goodness, is the motive of the manager: "walk the talk" and "care for employees." The employee is part of the larger family, trust is central, but the manager remains the respected leader. This is the vertical authoritarian leadership structure where employees glorify the leader. This clashes with the Western management style, which sees confrontation rather than unity as the engine of evolution. This kind of leadership somehow reflects the transformational leadership of the last century in the West, with charismatic visionaries who can motivate employees. But among employees this style can sometimes lead to disappointment, lack of expertise, and even unethical actions. These are the "godfather" type cultures, which operate a bit like the Sicilian mafia, but without any mafiosi of course. These companies are characterized by their tough founders such as Huawei's Ren Zhenfei, Liu Chuanzhi of Lenovo, or the "iron lady" Dong Mingzhu of Gree Electric, who reportedly hasn't taken a day off in the last thirty years. They are founders who, thanks to the opening-up of China in the 1980s and 1990s, made their breakthrough after first gaining experience in a state-owned company. They have been hardened by the China of the Cultural Revolution and are known for their tough, aggressive, and no-nonsense approach. Management through fear and love.

The paradox is that these tough leaders are in practice much more concerned with the people who work in their companies than human-centric leaders in many Western organizations. They are companies that trust individuals and people over technology, even though sometimes they are tech companies themselves, like Huawei or Lenovo. The Confucian concept of "*Guanxi*" is central here. *Guanxi* refers to all interpersonal relationships among colleagues with the core idea of taking care of each other, and the team taking care of you. Trust within the team is so strong that it's almost impossible to build it without making friends first, even if it doesn't give you an immediate advantage. In the West, on the other hand, especially in American companies, you can easily do business using legal contracts, without having to put time into people. But in China, there is usually an unspoken obligation to help each other and to give each other "face." The strength of "*Guanxi*" means that Chinese companies prefer to build teams that strengthen the personal relationships and trust within the group. Everyone motivates and keeps each other in check within the social fabric. The team is actually not a department, but a kind of family. Within the team there is a lot of freedom to experiment, but in the end the team has to prove itself to the manager.

In the West, we rely on technology to optimize our internal processes and their outputs, while in China, Confucian leadership trusts the team managers to increase the productivity of every team member. In Chinese "godfather" cultures, technology is seen much more as an end product with value in itself than as a tool or cost-center to increase the value of production. In contrast, in the West, companies are constantly looking for creative ways to engage employees and create stronger teams through team building, with trainers or coaches. Instead of organizing the regular training courses, company trips, and mediation, in the Chinese "godfather" culture, you as an employee become part of the family from day one and the company takes care of you. And you'll do anything for family, won't you? Together, the family is strong.

Example: The "Navy Seals" of business China

Huawei is the best-known example of a company that has been living in survival mode for thirty years. The survival of the business is more important than making money. Products or technology are mainly a means to that end. For example, in 2019 Ren Zhenfei proposed to sell their 5G patents to America to stop Trump's tech war with Huawei. For Huawei, it is only the customers that provide the lifeline, not the technology or profit, so Huawei mostly wants to outperform their competitors in customer focus.

I felt that strongly when I worked for their competitor Alcatel. The more customers Huawei has, the greater the economies of scale and the cheaper Huawei can produce, which in turn gives them more customers. The real power of Huawei is the brains of its employees—190,000 smart people. These are mostly also the co-owners of the company. Not the government, not the investors or the banks, not even the ex-board members. Top employee performance is rewarded. Each year they're allowed to use their own salary to buy company shares, determined according to their value creation. In addition, they're not allowed to earn anything outside of their activities at Huawei. A 100 percent focus on Huawei, and if the company does well, they earn annual dividends. If they leave the company, they have to sell their shares back.

This model is based on the Confucian meritocracy model where employees all work together closely as a team to survive. Everyone is motivated and monitored based on how good their performance is, and those who work really hard earn more quickly. This is the reason Huawei is still in business. No one wants to see their investment go to waste, and so will continue to fight for it. They are 100 percent committed. The main reason they keep doing this is because it's a big family—literally. If the employees are sent abroad, they all live together with their colleagues, eat together, cook together, go out together. Their own family members are rarely expatriated with them, as is the case with Western companies. For example, as a Western expat in China almost everything is handed to you on a plate. At Huawei, everyone is in the trenches together, and the more Washington attacks them, the more they make personal sacrifices and the stronger they become mentally. We could say they are the "Navy Seals" of business China.[66]

THE LEGALISTIC TRADITION

The legalistic tradition in China is strongly autocratic and commanding, with rules, control, and a lot of bureaucracy. We recognize this best as the "carrot and stick" and "follow rules and example" leadership, symbolized by the command-and-control approach of many managers. This style results in mainly transactional micro-managers who are less concerned with relationships, but are more rational and transparent, and driven by data, results, and efficiency. This places a lot of pressure on employees, which puts creativity and sustain-ability at risk because employees' emotions, needs, and confidence are much less important than their objective performance.

This is the "marshal" type of culture that functions like a command hier-archy of a highly disciplined army, without going to war of course. Businesses such as the insurance company Ping An, the courier company Meituan, and many Chinese state-owned companies have a strong legalistic culture. These are companies that place their trust in technology and their systems over their people. Here the Confucian value of "face" is key. This value refers to the social status people get in a meritocratic company or society, allowing them to enjoy respect and trust. This is not about "leading by example" as with godfather business leaders, but "leading by success achieved."

In the West, too, you can lose face, but in China the opposite is much more important: gaining "face" or recognition. You can therefore invest in someone's status or "face" by showing respect to make them feel more important. The reason politicians, bosses, and teachers are so respected in China, and less so in the West, is because they've had a lot more "face time" in China. In the West, business leaders often trust their employees, while in China, employees mostly trust their direct managers. Western managers motivate employees to get the best out of each individual. Chinese leaders build personal relationships of trust with employees and especially support those who are self-motivated— also because those employees give them more "face." By doing this they work mainly on intrinsic motivation, which is more sustainable than relying on extrin-sic motivation. Chinese leaders are dissatisfied when someone doesn't perform, while Western leaders are annoyed when an employee doesn't cooperate.

Modern "marshal" companies rely more on data than on the HR manager to find out if someone is motivated in order to justify a hire or layoff. As the HR manager in the Chinese relational context is more culturally inclined to be biased, the "human element" of the HR department in China to assess staff is disappear-ing, and in many companies the role of HR is now being replaced by AI algorithms. But what if, during HR assessments, precisely because of an artificial intelligence machine, even more prejudice and discrimination creep in? As always, China will give free rein to technology first and only regulate it later; while we take com-pletely the opposite path to protect the fundamental rights of citizens, especially in Europe. The war on talent will therefore be intensified from China.

> ## Example: More autonomy without losing control
>
> At the Chinese insurance company Ping An they have monthly key performance indicators. Each month the computer generates a performance card: green, yellow, or red. Green is good, yellow is less good, and three yellows will give you a red and then you're in the danger zone of getting fired. But in addition to employees, Ping An also has half a million insurance agents they need to find, train, keep happy, and retain in the case of the good ones. Because all these agents do all their work tasks via a smartphone, by following all their actions in real-time using AI, Ping An can track their strengths and weaknesses and provide solutions to the manager of a specific agent. For example, the data will show that the agent is selling policies that are too low value to financially well-off customers, then recommend a training course to learn how to sell higher value policies. By adopting this type of system on a large scale, Ping An has managed to sell forty percent more new policies than their competitors, make their agents almost twice as productive as their competitors, and sell almost twice as many policies with high profit margins. What agent wouldn't want that?

TAOIST PHILOSOPHY

The Chinese tradition of Taoist philosophy expresses a laissez-faire leadership, which strives for hands-off, self-organization, and fluidity. The "invisible hand" and "empowering" are the mantra of the leader, who is not actually a leader. This authentic, servant leadership style puts employees and customers first, within a community. It gives employees more freedom and autonomy but makes it difficult to generate responsibility and speed. Especially in China, godfather and marshal companies often grow faster because employees spontaneously follow orders in a business environment that favors collective discipline over individual volatility.

This is the favorite model of Western leaders because it symbolizes agility (ability to adapt in times of change) and innovation through creation. I call these companies the "fairy godmother" cultures, as in Walt Disney's *Peter Pan*, where their leaders are the personification of hope, committed to making dreams come true, just without a magic wand of course. These types of companies function as an irregular guerrilla network that thinks asymmetrically. Examples of this management style can be found at companies such as Haier, Alibaba, or Tencent. These are the companies that use technology to help people—internally and externally. Here, "human feelings" are at the heart. In

Confucianism we refer to "*renqing*" or "debt of reciprocity." If someone does you a favor, you have to repay it. This acts like a bank account of favors; the Chinese equivalent of "quid pro quo." In China, trust is based less on the capacity to help than on the certainty that the favors will be returned when needed; therefore not always immediately, but sometime in the future, sometimes even in the distant future. This Taoist leadership style is extremely efficient in times of crisis because people adapt quickly. Since COVID-19, this style has received much more attention in China, with companies building more flexible working hours, projects, and teams into their organizations. We see this phenomenon globally. With the world becoming a much more complex network, business leaders need to think like a node in the network if they are to succeed.

Example: Decentralization increases resilience

Today, Haier is the largest household appliance manufacturer in the world. Founded in 1920, this state-owned company was virtually bankrupt in 1984 when CEO Zhang Ruimin took over. He fired almost the entire middle management, reshaping Haier into a flat organization that today has thousands of micro-enterprises that form a kind of marketplace for ideas, talent, and resources. Every team becomes a company in itself, and every employee an entrepreneur. They're not paid by the Haier organization, but by the customer according to the value they create. [67]

Haier calls this disruptive model Platform Open Innovation, which increases the speed of communication by breaking down the walls and silos of the organization. Haier is constantly experimenting with new ideas in order to not get caught in a comfort zone or the past. Employees see constant change as very normal, part of the company's DNA, although good practices are indeed repeated. Sometimes teams are even in direct competition with each other. But they also strengthen each other through their resilience. It's magical!

Haier's customer-centric model makes every customer a lifelong participant in their digital ecosystem platform. They stimulate the involvement of users of their products to gain new insights that make it possible to implement the smallest improvements. This adaptive micro-innovation model, combined with a highly advanced Internet-of-Things (IoT) platform, makes it possible for Haier to allow customization on a large scale. In a market of functional products such as refrigerators and air conditioners, Haier has managed to delight customers worldwide and win the trust of millions of customers.

CHINA'S MARKET REQUIRES A MANAGEMENT STYLE
THAT ONLY WORKS FOR COMPANIES WITH A LOT OF STAFF

Ping An has one million employees and agents, Huawei has 190,000 and they work in 170 countries, and Haier has 8,000 departments. Chinese companies have the advantage of a huge domestic market and an infinite number of willing employees. This represents an army of cheaper, increasingly smarter people who can crush the competition. However, most of the companies that are radically changing China and the world are not yet on our Western radar screen. We rarely notice that these disrupters have managers who have studied abroad or were partly financed by foreign money. Just like in Silicon Valley, these unseen leaders are disrupting the established markets with high-tech or digital solutions. These are the next generation of global entrepreneurs from China, who are more similar to entrepreneurs like Elon Musk or executives like Tim Cook than the old-school bosses at Huawei or Lenovo. After studying overseas, or working in a multinational for a time, they came back to China. Not all of these young founders have had this foreign exposure, but key people in the executive management team usually have. This is why these firms are often very quick to enter international markets. Unlike their predecessors, profit is less important than growth, as in the Silicon Valley model. Some stay under our radar because they operate in industrial niche markets—but of course, in China given the scale of the country, the term "niche" is a relative one.

Bill Liu, founder of the paper-thin smartphone screen maker Royole, or Wang Jun of the biotech company iCarbonX are examples of China's new geniuses. They want to change the world, bursting with passion and relying heavily on their groundbreaking technologies and the charisma of the founder. They want to be unique. Other Chinese founders are entering the consumer market, and while they have international ambitions, they too are flying under our radar while they focus on conquering their domestic market first. They are digital marketers who, by using disruptive business models and huge investments, want to give a young generation of Chinese consumers more user-friendly or more relevant solutions.

Founders like Zhang Yiming of the video streaming app TikTok, or Colin Huang of the social e-commerce site Pinduoduo, or Li Xiang of the electric vehicle company Li Auto are the new business rock stars of the new China. Their universe revolves around speed and scale and they are successful in convincing investors to give them hundreds of millions of dollars to win the race to the top. It is these two categories of new entrepreneurs, the "geniuses" and the "rock stars," who are now making the leap onto the global market and creating a tsunami of innovation.

Because their management teams have often been educated in the West, they put much more thought into their going-global strategy than their pre-decessors. Their leadership style is usually a combination of the Chinese style as described earlier, but with a rather flat organizational structure like we're used to in the West. This makes them very resilient, as they aren't that different from the whiz kids of Silicon Valley, but they have the enormous advantage of China's "godfather" relationship culture or "godmother" network culture that accelerates them in terms of execution and flexibility. So, it is certainly not just the number of employees in the companies that determines the success of the new Chinese innovators. Salary costs are also no longer the main reason Chinese companies employ so many people. In Shanghai, the legal minimum wage is $250 a month, but the average worker under the age of thirty-five typically earns over $1000 a month,[68] which is also roughly the starting wage for a university graduate. For these companies, e-commerce roles in particular are the lifeblood and generate exponential growth. The salaries of these jobs can easily cost an employer in Shanghai between $5,000 and $10,000 a month. It is therefore no longer possible for these young "digital" companies to compete with Western competitors by simply hiring more and cheaper employees.

ARE CHINESE BOSSES TO BE TRUSTED?

If we were to ask the same question about Western business leaders, the answer would be that it depends from person to person. It is no different in China. All we can do is look at which corporate culture drives them to make certain decisions. The question we can ask is which of the four major influences is the strongest within their organization: Confucianism, Legalism, Taoism, or Western influence? To represent this visually, you can think of the Confucian "godfather" companies as vertical relational policies that protect employees; the legalistic "marshal" companies as rather horizontal exclusive policies promoting workers; and Taoist "godmother" companies as circular inclusive policies that involve employees. Chinese companies heavily influenced by the "West" have a rather horizontal policy that empowers employees.

Business leaders from a "godfather" culture are often seen as the master, who deserves respect and must lead by example. This "master-apprentice" model is the glue that holds the company together and builds a strong culture of a kind that has been lost in many Western companies. It is that reliance on "personal relationships" (*guanxi*) that provides the necessary resources and support, and it explains why their companies are able to build such massive ecosystems. So, we can learn a lot about strengthening team culture from companies like Huawei, Gree, or Lenovo. Managers from a "marshal" culture are viewed as kings, who command respect through their status. This "armed forces" model, which the Chinese are already introduced to at school, provides an enormous amount of structure and support to the organization that we in the West often no longer dare to or cannot implement because we are increasingly

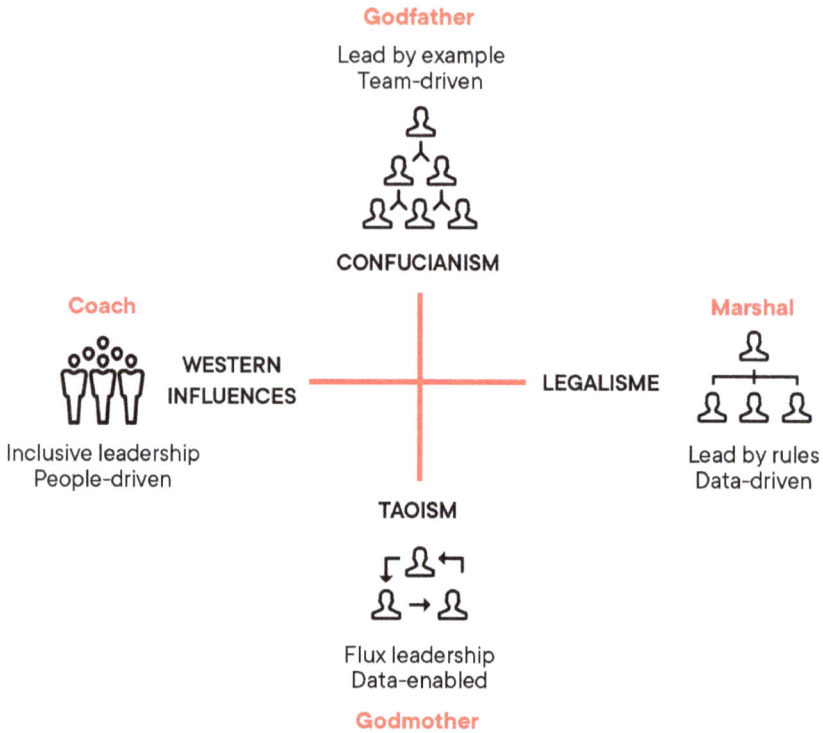

Godfather
Lead by example
Team-driven

CONFUCIANISM

Coach

WESTERN INFLUENCES

LEGALISME

Marshal

Inclusive leadership
People-driven

Lead by rules
Data-driven

TAOISM

Flux leadership
Data-enabled

Godmother

Figure 3 / The influence of the Confucian mindset, the legalistic tradition, the Taoist philosophy and the West on the Chinese corporate culture

striving for an ideal of open, diverse, and inclusive corporate culture. There's nothing wrong with that, but it's this confidence in a well-defined system that is the anchor and framework that makes the Chinese so fast and energetic. It makes your head spin to see how companies like Ping An, Meituan, or DiDi have gained hundreds of millions of users in just a few years. Managers from a "godmother" culture are seen as a kind of mother figure, who gain respect by giving trust. This "hands-off" model is a kind of Darwinian elimination model that turns every surviving employee into an entrepreneur. Confidence in their own capacity and the "network" leads to the enormous agility that Chinese companies often demonstrate. As I described in my earlier book, *China's New Normal*, companies like Haier, Alibaba, or Tencent show the world how they can keep becoming the market leader in every new market, service, or product.

You can't argue that one style is more effective than another, and no Chinese company is a pure godfather, marshal, or godmother company, although the founder often sets the trend. The Confucian godfather style is most aligned with traditional Chinese social norms and customs and is therefore most natural and powerful in China. The legalistic marshal style is closely related to the traditional system of government of the country and therefore often the most efficient in China. The Taoist godmother style is best suited to China's modern miracle and is therefore the most forward-looking. The real success of Chinese organizations is not down to any of these three leadership styles, but the combination of all three—consciously or unconsciously—with a touch of Western leadership on top. Similarly, successful Chinese companies have also been exposed to Western management models that they introduced into their organizations through consultancy firms such as McKinsey, or through its leaders studying abroad or hiring foreign managers. Younger companies such as Pinduoduo, ByteDance, DiDi, Royole, or iCarbonX are therefore breaking down all stereotypes of how Chinese companies run their businesses. Each of these examples is a compelling story in its own right but would go beyond the scope of this book.

Example: Gaining the trust of customers and staff

The Ctrip.com company (trip.com outside China) mixes a powerful cocktail by bringing together almost all of the leadership styles described above. It also shows that it's not just the Googles, Apples, or Zalandos of this world that are obsessed with employee and customer satisfaction. Unlike most Western companies, Ctrip.com not only measures the satisfaction of their customers (via the anonymous "net promoter scores"), but particularly the loyalty of the staff to the customers. To me, Ctrip.com is one of the best examples of how to put the customer first.

They are globally the second largest online travel company after Booking.com, and therefore have to deal with a lot of customers and problems: incorrect bookings, fully booked hotels, flight delays… As you can probably imagine, there is regularly a Chinese customer who is angry, disappointed, or even in a complete panic. At Ctrip.com, the management team decided twenty years ago that customer services would become the nerve center of the company. No way were they going to outsource that department, like many companies do in the West. Instead, they would have ten thousand people to answer phone calls 24/7 from thousands of travelers. Not only do they understand so much better what the problems are that they need to solve, but they create a bond with the customers. A remote call center in India or the Philippines simply can't compete with this approach. But more importantly, by doing this they have developed new products and services that make them unique in the industry. For example, through Ctrip.com you can apply for a visa, or they can arrange a refund of the VAT on products you bought abroad. If you're a Chinese person on vacation in Venice and you arrive at your hotel to hear that they're overbooked and can't give you a room, Ctrip.com will connect you to other Chinese Ctrip.com travelers in Venice to see if anyone can help you out. This is a butler service on a scale of a million travelers each day. Today, over eighty-five percent of their customer service interactions are through chatbots, but if you need to speak to a human, Ctrip.com still manages to answer the phone within twenty seconds.

When it comes to the employees, standards are no less than those of Western companies. CEO Jane Sun has ensured that more than fifty percent of the staff is female, compared to only twenty percent at tech companies in Silicon Valley.[69] Women at Ctrip.com get extra pay during pregnancy and as a young mother you get free services such as taxi transport, longer maternity leave than the legal minimum, flexibility to work from home, rooms to rest at work... The company even offers free egg freezing for the female employees who want to focus on their career before starting a family. The coronavirus outbreak and ban on travel in China came as a death sentence, just as for any other company in the industry. As a result, companies like Booking.com were laying off twenty-five percent or more of their staff in order to survive[70]. However, the founder of Ctrip.com, James Liang, came up with a different approach. He traveled to every province of China and, dressed in traditional Chinese clothing customs, decided to live stream every day to provide a personal introduction to all the unique places of China's history in order to encourage people to discover China while the national borders were closed. This was so authentic, personal, and successful that millions of Chinese people booked trips to these new hotspots. Ctrip.com has not had to lay off a single employee due to the pandemic. I would put Ctrip.com in the category of godmother companies, but with a strong Western influence. What makes them so unique is their focus on the individual and on the customer.

DO THE CHINESE TRUST THEIR SUPERIORS?

The trust employees have in their employers is more determined by their immediate superiors than by the trust they have in the company or brand. Most Chinese people, like us, of course prefer to work for companies that are seen as good employers, either because of the reputation of the brand or because of a positive culture. In China, the founder often embodies that culture. As we have seen, this can vary a lot and today is usually a mix of different influences. What makes China so unique is that since 1992—when Deng Xiaoping pushed structural reforms through the government—the whole country has experienced such a large and rapid change that every ten years there is a new generation of Chinese people who cannot be compared at all to their predecessors. In the West, there is a new generation every fifteen to twenty years. The baby boomers were born after World War II. Generation X, to which I belong, were born between 1965 and 1980; Generation Y (or millennials) between 1981 and 1995; and Generation Z were born between 1996 and 2010. As a rule, Western companies communicate in the same way to consumers within a generation. Every decade for the last fifty years, China has changed so much that it seems like a completely different country. In order to describe the different generations of consumers, in China they talk about children born "before 1980," "after 1980," "after 1990," and "after 1995." Those born before 1970 were greatly affected by the Cultural Revolution and underwent, much more than steered, the changes in China. The age of the employees and the companies therefore strongly determines the level of confidence in the superior.

Generally speaking, employees in the more traditional "godfather" and "marshal" companies are strongly driven by clear objectives and tasks. After China's economic reforms in 1992, this model was a good fit in a country where most Chinese people could earn more by working very "hard" towards a clear goal. Success or failure is personal, and directly reflects the trust they put in the organization and the company. Therefore, they were not very willing to commit to unrealistic goals. Certainly, the generation of employees born before 1980 are highly pragmatic, procedure- and goal-oriented, and fit well into this model.

With the start of the Chinese internet revolution after the SARS epidemic in 2004, more employees wanted to work for companies that gave them challenges and independence rather than tasks and objectives. These companies, often with a "marshal" and "godmother" culture, gave employees more room for "smart" working, innovation, or doing business, and judged them on their results. This was very attractive to a new generation of overambitious Chinese people who wanted to grow their careers in pace with the speed of growth of technology companies and China. Data points (key performance indicators, or KPIs) and customers would rate them, not their subjective managers. You have your destiny in your own hands, but due to the extremely competitive climate of China, many in this generation no longer had a real private life outside of work. This is typical for the generation of Chinese people born between 1980 and 1990, who were overambitious and full of self-confidence, and had little patience if they could succeed faster somewhere else. Young Chinese women were also more likely to build a career for themselves before having children.

In 2014, when the world of the smartphone and 4G arrived in China, at my company we had more and more young Chinese people born after 1990 who were looking for a powerful way to express their new identity. This digital generation, often spoiled by their parents, wanted to discover the world first. They needed both space and recognition. This fitted in well with the culture of "godmother" and "Western" models that they found in the new "genius" or innovative "rock star" start-ups that would conquer China and the world. Older companies like Ctrip.com also give the required attention and support to these employees to work in an "involved" way towards a higher goal for themselves and the company. The challenge of these employees is not so different from that of millennials in the West, but their need for attention and the need to manage their personal expectations is even greater. They are open-minded, proud, brand sensitive, entrepreneurial, and above all very outspoken. The manager is less and less the superior, but that certainly doesn't mean that they are disrespectful to business leaders with more experience, success, and status. This is ingrained in Chinese culture, even among the younger millennials. For example, at home, they still want to take care of their parents, but rarely are they really able to do so. It is this tension between all their individual opportunities and expectations, and on the other hand the desire to do good by their parents and superiors, that sometimes gives the impression that Chinese millennials have a split personality. But we shouldn't conclude that they feel bad about themselves, because it is often the opposite that is true. It is these modern young consumers and employees who look like Western millennials but that show the true Chinese cultural identity even more than their predecessors, who were much more influenced by Western ideals. These are the realists who don't worry about tomorrow and live in full freedom to make their own choices.[71]

By 2025, I predict that the new era of creativity in China will be in full swing. Generation Z employees born after 1995 are much more carefree than other generations in China, spending more and saving less. What makes China's Generation Z unique in China and globally is that they have never experienced a crisis, which makes them very optimistic. When the COVID-19 pandemic broke out, they were convinced that it would soon be over, and indeed this was the case in China. They were convinced that the economy would soon recover—and they were right. They are convinced that they will always have a job, that tomorrow will look better than today, and that they will make even more money in the future.[72] That is the biggest difference with millenials in the West. That's why they often refuse to work overtime and prefer to make the rules themselves. They are quick to express their dissatisfaction on social media and look for flexi-jobs and creative interpretations of roles. They look for companies that give them a sense of satisfaction and above all the comfort to maintain the lifestyle they are used to from home. They feel much more social pressure from their friends or colleagues than from their manager. They look for more personal experiences and happiness rather than confirmation.

In mid-2021, Chinese suddenly started using the term **tǎngpíng** (躺平),[73] which literally means "lying flat". It was a slogan adopted by the middle-class Generation Z to indicate that they were no longer interested in being a part of China's 9-9-6 rat race. They would no longer give in to pressure from parents to perform better, from companies to work harder, from the government to make the Chinese dream come true. The pandemic kick-started this process, as many young people spent weeks or months at home reflecting on the purpose of their lives. Many young people are comfortable enough in their own skin not to have to work. But this certainly doesn't mean they're lazy. They just want to decide for themselves when and how much they work. They want a better balance between life and work, as we're increasingly seeing in the West. This is the start of a freelance movement that is now expanding in China. The challenge for employers is that these young people are sometimes too sensitive to try things outside their comfort zone, but at the same time expect a job that gives them opportunities to discover new things, experiment, and that also gives them instant satisfaction. This environment is more likely to be found in the creative than the industrial sectors. Fortunately for the more traditional Chinese employers, it is only the upper middle classes that display Generation Z's "*tangping*" attitude, because the millions of poorer Chinese simply can't afford to "lie flat." The strength of this new freelance generation is its optimism, passion for hobbies, search for inspiration, and willingness to express themselves creatively, so long as it brings them new opportunities or friends. These employees want to be "discovered" by their manager. This fits in well with the cozy Western "coach" leadership style that employees trust from day one, but also finds similarities in "godfather" models that place importance on both the relationships and the local cultural values of China—just without Gree Electric's addiction to work or Huawei's survival instinct.

CREATIVE CHINA POST 2030

In the future, it probably won't matter which Chinese leadership style is used; employees in China will increasingly give free rein to their creative minds. The era of "Made in China," in which huge numbers of hard-working and very cheap laborers were workers in the factory of the world is now dying out after thirty years. In 2015, China entered the era of automation, which aims to turn every factory into a smart factory by 2025 with the help of 5G, AI, IoT, and Cloud computing. From 2030, the era of "Created in China" will take over thanks to the 210 million Chinese people born between 1996 and 2010 who will then form the new generation of employees, managers, and entrepreneurs. Even today, they're already driving the largest growth ever seen in China's domestic consumption. They represent the key to how China can slowly evolve from being an export country to a consumption-driven economy, and it is precisely why China is becoming less dependent on the West.

It is not only due to geopolitics and the Chinese government's strategic desire to decouple from the West, but because the new Chinese generation wants China to become smarter, more efficient, and more qualitative. The government can encourage and accelerate the innovation trend, but the real power to make China a global center of creativity and innovation will come from below. You could argue that fifteen years ago the West lost the battle against the millions of cheap Chinese workers; today it is losing the battle against Chinese infrastructure; and by 2030 it may start losing the battle against Chinese creativity. The reason I am so convinced is firstly because naturally, the Chinese are born just as smart, creative, or talented as we are. There are just a lot more of them, they are more hopeful for a better tomorrow, they are more open to trying something new, and they have the largest domestic market on the planet for selling their creations, innovations, and crazy ideas.

If you follow Chinese social media, you will see how creative, uninhibited, and clever China has already become. In a business context, we find the first signs of this out-of-the-box thinking in the surprisingly creative collaborations between different brands that at first seem very far apart. For example, Adidas is working with tea drink chain Hey Tea, and the fashion brand Karl Lagerfeld with Tsingtao beer.[74] KFC is partnering with insect repellant brand Liushen, and it's not just a one-way relationship: at KFC you can drink coffee with the insect-repelling aroma of Liushen; and online you can buy Liushen bug spray that smells like KFC coffee. The Chinese Generation Z and millennials are increasingly looking for products that clearly differentiate themselves from the well-known brands. This creates a new trend of innovative "collaborations" between different brands that seems increasingly extreme or bizarre.

The boundaries of what is "normal" are starting to blur, which also makes it more difficult to understand China. You can no longer put Chinese companies under the label of a single industry because they usually operate in a handful of sectors. You can no longer categorize business leaders under one style, because they have been influenced by all four of the leadership styles above. You can no longer label Chinese consumers as traditionally Chinese or Western-influenced. Well-known Chinese brands are also going beyond the boundaries of their traditional markets to surprise and delight consumers. Because younger Chinese consumers are much more individualistic than their parents, they are looking for more differentiation, uniqueness, and personalized offers. Unique events, pop-up stores, live streaming, gaming, and other ways to bring consumers closer to the brand are working very well in China. Brands are building these kinds of collaborations with other brands from other sectors in order to offer new experiences to increase the activity with and attention on the brand. Of course, it is not because Airbnb comes up with a staycation campaign with Hey Tea that China has suddenly become more creative. But creativity is about both originality and talent as well as energy. The more you try out, build, and research, the more the most creative ideas arise. By implementing new ideas, which China is an expert in, more new ideas appear. Therefore, we can be confident that China will become one of the largest sources of new ideas in the world. Smart Western companies will want to harvest these ideas by investing early in partnerships with Chinese companies, netizens, entrepreneurs, artists, and educational institutions.

CHINA REDISCOVERS ITS PAST

What reinforces this trend toward a more creative China is the search for China's cultural past. This national trend combines cultural creations with consumer nostalgia. Since the increase in political tensions between China and the West, Generation Z in particular have developed a very strong sense of national pride. We saw this in early 2021 with the consumer attack on H&M, Nike, and Zara, who announced they would stop buying cotton from China because of the hard-hitting statements and claims from the Better Cotton Initiative (BCI) that cotton from Xinjiang was being picked by Uyghurs in forced labor camps. When it turned out that the BCI office in Shanghai itself had already indicated that the allegations were false, Chinese young people stopped buying the Western brands that were following the politically charged BCI advice from New York. Western fashion brands that had cut ties with Xinjiang were also no longer even available on e-commerce platforms in China. The reaction from the West at the time was unanimous: if China is attacked politically, the government will use the economic power of 1.4 billion consumers to punish Western companies or even entire nations.

So, we hear that China really can't be trusted; because the government, companies, and consumers all work together when they feel threatened. This phenomenon is not new; for decades now, products such as Canadian lobster, Norwegian salmon, Australian wine, and even individual Western companies like Shell have been the victims of an intense geopolitical battle with China. What is not being mentioned is that Chinese consumers have the same vehement reaction to Chinese brands. Chinese influencers and even China's local governments who harm China or the Chinese people get the same treatment from local consumers There are many examples of this: the scandal when melamine was found in powdered milk products in 2008, and more recently, the overworked employees of El.me or Alibaba, or the rape scandal at the car sharing company DiDi. You see the same vigorous reaction against Chinese companies that abuse the personal data of consumers or scam them. Chinese consumers also don't give up easily, and usually Chinese companies or the government put things right again within twenty-four hours. When this turns out to the advantage of a Western brand, as with powdered milk brands, which since 2008 have mainly been imported from the West, nobody outside China complains about the strong united reactions of Chinese consumers.

In the West, you notice that some consumers do shout very loudly about Amazon, Ryanair, or Uber paying their employees far too little or treating them badly—some even report violations of human rights—but we're not quick to change our buying behavior. We almost always choose convenience over principle. We shout it from the rooftops that China doesn't play by the rules, but we are still happy to buy "Made in China" items. We still see the "Made in China" brands as "Western" designs, and strangely enough rarely blame these brands. By doing this we also aren't very concerned about the Chinese, but as a result we do lose sight of the great trend of "Designed in China." What you see happening is that Chinese products and brands incorporate a distinctive Chinese style that hankers back to the past, tradition, or sometimes even to a futuristic China. This really appeals to the young, Generation Z Chinese consumer.

Fashion and beauty products capitalize on this the most, but you could actually argue that since 2020 every Chinese brand is now seeing its chance to compete with the foreign brands by playing on the emotions of these young Chinese patriots. History is being revived, dusty museums are cool again, and China's NASA-style space program is enjoying its heyday. But it is not just the Chinese brands that are riding this wave. Western consumer brands from fashion house Moschino to Oreo cookies are incorporating Chinese culture to further embed their Western brand in the Chinese market. The days when the Chinese preferred to buy Western brands because they were trusted and radiated quality and history are numbered. China has rediscovered its own past and will use it as a weapon against any company that is insensitive to this.

Therefore, the very best strategy for further developing the Chinese market in 2022 is to do so with a local partner and to show genuine respect for Chinese culture and people. Not because it is still, as it was previously, mandatory to set up a joint venture, but because today it has become better, safer, and more effective to work with a local partner. Understanding what the Chinese consumer wants is now becoming essential for the survival of any brand in the Chinese market. Chinese millennials and Generation Z expect brands to constantly entertain them with creative co-branded products and VIP campaigns that engage consumers personally; but also by telling them about the values of the company and brand behind the product. That is why the choice of the right Chinese partner and marketing agency has become so crucial, to ensure that relationships with the new Chinese consumer remain sustainable by creating real value for them.

If there's one statement that truly annoys me, it's that the Chinese will never be as creative or innovative as Westerners. Leading Western thinkers and experts argue that this is because of China's highly collectivist culture, authoritarian system, or archaic education.[75] A society that rewards unconventional thinking will always be more innovative, while a more controlling hierarchical society that strives for conformity and isn't totally free-thinking will innovate only incrementally. I want to take a moment to expand on this, because it shows how blind or arrogant some Western experts are, as if Westerners are a culturally superior race.

Culture can certainly influence the way we innovate, but there are many other influences that support innovation, such as passion, curiosity, attitude, infrastructure, talent, resources, imagination, ecosystems, market demand, competition, and others. The biggest mistake the West can make is not to mistrust China, but to have a misplaced sense of overconfidence. It is belittling to the Chinese, morally shameful, and extremely dangerous because it gives a false sense of superiority. It is the ideal breeding ground for self-importance that can in fact kill our innovative power. Too many people still falsely claim that the West is better at innovation, while the Chinese are better at manufacturing or commercialization. However, it is no longer possible to innovate without thinking in a customer-oriented way; hardware and software can no longer be separated in the world of industry 4.0. They have become one.

If we look at Huawei's 5G products, it is difficult to argue that the Chinese cannot innovate. With their eighty thousand engineers in 2019, Ericsson and Nokia could no longer keep up with Huawei in terms of R&D, patents, and 5G installations. When Trump cut off Huawei's access to American microchips and the Android operating system in 2020, their rapidly increasing lead was suddenly under threat. The Western press was very clear that even the hero of Chinese innovation was dependent on American technology. What they forgot to say was that Huawei's European competitors had the exact same weak spot, and probably wouldn't survive a similar ban.

Huawei is just the tip of the iceberg of Chinese product innovation. There are plenty of others, but they aren't very visible to the West as most are less than twenty years old and still have their hands full, first trying to conquer their huge domestic market and China's neighboring countries. We only know a few brands such as DJI's drones, Geely-Volvo's electric cars, or Haier's smart refrigerators because they have already become world leaders. But every year we discover some new names like TikTok, Ant Group, Xiaomi, or Shein, who, without us having heard of them, have become the most valuable companies in their sector. What we need to watch out for the most is their innovative strength in service innovation, customer innovation, and business model innovation. This has nothing to do with the culture of innovation, but the combination of three things that puts China ahead of the West: infrastructure, consumer adoption and domestic competition. China has a highly advanced and excellent infrastructure that facilitates innovation, for example the 5G and IoT networks. On top of that, the Chinese consumer is extremely demanding and impatient (consider for example how quickly mobile payment was introduced in China). But the real driver for Chinese innovation comes from the truly fierce competition between companies in China, partly due to the large market, which means that even Tencent or Alibaba are never really safe from emerging companies such as TikTok or Pinduoduo that have only been around for five years—innovative start-ups who attack the bigger fish.

START-UPS IN CHINA

In 2005 I founded my first start-up in China. But how do you go about this? My first thought was to hire someone Chinese who I trusted 100 percent: Dave Wei. In 2000, when I was working for Alcatel in Shanghai, I spent more days with Dave than with my own wife, so you could definitely say we were close friends. Having convinced him to leave the multinational Alcatel, he became the first salesperson and also my right-hand man in my technology start-up. Our customers were top universities and research institutions as well as development departments of major companies such as Lenovo. Since most of my clients got their budgets from the government, my biggest challenge was not in getting sales or being paid, but the level of support that was expected with every deal. These customers soon demanded that I hire a whole team of engineers to help them every step of the way, from concept to final application. I quickly hired a handful of local rocket scientists, which really wasn't cheap. What my team liked best was testing the latest 4G application together with the customer or improving the signal-to-noise ratio. After a year, my early euphoria over easy sales turned into a panic that my customers were eating up my entire profit in after-sales service. I no longer needed salespeople, but people who could manage customer expectations. The biggest challenge for foreign companies in China is less about gaining the trust of their staff, and more about building up the trust of customers so that they're able to say "no." The challenging thing about Chinese customers is that they often behave like little emperors. They're paying, so you need to do what they want right away. As a Westerner in China, it is sometimes shocking how badly Chinese customers treat their suppliers. There are lots of reasons for this. Culturally, you can go back to the Confucian idea of subject-master. Socially, it makes sense given the number of people all screaming for attention. We consider hounding suppliers and service staff as disrespectful, but the Chinese see it as necessary to get attention. Everyone wants to make money, which makes the Chinese very impatient. But Chinese suppliers are also very often submissive because they see their top customers as a leverage to the next level.

As a result, the Chinese have gained a reputation for being extremely pragmatic and assertive. But this is more about China than the Chinese. When I returned to Belgium in 2016 after twenty years living in China, I noticed that I had changed too. I had very little patience if I had to wait for food in a restaurant or if it seemed like the waiter was ignoring me on purpose. I couldn't understand why I had to wait at least fifteen minutes to be served at the post office or train station when there were only a few people in line. Making an appointment with a plumber or optician felt like planning a trip to Mars. I got angry that companies sent me an invoice before we even had a contract or agreement. That's an easy way to make money, I thought at the time.

During my first months back in Belgium, I often thought that in twenty years the country had become much more cunning and lazier than before. Here the supplier seemed like the emperor and you as a customer could consider yourself lucky if they even made time for you. I had come to the conclusion that you really can't trust Western suppliers. Scared of receiving an invoice, I stopped asking people for advice, and hired a lawyer for each contract—who sent me another eye-watering invoice. I really missed China.

But when I thought back to my life as a start-up founder, that thought quickly passed. As a start-up in China, it is a completely different story. You have to constantly prove yourself before you build up a reputation so that customers and their employees trust you. Many other expats in Shanghai knew me as the "Digger," because like Chinese start-ups I turned over every stone to find business. I was available 24/7 for my customers. I could write a whole other book full of absurd stories like how a customer harassed me for four hours because the blue color in our app wasn't blue enough, or how another customer wanted a ten percent discount because one of the thirty hostesses at our event had showed up with a Band-Aid on her leg. If you take this to heart, you won't survive long in China. The best solution is to build up a personal relationship with the manager of your customer and make good agreements and a watertight contract. When I compared the start-ups in China with those from Europe or North America I met in 2016, I saw little difference in knowledge, experience, or dreams. But the difference in fighting and toughness and resilience was like comparing a squad of Chinese Navy Seals to a group of young Boy Scouts. Chinese customers are so demanding that you are hardened and trained to survive, but also learn to operate in a very clear structure, which helps in scaling up later. The managers of Chinese start-ups today have mostly studied or worked in the West, and sooner or later the founders parachute them over our Western markets to take over our customers—and they do it ingeniously well.

EVERY CUSTOMER IS A FRIEND

My most flamboyant right-hand employee was Jennifer. She was the opposite of Florence. She could wrap any man around her finger, and any woman became her best friend. She was a pit bull saleswoman who never let you go. Every start-up needs a Jennifer. She wasn't just smart and determined, but also very loyal and empathetic towards customers. She simply became every customer's best friend. More than half of our orders were placed because customers wanted to do her a favor. Her secret was to make business as personal as possible and she did that with… WeChat. As a manager you did need to have patience, because seventy percent of her working day was spent on her cell phone. You don't want to know how many times in the first few months I went up to her annoyed to ask her when she was planning on starting work. Every morning when she came to the office, she would also spend half an hour in the bathroom before getting started. It drove me crazy and more than once I was close to firing her during her probationary period.

But that changed when I went to meet clients with her. She knew every customer as if they were her best friend. She had been following that customer's social media posts for weeks and mapped out their interests down to the smallest of details. She had proactively invited most of the customers to an event that would interest them or put them in touch with one of her friends or even other customers. That all happened in the evenings after working hours and from her posts I could tell that she was sometimes still partying with a customer at two a.m. If she spent too long in the bathroom in the morning, it was because she had only just got out of bed and hadn't eaten breakfast yet. My office was the place for her morning routine. Whenever I spoke to her about her casual work ethic, her response was that her sales figures were all that mattered to her—and so I lost the argument.

In 2015 my wife and I decided to leave China. Our daughter was going to study in Belgium and so we would put our China story on hold for a while. It was with great sadness in my heart that I had to let my team go. When Jennifer heard this really bad news, she was quick to react. That same evening, she wanted to invite me to her parents' place in Shanghai as a goodbye. I accepted, of course. Although I was her manager, she also considered me a friend, just like her customers. My wife, daughter, and I would be meeting her parents for the first time. Jennifer was always very fashionably dressed, so of course we were expecting a luxury apartment. But nothing could be further from the truth. On the twenty-fourth floor of an apartment block among twenty neglected skyscrapers, she lived with her parents in a 700-square-foot musty apartment that was crammed full like the home of a hundred-year-old hoarder. Her mother had spent the whole day cooking all kinds of Shanghainese dishes for us. Her father had clearly been given the task of getting me drunk—which he did very well. We received a really warm welcome and it got very emotional when her parents gave a speech about how I was the best boss Jennifer had ever had. They both had senior positions in Shanghai's local government. Her father was also a painter. As a thank you, we were allowed to choose any of his paintings to take home—although he very subtly made clear which one was intended for us. Once her father was properly drunk, he showed me his huge collection of jade gemstones with price tags still in the boxes. I was just about sober enough to calculate that, among all that junk, their jade collection was worth as much as my house in Belgium. As with Jennifer, in China you can't always come to conclusions based on first impressions. When I went to the office the next day with a bad hangover, Jennifer suddenly came to my desk to get me to sign something. It was an agreement with the calculation of her severance pay and bonus that she was still owed. She didn't want to leave anything to chance, and I was far too tired and too emotional from the night before to argue about it. I trusted her. It all turned out to be correct in the end, but this story speaks volumes for me. Trust is the common thread; it's just that we don't always see it.

流

liú

Meaning: **flow, drift, move, spread, current, stream.** This character is built up of one symbol meaning **water** and one for **fast flowing**. It symbolizes everything that is constantly moving, as well as new trends. If you trust the movement, flow, and direction, you can fit in and bring about change yourself.

4.

Collective trust. Why doesn't China seem to trust minorities and nonconformists? Are the Chinese actually hospitable or is this just for show? Does the opinion of Chinese people really count? How can the Chinese bring about change if they're not allowed to protest openly? Do the Chinese have role models they trust? How authentic and self-aware are the Chinese?

Network and tribes

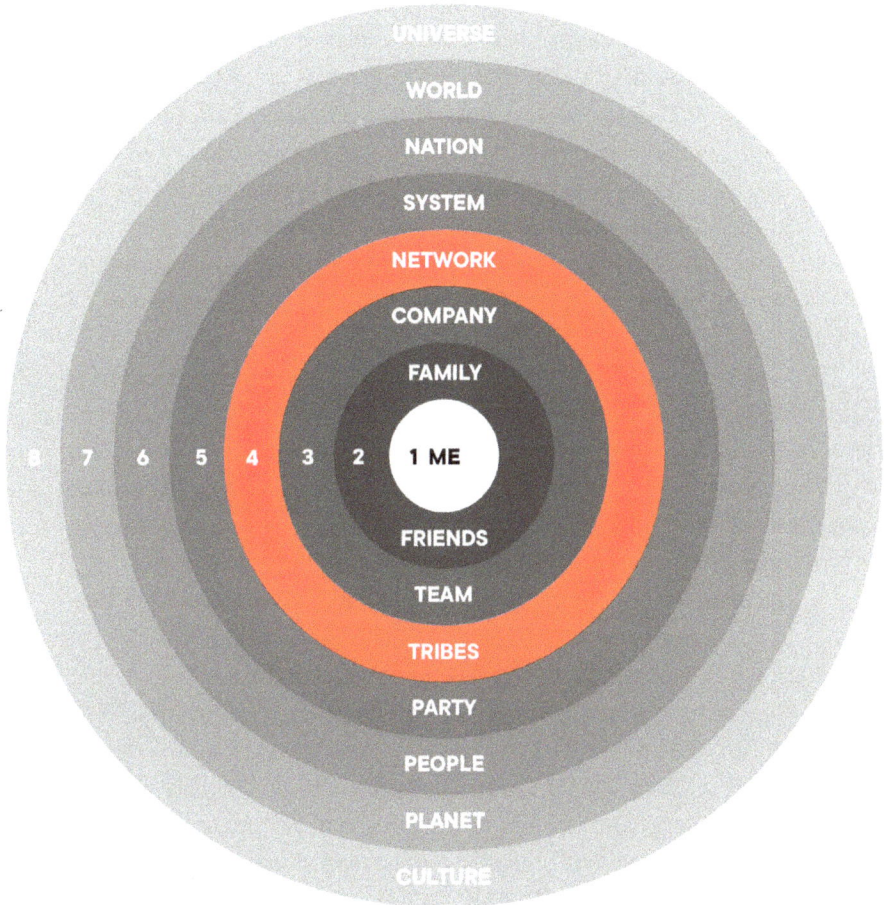

UNIVERSE
WORLD
NATION
SYSTEM
NETWORK
COMPANY
FAMILY
1 ME
FRIENDS
TEAM
TRIBES
PARTY
PEOPLE
PLANET
CULTURE

8 7 6 5 4 3 2 1

The year 2020—the year of the rat—will forever be remembered as a year of global disaster due to the coronavirus. The rat is the first sign in the twelve-year cycle of the Chinese zodiac—it represents curiosity, resourcefulness, and survival instinct. Astrology aside, the last of these characteristics is very significant for the Chinese people. That instinct was sometimes needed in previous rat years too. For example, in 1960, during China's worst ever famine under Mao Zedong when many millions of people died of starvation.[76] But in fact, 2008, the previous rat year, also started out badly, with winter storms, violent clashes between rioters and the police in Tibet, a boycott of the Beijing Olympics, a magnitude-8 earthquake in Sichuan, floods in the South, the milk powder melamine scandal, shocking gas explosions, terrorist attacks in Xinjiang, and the global financial crisis. In a year that held so much promise due to hosting the Olympic Games, Beijing had its hands full with national crises and international criticism. The recurring theme was that it was mainly society's weakest that were affected—the poor, farmers, laborers, children, minorities. If you lived in China at the time, the newly urbanized middle class gave you the strong impression that they really didn't care about the weak in their own country, let alone having any global concerns. "Everyone for themselves," seemed to be the motto.

Then, on May 12, 2008, a massive earthquake in Sichuan killed nearly 70,000 people, including many children, injured 370,000, and left five million homeless. In the days after the quake, all of my Chinese friends, young and old, donated money or blood for the relief effort. Volunteers from all over the country descended on the region. More than $4.7 billion[77] in public donations were collected within two weeks—the same amount as the entire year of 2007. Had the Chinese suddenly discovered altruism and compassion? My own explanation is that the proximity and scale of the crisis had caused millions of Chinese people to stop and think for a moment about "life." Sometimes it does feel like a real crisis is needed, like sadly the coronavirus, to put things into perspective. For China, May 2008 was the first time this had happened since the opening-up of China in 1978. This might seem strange, because even as early as 1989 the world was predicting the beginning of an internal social crisis in China, partly due to the mass protests on Tiananmen Square and later those of the Falun Gong spiritual movement in 1999. However, these events did not lead to a wider national crisis, in part because of the repressive actions of the government, but also because most Chinese didn't identify with these "rebels" or "heretics."

At that era, China's first priority was to move forward, and any crisis was seen more as an external challenge than a serious internal problem. The West, on the other hand, wanted to draw attention to China's human rights violations, for example by awarding the Nobel Peace Prize to the Dalai Lama (1989) and human rights activist Liu Xiaobo (2010). It was a noble goal but had the opposite effect. Instead of encouraging the Chinese to revolt against the regime, more and more of them were convinced that the West wanted to hold China back. However, the 2008 Sichuan earthquake was not a Western narrative. The high number of casualties was partly due to Sichuan's badly built houses and schools (called tofu buildings). Chinese critics pointed out that the government's incompetence and corruption had been allowing this to happen over many years. The enormous speed at which the government then started building new and better houses for the recently homeless in Sichuan was a clear sign that this crisis had put enormous grassroots pressure on the Chinese government. The difference between the response to the Sichuan earthquake and other national disasters lies in the extent to which many Chinese people felt concerned with the disaster, and how personally they identified with it. This was less the case with the troubles in Tibet, Xinjiang, Inner Mongolia, Hong Kong, or Taiwan during the same period, despite the fact that the last two are mainly inhabited by the Han Chinese. A common view in the West is that China oppresses people of different ethnic, religious, or ideological backgrounds within the country. When I think back to lessons of the 2008 disasters, China's repressive actions seem to have less to do with nonconformists and more to do with the people or groups who represent a threat to China's progress or national security: corrupt politicians, reckless factory managers, fraudulent traffickers, radicalized terrorists, separatists... In the next chapter I will discuss the ways China, in fact, assesses and tackles these risks differently.

WHO ARE THE HAN CHINESE?

A mistake we too often make in the West, consciously or unconsciously, is to assume that China can't be trusted because the regime is a potential danger to anyone (including us) who is not Han Chinese. One wonders if this isn't an old colonial way of thinking. It is true that China's population is ninety-two percent Han Chinese. Even within the ethnic Han Chinese group there are of course significant genetic, linguistic, cultural, and social differences as a result of millennia of immigration and assimilation of different regional ethnic groups and tribes within China. Between the Han Chinese, one Chinese person will look down on another for class or other cultural reasons. I lived in both Shanghai and Beijing, which have very similar economic, cultural, and social backgrounds. In both cities, people generally speak Mandarin outside the home. But the Shanghainese find Beijingers arrogant and unrefined. In their minds, Shanghai is the refined fashion capital, while Beijing is full of uncouth, common people. Beijingers, on the other hand, find the Shanghainese pretentious and selfish. In their minds, Beijing is the cultural and political center, while Shanghai is a crass shopping mall. Before 1949, Shanghai was the more modern and appealing city; under Mao it was Beijing's turn; and since the actual settling of capitalism in China in 1992, the spotlight is back on Shanghai. But both cities need each other, like yin and yang. Beijing provides stability while Shanghai (and South China) ensures economic growth.

Can't we draw a parallel here between China and the West? We also see these dynamics between Amsterdam and Rotterdam in the Netherlands, or between Ghent and Antwerp in Belgium. Ghent, for example, is a hipster city, more progressive, while Antwerp's large port makes it more cosmopolitan and therefore more conservative, and it claims to have a better understanding of the problems of globalization. Even between the provinces there's jealousy over the distribution of funds, and there is even a complete polarization between many ethnic communities, as well as between the Dutch-, French-, and German-speaking regions of the country. In a small country that has less than one percent of the Chinese population, with a diversity and population that is many times smaller than a city as Shenzhen, this is quite a confounding observation.

When you also take into account the social context between the cities in China, you see that many Shanghainese, for example, are quick to look down on Han Chinese from the poorer neighboring province of Anhui. China is much less uniform than we might assume. To really learn more about China, I really recommend not automatically assuming that any rivalry between the Han Chinese and non-Han Chinese ethnic groups is determined by race, religion, or culture, but by a personal assessment of each individual or group as a result of jealously, fear, or self-image—just like anywhere else in the world. In the past, Chinese also created a self-image of themselves inferior to the image they had of the rich, successful, and efficient Westerners. They held the West as a mirror up to themselves as how they could evolve. But there are too many cracks in that Western mirror now. The more problems of conflict, inequality, and stagnation arise in the West, the more Chinese people think that China has a better way and is doing better. The Chinese have become visibly prouder of the rise of China; while right now, more than ever, the West continues to look down on China and the rulers in Beijing, who are congratulating themselves about China's evolution. Since 2021, "the East is rising, and the West is declining" has been a common mantra on the lips of Chinese officials, usually for domestic consumption. Although this statement sounds populist, it is also important to point out that it is not about China or exclusively the Han Chinese, but about a shift of the global economic center from West to East. People are already completely convinced of this in Asia, but not in the West. Is the mistrust in China the result of the unfounded overconfidence of the West? I am not at all convinced that the West is going backwards, but Asia is certainly advancing faster than the rest of the world.

Other than the Han, China has fifty-five minorities who are considered integral to China's identity and cultural heritage. The epicenter of the 2008 earthquake was in Wenchuan and Beichuan counties of Sichuan, with a total population of 340,000 people, 190,000 of whom were Han Chinese. The other 150,000 belonged to minority groups such as the Qiang or Zhang.[78] About 30,000 Qiang were killed by the violent earthquake. The Qiang are a very ancient Chinese ethnic "clan" of nearly 300,000 people who are ancestors of the Han Chinese. They live in the mountains in self-sufficient units of patriarchal families. They have a rich polytheistic religious faith that worships both their ancestors and objects (such as white stones). Historically, in their rather isolated villages, ancient religious and traditional social customs were well preserved. Their allegiance to the clan is much bigger than their interest in the individual. Although we often describe the Han Chinese as a highly collective society, compared with the Qiang, they are much more individualistic. The Qiang's traditional social structure greatly helped them recover after the earthquake. Generally speaking, studies have showed, for example after Hurricane Katrina in America,[79] that ethnic minorities (mostly African Americans) with an economic status similar to the (usually Caucasian) majority population are more severely affected by natural disasters. The opposite held true for the Qiang and Zhang, as after the earthquake they got back on their feet slightly quicker than the Han Chinese living in the same areas. At the time, the Chinese government gave Han Chinese the same levels of financial support and assistance to rebuild as they gave the Qiang and the Zhang minorities.

According to the Chinese, the Western narrative that China wants to destroy its ethnic minorities is the exact opposite of the reality on the ground: China encourages many minorities to preserve their traditions, buildings, and dress. If China really wanted to destroy all these cultures, why is it putting effort into rebuilding these villages and offering support to preserve their traditions? You sometimes do hear that it's for Chinese tourism, as a minority village is more of an attraction. If this is the big incentive, then at least we can forget about China forcing all ethnic minorities to give up their traditions, beliefs, culture, and language—as these have economic value. If, on the other hand, they would have no economic value, we could also ask why China so often pursues policies that actually favor minorities over the Han Chinese. The fifty-five ethnic minorities in China were never subjected to the one-child policy. They are allowed to speak their own language at school. The grades they need to get into university are lower than for the Han Chinese. They often receive more financial help, loans, scholarships, and even job opportunities. And the list of positive discriminations that favor the minorities over the Han goes on. I have visited dozens of ethnic minority villages in China and the energy of these people tells me a different and certainly more nuanced story than what I read in the Western press. Maybe I picked the wrong villages? This said, we cannot discard that all minorities have not always been treated equally. Minorities such as Tibetans, Inner-Mongolians and Uyghurs have clearly experienced more repression than many other minorities. At certain times they were more of a liability for China. At other times they were more an opportunity for China to show their heart. My belief, however, is that generally speaking the situation is improving for all minorities today. Or perhaps in the West, however, we just can't seem to believe that China would do a good job of valuing and integrating the minorities? Because Western and Chinese media reports tell a completely different story. Who can we still believe? Both views are somehow true. The challenge we face in believing China's story lies in the directness of its integration policy. For example, for a long time, the Han Chinese were financially incentivized to move from the interior provinces to Tibet or Xinjiang or to marry a Tibetan or Uyghur. China has also used a similar strategy to incentivize people to move to newly built "ghost towns," for example. We see this and other examples as being forced on people, but for many of the pragmatic poorer Chinese it is a life choice, the Chinese equivalent of "Go West, young man." It is normal that we in the West have our reservations about this.

But when I think about China's 302 dialects, fifty-five minorities, eight major cuisines, all the different natural environments, and its socio-economic diversity, at the end of the day there really is no such thing as "the Chinese." Even on Chinese banknotes you'll find five different languages: Chinese Pinyin, Mongolian, Tibetan, Zhuang, and Uyghur. It may seem like a small thing, but to me this kind of multilingual messaging seems counterproductive if you want to destroy the culture and language of the minorities.

ALL FOR SHOW OR A GOOD IMPRESSION?

Every year at Chinese New Year or the National People's Congress, minorities are celebrated as central China's cultural heritage. It might look like a highly staged display, but what it shows is that the Han Chinese in general value minorities far more than we give them credit for. Especially since the 2008 earthquake, the Chinese have made a major mental switch to being interested in helping minorities and victims of natural disasters and the less well-off in society. We saw the same phenomenon with the floods in Western Europe in the summer of 2021, where solidarity was not a given, but still came about when governments reacted slowly, and especially because it was the socio-economically weak that were affected.

If we return to why the Chinese suddenly opened their pockets and made donations after the 2008 earthquake, we need to place what happened in the context of China's global image. The year 2008 was to be the year when the whole world would focus its (positive) attention on China as host of the Summer Olympics. Everything had to (and would) run smoothly. It was a unique moment for China to clean up its image and show the whole world how different, better, and more beautiful China was now. The image of China as a country crawling with copycats, thieves, and scammers would be replaced by a technology-inspired, smart, talented China. China's image as a polluter and heartless country full of sweatshops could finally give way to a more balanced view of a responsible, empathetic, and inclusive China. The Olympic Games would shine the spotlight on a new and modern China.

But the Sichuan earthquake had other ideas. The beautiful image that China intended to show the world and its own population of 1.3 billion citizens was suddenly shattered by the earthquake. In 1976 there was a devastating earthquake in North China that killed 242,769 people, but at that time China was largely isolated from the world and therefore the disaster got much less media attention. The 2008 earthquake in southwest China left 69,227 dead and 17,923 missing. In the West, the reasons for the high death toll were seen as the power-grabbing politics of corrupt leaders and managers, and the selfish attitude of those in power toward the poor, the weak, and the minorities. Many Chinese people felt the same. Many Chinese people really didn't want to be associated with the pure profit-seeking, corrupt elite who had built schools out of poor quality "tofu" concrete. They saw the earthquake as an opportunity to show China and the world that the Chinese really do have their hearts in the right place.

In a way, the year 2008 marked a crucial turning point for the Chinese as they began to see how the world viewed their country for the first time. This was brought about by social media and smartphones, which had really started to become popular at that point, but it also reveals one of China's core values: to give guests a good impression. All Chinese people are familiar with this saying by Confucius: "Is it not a joy to have friends coming from afar!" It is deeply rooted in Chinese culture to show guests that no effort has been spared to demonstrate Chinese hospitality. Business leaders and politicians go the extra mile to show foreign visitors their warmheartedness with gifts, expensive dinners, beautiful hotels, and VIP service from the moment you arrive at the airport until you leave China again. Foreigners never complain about this, because it is something they're not really used to in other countries, at least not to the same degree. But back home, lots of foreign business travelers think it is a Chinese trick to get a better deal or, worse still, to cheat them. Many times, I have been welcomed like a king by Chinese mayors, business leaders, professors, farmers, or families of friends. I never felt that this was insincere or that I was being played. You could just as easily reverse the logic: In fewer than ten percent of the cases where Chinese people gave me the VIP treatment did

I go into business, help, or even keep in touch with them. Does that mean that as a foreigner I took advantage of almost ninety percent of the Chinese who rolled out the red carpet for me? Surely not.

With the odd exception—just like anywhere in the world, there are people with bad intentions—hospitality is so deeply rooted in Chinese culture that for the Chinese it goes without saying that guests receive a warm welcome. Giving a good impression is extremely important to the Chinese because they genuinely care what the outside world thinks about them. They want to show their "face" and know that they often don't get a second chance to make a good first impression. This is especially important towards people that they respect: politicians, teachers, the elderly, bosses, family, friends...and Westerners.

However, there is some friction now emerging when it comes to this last group. Since 2020, the Chinese increasingly believe that Westerners have way too many double standards, as they accuse China of wrongdoing without living up to their own higher values of democracy, freedom, equality, solidarity, and human rights. The traditional storyline in China about the innovative, wealthy, and socially just Western world is now giving way to a more critical view of Black Lives Matter, corona deaths, Brexit, police brutality in Catalonia, migrants drowning in the Mediterranean, and on and on. In Chinese Confucian morality, you can only promote social justice and equality if you lead by example. Of course, we hasten to explain that the situation in America or Europe is different, and not really comparable to freedoms in Hong Kong or human rights in Xinjiang, but many Chinese people don't see a big difference. Just as we tend to take a black-and-white view of China, the Chinese today also jump to conclusions without fully understanding the situation in the West. This is not surprising, but it is important to understand because the West is quickly losing its automatic VIP status in China. As a country, China feels less of a need to make a good impression on the West, and the Chinese people are less concerned what Westerners think about China. So, we become disconnected from each other, dehumanize the other side, and increasingly categorize each other as inferior—less sincere, less human, less respectful...less trustworthy. As a result, the circle of trust between China and the West is now largely broken. We have been pushed out of the network of close friends and relegated to a more distant, less tight circle of trust: the more anonymous world (more on this in chapters 6 and 7).

CHINA IS LOOKING FOR ANCHORS

Until the middle of the nineteenth century, China was the largest economy in the world. This is why many in the West claim that China will turn in on itself again, become 100 percent self-sufficient, and slowly push Western "barbarians" out of the country, as it has in the past. You sometimes hear that China wants to return to its independent isolated status from before the Opium War of 1839. Long before that, the English bought a lot of porcelain, lacquer, and tea from China, while the Chinese had little need for or interest in European products. As with America today, England's trade balance with China was negative. After 1800, the English began smuggling Indian opium into China, which left millions of people, even the upper class, addicted. When the Chinese took action against this, the British saw this as a threat to their commercial interests that had to be resolved with a war. In 1842, the Treaty of Nanking was signed in China, capitulating to all the British demands, including the annexation of Hong Kong and four other ports in China, and reparation payments.[80] The war was over, but China was humiliated, weakened, and impoverished, while the opium trade continued to grow. More recently, the US trade war with China, claims for damages for the COVID-19 outbreak in Wuhan, or interference from the White House in the Hong Kong issue all immediately remind the Chinese of 1842.

China does not want to make that mistake again; certainly not in the era of a globalized world. For the Chinese, foreign cutting-edge technology, crude oil, and Western quality brands sometimes seem like the opium of today. Contrary to what is sometimes claimed, China and Chinese consumers do not want to become independent from the West. As the world's largest exporter, Beijing is well aware that the world can no longer be separated—political scientists call this the multipolar world order. Washington, on the other hand, had a very different idea under President Trump. The cold war approach that, thirty years later, America resorted to again with its new enemy China sent a shiver down the spine of Chinese policymakers. Like the Soviet Union before it, China is increasingly seen as the evil, authoritarian, and militarized enemy of the free Western-democratic world.

The thinking in Beijing is that, unlike 150 years ago, China can never again allow itself to be completely dependent on the West. This is a core objective of China's geopolitical strategy. We can also better interpret Beijing's actions by understanding deep-seated China's fear of the West. However, China's fear of Western influence or over-reliance does not mean that it now wants to do everything itself. The Chinese producers are too practical for that, and Chinese consumers will only change their purchasing behavior if they can afford to. Consumers do not simply choose Chinese brands over Western brand alternatives out of principle. What Chinese consumers want are quality products at the best prices; but also fast, excellent service. They want to buy from reliable brands that are relevant to their identity and lives. As consumers, they want to be understood and become part of the brand's story. Foreign brands are often better prepared because Western consumers have been demanding these high standards for much longer, and because consumer regulations and protection are more advanced. Chinese brands, on the other hand, thrived mainly due to a lack of regulation and transparency in a society that was growing faster than legislation and auditors could keep up with. Counterfeit products, scams, lies, theft, empty promises, and falsification of numbers were sadly all too common in the past. Those who were smart about it could get very rich very quickly.

However, if you live in a world of high mistrust amongst strangers, like the 1.4 billion Chinese, you of course look for close-knit networks and tribes to reassure you: friends, family, schoolmates, people from your hometown, cultural groups, authentic influencers, social communes, the Communist Party, a religion, foreign brands... whatever you relate to the most. Every Chinese person will find their own anchor. In 2013, I had ten very different Chinese employees at my Shanghai start-up: including a deeply religious Christian, a very loyal CPC member, an openly lesbian woman, someone so traditional that all she cared about was getting married and becoming a mother, a rocker covered in tattoos, a femme fatale who was always the center of attention, and my best engineer who was secretly a fanatic human rights activist and had seen a lot of suffering. Everyone had their own anchor. What struck me the most was that they all got along like one big family. Each had their own clan, tribe, faith, and authenticity, but really wasn't bothered by those of their colleagues.

Thanks in part to my Shanghai team, I've come to see China much more as a country with 1.4 billion frameworks rather than one big framework. I prefer to call them circles. Within your own circle, big or small, as you prefer, you can be completely yourself. Outside of that you have to take other circles into account. This is of course not uniquely Chinese, because the whole world is colored by a diversity of tribes, networks, and clans. However, the mistake that is too often made when it comes to China is to assume that there is only one clan: the Communist Party. Nothing could be further from the truth. The Party is just one—albeit a very large one with its 95 million members—of an infinite number of networks. In order to frame China correctly, we may first need to review that monolithic framework. Every framework in China offers primarily a protection from the outside rather than a border to trap the people inside—although one can't exist without the other. The reason we usually see the Chinese framework as very restrictive, conformist, and authoritarian is that we are looking at that Chinese framework from the outside in. We see it as a cage. We therefore don't quite understand why the Chinese don't oppose the system and government more vigorously. We often think that, as soon as economic growth in China stops, the Chinese will want to get out of that golden cage. I don't believe this for a second. For decades, we also mistakenly thought that as soon as the Chinese got a taste of the economic freedom of the West, China would also become a liberal-democratic society. We too often project our own framework onto China and predict that the Chinese will one day want to take "refuge" in our framework. The reason for this misconception is that we don't really understand how the Chinese can be so happy in their "restrictive" environment, or their "framework." That same Chinese framework provides the security that is important to many Chinese people in a new society that is evolving so quickly that it's hard to keep up.

CONTEMPORARY NOMADS

The best way to think about the Chinese people is as modern nomads who are constantly moving from one future to another. As discussed in the previous chapter, China has a new generation every ten years, and therefore a different landscape and a different future. The Chinese move around from one city to another, from one job to another, from one generation's lifestyle to another, from one group to another. The search for relevant tribes and networks is central to their life's journey. When I think back nostalgically to China at the end of the last century, then it is precisely those moments that are the emotional images that first spring to mind.

In 1997, I was introduced to Chinese underground rock bands and the Midi Music Festival in Beijing. I also went to controversial modern art galleries and performances. When you see thousands of young Chinese people headbanging together, or a provocative artist taking off their clothes during a public performance, you don't feel like you're in China at all—and certainly not in the capital city of the Communist Party. But this was also China. My experience in the 1990s was that people constantly wanted to push the boundaries, and that the government would constantly redraw those boundaries. You could call it a cat-and-mouse game, but to me it's more like a sine wave over time with the y-axis showing the intensity of control. When there is a lot of tension emanating from the government, such as during a National Party Congress, the Olympic Games, or the visit of a world leader, every Chinese person knows that you need to color within the lines for a while. Then the floodgates re-open for a bit, and everyone starts experimenting again.

My observation is that this experimentation quickly spirals out of control and erupts the social restlessness of the Chinese. Twenty years ago, Shanghai had the famous Maoming Road nightlife zone, not far from where I lived and the same distance from the Shanghainese government headquarters. In just a few years, this nightlife district had exploded into a jungle of so-called Western decadence—excessive alcohol consumption, deafening music, drug dealing out in the open, prostitutes, and so on. Paradise on earth, or a sewer of depravity, depending on how you looked at it. The police did nothing about it for many years, presumably because they were paid to look the other way, until pressure from the locals got so great that the police had to act. Within a few months, the entire street had been shut down. That was the end of nightlife on Maoming Road. The party then moved to a new street somewhere else in the city. Every two or three years, the same thing would happen, and the same bars, crowds, and nightlife would get closed down and move on to the next hotspot. This was a cycle that most foreigners in the city really enjoyed.

The moral of this story is that in China, a lot is possible until it is no longer possible. Then a new framework is created that again leads to new discoveries—a nomadic journey to the next place, the next future. It is in that vacuum between two frameworks that Chinese social groupings, networks, and tribes arise and flourish, a time when China's creative, heroic, and opinionated individuals show themselves. We should also not forget that for many Chinese people, daily life, even today, is not at all straightforward, as discussed in previous chapters. Social expectations, competitiveness, the cost of living, and much more are what cause many of the Chinese to flourish and be free and creative within their own environment or self-designed framework. Not all tribes are loved.

NOT ALL TRIBES ARE LOVED

Twenty years ago, my wife was involved in the Shanghai art scene as an artist. Every weekend we would go and discover an upcoming young Chinese artist in a gallery, at an arts platform, or in a dilapidated factory. All very raw, pretty provocative, and shocking. What is striking today is that this young generation of Chinese artists is now known all over the world for their works of art that have become extremely valuable and sought after. Their candor is often gone, and with it usually their provocations too. But their creativity is still there. At a later stage in their careers, these artists often found a certain peace of mind and reconciled themselves with the framework China provides today. But this is certainly not the case for everyone. Conceptual artists such as Ai Weiwei have continued to fight against social and political injustice in China. As the son of the well-known Chinese poet Ai Qing,[81] for a period Ai Weiwei was much loved in China, and he even got the chance to design the "Bird's Nest" for the 2008 Beijing Olympic Games. But when the earthquake claimed many victims in 2008 and exposed deep issues in Chinese society, Ai Weiwei emerged as a nonconformist and political activist critical of the same Chinese regime that his father had been loyal to. He says he hates the enforced uniformity of the Chinese people under the Communist Party, which he believes is how it survives. He is convinced that freedom of expression has never existed in artistic China, and that those who do not belong to the establishment are discriminated against or persecuted, something he experienced himself when he was detained and his Shanghai studio was destroyed. The systematic suppression of artists, journalists, intellectuals, and lawyers who question China's system leads Ai Weiwei to reject the legitimacy of China's government. He sees it as proof of Beijing's vulnerability and weakness, and as a result he quickly became popular in the West and a pariah in China. His art is much less driven by a belief in progress than a desire to bring about real social and political change.

And this is where it starts to hurt in China, where change is more evolutionary than revolutionary. Few in the West still believe in social change, especially when it comes to China, if it is not disruptive. Our modern history since the first industrial revolution has shown us that it is mainly revolutions, regime changes, and uprisings that have led to the biggest social change. However, China's modern industrial history over the last forty years has shown exactly the opposite. No country has enjoyed as much socio-economic progress as modern China, despite the absence of successful uprisings or revolutions. Over forty years of rapid change, most Chinese people have achieved a significantly better standard of living, better life and study opportunities, better healthcare and care for the elderly, better working conditions, better consumer protection, less discrimination, much more inclusion, and the list goes on. The question we don't ask is how China is improving socially without any strong opposition demanding change.

That opposition does exist in China—but just like icebergs, it is mostly below the surface. The Ai Weiweis and Jack Mas of China who are not afraid to openly criticize the status quo are quickly reined in. But this doesn't mean their criticism is lost, because it also lives on below the waterline—and China's rulers know that too. However, we usually see this as Beijing's heavy-handed control over potentially dangerous subjects. That's certainly how Ai Weiwei sees it. But are we not insulting the intelligence of the Chinese authorities a bit here? Why do we believe they would fail to notice and take into account those strong signals? With this thinking, are we not also indirectly insulting the intelligence of any Chinese people who conform to Beijing's control?

I ask this as an open question because the Chinese usually see it that way—as an insult to the intelligence of the people and their leaders. Do people really still believe that it is possible to suppress 1.4 billion people, with no one in China knowing what Ai Weiwei is saying and no one daring to express their own opinions? This narrow-minded thinking reminds me of a quote said to be from Abraham Lincoln: "You can fool all the people some of the time and some of the people all the time, but you cannot fool all the people all the time." Hundreds of millions of Chinese people, including most government employees, are remarkably well aware of the criticism of China and the Party. Many of these people understand the accusations better than anyone as they live in China's reality on a daily basis. People like Ai Weiwei may not be loved by

China's establishment, but the voices of people like him do not go unnoticed. Beneath the surface, on social media, and in the political corridors, echo chambers emerge that amplify the opinions of people with similar views. This is how the majority of silent like-minded people grows, making the iceberg more visible to the government.

This is the power of Chinese tribes and networks. Not to be more visible, like in the West, but to remain invisible while growing in size. This is precisely why the Chinese government is more concerned about the scale of any emerging Chinese tribe than about a few whistleblowers, rebels, or nonconformists. Since 2012, the heat has been turned up on those "rebels" because social media can quickly make the iceberg so large that it is more difficult for Beijing to handle. You may wonder whether this is primarily due to the new, more autocratic leadership of Xi Jinping or the arrival of 4G. Take, for example, the more than 50 million officially registered Christians in China. Growing by seven percent each year, this Christian community is set to become the largest in the world by 2030. All this is happening in a country which is officially atheist, and where, at the end of the nineteenth century, it was the Western missionaries who were blamed and persecuted for the bloody Boxer Rebellion against Western imperialism. Today, the Protestant Church is China's largest tribe after the Communist Party. After the expulsion and persecution of religious tribes under Mao Zedong, today all Chinese people enjoy, nominally at least, religious freedoms protected by law, which has resulted in the explosion of Christianity in China. Since 1978, each religion has had to integrate into Chinese society.

In concrete terms, this means that Christian communities in China come under the umbrella of one of five Chinese Patriotic Associations, which is led by a group of Catholics or Protestants—not the Pope. You could argue that Christianity in China is separate from Western doctrine and is considered universal or global. Not every Christian in China would agree. The church is part of Chinese society, but Christianity is not really part of Chinese culture. China does value structure, rites, and traditions, and that's where they find common ground. However, the most recent Western story lines about the Christians in China focus on the persecutions, restrictions, and victims of the Xi regime. Rooted in the secularized thinking of a separation of church and state, the West sees any participation by Beijing in the ins and outs of religion as a political problem. It tends to portray Chinese Christians as victims of the regime, while Chinese Christians are often more devout than Western Christians, who are going to church less and less. Chinese Christians have enough resources, members, places of worship, and online communities, and it also doesn't appear that churchgoers really want to change China's regime or culture. This view is a generalization based on my personal experiences with the Chinese Christians I know. But because the narrative from the West is always about the repressive Chinese church, we never hear anything else about the largest emerging religious community in the world.

Compared to the years under Mao's highly atheistic rule, today believers of all five officially recognized religions in China—Christians, Protestants, Muslims, Buddhists, and Taoists—have freedoms to practice their religion, but not to the same degree they are accustomed to outside China, and many tensions remain. The church in China will not really change and will continue to be subject to strict state supervision because of its reach and its links to Western political agendas. Throughout China's history, faith and religion have always been subordinate to political power. The West sustained a direct relationship between church and state until the American Revolution and the French Revolution resulted in a separation of powers. Therefore, the religious believers and their leaders in China won't be quick to break the rules or enter into a power struggle with the authorities. What can be changed, though, is our perception of the situation. The story of how more and more Chinese people are becoming religious is really not about people turning against the Communist Party, but rather about the search for more meaning in a modern way of life that has become much faster, more anonymous, and more materialistic. However, the larger the church community gets in China, the harder Beijing cracks down on individuals who use the church to fuel political anti-China agendas. But actually, that approach will hopefully also give Beijing more time to solve the real underlying problem—the better integration and/or increased independence between church and state.

Too often we assume that Beijing wants to hold on to power by keeping everything as rigid as possible and not letting anyone get in its way, while—conversely—the Chinese see Beijing wanting to change everything as quickly and effectively as possible in order to gain as many supporters as possible. From our Western perspective, this seems like a utopia, which is of course why there's an outcry when activists, nonconformists, or journalists are silenced. The Western response is that Beijing is doing this to mask or dissolve problems in order to maintain power; the same message Ai Weiwei shares in a poetic, confrontational way with his art. Keep in mind, it is not just China that Ai Weiwei targets—he also criticizes Europe for its violation of human rights and freedom of opinion with respect to the migration crisis. He is convinced that it is the West that is mainly to blame for keeping the authoritarian regime in China going, because it makes a lot of profit from China.[82] Ai Weiwei says that dictators never voluntarily give up their power or control, and therefore that change must happen abruptly, through revolution or some disastrous event. In his view, there is no precedent for this shift to take place gradually. It is therefore also not a surprise that he chooses disasters as the subject of his art. I do not agree with Ai Weiwei, although I am a big fan of his work, motivation, and willpower.

DOING NOTHING CHANGES CHINA

Jin Xing, China's most famous contemporary dancer, represents a very different approach to bringing about social change not through confrontation but through integration and leading by example.[83] In the West, she is best known for being the first transgender celebrity from China. As a nine-year-old boy with a phenomenal talent for dance, Jin Xin was given the opportunity to join the dance ensemble of the People's Liberation Army (PLA). When we talk about the Chinese army, we automatically think of soldiers marching, North Korean-style, perfectly in time across Tiananmen Square in Beijing. With its bayonets and missiles, China's huge military parades are a public display of force that makes us think of war. But the Chinese are more familiar with the more humane side of their soldiers, created when they are deployed *en masse* during natural disasters like the 2008 earthquake or the floods of 1998. The Chinese experience their army through their medical interventions during biological crises such as SARS, Ebola, or COVID-19. Many Chinese people become emotional when they listen to the operas and songs by the song and dance ensembles of the Chinese army on central CCTV and local television channels.

Military musical ensembles have produced some of China's most famous and powerful artistic figures, including Jiang Qing, Mao Zedong's last wife. She is better known as the leader of the infamous Gang of Four who, after the Cultural Revolution, were all convicted for the wrongdoings of the Party, like using leftist cultural propaganda and persecuting their political enemies. For that reason, since Jiang Qing's death by suicide, every Chinese first lady has kept a low profile. The current first lady is Peng Liyuan. Before marrying Xi Jinping in 1987, she was well known in China as an actress and an opera and folk singer in the PLA's song and dance ensembles. From 1983, when she was twenty-one, she performed every year—for twenty-five years—on the most-watched TV show in the world—the Chinese New Year Gala. With her additional 350 performances a year all over the country, Peng Liyuan became a superstar in China[84]. When she married him, she was much more famous than Xi Jinping. Even today she is often in the spotlight both at home and abroad. She reminds me of Jackie Kennedy, Princess Diana, or Michelle Obama, although many Chinese probably wouldn't agree. She expresses the gentler and humane side to her country and government, including as a goodwill ambassador for the World Health Organization, and she is a role model for every Chinese girl today.

The ballet dancer Jin Xing has now also become a true role model for millions of young Chinese people. The Western media and important global stages like the World Economic Forum portrays her as a strong Chinese woman, which she is. But her fame in China is less due to her being open about her gender transformation. In a country that still often sees transgender identity as a mental disorder, she is respected because she uses the strengths of China's traditional family culture to help millions of young Chinese, and indirectly China's LGBTQ community (and for the sake of completeness, LGBTQIA+). I'm describing below how she achieved this without being an outspoken champion of more LGBTQ rights in China. Like Ai Weiwei, Jin Xing has become a focus of "Western" interest with her story highlighting China's restrictions on freedom. But as a result, we actually miss the essence of her story.[85] We pay too much attention to how Jin Xing breaks through the Chinese taboos of the binary gender categorization of man and woman. Homosexuality has only been legal in China since 1997, and since 2001 is no longer considered a disorder. But being openly gay is still very rare in the Chinese family context, with continued pressure from many parents to marry someone of the opposite sex.

An alternative view is that, throughout Chinese history, homosexuality has been seen as a normal aspect of life and it was only in the nineteenth century, during the Qing dynasty, and mainly due to Western influences, that the opposition to homosexuality came about. In general, today, people in China are not too interested in having public conversations about non-binary gender. There are LGBTQ movements in China, but they still have a long way to go to match the freedoms of Western European countries, for example. Homosexuals in China are now allowed to live together, become each other's legal providers, and serve in the military. I still remember Shanghai Pride being one of the city's major events each June. Not as big as in Berlin or Amsterdam, but Shanghai Pride colored the city with art, film, and activities that showed how tolerant the city was. However, China still has a policy of silence on this, which means that LGBTQ gender identity topics are neither encouraged nor discouraged, but certainly not promoted. Most activities by the LGBTQ networks take place behind closed doors in order not to draw too much attention from the authorities. In terms of acceptance, same-sex couples in China still cannot marry. China is certainly not bottom of the Asian class here, as this is currently only legal in Taiwan; but there is still work to be done to improve LGBTQ rights in China. That's precisely why personalities like Jin Xing are so important. When, as a Chinese superstar, Jin Xing moved to New York to study contemporary dance in 1987, she was suddenly confronted with a new reality. She was completely unknown in the city that never sleeps, but it was precisely this new environment that gave her the space and freedom to reflect on her sexuality and to discover that she was not gay, but transgender. She returned to China, and at the age of twenty-eight had a sex change operation, which was not that straightforward in 1995. She was determined to have this done in China so that she could make a difference to her country by having the press cover her transition and the fact that she was the first openly transgender celebrity in China. Her goal was not to point the finger at China, like Ai Weiwei, but to use her stardom to find a natural way to show millions of Chinese people a different reality.

Jin Xing claims that in 1995 only thirty percent of Chinese people supported her decision, while now it would be more than eighty percent—this is the social process she has brought about. Her genuine personality, incredible talent on the dance floor, and outspoken views made her a national icon that attracted millions of viewers each week to her hit TV shows. Her biggest hit was a dating show where couples were invited to talk about their marriages, together with their parents. And this is the real strength of Jin Xing: using her role as a TV host to magnify China's family values. In doing so, she reconciled deeply rooted traditional Chinese values with the individual expectations of a new generation. That's why she gained so much respect and admiration—and the Chinese don't see Jin Xing as a rebel, not even as a transgender person, but as an inspiration to be yourself in a traditional society. Working hard, being yourself, showing patience, and chasing your dreams can bring about change both for yourself and for society. The key element is time.

In China, a lot of things are not talked about because people don't like to change their habits, but with enough time and energy you can convince or change a lot of people. This is quite unique to China. In the West, we look too much at the facts and not enough at the process of natural evolution. We love to label things because that helps us get the debate started. In China, this categorization is much less pronounced and you see that boys really do behave in a very feminine way, and vice versa, without anyone or themselves having to ask which group they belong to. The world through Chinese eyes looks much more complex and also more in flux than it does to us, taking context more into account than lists and rubrics.

But it is precisely because of exposure to Western influences of the last decades that the Chinese have also become much more informed and mindful of the challenges LGBTQ encounter. You would think this is a positive evolution, but it has actually made the Chinese less confident, which makes the natural transition in China more difficult. If something naturally moves in a certain direction, like LGBTQ rights, you can speed it up or slow it down. By rebelling or questioning everything in China, you are more likely to slow or block the process than you are to speed it up. A growing awareness among the general population could speed up the process. Jin Xing's fans have speed things up for the LGBTQ community in China. Time explains and changes everything in China, and most of the Chinese believe that the future will always be better than today. Few Westerners believe that or want to allow China's leaders that time. But we forget that it has taken the West more than 100 years to really protect LGBTQ rights—and it is still not the same in every country in Europe even today, with Hungary as an obvious example. When you see Chinese state media writing about how companies are now actively trying to improve the situation for LGBTQ workers,[86] it seems likely that modern China will need less time. Even without revolution, society appears to be changing much more quickly than in the West.

This is why I believe, when it comes to understanding China's future, that we can learn more from Jin Xing's story than from Ai Weiwei's example. It goes back to the Taoist philosophy of "*wu wei*." **Wúwéi** (无为—literally: inaction, acting by not acting) means that you know when to act and when not to. The term "*wu wei*" actually means acting, but without placing importance on the result. The road is more important than the destination. That may sound a bit vague, but it is enormously powerful when 1.4 billion people take their own path. One might call it "leading by example."

CHINA'S SILENT REVOLUTIONS

There are a lot of *wu-wei* style gender revolutions and women's liberation movements going on in China today, including #MeToo and LGBTQ. Some of these developments are exemplified by trendsetting companies such as lingerie brand Neiwai ("*neiwai*" literally means "inside out"). Their focus is on the liberalization and empowerment of Chinese women through the promotion of comfortable, functional underwear that, in their words, accentuates the natural shape of the body. In Chinese media, the idea is repeatedly emphasized that beauty means a slim waist and legs, and stark white skin. As a result, many Chinese women are very self-conscious about their bodies. On March 8, 2020, International Women's Day, the Neiwai brand launched a marketing campaign called #NoBodyIsNobody after carefully listening to the younger generations on social media. The hashtag resonated with millions of young Chinese women who are seeking ways to defy China's traditional social expectations. The brand is already known as the driving force of a social movement for women's emancipation and liberation from the suffocating cultural norms of China's patriarchal past. Neiwai challenges China's cultural stereotypes, but without rebellion; instead, by simply embracing people's many imperfections, and helping millions of women in their struggle to not always "have to" conform.

Influenced by foreign brands, Chinese shoppers are increasingly looking for beautiful designs, but it is less and less important to them whether they come from a brand that is French or Chinese, like Neiwai. Since the pandemic, Chinese consumers increasingly assume that it is not just Western brands that can deliver what they desire: top-quality products, beautiful packaging, effective marketing, emotional messaging, fast deliveries, pure customer focus, and a high level of professionalism. It is a misconception to think that Chinese consumers buy "Made in China" out of pure patriotism or anti-Western feelings. Increasingly, they choose to buy Chinese brands simply because they have gotten better. We often hear that Chinese consumers increasingly prefer local brands. This is called the **guócháo** (国潮) movement.[87] The term *guochao* or "national tide" refers here to modern Chinese brands that are challenging the top foreign brands in China. Cultural elements and symbols from China's past are incorporated into the design of products or seasonal fashion. The Chinese government also supports this trend as it aims to bury the still negative connotation of "Made in China" for good. But this "buy local" trend is being driven by the consumer base, not China's government or the Party. The real strength of this new trend came about because Chinese brands now can and do dare compete against foreign brands. In fact, the trend has only become possible because many Chinese brands can now rival the well-known Western labels. It is therefore certainly not the result of the negative view of the Chinese toward the West, but it fits in perfectly with the new trend of not seeing everything as better just because it comes from the West. It also raises the question of why the Chinese no longer see their brands as inferior or unsafe.

In particular, we should reflect on the fact that China is moving faster toward quality than we can tell from our past experience. The Chinese market is very quickly reaching a level playing field with the West, with each Chinese brand aiming to become a global best-in-class leader. I rarely give advice on buying stocks, but I would keep a close eye on the "Designed by China" brands that are going global. In their domestic market they might of course have an even bigger impact because of their detailed understanding of Chinese culture and consumers. I wouldn't therefore really call *guochao* a trend, but a statement that many Chinese brands are no longer inferior to Western brands. It's not a real trend because it will never go away. In categories such as lingerie or cosmetics, this development is a given because consumers there are even more attracted to local brands that intuitively understand the Chinese body and beauty ideal.

The other silent revolution that China has experienced is the digital revolution, which was driven by curiosity and the desire for more comfort: a billion internet users all looking for more information, better experiences, sustainable self-realization, and a strong identity reflecting Chinese culture and ancient traditions. It is this endless desire and diligent search for a new, individual identity that makes the Chinese consumer hyper connected, sophisticated, and difficult to convince. From our Western perspective, we easily view the Chinese through the typical scenes we see in Venice, airports, or luxury shops in Paris: hordes of Chinese people weighed down with bags from very expensive brand names, Godiva chocolates, or statues of the Eiffel Tower. It reminds us of the image of the *nouveaux riches*, who have suddenly become rich and flash their cash around. That group does exist in China and, as early as thirty years ago, earned the nickname **tǔháo** (土豪), or "rich peasants," a word from China's feudal past that refers to the powerful landowners in remote places who harassed the poorer peasants. Today's tuhao usually come from China's less populous cities, but suddenly became very wealthy with the opening-up of China in the 1980s and 1990s. The term is also sometimes used for poor people and factory workers who make impulse buys.

The majority of Chinese consumers are no longer *tǔháo*. Tom Nunlist, in his book *China's Evolving Consumers*, described consumer types that are actually quite sophisticated and think very carefully before buying products or services. These consumers are the new middle class, millennials born after 1980, the post-2000 generation, young singles, post-1995 men, white collar women, young urban couples, and young mothers. These eight categories of consumers also need an average of eight touchpoints with the brand before buying anything. That is four more than typical Western consumers.[88] They also often check with friends and relatives before deciding to buy. As we saw in the previous chapter, the Chinese "interpersonal" link, known as *guanxi*, creates a social bond of trust between people from within the relationship circle. That *guanxi* reveals itself in a debt of "reciprocity of favors" known as *renqing*, where involving friends, family, and connections in a buying decision is natural rather than inappropriate. Not asking your friends about buying and spending on something substantial is a rather strange concept for many Chinese people. They make their purchasing behavior highly dependent on their socio-cultural environment and circles of close friends. They look for those anchors, impulses, and references more proactively than Western consumers. As a customer, they therefore look for a bond of trust with a brand more than we do—according to their unwritten laws of social reciprocity. Ideally, each purchase comes with acknowledgment from the community that the buyer identifies with, that a product or service is valuable, and that the brand can be trusted. But how should a Western brand in China communicate effectively given the complexity, relationship networks, and cultural sensitivity of consumers? Brands can use China's social context to their advantage by appealing to Chinese customers. This is the wonderful Chinese world of the KOL (key opinion leader) and the KOC (key opinion customer), which every business or communications manager should have on their radar.

MY OPINION COUNTS

The key opinion leader (KOL), better known as a social media influencer, has already become essential to the communication between consumer and brand, and this has a lot to do with trust. For millions of consumers, the key opinion leader is their source for getting the right reviews, comments, and feedback before making a purchase. To a certain extent, the Chinese key opinion leader can be compared to influencers on YouTube, TikTok, or Instagram in the West. Their fame gives them real market power, so the brands are trying to please them, rather than the other way around.

This key opinion leader trend is an important part of the social sales strategy for many brands in China. Influencers promote branded products in live sessions lasting five to eight hours a day. Livestreaming has become the single most important sales channel in China. In some provinces, already more than fifty percent of all agricultural products bought online were sold directly to consumers via livestreams. Department stores in China have built in-house livestreaming studios, and they are training their staff to broadcast live shows on a daily basis. Sometimes you see a key opinion leader standing in a studio with more than 100 smartphones angled at them in order to maximize the reach of each livestream through as many livestreaming accounts as possible. They are a modern-day version of the Hollywood star. Livestreaming has become the most in-demand expertise in China. A true fad, but also deadly serious—because there is a lot of money involved. But key opinion leaders can also damage a brand. Chinese consumers demand that key opinion leaders are sincere, their stories are authentic, and that they uphold social norms and cultural values. In 2021, many key opinion leaders suddenly lost their spot in the limelight after being discredited for anything from #MeToo incidents, to a lack of respect for China's cultural values and past, to boasting about their wealth, to tax evasion. Chinese key opinion leaders are supposed to set an example for society, and the influencers who don't, get a slap on the wrist from both the netizens and the Chinese government. Once that happens, well-known brands in China will drop the key opinion leader like a brick. An expectation has been set in China that those popular within large networks and tribes must stick to behaving in a way that benefits society. Beijing is once concerned that large tribes can disrupt society, but recognizes that key opinion leaders who have a positive impact on society can make a big difference in China. This promotes, among other things, the integration of minority tribes that previously faced discrimination. The biggest difference with the West is that Chinese influencers are not just top entertainers with a large number of followers. Many of them promote new brands or products to smaller groups of followers, making their stories so much more authentic and intimate. They have also become real entrepreneurs; their visual storytelling determines their brand value. In China, a key opinion leader only needs 1,000 super fans who share content on Chinese social media, and who trust the influencer and therefore make purchases that they recommend, in order to generate the same sales as a Western influencer with a million social media followers. The real difference with the West is mainly that Chinese consumers want to build trust in their relationships with influencers, and don't just see them as an authority on social media.

The key opinion customer (KOC) is the trend that all marketers in China have been talking about for several years now. The key opinion customer is often misunderstood outside of China as a micro-influencer or long-tail influencer, but actually a key opinion customer is not an online authority, but rather a customer and a brand ambassador. This isn't a trend started by China as we know this better as word-of-mouth marketing promoters. But China has turned key opinion customer marketing into an art form and a business process. In contrast to the key opinion leader, who makes use of their popularity among online followers, the key opinion customer often starts from their own community of close friends: family, friends, and friends of friends. The key opinion customer is like the Tupperware hostess of the past. In case you're not familiar with this hugely successful concept, the American company Tupperware came up with the idea in the 1950s of Tupperware parties to promote their airtight plastic containers for storing food to new customers. An existing customer would invite their housewife friends to their homes to see the products in action. The hostess would sell a range of Tupperware bowls, dishes, and trays to friends, neighbors, and family, and was rewarded with products from... Tupperware. Move that overall concept online in China and then you'll understand the concept of the key opinion customer.

Just as for the Tupperware housewives, it is not just the financial benefits that are important for today's key opinion customers, but also the commitment and affinity with people you know, where a brand's products become the reason to get together. Another aspect the Tupperware parties have in common with today's online key opinion customer sessions is that the direct communication is very authentic, creates a deep relationship with the brand, and automatically produces new ambassadors or key opinion customers. This sales process creates the purest form of trust in a new brand, as key opinion customers are promoting a brand that they love to close family and friends. This form of brand communication is also much closer to the age-old Confucian mindset that the family is the foundation of a moral society. It is also common that a key opinion customer only has about 100 loyal followers online, so a lot of this takes place at a relatively small scale.

The marketing that more and more brands in China are using to identify, motivate, shape, and reward their select group of key opinion customers is so significant that it has become the logical trigger for Chinese brands to position themselves against more well-known Western brands. In the past, foreign brands have stolen the hearts of Chinese consumers, but Chinese brands are now stealing back that emotional connection with customers, based on their own cultural values. Western brands, stubbornly clinging to the marketing tools that they have perfected over the years, are now involved in guerrilla marketing warfare in China. Western strategies based on collecting big data through digital campaigns and hiring superstar key opinion leaders with lots of followers are now facing "unfair" competition from Chinese brands working from the bottom up. These brands are turning customers into key opinion customers that offer personalized services to millions of customers.

The shift in mindset from big data and key opinion leaders to small data and key opinion customers will be much more difficult for larger brands, because they will have to let go of their control over communication, something which is difficult to guarantee with key opinion customers. The aim is not to let key opinion customers communicate the way the brand wants (as with key opinion leaders), but to reward key opinion customers for communicating in a way that the brand cannot: by combining loyalty, community, and recommendations. By putting their faith in key opinion customers, Chinese brands gain the trust of millions of customers.

Western brands, especially new brands in the Chinese market, will have to build better relationships with Chinese consumers from now on. Not only do Western brands in China need to have strong branding, product quality, and customer focus, but they also now need to pay much more attention to their emotional relationships with Chinese consumers and their cultural values. Brands that are not prepared to do this are better off staying out of the Chinese market. Brands that are open to a demanding consumer who wants to be understood can learn a lot in China from how Chinese brands engage and understand their customers. These insights and experiences can even provide a competitive advantage for Western brands in their own domestic markets.

Example: transforming clients into brand ambassadors.

One success story of the key opinion customer trend is the five-year-old Chinese cosmetics brand Perfect Diary. They have an almost perfect combination of relevance, reliability, and relationships with their customers. Consumers simply love the brand: their prices are better than Western competitors, they engage customers in a close-knit community, and the packaging and product quality are as good as the L'Oréal or Estée Lauder level brands of this world. Compared to these competitors, Perfect Diary is not playing it safe. In their PD logo, the P stands for Perfection, and the D for Discovery, Different, and Diversity. It could have just as easily been the slogan for Apple or Benetton.

While their Western competitors focus purely on key opinion leaders, Perfect Diary mainly works with key opinion customers. They hire their customers and turn them into their brand's most loyal livestreaming ambassadors. The strong relationship of trust that consumers have with Perfect Diary's key opinion customers encourages private communication about the brand on social media. They've even created a virtual online influencer, based on Perfect Diary employees, to maintain one-to-one engagement with millions of customers at the same time by inviting them to a community group chat where they share their interests, lifestyle advice, and beautytips. When all non-essential stores were forced to close in China in early 2020 due to the pandemic, Perfect Diary employees were trained to hold livestreaming sessions with customers. It wasn't a PR stunt, but rather a way for the brand to tell their customers how to stay safe and healthy during the pandemic, as well as offer support to a friend in a difficult period of loneliness and mental anxiety. Through their strong proactive involvement, empathy, and personal approach in times of crisis, they proved—without any campaign—that they really cared about their customers and their health. In short time they had built a top reputation. The fact that this "partner for life" trend between brand and customer became such a successful formula in China is all about the online environment of the social e-commerce internet platforms that have seamlessly integrated community and communication applications with e-commerce. Amazon, on the other hand, is not a social communication application; and Facebook or Instagram didn't even have an online store at the time. We are much more focused on becoming best in class, while Chinese platforms invest more of their time in looking for the links between the different classes.

GROWING SELF-AWARENESS

A second Chinese cultural revolution is now being fought through social e-commerce apps, for example powered by entrepreneurs Charlwin Mao (sounds like Chairman Mao) and Miranda Qu, who co-founded the company Xiaohongshu in 2014. *Xiaohongshu* is Chinese for "little red book" and the shorter English name for it is RED. The idea was to provide a lifestyle platform for Chinese consumers to share what they've bought online. RED therefore became a combination of Instagram, Pinterest, and Amazon through its unique integration of communities, content, and commerce in one platform. On RED, every internet user can tell their lifestyle stories via photos, video, or streaming,[89] and visitors feel like they're on a journey, discovering the lifestyle of others. By reading the reviews in the little red book, similar to the book review site Goodreads, explorers on the RED platform are encouraged to make impulse buys based on what they stumble upon.

The platform mainly attracts Chinese women between the ages of twenty and thirty-five who trust the platform more than search engines, ads, or recommendations on e-commerce sites. RED therefore focuses on building trust between the platform and its users by rewarding those who share authentic recommendations and advice with their followers. Of the women using the RED platform, more than 250 million tend to live in the largest Chinese cities and are no longer completely financially dependent on their family (father, boyfriend, or husband). They spend their free time on RED reading lots of recommendations about top-quality products before then making a purchase and sharing their experiences. The founders compare RED to a kind of online Disneyland, where you can step into another world for a while, have fun, and discover self-love. Authentic stories about a product make you love the brand more, which then makes you want to read even more stories about that brand. This then leads to you buying the product and wanting to share your story with the community. It creates a vicious circle reinforced by artificial intelligence algorithms that develop the quality of the stories, show you personalized stories based on your browser and GPS history (online and offline travel), and prioritize key opinion customers who mainly share authentic and objective stories. Through key opinion customers, RED has provided millions of women in a rapidly changing China with a magical world of hopes and dreams where they can find a new identity and self-confidence. RED is an example of the wonderful world of what is known in China as social e-commerce, and something that is now also making its way to the West.

Hundreds of millions of Chinese strangers trust each other by sharing authentic lifestyle stories. Meanwhile, we don't trust the Chinese. This new trend is less about promoting a product and more about people seeking trust. Perhaps this is where we'll find the answer to the question about whether we can trust the Chinese. We don't know their stories, and we understand them even less. And maybe we also simply forget to share our own stories? There is proof that a good story changes our emotions and creates a connection with the narrator, but at the same time the love hormone oxytocin indicates that we can be trusted, which is needed to build a relationship. However, if we look at Chinese marketers, business leaders, journalists, or politicians, they don't really come across as very emotional or charismatic. Maybe we lack trust in the Chinese because they're not very good at telling stories that we Westerners can relate to?

Social e-commerce platforms such as RED offer China a business model for the growing middle class, who have gained much more self-confidence since 2013. This is the result of a much higher level of self-awareness, as the Chinese today do much more self-reflection, and therefore have a better understanding of who they really are; they reflect more on how others view them and how they can fulfill their own role in society. This may be the single greatest strength China has today. The West should be a little less scared of Xi Jinping's dictatorship, the Communist Party, or the all-controlling government, but be ready for a China that is more self-aware. It is that growing self-awareness that gives Chinese people confidence, makes them successful and satisfied in themselves, forms healthier relationships, and makes many of them increasingly creative. It also appears true that people with more self-confidence lie, cheat, and steal less. In light of this, I would like to move beyond the well-established stereotype of the unreliable Chinese, and challenge everyone to view the Chinese more from an evolutionary perspective of increasing individual self-awareness. A transformation that is happening at lightning speed and is being driven very pragmatically, which makes it even more intense.

According to psychologist Tasha Eurich,[90] self-awareness is not about introspection—asking ourselves why we do or feel things—but rather about each of us asking ourselves what is important to us and what we can do to become more aware of our contribution to the world around us. It is precisely this new worldview that represents a fundamental transformation for the majority of Chinese over the past ten years. Each year from 2013 to 2019, more than 100 million Chinese people traveled abroad.[91] Nearly half a million Chinese students graduated from universities in the West, ninety percent of whom returned to China. In 2019, ten times as many Chinese tourists and students were abroad than in 2000. As a result, Chinese millennials today have much more in common with Western millennials than with their parents or the previously conformist Chinese tradition. These young people are often still financially dependent on their parents, but they are broadening their horizons more and more by traveling the world, and also within their own country. They are looking for unique experiences and adventures by staying in Airbnbs, discovering the North Pole, or sampling local cuisine. They often travel in pairs, speak a bit of English, and above all want to be able to share their own stories with friends on social media. They are also better informed than the average tourist from other countries. If you want to get to know your own city better, I always recommend talking to a Chinese tourist.

The life of a typical middle-class Chinese person has become a journey of discovery in search of a unique identity; a search they carry out with passion, energy, and perseverance. A tireless search for uniqueness—and all in a country where the general perception is that everyone is just blindly following the "authoritarian" regime. In recent years, the Chinese middle class has undergone a real transformation in building personal values that determine new life choices relating to social and intimate relationships, financial goals, health and well-being, careers, the environment, personal development, and leisure.

信

xìn

Meaning: **honesty, reliable, believe, credibility, trust, certainty, true.** This character is built up of one symbol meaning person and one for words. It means that trust and reliability are based on someone's word. To trust the system, we need to trust people's words.

5.

Trust the system. What does freedom mean to the Chinese? Do the Chinese trust the Communist Party? Is the Party a danger to the Chinese and the world? Why don't the Chinese want more freedom and democracy? Do all Chinese people live in fear and in a dystopian reality? Is China a Big Brother state and Xi Jinping a dictator?

System and the CPC

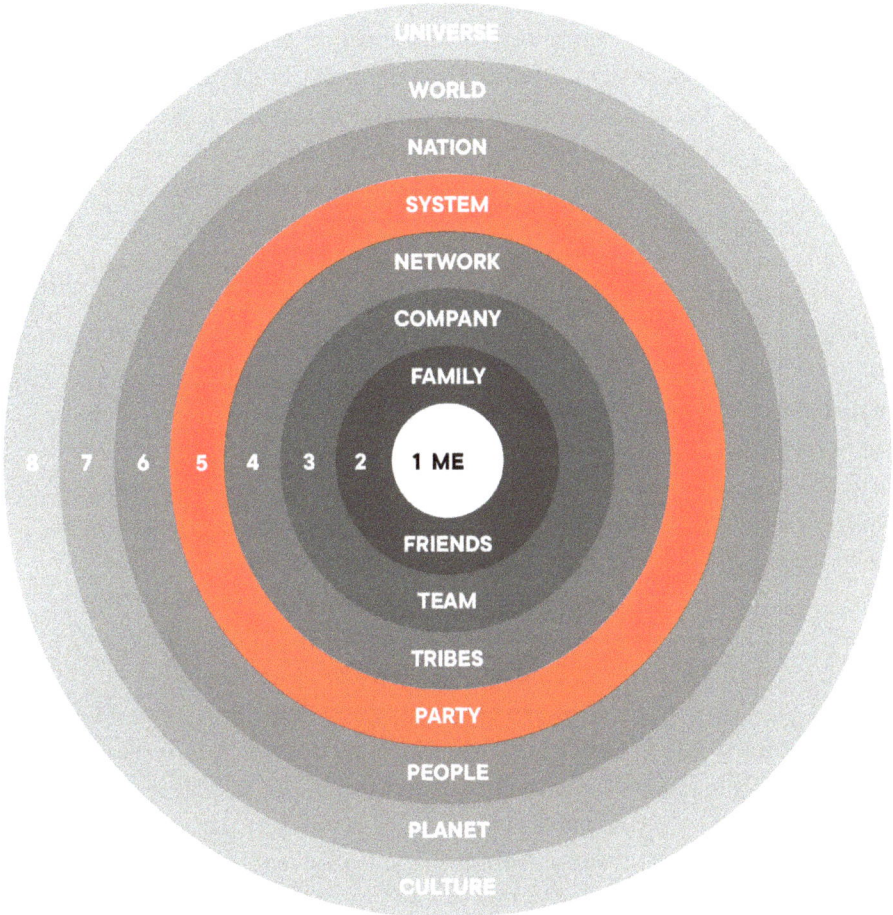

UNIVERSE
WORLD
NATION
SYSTEM
NETWORK
COMPANY
FAMILY

1 ME

FRIENDS
TEAM
TRIBES
PARTY
PEOPLE
PLANET
CULTURE

8 7 6 5 4 3 2 1 ME

A WILD ADVENTURE

Ever since I was a child, I wanted to be a biologist and travel the world like David Attenborough. When I started university in 1988, studying biology seemed much more theoretical than I had imagined it would be. In truth, I found it really boring and quickly lost interest. One day I decided to stop and study something else. But what? I flicked through the huge book of the eighty courses the university offered, but hardly any of them really inspired me. Until I got to Eastern languages and cultures. As a child I had done karate for years and was Bruce Lee's biggest fan, so studying sinology felt like a natural step. However, when I was in my second year, I started to doubt my choice again. China had received a lot of bad press since the Tiananmen Square incident in 1989. My friends really couldn't understand how I could be interested in a country with a regime that had so brutally crushed a peaceful student protest. Even then, China was labeled a dictatorship without any freedoms, despite the fact that ten years earlier the country had been opened up to the world by Deng Xiaoping. Thirty years later, we again are faced with the same mistrust and the same disappointments. Back then, it was about the future of China; today, it is about the future of Hong Kong. Even though not many Chinese people in their fifties have happy memories of their crazy student years in the late 1980s, that future didn't turn out so badly. Will it be the same for the Hong Kongers in thirty years' time? Today, Western confidence that everything will be all right in Hong Kong is gradually disappearing, which reminds me of the same uneasy feeling I had in 1990. Back then I was also very worried about China and its authoritarian regime. What I really wanted to know was if I would like China and whether it had a future, and therefore whether I should continue studying Chinese. My grandfather bought me a return plane ticket to Hong Kong and I scraped together all my savings to pay for my first trip to China. With just my backpack and a *Lonely Planet* travel guide, I arrived in South China on February 1, 1991. This was the start of my wild adventure.

Two years earlier, my father and I had visited the Berlin Wall, just before its fall. We could see East Germany in the distance, and this is how I imagined China at the time. A very closed society, uniform, colorless, people enduring a difficult existence. On day one of my trip to China, I ended up in a local wet market in Guangzhou. It was an eye-opening experience. The traders were loudly selling their goods, cleaning fish, or plucking chickens, and you could tell they were having a lot of fun. In the parks, the elderly played mahjong or danced to Chinese music, children played tag or jumped rope, and adults played badminton or strolled hand in hand. It looked like everyone was happy. As there were far fewer foreign tourists at the time, I did attract a bit of attention; people were interested in talking to me and offered me a tea or even a beer. Everything was bustling with life, and everyone seemed so "free." When I arrived at Guangzhou station to take the thirty-six-hour train ride to Shanghai, I suddenly saw a completely different side to China. Thousands of people from all over the country were arriving in Guangzhou by train with all their belongings in a very big bag. They were coming to South China in search of a better life. The city of Shenzhen near Guangzhou was one of the first economic zones in China to allow private companies and international trade. The travelers came from the countryside, where their future as farmers looked much bleaker. They had a choice: continue working hard on their often barely fertile piece of land and stay poor; or spend years working hard in the factories and on the construction sites of Shenzhen and get rich in the process. Tens of millions of them chose economic freedom.

FREEDOM

One of the biggest barriers in trusting China is changing our own view of what freedom means to the Chinese. We point to events in Hong Kong, how journalists or activists are being silenced, how the state uses millions of cameras to follow your every move, and how suffocating the education system, family, or social control is. We often hear that the Chinese are not free at all. Then we hear that there is no real freedom of opinion, religion, association, press, or movement, or any academic or political freedom. And it is indeed true that Chinese citizens living in China cannot express their dissatisfaction or protest as freely as citizens of many Western countries.

However, the question we don't ask enough is why so few of the Chinese are bothered by this. The opinion that all of the 1.4 billion Chinese people have been thoroughly indoctrinated by the authoritarian regime to accept their limited form of freedoms as "normal" is too Orwellian to be true. Another view to life is the reason why most Chinese are at peace with a different set of liberties. Westerners like myself, who speak fluent Chinese and who have lived in China, are unlikely to argue that government indoctrination or information censorship is the primary reason their Chinese friends don't demand more freedoms. Looking at the images of the violent clashes in Hong Kong, Western intellectuals are too quick to conclude that Hong Kongers are taking to the streets to preserve their freedoms because they know what freedom is—in contrast to the Chinese on the mainland. There are ten times more students from mainland China living abroad today than there are university students studying in Hong Kong. And the majority of all Chinese students abroad voluntarily return to their home country after their studies. The question then is why these students don't think it is necessary to stand up for more freedoms? If we then look at how immense China is, the flow of information from the West is of course not up to the same level everywhere. But many Chinese people from all over the country have lived, studied, or traveled abroad and have had a lot of exposure to Western society. I can confirm that the Chinese who have studied abroad are just as well-informed and opinionated as my Belgian friends. So why don't these highly intelligent Chinese people mind the restrictions on their freedoms in China?

My conclusion is that there are three key reasons:
- The Chinese grow up with rules;
- China has come a long way;
- There is more freedom in China than we think.

THE CHINESE GROW UP WITH RULES

In this ancient culture, rules play a very strong role in maintaining harmony within society. It starts with the father of the family and ends with the father of the homeland. Since time began, China has had a cosmological rule system that dictates the order of respect among the Chinese: heaven, earth, emperor, father, and teacher. In traditional China, the Chinese honored and respected, even over their own father, the emperor as father of the homeland—and today this is Xi Jinping. It is culturally "normal" that some things should not really be discussed or questioned. This is much less so in the West, although we also unconsciously avoid certain subjects or approach them with extreme caution because they are politically incorrect. Over the centuries, these "acceptance rules" in China have grown out of a fear of being overthrown by the indomitable Chinese rebels who emerged to overthrow dynasties. Chinese citizens tend to accept the rules because they intuitively sense that if they don't, there will be chaos. This mindset reveals the vulnerability of the country.

Another China paradox is that they have many more ways to enforce the rules, but don't actually need to use them as much as we do. During the pandemic, this cultural difference with the West became very obvious. Most Western citizens, just like Chinese, were at times forced to strict lockdowns, social distancing, and prohibitions of gathering.

With its control over its people and its many cameras, China should have been able to catch offenders faster than Western countries. But rarely did you hear on Chinese social media of anyone being caught (and the Chinese certainly don't hold back when it comes to sharing online people who break the law). In Belgium, where I lived through the lockdowns, the police and regulators were working overtime to cramp down on lockdown parties and check whether companies followed the measures correctly. It is not because there are more means of control that there is also more need to deploy them.

The other difference with the West is that those rules are not just there to protect the individual against injustice or crime, but also to maintain China's civilization and social system—which of course includes the Party. If you were to look at the cybersecurity law that China introduced in 2021, you would soon notice a lot of similarities with the European GDPR[92], (but with more emphasis on national or collective security. This new law meant that, in the summer of 2021, twenty-five apps, including that of car-sharing giant DiDi, were suddenly removed from Chinese app stores. With its 600,000 vehicles, DiDi was in a position to gather even more information than the Chinese government. You might think that this would be a goldmine for the government to exploit to control the Chinese even more, but their main concern was that this data could end up in the hands of other countries, so it became a national security risk. In most cases, the rules that apply to the Chinese are not that different from those in the West.

What is different in China is that it's best not to attack the "system" itself, nor the guardians of the system—the Party. In China, attacking the institution itself or undermining its key leaders is crossing a major red line. China takes firm action against terrorism, separatism, conspiracy against China, and undermining the nation by, for example, setting fire to a Chinese national flag. Furthermore, in China it is not a good idea to create social unrest through hate messages, wild rumors, conspiracy theories, or even negative economic reports if you don't have authorization to publish these. This is very different to Western democratic countries: we have to put a lot more effort into damage control, while China focuses more on prevention control, which leads to Western questions and accusations about the violation of human rights in China. The reason that the average Chinese person isn't really bothered by this, and therefore supports the system, is that they feel that these rules bring them more advantages than disadvantages; and not because they have never experienced or are unaware of other freedoms.

When it comes to China's governance and system, many millions of Chinese people read the daily negative, attacking, and hateful reports from the West about the Communist Party and its leaders. What bothers the Chinese most is not always the content of the articles themselves, but the extremely condescending attitude of the West, as if the Chinese are unaware or unable to think for themselves or to think freely about political and ideological issues. While we are quick to see the Chinese as indoctrinated and uninformed, the Chinese look at us as ignorant and arrogant. What is really absurd is that we are accusing each other of tunnel vision.

CHINA HAS COME A LONG WAY

Thirty years ago, all Chinese people enjoyed far fewer individual freedoms. There were a lot of limits on property ownership, quality of education, job opportunities, food supply, healthcare, information, media, mobility, use of personal time, private initiatives, entrepreneurship, entertainment, travel, religion, and more. We can no longer picture the China where almost everyone wore the same blue Mao suit to cycle to work every day at a state-owned company, and where everyone would hang out in the park on the weekend because they did not have any disposable income to do anything else. I saw this for myself thirty years ago in the smaller cities of China. At that time, almost all Chinese families still lived together in their parents' homes, and their lives were literally at a standstill. In 1990, China had 754 million people living in extreme poverty. China's GDP per capita was $314. In 2020 it was $10,000. This is a growth of 3,137 percent, compared to 173 percent in the United States and 113 percent in Germany over the same period. This is called the "lived change index," which measures the economic change that a population has experienced over a period of time.[93] If you were to project that rate of lifestyle change onto most developed countries of thirty years ago, where for example in my home country Belgium half of all families owned a house and a car, and most people already had a good amount of savings, then half of all Western citizens today would probably be millionaires and own a castle with a few expensive cars in the driveway. Maybe if this were the case, we'd also give our own government more credit? Of course, it is much easier for China to grow by catching up to the West than to grow as an advanced Western economy. Taking the different stages of economies into account, the earlier comparison between China and Belgium therefore isn't correct, but from a feeling of perceived acquired wealth for Chinese over one generation the comparison is representative. Just think about the elections in the United States, the outcomes of which are regularly predicted by economic progress. Had the COVID-19 recession not happened, Trump would likely have been re-elected. In around thirty years, modern China has enabled more than a billion Chinese people to make a giant personal leap in terms of wealth and new freedoms, and even individual human rights have seen the same progress. The international community completely disagrees with that last part and is putting increasing pressure on China to respect human rights the same way they are interpreted by the West. When it comes to this topic, all Western fingers, from Amnesty International and Human Rights Watch to journalists and politicians, are pointing in the same direction.

I agree that we should address all human rights violations and try and put an end to them as soon as possible. But when it comes to China, we run into problems. China has in the last years repeatedly denied most of the current human rights violation allegations, with the response that what is happening in Xinjiang, for example, is a sovereign matter that is purely about national security. The global challenge is that China doesn't often release a lot of data when it comes to a topic of national security. The same applies to the United States and other countries. China claims that the evidence from these international organizations, media, reporters, and so-called China experts on human rights violations has been made up, politicized, and misused by interest groups primarily in the United States, trying to undermine the sovereignty of China or the Communist Party. Since 2021, China has become so annoyed by what it views as made-up evidence against the country that it has started to share counterarguments and evidence despite the risk to national security. But the response has fallen on deaf ears in the West, which has in turn accused China of even more state propaganda. China's previous lack of transparency is still feeding the mistrust we have in China today. We are talking past each other: we simply no longer trust the evidence provided by the other side. But isn't it strange that the West, which insists on freedom of opinion, is not interested in China's opinions or counterarguments? Is it laziness or do we just subconsciously not discuss this information in the Western media? Isn't it strange that China, which places so much importance on communicating prudently to not losing face, is now as outspoken as the US? This spectacle is more like a boxing match than a real debate. The reports suggesting COVID-19 was leaked from a lab in Wuhan were the low point of this dialogue with China—even global health was being put at risk to score political points. This put an end to the collaboration with China to find out where the virus had come from and to develop vaccines. If we tackle global warming in the same way, we will never save the biodiversity of the planet—or ourselves! The world order may be multipolar in terms of economic relations, but geopolitically it is becoming more and more of a duopoly with familiar cold war dynamics, in particular the use of propaganda to discredit the opponent.

Today it is impossible to have a truly honest conversation about human rights in China without being accused of being either a Chinese Communist Party propagandist or a Western imperialist. You can't be impartial anymore. If, on the other hand, you ask the Chinese in confidence about their personal situation, you will get a surprising answer. They believe that the protection of their rights as individuals is only ever improving in China. They will then give you examples from ten, twenty, or thirty years ago about the terrible and extremely dangerous working conditions for employees; about the lack of consumer protection, privacy, and women's rights such as with the one-child policy or discrimination when looking for a job; about crime, scams, and corruption; about extreme poverty and poor social security; about the shortage of pensions and health insurance; about the poor quality of products, services, and healthcare.

In other words, barely twenty years ago it was much easier for rich people and politicians to exploit, violate, or even have the average citizen locked up. For many of the Chinese, including the poor and minorities, China seems to have become much better, safer, and a more just place to live. It is important to note here that this was not a period of improved quality of life and extra rights for all the Chinese. For the people of Xinjiang, and in particular the

Uyghurs, life after September 11, 2001, was marked by increased anti-terrorist actions, checks, and restrictions. But for the majority of the Chinese, they had the Chinese government and the system to thank for the improvement to their rights as individuals. In recent decades, for most Chinese, improving their standard of living has also been much more important than fighting for a freer political voice. If the system works well, and keeps improving, why is there a need for a political vote that undermines that system?—this is how the pragmatic Chinese think. Of course, there are also a lot of things in China that don't work well, but that's why the Chinese don't necessarily want to change the system—rather, they want to improve it. More and more Chinese believe that the West wants to change China, not improve it; and that the human rights debate is not really about improving the rights of the Chinese, Uyghurs, or Hong Kongers, but about changing China's system, which they see as a more and more efficient and evolving work-in-process. There is no country in the world that in the last thirty years has undergone so much internal reform with new laws and standards to give greater freedom and protection to its people and businesses. So, it is too easy to pass judgment that the Chinese should have more freedoms, but we cannot deny that China has in its own way brought prosperity, opportunities, and stability to more individuals than any Western country over the last forty years. From a trend analysis point of view, if China continues in the same way, in thirty years' time the West may well be less free than China. After all, more and more authoritarian forces are starting to develop within Western liberal democracy. Just imagine!

THERE IS MORE FREEDOM IN CHINA THAN WE THINK

There is a big misconception that you can't criticize the government in China. But there are plenty of examples that show otherwise, like the one-child policy. The government was heavily criticized for this, so the policy was eventually abolished in 2016. The other reason to get rid of it was that, with the working-age population declining every year, demographic trends presented a new economic challenge for China. Since then, there has been a lot of criticism about the pressure the government is putting on women to suddenly have more children. Chinese people's voices make it quite clear to the government that women are not merely "reproduction machines" that the government can just switch on and off as it pleases. In the early days of the coronavirus pandemic, there was also a lot of criticism on social media about the Wuhan government's response, which were taken offline quickly and some citizen journalists were detained. But it attracted the attention of Premier Li Keqiang himself.[94] China is surprisingly proactive in welcoming comments from the entire population online about new rules and legislative proposals that are being drawn up.[95] This doesn't take away from the fact that masses of online messages, from hate messages to pornography, which are labeled as toxic to Chinese society, are quickly censored, including political discontent of course. China therefore has an international reputation as the country with one of the most restrictive censorship laws in the world.

We also have online censorship in the West, but to a different degree and in a different form. All over the world, online content promoting or glorifying scams, suicide, hatred, extremism, violence, child nudity, political advertising, and social or racial inequality are increasingly being taken offline. This is less determined by the government and more by the social media platforms that create their own rules. A company like Facebook employs 15,000 people to monitor the internet.[96] The Chinese social media giants have not many more people in this line of work.[97]

At the end of 2019, I visited TikTok in Beijing and asked whether their experience with China's strict censorship laws gave them a competitive advantage when monitoring TikTok videos around the globe. The answer was no: "In China it's less difficult to know what is allowed and what is not allowed, while in the United States nothing is clear. That's why we sometimes run into problems. Not for taking a different approach, but because the US government doesn't provide any clear guidelines." I could sense their frustration that the United States not only does a lot of censoring but is also very ambiguous about that censorship.

We can't imagine not being allowed to criticize or insult Boris Johnson, Donald Trump, or Joe Biden on the World Wide Web. Don't the Chinese need this in the same way we do? It is difficult to show whether or not the Chinese are scared to attack the system or Xi Jinping personally, as there aren't many examples of political nonconformists being allowed to voice their opinions openly in China. But to conclude that all Chinese people are scared to voice their opinion is like claiming that all Westerners are scared of their government because we're not allowed to walk down the street naked. Most citizens can agree to only partially revealing themselves in public. It is no different in China when it comes to your personal opinion of the government. The Chinese simply do not publicly share their dissatisfaction with the top leaders of the country or with the system itself, but rather with local governments, companies, or regulatory bodies. They also do it more privately, and both online and offline.

In this respect, they are much more pragmatic and strategic than we are, because you can't keep hundreds of millions of internet users quiet. If there's a lot of you, like the Chinese, you can also indirectly bring about a lot of change by not wanting to destroy the entire machine, but by having certain parts replaced or upgraded. The anger of many Chinese internet users about wrongdoing in the country is therefore mainly aimed at individuals, companies, and local authorities. They are the visible victims of the proxy war between internet users and Beijing. Those vicious and personal attacks on the Chinese Twitter Weibo are certainly no less violent than what happens in the West. Well-known examples are the strong reactions to the statement by Jack Ma about the "normal" seventy-two-hour working week (9-9-6) in China, or the outrage of Chinese internet users when Robin Li, the founder of Baidu (the Chinese Google), claimed that Chinese people place much less importance on privacy, or the mayor of Wuhan who was blamed for his cover-up and slow response to the coronavirus outbreak. What internet users really want is for Beijing to tackle the virus, privacy policies, or labor laws from these examples, and it often does take concrete actions. In many cases, Beijing will take decisive action within twenty-four hours, also to avoid being attacked. Building hospitals in Wuhan within ten days and the sudden restrictions imposed on the largest technology companies can be viewed in this light. The greater the online anger, the quicker the government response. Western news reports like to talk about Beijing's control as netizens have little direct impact to change the priorities in Beijing, but the internet users have more influence on the narrative in China than we might imagine. Put simply, it is usually more efficient for the government to quickly address a problem that has been raised than to censor all online conversations in order to bury the story. Because Beijing has so much power, it is also a lot easier for the government to take decisive action than it is in Western democracies.

In contextual China, the government reads between the lines that the system needs updating, new legislation, and better control. This is how the system, or machine, repairs itself. In the West, we see a broken Chinese machine, while the Chinese see a machine that is constantly improving. So, internet censorship works more like a valve that regulates the pressure of society, and not as a tap that is half turned off. You could argue that the West is mopping the floor while the (internet) tap is still on, while China is trying to catch the water in buckets. This is why I like to compare the Chinese internet with a greenhouse. It is precisely because plants in a greenhouse are protected from the strongest forces of nature, like the sun, wind, and rain, and that the greenhouse is regulated in terms of temperature, nutrition, and fertilizers, that the plants will flower and be healthy and diverse. As long as the Chinese stick to the basic rules in China and do not attack China's system itself, they have a lot of freedom. Via virtual private networks (VPNs), which are officially banned but tolerated, internet users who speak English are also able to explore the "free internet." But many of them don't spend the whole day on YouTube, Google, or Twitter, and instead quickly return to their trusted and extremely informative Chinese greenhouse. They do this because China's closed internet is much freer than we think. The Chinese are highly opinionated and critical, and the Chinese internet is the main driver of the speed at which China is developing as a modern society.

On July 1, 1921, the Communist Party of China (CPC) was founded by a group of revolutionary intellectuals, including Mao Zedong. Against all expectations, the CPC survived all internal and external battles and disasters for 100 years. Today, this makes the CPC the world's longest reigning and largest political party, with ninety-five million current members. The total of CPC members is also due to the population size of China, as we also see in India with the BJP with the same impressive numbers.[98] That all gives the CPC enough reasons to celebrate. However, the enormous trust that the Chinese people have in the CPC is as great as the enormous distrust that the West has in the CPC. This stark divergence makes the CPC a fascinating topic. The West prefers to label the CPC as an authoritarian, totalitarian dictatorship that monitors all 1.4 billion Chinese people, and oppresses many of them too. It appears that the West is also scared that the CPC is exporting its influence and could affect the democracies and ideological freedoms of the West. The United States and its allies are all singing from the same song sheet on this. Meanwhile, China is scared that the West wants to limit the power of the CPC, as well as change China's governmental structure and economic system. At the CPC's hundred-year celebrations, Xi Jinping reiterated that China will never again allow itself to be intimidated, oppressed, or subjugated by foreign powers. He also said that China historically has never oppressed other countries. These statements aside, most of us remain convinced that China wants to influence the world with its propaganda, like as with its own people. On the other side, many Chinese remain convinced that the West wants to keep exerting its imperialist influence on the world and China. And they don't need to look that far back in time to show that the United States still either has a military presence, or at some point has carried out a military intervention, in half the countries in the world.[99]

To win their main argument, both China and the West search for justification in the modern history of the Chinese nation, but each is looking at a different time period. The West mainly looks at the CPC in the period from 1949 to 1976 under Mao, and then at the Tiananmen Square protests in 1989. Post-1949, the first milestone was Mao's failed Great Leap Forward (1958-1961), which plunged the country into famine. Later, when his position and ideology came under threat afterwards, Mao launched the great proletarian Cultural Revolution (1966-1976) against the old capitalists and what he called the new bourgeoisie, which included his political opponents. These two CPC campaigns are said to have killed tens of millions. Later, when Deng Xiaoping came to power as vice chairman of the CPC in 1978, he launched a process to gradually open up all of China to world trade. Deng's darkest moment came in 1989, when he apparently instructed supported Chinese Premier Li Peng to suppress the student protests in the same year, this confirmed to the West that the CPC was merely a cynical authoritarian dictatorship more concerned with preserving power than with the prosperity and needs of the people. The Chinese version of CPC history about that same period mainly glorifies the heroic acts of Mao Zedong, who reunited China and saved all Chinese people from the corrupt nationalists (Guomindang) and brutal Japanese invasion; within just fifty years, the CPC had almost doubled the life expectancy of the people, raised the literacy rate to ninety-seven percent, and, since 1978, brought about an unprecedented economic miracle in the country.

For most Chinese, it's simple: China's success is inextricably tied to the CPC. Until 1978 thanks to Mao's liberation and modernization of China, from 1978 thanks to Deng's economic push, and since 2013 thanks to Xi's dream of greater prosperity for all Chinese people. For the West, it's also a very simple story: Until 1978 China was a communist dictatorship that was stagnating. Since 1978 it has turned into a capitalist country that is progressing rapidly but where life remains hard and unfree because of the communist dictatorship. Under Xi since 2013, things have gone from bad to worse as he is trying to scale back capitalism and strengthen the communist dictatorship. The Chinese see the CPC as the winner emerging from battle, now allowing every Chinese person to dream of a better future. The West, on the other hand, sees the CPC as an extreme totalitarian system of control, and a growing nightmare for all Chinese people.

The Chinese are more scared of being controlled by the West than by the CPC. This fear comes from previous experience: the 100 years of humiliation of China by the West that started in 1840 after the Opium War. In his speech marking the 100 years of the CPC, Xi Jinping said: "Gradually, China was reduced to a semi-colonial and semi-feudal society. With our country humiliated, our people subjected to great pain, and our civilization plunged into darkness, the Chinese people and nation suffered greater ravages than ever before." As a result, China suffered three major losses: the loss of control over its own territory, over its governance, and over its reputation. It is in this context that we need to understand the taboo topic of China's territorial and governmental sovereignty.[100]

The reunification and control of the entire country, including Tibet, Xinjiang, Hong Kong, and Taiwan, is seen by the West as proof of the CPC's voracious drive for power and control, while the CPC justifies it as the legitimate righting of historically unjust wrongs. However, the international reputation China had as a world power before 1840 has still not returned. The question is how much international power China wants to achieve in order to get over its past humiliation. The West is much less confident that China's intentions are just about recovery. The West is less convinced that China is sincere in its defensive position to let multiple systems of governance coexist peacefully and harmoniously in the world.

DOES THE CPC HAVE TOO MUCH POWER?

In the West, the CPC is accused of not being a legitimate representative for the entire population. The reason for this is that China doesn't have democratic elections like in the West. Another reason is that the highest-level decisions are often made behind closed doors, so it feels like the opposition has no voice. In addition, in 2018 the term limits on the role as President of the People's Republic of China were removed from the constitution, giving Xi Jinping potentially the title for life. He is also the highest leader of the army, police, and CPC. All the power is in the hands of one person, who is often referred to as a dictator. Since the CPC is also the highest supervisory body in China, China has no counter-balancing political mechanism to monitor it. The lack of elections, transparency, checks and balances, all the power in one party, and the CPC with President Xi as its supreme leader are some of the reasons we call China an "authoritarian dictatorship." The authoritarian regimes we are familiar with are countries where it is one party or the army that have complete control, and where their power is based on spreading lies and fear. It is therefore not surprising that, with that enormously negative image in mind, the West doesn't trust China easily and instead sees the country as a threat to democracy. Although democracy is placed opposite authoritarian regimes on the spectrum of the democracy index,[101] more and more democracies are also displaying more authoritarian elements and leaders. This is closely linked to the fact that, historically, authoritarian regimes have usually been created out of the crises and chaos that characterize the West today. Using that same logic, we could also argue that authoritarian regimes that become economically stronger and more stable would lead to more liberalization and democratization, and ultimately the decline of the authoritarian regime.

At the end of the last century, the West was firmly convinced that the Chinese would demand more freedom and democracy once China became economically prosperous. This is why we're surprised that today, China is still governed by the CPC, which is stronger than ever before. The strange thing is, we're drawing the same incorrect conclusions today. We still look at China as a battle between conflicting interests, those of the CPC and those of the people. We still see the CPC as a purely authoritarian regime that wants to severely restrict the freedoms of opinion, association, and mobility of the people, that doesn't tolerate opposition or contradiction, that censors, that has no independent legal system, and that has self-preservation as its only priority. According to Western logic, this is a power struggle between the population and the CPC, against the will of the Chinese people who don't dare rebel openly against the regime because they are scared of retaliation.

In reality, the vast majority of Chinese citizens don't live in fear at all, and the power of the CPC is therefore not based on fear, but on promise of sustained progress. If the progress were to stop, the CPC might indeed lose some of its power. That is certainly not the situation today, but it does explain the CPC's focus on creating even more prosperity. That doesn't fit with our usual explanation of how authoritarian regimes make their people dependent on the government. It is our Western dualistic reasoning (A or B) that misleads us into using opposites to look for truth. The fact that the government doesn't necessarily think differently from the people seems almost utopian to us. The Chinese are also dualistic thinkers, but they don't see these opposites as mutually exclusive, rather as inclusive data (A and B) that must be reconciled to generate any positive change.[102] The population is therefore not in conflict with the CPC, but the opinion of the people is equally crucial to facilitate any change in China for the CPC. Within the Chinese circles and the CPC, there is also contradiction in the several political movements. Debate takes place between those who are more interested in socialist politics and those who accept economic growth with more polarization. In contrast to the ideological struggles seen between the various parties in the West, China is still much more concerned with the struggle for economic growth and prosperity than with ideology. China has many identities, which sounds contradictory to us. China can give us the impression of being anything from peaceful to assertive, from willing to disruptive, from engaged to disinterested.

The reason we don't trust China is often about this contradiction. We find it difficult to accept that a country or a population simply accepts these contradictions. The Chinese see these contradictions as normal and to be expected within the natural evolution of the system. In every contradiction, they see both truth and error, and are therefore perfectly able to live with these contradictions. The Chinese can live with a stricter authoritarian system, and the CPC can live with highly pragmatic and impatient citizens. When we witness China cracking down or talking tough, the Western media usually immediately concludes that the CPC wants to demonstrate its power or exert control over companies, individuals, or institutions. We talk about repression or oppression. This would be correct if we put the CPC directly against the population and organizations. But it's not so black and white. Most Chinese citizens support the CPC, many business leaders are party members, and CPC leaders all have family members who are not CPC members or who run companies that are all about capitalism. The CPC is an inherent part of society; it does not exist to control everyone. You grow up with it in China, just like elsewhere in the world people grow up with a village priest, imam, or rabbi—a trusted person you can look up to. That's where the comparison with religious groups ends because the CPC is completely atheistic. But it is important to understand that the CPC is not seen by the vast majority of Chinese people as an enemy or something to be countered.

The best analogy I can make for the CPC is that of an extremely loyal watchdog for the population and the Party, and not a predator. As the CPC barks, it usually doesn't bite. When the CPC bites, it usually stops barking. If China is firm in its statements, or barks loudly, then you can almost automatically expect it to be flexible in the implementation of its words. Just think about Taiwan or even Hong Kong. Imagine for a moment, purely hypothetically, that the United States is in the same situation, with a rebellious Alaska or Hawaii, then I fear it wouldn't just be about talking tough. They would have their troops lined up in no time. China, on the other hand, is much more patient. China spent fifty years reuniting Hong Kong with the mainland. For Taiwan, more than a century. If, on the other hand, China continues to bark, while the recipient of the message—the troublemaker or intruder—won't listen, then it will bite. China bites to give a very clear signal that this is where they're drawing the line, and that you should stay well behind it. This is what has happened in Hong Kong. When Hong Kong's status as a special administrative region comes to an end in 2047, the city and its people can be protected by the CPC.

However, it is difficult to explain this to a protesting Hong Kong student who currently sees the CPC as their worst enemy, an invader taking away their democratic freedom, hopes, and future. From a Chinese point of view, the CPC will give the Hong Kongers a much better future than they had under the British. An endless discussion…that will last until 2047. So, if Beijing takes a heavy-handed approach to law enforcement, we can read between the lines that they are doing this to draw a line somewhere, to give a signal, but also not to have to change the system too quickly. You can also read into this that the system, and therefore the legislation, will get adjusted. For example, the crackdown on bitcoin mines in Western China as a signal for stricter environmental regulations. Or the blocking of the Ant Group stock launch (IPO) at the end of 2020 as a sign of the new fintech and later anti-monopoly laws. Or the removal of the DiDi apps (the Chinese Uber) from Chinese app stores as Beijing getting very serious about cybersecurity.

This actually means that China is changing, and not necessarily that China is getting tougher. It is not a fist, but a new hand opening up. The real controversy about these moments of change is that it also makes honest victims in the process like human rights lawyers serving prison sentences for asking Beijing to uphold its own laws. These victims do not in any way view Beijing's repression as a process in time or a new hand opening up. Time can solve many challenges, but not all challenges have the luxury of time to heal. That said, China is ramping up its controls on data, privacy, finance, monopolies, pollution, corruption, etc., but we see the same phenomenon all over the world. The difference with Europe is that China usually spends more time preparing everything properly, which means that companies stay under the radar for longer, but then ultimately acts more firmly and tougher. So, in China, the regulation comes later. That vacuum allows more innovation and faster growth, but that also creates many more shocks and aftershocks. This change to the system or in the legislation must be well thought-through, and not done too quickly. This is why it's better for us to look at evolutions and trends in China, rather than at statements or actions.

These signals tell us much more about the CPC than the statements, propaganda, or actions you read in the media. The reason the Chinese are not easily put off by the enormous power of the CPC is certainly also that they have faith in the self-correcting nature of China's political system. The best proof that the CPC can change can be found in modern history. In 1978, China suddenly decided to introduce many elements of the cap-italist system. We thought this was the right choice for China because it reflected our own system. What we have not often thought about is that it was a drastic ideological decision for communist China at the time. This would be like Washington deciding to slowly turn the largest US businesses into state-owned companies to solve a social crisis. Never going to happen. But the CPC did in fact make this kind of U-turn, in order to help the people. So, the CPC's greatest strength is less its communist or Marxist ideology, and more its enormous ability to pragmatically self-regulate, which has its roots in the meritocratic system of ancient China. This traditional meritocracy fits together very well with the ideology of socialism, or rather, socialism with Chinese characteristics.

CHINA'S MERITOCRACY

How can the CPC guarantee that it has the well-being of the country and the people in mind? Take, for example, a large city like Beijing or Shanghai, where the sixteen representatives of each of the sixteen districts are directly elected by citizens from a list that is based on qualifications and put forward by an organizing committee. This electoral system is described in the Constitution of the People's Republic of China, and therefore determines how the country is governed. Voting is not compulsory for Chinese citizens. The electoral system in itself is not that different from local elections in Belgium or the Netherlands. The sixteen districts in Beijing together have as many inhabitants as the entire population of the Netherlands. So, is Beijing just as democratic as Belgium or the Netherlands? You could say that, but one big difference is that candidates can't just put themselves on the list. Instead, this is decided based on certain qualities and also loyalty to the CPC, not on popularity or promising a lot, even when delivering very little in the past. So, there is a watchdog—the CPC. But this doesn't mean that the only people on the list are friends of politicians. We should certainly not underestimate the value of China's meritocracy; a hybrid model of control by the CPC with a unique system for the selection of officials that is more than a thousand years old.

When you consider how anyone in China, regardless of their class, historically could work their way through the imperial exams and become an official in China's national government, you could say that China invented meritocracy. In terms of individual participation in politics, their system is also much broader than we usually think. In addition to the CPC, China has eight other much smaller democratic parties, and as independents, people can also vote for one of those eight parties. According to the constitution, this multi-party system falls under the CPC and the parties must cooperate and evolve with the CPC. So, the power of the CPC is described in the constitution, and cooperation with the CPC is expected, but that does not prevent each party from having its own social priorities even within the CPC's well-defined limits. This is often done through China's consultation model where people from the various parties, chambers of commerce, business leaders, and citizens are regularly consulted to get honest feedback. Members of the eight other parties are also elected to the various local and national parliaments and have senior political positions.

On the one hand, China is not very democratic because it is very streamlined to keep the entire nation heading in the same direction, led by the CPC and President Xi. A country that wants to move forward needs clear direction. On the other hand, China's system is often more closely involved with citizens because political ambitions are decided based on a meritocracy that is co-determined by the citizens, and not on the basis of a popularity contest, election campaigns, or showdowns. China calls this a democracy with Chinese characteristics. For the highest office, the President of the People's Republic of China, the best and only candidate is proposed by the CPC and then confirmed by the National People's Congress. This is unthinkable for Western democracies, but China is comfortable with this system, which is more like how a company's CEO is elected by the board of directors. The people have no direct way to change their leader. It's that uncertainty that the West often has reservations about because our own past has taught us that if too much power is in the hands of one person or party, it easily leads to corruption. China has also had experience of this in its recent history. I personally saw Chinese people with political or military power having no problem lining their own or their families' pockets. In the three decades before Xi Jinping came to power, China experienced a real boom in corruption, decadence, and nepotism. The people really didn't appreciate this, and the very unequal treatment caused a lot of dissatisfaction.

When Xi Jinping came to power in 2013, the fight against corruption within the CPC and government became his top priority. He said he would fight the "tigers and flies," which referred to "senior and local officials." To this day, he is fighting that fierce battle with more than 100 tigers and 10,000 flies that have already had charges brought against them. The anti-corruption commission is under the control of the CPC, and so is not politically independent. The commission might have a goal of self-purification for the benefit of Xi Jinping and his supporters rather than a goal to remove corrupt party members for the benefit of the population. However, Xi Jinping's anti-corruption campaign has hit so many officials, including his own supporters, that it seems clear by now that pushing out political rivals was not its sole purpose. Since this commission is much more powerful than similar anti-corruption institutions in the West, it is also a perfect example for us to get a better understanding of how the CPC keeps itself in check. One accusation that is often made against China is that the CPC lacks the checks and balances to regulate itself, which can easily lead to unrestricted power. The difference in the systems reveals how the West and China work differently to control those in power. In the West, the citizens or independent entities will monitor and correct political power, while in China there is a Central Commission for Discipline Inspection (CCDI) within the CPC that monitors all members of the CPC. This is like the internal affairs department of the police or army. Regulatory bodies can be regulated themselves by putting a higher body on top of another, so the CCDI is the highest disciplinary body within the CPC in China. In addition, China's legal system has exactly the same role as in the West, to punish corruption, with the CPC no longer above the law. Another method of regulation is more horizontal, as is common in the West, where competition between independent institutions is used to keep each other in check. The advantage of this Western cross-checking system is that non-governmental organizations voluntarily take action to expose any abuses of those in power. The disadvantage of the Western system is that regulatory institutions often have less power, for example the World Health Organization or Amnesty International, and are therefore less efficient at fighting corruption or wrongdoing. In a democratic country like India, which was economically comparable to China forty years ago, the inability to fight corruption at the top is still a huge challenge. This is precisely the advantage of the Chinese system, which has enabled the CPC to tackle corruption in the country much more effectively. The disadvantage of the Chinese top-down regulatory system is that you have to have faith in the very top, the CPC. And this is where we end up in a catch-22 situation. If you trust the CPC, you can assume it will regulate itself to justify its legitimacy to the population. If you don't trust the CPC, then you can assume that the CPC will abuse this system to keep hold of its own power. Therein lies the answer.

CAN WE TRUST THE CPC?

The question of whether the CPC can be trusted is actually a question that should be put to the Chinese people, not the West. The West is experiencing a crisis of confidence; a post-truth world in which objective facts have less and less influence when it comes to public opinion. We are letting our opinions be guided by our emotions, but our Western system, on the other hand, is increasingly governed by capitalism, which has turned citizens into consumers rather than people with feelings. The more the system ignores our emotions, the more emotional the individual becomes. When it comes to the subject of China, populist politicians in the West easily play on our emotions, while those same politicians are also happy to let Chinese factory workers quench our thirst for more things.

As consumers, we have partly lost sight of the social values of communities, which are the cornerstone of trust.[103] We have moved from a relationship economy to a transactional economy, and that means we don't trust leaders, partly because they also don't seem to trust us either. In addition, all people and organizations that are physically and culturally further away from us, like China, are by definition less trusted than what is trusted and known to us. We have less trust in the countries that are physically further away from us. The same goes for regimes and ideologies that are too "different." It is therefore not surprising that we do not trust the CPC. But that does not mean that the CPC cannot be trusted. Where we have experienced a crisis of confidence in our Western political leaders over the past forty years, China has experienced exactly the opposite: a confidence boost in its leaders. After Mao's death in 1976, the Gang of Four was impeached, tried, and convicted as the main people responsible for the violent actions of the Cultural Revolution. Mao himself got a final rating from his successor Deng Xiaoping as having been seventy percent good, thirty percent bad.[104] That moment marked the revival of public confidence in the CPC. Against all expectations, and for almost all the Chinese population, each year was better than the previous one. The miracle is mainly credited to the hard-working Chinese people, but it is the CPC who paved the way for this with a pragmatic-evolutionary plan and near-perfect execution. The CPC has provided opportunities to more than a billion underprivileged people: a true transformation in the quality of and access to education, healthcare, infrastructure, food, housing, private property, information, entrepreneurship, mobility, leisure, security, etc.

The big difference between Western political parties and the people in power in Beijing is that the CPC has seen its citizens more as real people with basic needs, and less as consumers with habits. It is a fact that the CPC has not helped all Chinese people through this mega transformation, and a lot of people were also harmed or oppressed. But when we look at it on a large scale, those who are not happy are almost invisible in terms of the growth in confidence in the CPC. The system's vertical structure of control, with the CPC taking ultimate responsibility as the regulatory body, has proved so efficient in recent history that the Chinese people have full confidence in that same model for the future. But it is also the resilience of the CPC that gives them yet more confidence. This is something we rarely see in the West. We forget that the Chinese political system, the Chinese state-owned enterprises, and the Chinese CPC have undergone constant change and reform in recent decades. Too slow according to the West, but still much faster than any government in the West. We take "our normal" as a starting point for comparison; but China has come a long way and sees that reform as an internal evolutionary process, and therefore doesn't view the Western model as the end goal. The CPC has also shown in its recent past that it isn't scared to self-correct during this process; for example, by cracking down on corruption within the CPC, by exposing local governments that falsify figures, or by firing officials who gave companies the freedom to harm citizens, the environment, or to line their own pockets.

This exposes another misunderstanding about China: that China is always manipulating the numbers and their data can't be trusted. This became very clear during the coronavirus outbreak. We didn't trust the numbers. And if you don't trust the numbers, then by definition you also have to reject everything China says using those numbers. It makes it very difficult for China to prove anything. Something that is incompatible with the idea that all data from China is fake is that the Chinese are in fact obsessed with data. The CPC is spewing out numbers with its five-year plans, and the entire nation is trying to work toward those numbers. The officials are evaluated by the CPC and the government on the basis of these figures, but also held accountable for their correctness. The contradiction is that, if the figures in China were false, the CPC would not be able to trust the figures from local governments and, as a result, could not evaluate or hold officials accountable.

Of course, we can ask whether the embellishment of figures sometimes still happens at the top. We have seen this with Western officials and politicians too. The question is whether this is widespread in China, or the actions of a few individuals. The argument against this logic is that China would never have grown so quickly if falsifying data was systemic to the CPC. Wouldn't a system that is always and entirely based on false data sooner or later cause China and its social system to implode? After forty years of growth and prosperity, the Chinese therefore think that the West likes to believe this story because it supports our narrative of mistrust in China without us having to provide data for it ourselves. Either way, Xi Jinping is proving with his anti-corruption campaign that he is cracking down on officials who falsify data, regardless of their position. We can confirm that the control over correct data has been tightened in China, but then it is difficult to claim that the same data is becoming increasingly unreliable. The Chinese people's confidence in the accuracy of the data that the government shares with its citizens has grown a lot in recent years. All these improvements and facts only give the average Chinese citizen more confidence in the CPC. It is sometimes difficult to understand how a body that has such tight control over its citizens can be rewarded with so much confidence.

The answer lies in the fact that the CPC is also responsible for the security and order of society. China remains one of the safest places on Earth. I lived in China for almost twenty years and never had the same unsafe feeling I get in a big European or American city when I walk around certain neighborhoods at night: that instinctive tense feeling that makes you walk faster or even avoid a neighborhood. You feel safer in the run-down neighborhoods of Shanghai or Beijing than almost anywhere in Paris or San Francisco. In twenty years, the government's CCTV footage was also never used against me. The only time this came in handy was when my bike was stolen. The Chinese know that there is a lot of control, but decent citizens forget the cameras are there. This also shows the power of government in China versus the power of the technology giants in the West. In the West, the rollout of cameras is usually done in collaboration with private partners and US technology. Our governments also don't invest enough resources to process all the images themselves. Sharing them with third parties increases the risk of privacy violations. In addition, Google also collects data from the cameras, for example to make predictions about how busy shopping streets and roads are. So, it seems only logical that we are more worried about privacy.

This doesn't change the fact that in the West, we are also much less concerned about privacy in large crowds or megacities where guaranteeing security comes first. There are 700,000 security cameras in London, and the Tomorrowland festival employs 700 security staff. Visitors and festival-goers don't seem to be put off by it. This type of control rarely feels like an invasion of privacy to the Chinese and is therefore not really associated with the CPC as a system of control or China as a control state. In China, the Big Brother narrative about the CPC does not take on the Orwellian proportions that the clickbait titles suggest. Instead, it feels much more like the people are grateful to have an "older brother" to protect the good citizens. And doesn't everyone have complete trust in their older brother? The fact that many in the West don't believe the CPC has the people's best interests at heart is something that the Chinese put down to our own, different experience. We of course look back at how authoritarian regimes in our modern Western history pushed their nations into decline, decay, poverty, or war. However, the Chinese generally believe that the CPC really does want the best for its citizens, precisely because during their modern history it has lifted the nation and its people out of decline, corruption, extreme poverty, and war. The West can't follow this reverse logic, but for the Chinese it makes perfect sense.

What is China's main system of governance? Communism? Marxism? Leninism? Socialism? Capitalism? Mercantilism? Technocracy? Dictatorship? A Chinese form of democracy? What is the main thought system in China? Confucianism? Taoism? Legalism? Atheism? Utilitarianism? It's certainly not simple to define what China is or how it operates. Nor is it easy to give a conclusive answer, because extensive and sometimes divergent ideas have been put forward about each of these definitions. I will therefore share how I define the Chinese system: pragmatic, adaptive, and evolutionary.

PRAGMATIC CHINA

I believe the answer lies partly in Deng Xiaoping's legendary statement from the early 1960s: "It doesn't matter whether a cat is black or white, so long as it catches mice." Deng Xiaoping used this quote again in 1978 as a signal to reform China's domestic economy and open up the global economy to the Chinese. He believed that an ideology is only useful if it solves problems. The result, and not the political system, determines how resources are used. This cat quote is used in the West to show how pragmatic China is, and that the end—get rich, gain power, and maintain control—justifies the means. If we look at China's new middle class and super-rich, we could even say that China has become more capitalistic than the West. But if we look at how Beijing limits the power of technology companies and their founders, and how Marxism-Leninism under Xi seems to thrive, then we notice that the Communist Party is also very pragmatic, including when it comes to maintaining its power. Nothing is allowed to rise above the Party and President Xi rises above it: no China without the CPC, and no CPC without China.

It would seem that the market is the white cat and the CPC the black cat. Actually, they are both black and white cats, in other words a socialist market economy. But in his speeches, Xi also constantly refers to Chinese culture, using ideas and principles from the past. So, China's leaders often seem more concerned with safeguarding Chinese civilization than with preaching Marxist ideology. China is more of a civilization state than a nation state. We must not forget that China is the oldest living culture in the world. China's pragmatic nature is not only there to advance the nation, but above all, Chinese civilization, which in turn strengthens the nation. That Chinese pragmatism combines all systems of governance because they all have advantages and disadvantages. The intended result partly determines which governance system is best suited to a situation. That's why I sometimes find it strange that the West is scared that China wants to export its system, values, and culture to the West, when we don't even understand the Chinese system and have a hard time even defining it.

ADAPTIVE CHINA

China's greatest strength is its ability to adapt. We see this clearly in the world of business. It's what we call being agile. Chinese companies are very capable of constantly adapting to a new environment, regulation, competitor, or opportunity. This is mainly due to the constant change that is inherent in China, but also to the enormous amount of competition among the Chinese. From an early age, Chinese children are taught by their parents to be better, faster, more cunning, or smarter than their classmates. When it comes to doing business, the Chinese have to fight to survive.

Every Chinese person learns to adapt to new rules in order to survive. In the West, we prefer to adjust the rules so that we survive together. The Chinese see their system and way of thinking as guidelines for dealing with change. We see our system and way of thinking much more as fixed values in society that we need to follow. For the West, those values are absolute. For China, they are much more relative. Relative in the sense that the context determines which values are more important, not in the sense that they wouldn't be closely followed. The CPC shows the Chinese which system of governance or thought system is best suited for each situation. In Chapter 3, we saw how Chinese business leaders can easily switch between four different leadership styles depending on the situation. The CPC and the Chinese government do the same. They adapt to move the country forward. After 1949 this was mainly ideological, after 1978 mainly economic, and since 2013 under Xi Jinping mainly social.

China's system today has become a real Chinese feast in which many different dishes—or systems—are placed on the rotating table. Everyone wants to turn the table to find their favorite dish, but the CPC indicates the direction and preferences. What doesn't work well is if we use our Western perspective to look at China's system as if it is a Western menu. If we do that, we put three dishes on the menu: the ideology of Marxism, economic pragmatism, and Confucian traditionalism. Worse still, we feel that those three dishes definitely don't go well together, and in fact mostly compete with our system. We only look at those three dishes, not at all the many other options on the table. We see China's system as against our principles of equality, freedom, democracy, civil rights, human rights, and international cooperation, although even in the three major systems we associate with China we can find an equivalent for our Western values: Marxism promotes equality and civil rights, economic pragmatism certainly doesn't want to limit individual freedoms and international cooperation, and Confucianism preaches more democracy and human kindness. The conclusion could be that China selects the way of thinking that works best in any situation—that's more of a Western mindset that assumes the control of the CPC. Another conclusion could be that China's system is so diverse that it can adapt to almost any situation—that's much more of a Chinese mindset based on the fact that the CPC scans the environment before changing anything. The assumption we put forward determines our trust in China and the CPC.

EVOLUTIONARY CHINA

We must view China as a system in continuous transition. Let's not forget the Chinese saying that, in China, change is the only constant. The same is true for the CPC and the system. This is much less visible to us because we see little difference in the political leanings within the CPC, and their internal deliberations are hidden from us. In the West, on the other hand, we seem to prefer a cadence of opinions, with elections bringing about a possible change of power at least every four to five years. The surprising thing is that, despite this regular changing of the guard, the system changes less quickly for the people in the West than it does for the people in China. Even the Western media constantly reports on how China is always issuing new rules and laws.

Another reason we don't notice that China's system is constantly changing is that we see our system as being the end goal that China should be aiming for, which simply is not the case. If China doesn't evolve in our direction, then we think China simply isn't evolving, but rather stagnating. We then observe the delay in China working in exactly the same way as we do in the West—from market access to transparency—and, if China doesn't reform quickly enough according to the international model, fail to see any evolution. China's system could therefore be better placed in a non-linear evolution from traditionalism, to socialism, then economic pragmatism (capitalism), and with the ultimate goal of achieving communism. The older the system, the deeper the roots are embedded in the system. The mistake we can make here is to think that state property (under communism) is completely separate from private property or private initiative. The two are actually related to each other, like yin and yang. They depend on and blend into each other.

This evolutionary economic system of governance can be seen as a long transition after centuries of empires without much private property for the average citizen among the landowners, to a more socialist state-driven system under Mao, to Xi's state-capitalist system today where private and state-owned property is being merged under the administration of the CPC. This system is now looking for the ultimate Chinese communist dream—what the Chinese call a *datong* society (great unity)—the last phase of their evolution expected to be reached before the year 2121. According to and thanks to the CPC, through its earlier modern evolutions, China already reached the penultimate *xiaokang* phase (a moderately prosperous society) in 2021: an economically, politically, culturally, socially, and ecologically prosperous country. The terms *xiaokang* and *datong* are 2,000 years old. *Xiaokang* is the penultimate stage on the path to utopia—*datong*. According to the ancient writings in one of the five Chinese classic texts, the *Book of Rites* (liji礼记),[105] *datong* will be reached when everything under the sun is for the common good. An egalitarian world without borders, unnecessary suffering, crime, or waste, where everyone is safe and being looked after.

This great unity or *datong* shows us that the CPC is still pursuing communist ideals.[106] Because China opened the floodgates even wider to the world at the start of this century, China's current economic growth is already being much more impacted by China's private sector than its public sector. As a result, the CPC is left with a reality where privatized capitalism triumphs and the idea of pure communism is more of an aspiration. This is why we call China "communist," while China calls itself "socialist." The CPC still sees China's current system as imperfect, unequal, selfish, and lacking in public character. In the coming years and decades, the CPC will therefore focus on the humane aspects of society, which is certainly not a common phrase in the rhetoric of the West to describe China. If we want to get a better understanding of China's ideologies, we can take an evolutionary view of three areas—traditionalism, (state) capitalism, and communism. "Traditionalism" provides the CPC with a nostalgic reference that they can learn from. "Chinese-style socialism" is the reality of the CPC that can be enjoyed today. "Communism" embodies the ideal of great unity to aim for. The CPC keeps the country's nostalgia alive, is pragmatic in its approach, balancing capitalism and state control, and feeding the population with propaganda about an even better future. The CPC is therefore mainly concerned with solving China's very real social problems, and much less with ideological battles. This reminds me of the very wise turtle Master Oogway from the film *Kung Fu Panda*: "Yesterday is history, tomorrow is a mystery, but today is a gift. That is why it is called the present." Chinese citizens are therefore not bothered by nice old Chinese stories or the CPC's hollow propaganda slogans about the future. It's like a prologue and conclusion to a book, but not the true content or depth of China. The challenge for the West is to read not just the introduction and conclusion, but to dive deep into the story itself. But most of us just read the back cover and the negative reviews. We urgently need to break down these walls.

CHINESE WALLS

Gates and walls have long been part of the Chinese urban landscape. Cities had outer walls for defense and inner walls that divided them into districts, which in turn were divided into sectors, each sector containing a number of agricultural plots and buildings. This architecture of China reveals a lot about how the Chinese construct their lives. In the West, we see a lot of open residential buildings, while in China, traditional architecture is more enclosed or private. Although closed communities can also be found in the uptown neighborhoods of the United States or Europe, a fence or wall is more of a protection or shield against the outside world. In China, the walls are instead designed to make the best use of the open space within the walls as something unique to that community. The closest comparison for us in the West is the modern concept of cohousing, where different families with the same values and intentions share a housing complex. The objective is not to protect themselves from the outside world, but rather to enrich their own world and make it much more sustainable. It promotes comfort and a sense of belonging. We do this in the West mainly because the cost of living in the cities has become unaffordable, but in China it dates back to the ancient history. It later reappeared in the Mao-era "work unit," or *danwei*, and more recently in the urban layout of the apartment building complexes in modern China.

The term **dānwèi** (单位) took on a negative connotation in the West during the era of Mao's communist China. The Maoist *danwei* were therefore mistakenly seen as a method of control for the state to organize urban society, monitor political loyalty, and limit the mobility of workers—who had little chance of being able to work in another *danwei* without permission granted in their personal files. This all sounds restrictive, but the Chinese were living in a time of few economic opportunities to improve their lives, and in a purely planned economy where loyalty to the Party was the norm. If you live in Bentonville, Arkansas, in the United States, there is also a very good chance that you work for Walmart, with no union to defend you, and your whole life is indirectly yet heavily influenced by the Walton family, who you are faithful to because you have almost no other choice. It's not exactly the same, but the feeling and happiness that the Chinese employees felt working for a Chinese *danwei* would not have been all that different. So, the *danwei* became a small society within a society. You can see it either as people being locked up or as a really close-knit community. I want to focus on the second interpretation, and how the social function of the *danwei* has created a socio-cultural fabric that has brought about so much solidarity in today's China.

Unity and solidarity are China's most undervalued qualities. They can be seen on a national state level, but also in everything that used to fall under the *danwei*: company, colleagues, family, friends, and community. The *danwei* mixed together all the activities of a worker and his entire family. The *danwei* gave a Chinese person a permanent job and a decent pension later on, and for the whole family: a house, medical care, education, and subsidies for transport and food. The *danwei* was also responsible for the political and social well-being of its inhabitants, as well as having a say (as it still often does today) in private matters such as health, marriage, reproduction, family, relationships, studying abroad, etc. We see this outside of China too, in highly closed religious communities where the rabbi, imam, priest, guru, or chieftain takes care of their subjects by listening to them and giving them wise advice.

At that time, almost all housing units in the cities were managed by a *danwei*. You had different forms: corporate *danwei* that were later often privatized; the non-profit *danwei* for education, research, sports, health, or culture; and administrative *danwei* that we know as trade unions and women's federations.[107] In the mid-1990s, there were still more than 200 million Chinese people who, thanks to the "iron rice bowl" system, had a fairly secure future by working for a Chinese *danwei*. But then the *danwei* work units collapsed. This was partly due to the privatization of many inefficient state-owned enterprises that provided the housing, the land reforms of the 1980s, and partly the modernization in the 1990s, which broke down the communist-era monopolies and created a private housing market. The safety of the *danwei* walls made way for private homes that were in sudden high demand in China. Land was dirt cheap, which led developers and local governments to start China's building frenzy. This created a real estate market in China in which almost all new urban homes that were built were again built within a wall or fence. Back then, every Chinese person wanted to buy a house or apartment in one of the many apartment or housing complexes that had recently shot up.

The new wall suddenly embodied a new meaning of "private property" in contrast to the "public property" of the Chinese state or the *danwei* of earlier times. The wall also served as a way to escape public scrutiny or to keep different classes apart, and it reflected the Chinese mentality of a society in a gradual transition from collectivist to more market-driven individualism. So, the wall was a constant between the rigid organization under the *danwei* and a whole new individualistic and open consumer world. Due to the urbanization frenzy in China from 1990 to 2010, the number of people living in cities doubled from 26.4 percent to 49.7 percent of the entire population.[108]

The concept of community, as previously familiar under the *danwei*, was therefore reintroduced in the 1990s in response to the new challenges of the anonymous city. To preserve the stability of the country and the Party, among other things, a "committee of residents"[109] now took over the welfare of the *danwei* for the whole neighborhood or building complex. The residents of these new walled neighborhoods and complexes saw these communities, which were highly focused on themselves, as part of the urban infrastructure of their past, and not as an invasion of their privacy, despite the link between these neighborhood committees and the CPC, a party that prioritizes social stability and security, and that—thanks to the walls and neighborhood committees—had a convenient infrastructure to achieve its goal. You can see this as being about social control or as social involvement and security, but it contains all those things. One thing is certain: during the COVID-19 lockdown at the start of 2020, this infrastructure ensured that all Chinese people stayed within their own walls. On the one hand, these residents were monitored by their committees, but on the other hand, they also received a lot of help for practical things like grocery shopping, getting medication, and even mental support.

We rarely see this human, solidarity-driven side to China, but it helps explain how they were able to suppress the pandemic so quickly. The government didn't force companies to mass-produce masks, or farmers to donate products to Wuhan, or send nurses and doctors to the affected area as volunteers; nor did they ask local residents to look after the children of parents who were in hospital. What was also very noticeable was that the very first people to do their bit were the CPC party members.

The question that arises is whether the social fabric, which is of course built by putting up walls around certain communities, makes the solidarity of a nation stronger or weaker. The Chinese really are stronger together, supporting each other through the bad days, and sharing the enjoyment of the good days. The Chinese became volunteers during the pandemic. They did that mainly because it is honorable, gaining them the respect of society and their immediate social environment—family, friends, neighborhood, tribes, the CPC. It gave them "face" points. In the West, we saw this solidarity and contribution much more in terms of a personal conviction, an individual responsibility, or sometimes a feeling of guilt. It often starts from an individual who really wants to do something good, regardless of whether they are directly involved in or personally connected to those in need. We call it empathy. We are happy to cry at a distance; the Chinese prefer to dry someone's tears themselves.

NOT EVERYONE HAS BEEN LIFTED UP

China's expanding middle class has grown in confidence in recent years; but the social and economic inequality between the Chinese urban residents and migrants living in the cities from all over the country is now also suddenly in the spotlight after decades of economic growth. While cities such as Beijing, Shanghai, Guangzhou, and Shenzhen (BSGS) symbolize China's economic miracle, the real miracle is not the newly wealthy people living in the cities, but the 730 million people who were lifted out of extreme poverty over a period of twenty-five years.[110] It is precisely these people who built the cities and got the factories going. Today, and for the first time in history, extreme poverty (an income of around $2 a day) has been officially eradicated in China.[111] But by the end of 2020, 600 million Chinese people were still living on around $5 a day. Since China is now considered an upper-middle-income country, the poverty line should be $5 a day.[112] Under this definition, a third of all Chinese people are still living in extreme poverty. This rises to more than eighty percent if we use the US poverty line of $35 a day, which is a better comparison in terms of GDP figures.[113] So you could argue that the CPC is using the eradication of extreme poverty as a propaganda stunt, since it is comparing China to Third World countries. But we also cannot deny that more than 800 million people used to live below that lowest poverty line, and now they don't. In addition, there are 150 million Chinese migrants who still work around the clock in cities today, with an average monthly income of $520 ($16 a day). As low-income earners, they are among the lucky ones,[114] even though they pay a huge social price: more than half of them left their families behind to go in search of a better life. There was plenty of work, but the real struggle for them was to socially integrate into a new, unknown city.

The main reason for this social integration problem is not just poverty or the class division, but China's discriminatory registration system, known as **hùkǒu** (户口). This system was introduced in 1958 to register every family, and in 1985 everyone was given a personal identity card. The main function of the *hukou* is to control internal migration between the rural areas and the cities in order to maintain the basic social safety-net and stability of the country. Had the government not introduced this system, the rural exodus would have been much greater and faster, and the BSGS cities would not have been able to cope with the influx of migrants from rural areas. At the same time, the very strict classification by the government of all Chinese people into two classes did increase social inequality. After the founding of the People's Republic, this classification was introduced to grant all farmers the right to work a piece of land, while people living in the cities had no right to land. The farmers also had no other rights outside their district. When urbanization in China exploded, this dual classification became especially challenging for the rural migrants who were working in the cities. Many migrants do not want to give up their rural *hukou* as they want to keep their land and if possible, rent it out. Under the current rules, rural residents are allowed to travel to the big cities for work, but in the city they have no right to education, healthcare, social benefits, or many public services for themselves and their children. As a migrant worker it actually almost feels like you're living illegally in your own country. The *hukou* system has also been used by major cities to attract good laborers by giving them an urban *hukou*. Since 2014, the law has been relaxed and has even disappeared in smaller cities and municipalities. Despite this, today up to sixty-five percent of migrants in the major cities continue to wander around without a local *hukou* or legal access to essential services.

China's urbanization rate has increased from twenty percent in 1980 to sixty-three percent in 2020, and the larger cities have grown into megacities with ten to twenty-five million inhabitants. In some of these cities, half of the local population do not have any local social rights. Although these migrants often share the same language, culture, national identity, and ethnicity as those from the city, they are often still discriminated against, and they are described as **xiàrén** (下人), Chinese for "servant," a pejorative associated with theft, poverty, and a lack of education.[115] This situation would be enough to make Mao Zedong turn in his grave. This is also part of the imbalanced and incomplete image the world has of China. A lot of people got rich, but at least as many got left behind. When people talk enthusiastically about China's wealth, businesses, and innovation, the comeback from the West is often that the BSGS cities are not the real China, and that China still only has twenty-five percent of the GDP per capita of the United States. Let's just imagine for a moment that we split China into two. Then the middle-class urban *hukou* residents in the east of the country would have as much purchasing power as the Americans, while the lower-income classes in the west of China would be as poor as those in Bangladesh. This is of course hypothetical, but it illustrates the importance of population size.

The best way to look at China is two regions with one government. One region has a standard of living equal to Europe or America, and the other is yet to be lifted out of extreme poverty by the CPC. Half of China's population is the size of Europe and twice the size of the United States. The Gini coefficient, which measures inequality, is now 0.465, compared to 0.3 in 1980.[116] The higher the number, the greater the inequality—and levels above 0.4 are considered to represent a social problem and risk. The United States has a Gini coefficient of 0.48, while many European social-democratic welfare states are under 0.3. In the words of Confucius: "In a country well governed, poverty is something to be ashamed of. In a country badly governed, wealth is something to be ashamed of."

A WOLF, A SHEEP, AND A CABBAGE

This large wealth gap does not fit with the ideal of a Confucian-communist government that wants to be inclusive for all citizens. This reality has given China and the CPC a reputation for being heartless, irresponsible, and selfish in the minds of some observers. There are plenty of stories that illustrate this: farmers moved to make way for a mega dam or highway, workers who were exploited by competition or for profit, fatal work accidents because safety or quality was not important, the elderly who lost everything because the law didn't protect them, mental exhaustion or addiction because of the pressure of overworking. China's extremely pragmatic system has fueled this growing inequality and has been obviously described as inhumane. It's puzzling why a system that prioritizes equality and inclusivity leaves so many people out in the cold. But it makes a lot more sense if you know the "river crossing riddle." In this traditional tale, a farmer has to cross the river in his boat with a wolf, a sheep, and a cabbage. But the boat can only carry the farmer and one item at the same time, otherwise it will sink. You can't leave the wolf and the sheep on the same side, nor the sheep and the cabbage. The farmer is the CPC, the boat its resources, and the river the barrier to the other side which represents greater wealth, comparable to the West. The Chinese solution to this riddle is to take the sheep—the poor people—over first to get the factories going and build the cities: they built China. Then the farmer—the CPC—crosses the river again to take the wolf—the entrepreneurs and their employees—to the other side. They made China rich: the new middle class. But then the farmer has to go back to the other side with the sheep, because he cannot leave the wolf alone with the sheep. In doing so, he protects the sheep—the period of improving social legislation at the start of this century. But the wolf is left alone. This was also the period of increased corruption, profit-seeking, and growing inequality at the start of this century. Then the farmer leaves the sheep alone for a while and takes the cabbage—the rules for the rich and companies—to the other side. This is the phase we're in now. In the final phase, the farmer has to cross the river again to go and get the sheep and bring it permanently to a better life on the other side.

Because when we look at China today, we see the CPC, the middle class, and the rules on the same side of the river, but with another 600 million Chinese people still stranded in relative poverty on the other bank, we conclude that the CPC wants to focus its power on the rich—and limit capitalism. But actually, the CPC is busy getting all Chinese people to the other side. And to do that, from now on the rich will have to live with much stricter rules. China's system is more inclusive than people think, but to achieve that, exclusivity is needed first. China is also much more equal than people think, because in addition to income, there is also social equality: the equality of opportunities and access to services. All forms of inclusivity, including financial ones, are Xi Jinping's top priority today. China is now trying to achieve income redistribution through lower and differential tax rates, financial aid, and a lot of investment in the poorer regions. For the left-behind population, healthcare and education will get more attention and pensions and social security will improve, including by ending the *hukou* system in cities with fewer than three million inhabitants. This is how Beijing aims to widen the middle-income group across the country. The trend is that high-income groups will be more tightly regulated and taxed on real estate and capital gains. It is expected that China will do this very pragmatically and step by step. And this change is not just being initiated by Beijing, but also widely supported by a majority of the population. Change in China does not often happen through confrontational actions, as is often the case in the West, but by first creating constructive social support. The Chinese term for this is **jiànzhì** (建制), or "organizational system," a system that is constantly changing in an organized way. It is much more about influence than power.

In my view, the idea that China is not free because the Chinese government constantly exerts its power against the will of the people is a half-truth. Not only do Chinese citizens often think the government's decisions are justified, and are therefore happy to follow them, but the government also tries, like a physiotherapist, to look for their pain points in order to avoid as much tension as possible later on. The Chinese, therefore, believe that their country is the most self-regulating political order in the world. They see citizens in democratic countries only briefly having control and power every four years, and then having to give it back to the politicians. They don't necessarily see our system as a better form of democratic participation by citizens. They often view the changes in Western policy as sometimes being very abrupt, as with Trump, or as simply stagnant, as with the European Union. In China, when the CPC decides something, the change seems to happen quick, but the Chinese also see the extensive preparations that happen sometimes over years beforehand, something which is much less visible to us. Not all policy from China is about secret agendas, and progress is often prioritized over control. In Chinese there is a saying: "Trees you move die; people who move survive."[117] I interpret this as meaning: you really don't want to rip out the roots of the Chinese system that provides the fruits, but people can adapt to changes in the system to produce even healthier fruits later on. Change brings life.

爱

ài

Meaning: **love, like, be fond of, cherish, take care of, be suitable for, affection.**
The ancient character is built up of a symbol of a person holding a heart. It symbolizes the love you have for someone who you want to protect. Good leaders should
love and protect all the Chinese as if they were family.

6.

Trust China. Why should we trust a regime that violates human rights? Isn't Hong Kong proof that China can't be trusted? Is China going back to being more nationalistic, totalitarian, and closed? Is the Communist Party restricting private businesses again? Does Beijing want to knock the US dollar off its throne?

Nation and people

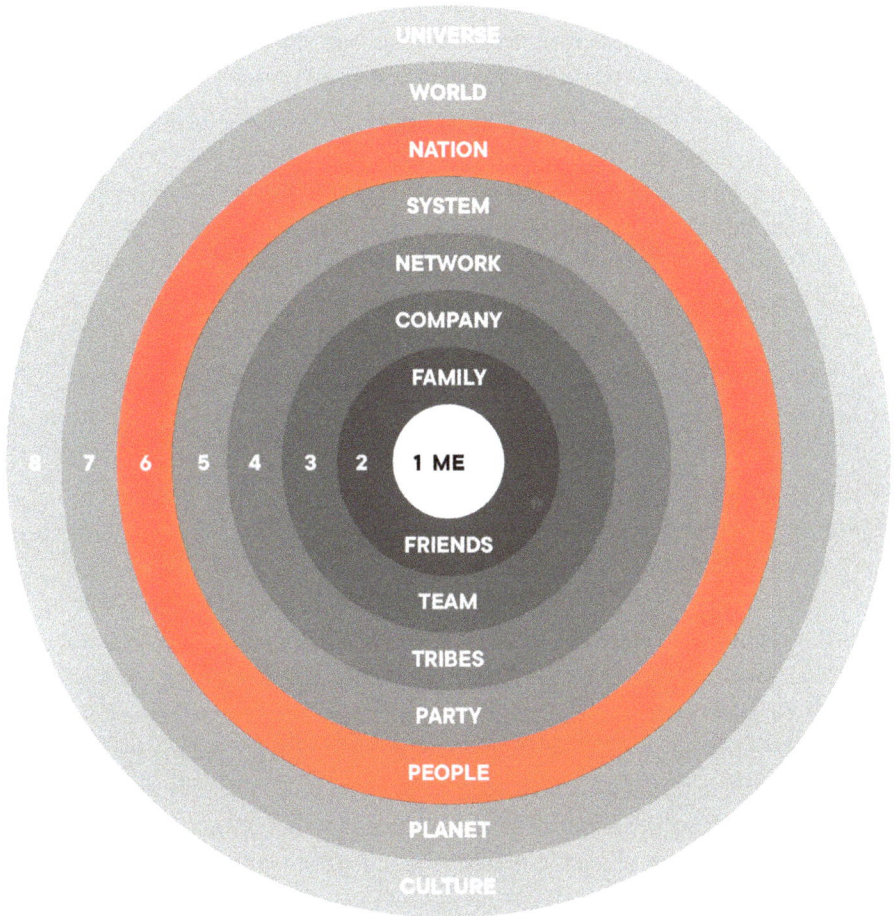

UNIVERSE
WORLD
NATION
SYSTEM
NETWORK
COMPANY
FAMILY
1 ME
FRIENDS
TEAM
TRIBES
PARTY
PEOPLE
PLANET
CULTURE

8 7 6 5 4 3 2 1 ME

TWO UYGHURS SAVED MY LIFE

On my first trip through China in 1991, I was a real tourist and visited all the most famous sights. I went to Hong Kong, Guangzhou, Shanghai, Hangzhou, Suzhou, Luoyang, Beijing, Tianjin, Datong, Xi'an, Chengdu, Guilin, and Wuhan. I stepped inside more temples during that trip than all the churches I have visited in Europe, took more sleeper trains, and photographed more landscapes than any time before or since.

In 1993, for my second trip, I thought I would slow down a bit, taking more time to get to know the culture and the people. I bought a one-way plane ticket to China and wanted to come back to Europe overland, following the Silk Road. I planned to start in Xi'an, the original capital of China where the terracotta army of the first emperor of China was discovered. My first stop was Dunhuang, to visit the astounding cave temples at the edge of the Gobi Desert. When people ask me what's the most impressive thing I've ever seen in China, I always say the caves near Dunhuang. They house the largest collection of Buddhist art in China with well over 1,000 Buddha statues. This 1,700-year-old site served as a gateway to Buddhism along the Silk Road, reflecting the meeting of cultures between China and India, stretching all the way to Europe. I really couldn't imagine a better place to start my adventure. From Dunhuang, I bought a bus ticket to Turpan in China's autonomous region of Xinjiang and then took the bus further west to Kashgar, the last major city in Xinjiang before the Pakistani border—and the heart of Turkestan, according to the Uyghurs. The Uyghurs are a Turkic ethnic group native to the Xinjiang Uyghur autonomous region northwest of China originating from and culturally affiliated with the general region of Central and East Asia. The bus journey lasted three days and two nights and passed through one of the most inhospitable desert areas in the world. Soon after leaving Turpan, I didn't feel so good, and my stomach was starting to make strange noises. At our first stop in a small village it soon became clear that I had a severe case of diarrhea. What now? Hot Chinese tea wasn't a good idea, but besides Coca-Cola, Sprite, and Fanta, there was nothing hygienic to drink at all—not even any bottled water. Back then in China, people usually drank water hot for hygienic reasons as tap water was unsafe. Obviously, there wasn't any alcohol either in these Muslim villages. As I don't like sugar, the lack of options for hydration was a big problem for me. In fact, I have a hereditary fructose intolerance, which means my body is missing an enzyme it needs to break down fructose. This genetic abnormality is called HFI, and it can even kill you if you eat fructose regularly. I really didn't want to take that risk, so the alternative was to drink as little as possible. However, that was a very bad idea in this endless Taklamakan desert with temperatures up to 104 degrees Fahrenheit combined with the bumpy ride. I've never felt so bad. But the worst was yet to come. The bus ran into engine trouble a few hours from our destination, Kashgar. The driver pulled out his screwdrivers and everyone had to get off the bus—even the chickens and goats.

At this point, I was completely dehydrated and really sick. After two hours I really thought I was going to die in the desert, so I stopped the next car that passed. Two Uyghurs with long beards got out, and immediately saw that I needed urgent help. They gave me a lift to the hospital in Kashgar where I stayed on an IV drip for two days. So, I will always be grateful to the Uyghurs for their help and how well they took care of me. Once I was back on my feet, I was able to fully enjoy the region and the local culture. My portraits[118] of this Turkic people, the Uyghurs, are some of the most beautiful I made in China. What struck me, aside from the men with long goatees, women in robes, and children playing in the street, was that there was a different energy in the air compared to the China of the Han Chinese. I immediately recognized it from the Turkish neighborhoods in my own hometown of Ghent, where the Turks, after four generations, are the largest and most integrated migrant community. They are hospitable, polite, uncomplaining, enterprising, and respectful. But when you drive through these Turkish neighborhoods in Ghent, you still notice that even in winter they prefer to be outside with their Turkish friends than inside, that they rarely pay any attention to the traffic rules, and that they are a strongly macho-patriarchal nationalist society. I sensed this familiar cultural atmosphere during my stay in Kashgar. While the Han Chinese tend to give a more reactive, accommodating impression, many of the Uyghurs in Kashgar seemed to have more of an active, impulsive Turkish spirit.

DO WE WANT TO SAVE THE UYGHURS?

The western region where the Uyghurs live was annexed to China in 1754.[119] In 1884, during the Qing dynasty, it was given the status of province; the name Xinjiang means "new border." Ancient Chinese writings tell us that 2,000 years ago, during the Han dynasty, the Chinese emperor protected the region with a system of officials, garrisons, and decrees as part of China's national sovereignty. This means that many Chinese see Xinjiang as a region that the Qing dynasty recaptured, not conquered. On this basis, China therefore sees Xinjiang as an inseparable part of its territory. Since the twentieth century, separatist Uyghurs have called the region East Turkestan. Any attempt at militant separatism is considered terrorism by China. After the fall of the Soviet Union in 1991, and the independence of Uzbekistan, Kazakhstan, Tajikistan, and Kyrgyzstan, tensions started to escalate in the region. In 1992, the region's first terrorist bombings took place at a hotel in Kashgar and on a public bus in Xinjiang's capital Urumqi. During my 1993 trip, I couldn't fail to notice the most horrific billboard images of the victims of these terrorist attacks at every entrance to train stations all over the country. Even back then, China was clearly fearful of the militant Uyghurs, a negative image that was spread as propaganda to scare the entire Chinese population. Let's be clear about it: many Han Chinese do not see the Uyghurs as real Chinese people. Try renting an apartment in Beijing as a Uyghur, and you'll get the same reaction the Roma or Bulgarians get in Western Europe. After the 9/11 terrorist attacks, the United States and the United Nations also declared militant Uyghurs a terrorist group linked to Al-Qaida. As a result, the United States locked up twenty-two Uyghur fighters captured in Afghanistan at Guantanamo Bay. China has always viewed and justified its actions in Xinjiang as counterterrorism or deradicalization. At that time, the West hadn't yet set its attention to what occurred in Xinjiang as it was too busy fighting terrorism elsewhere.

However, after 2007, acts of terrorism escalated very quickly in Xinjiang, and so did China's counter-repression, which then fueled the terrorism again. There haven't been any further attacks in Xinjiang since 2017. However, this success in stopping terror attacks strongly suggests that China must have taken a very repressive approach, given that the West has been trying and failing to stabilize the Middle East for over twenty years. China claims this success is due to investment, proactive integration, and raising awareness, and denies it is because of repression, genocide, or indoctrination of the local people. China is convinced that it had the right approach to tackle the root causes of radicalization. Now that US troops have left Afghanistan, perhaps we will soon find out which approach works best, as China will increase its investments in the country and intends to help the Afghan government with materials, humanitarian aid, weapons, and technology to fight terrorism in order to restabilize the region. China has every interest in this, because Beijing fears that terrorists in Afghanistan are supporting the East Turkestan Islamic Movement (ETIM) in Xinjiang. When the Trump administration decided in 2020 to no longer class the ETIM as a terrorist organization, the world suddenly started to see China's counter-terror activities as ethnic persecution and violations of human rights. The allegations against China depicted the unwillingly locking up of large groups of innocent people. Instead of fighting the global war on terror together with the West, China suddenly got portrayed as the bad guy, and the United States as the judge. Since that time, Western institutions, the media, and experts have targeted China's repressive regime in Xinjiang, writing about "genocide," "forced sterilization," "re-education camps," and "forced labor." We're familiar with these stories, and they affect us very deeply.

China's human rights issue is certainly not made up; but the scope and scale of the violations being blamed on China today are horror stories that have also taken on a life of their own. China has denied many of the allegations, provided information that they are false, and unraveled some of the Western lies about Xinjiang through embassies, the media, and experts.[120] Either we are not aware of these elements of proof, or we don't believe them. As a result, we are tangled up in a hyper-emotional geopolitical relationship where the Uyghurs have become plaything or pawns to show that the other side is lying. Other sensitive topics like Tibet, Hong Kong, Taiwan, or the South China Sea relate more to power. The topic of Xinjiang is mostly about lies. Anyone who dares to question the veracity of reports about human rights abuses in Xinjiang is quickly regarded in the West as a supporter of China's totalitarian regime. Similarly, anyone outside China who doesn't openly admit that the West is lying about Xinjiang is generally seen by the Chinese as a lying Western imperialist. The problem with this emotional deadlock is that we are no longer debating with China the most important issue of how to improve the lives of Uyghurs in Xinjiang. Instead, both sides are abusing their own closed narrative to reinforce anti-China or anti-Western attitudes. This leads to increasing racism in the West against Chinese and Asians, and as a reaction, an even stronger nationalism in China against the West. It increases our mistrust of China when the conversation should be about the Uyghurs.

If we really want to help the Uyghurs, then we need to move away from the highly toxic narrative about Xinjiang and also look at the positive changes in the region to get a more nuanced picture of the future of the people there. But to do this, we first need to recognize that the Uyghurs have become a political football caught up in the geopolitical tensions between China and the West. Why did the United States simply remove a known terrorist group from its terrorist list? At the same time, why is it so difficult for Uyghurs to get asylum in the US? Surely, we could also be exposed to more positive reports about conditions for the Uyghurs in Xinjiang, which has achieved a seventy percent automation level within the cotton-picking industry, more employment than ever, and a literacy rate of 99.91 percent. The Uyghurs have been lifted out of extreme poverty, have on average twenty-five percent more children than the Han Chinese, a higher GDP growth than the rest of China, the region has become a tourist magnet for all Chinese people, and have received a large investment from Beijing to further promote local ethnic cultures. This type of news isn't reaching us in the West. It is not about having to close our eyes to cases of repression in Xinjiang, but to have a balanced view by keeping our eyes open to examples of China's humanity toward minorities. We must dare to discuss China's response to Xinjiang openly and honestly. If China can produce evidence that ninety percent of the horror stories about the Uyghurs are made up by the West, then you can argue that even if only ten percent of the facts are true, it is still a humanitarian crisis, and rightly so. But you can also ask yourself: if even half of it were made up, isn't this a tragedy for the West that places so much value on morality? This research doesn't get any coverage in the Western press. Western companies should continue to invest in Xinjiang in order to give the Uyghurs work, instead of turning their backs on the region. This is also a matter of principle. We must avoid turning every discussion about China into one about human rights, because we don't do this with the United States. Every time we talk about the US, why don't we point to the drone strikes on civilians in Afghanistan, the police brutality or the number of African Americans in jail? Whenever we talk about Europe, why don't we refer to the inhumane treatment of migrants in the Mediterranean Sea? We need to think in a solution-oriented spirit, and not a reductionist way. I believe this is the only way we can really help the Uyghurs. And it will take a lot of courage.

When it comes to the Taliban, China thinks pragmatically and based on the belief that economic prosperity works against radicalization. Although the European Union takes the same approach in some countries (mainly former colonies), it seems to be increasingly favoring sanctions in others (as against Iran), but these actually promote radicalization. By doing this, the West is actually perpetuating an unstable world order that gives it quite a lot of power, but sometimes with wafer-thin moral authority. I believe that if we change the focus of the dialogue about the Uyghurs to a more positive narrative about the evolution of the entire region, China will also be more transparent in showing us the facts we are looking for. Not everything is black and white in China, and neither is this the case in Xinjiang. Since there has been extensive world-wide focus on Xinjiang, there has been indirect positive change. The average Chinese person has started to appreciate and support the Uyghurs more. But at the same time, they have started to appreciate and believe the West less, which was certainly not the goal.

We have probably forgotten that, less than thirty years ago, around half of all Chinese people were living in even more basic and inhumane conditions and often working for terrible bosses. Back then, you could say that China was actually violating individual human rights across the country even more, compared to our Western standards. This is very different today, especially in cities such as Shanghai or Shenzhen. The poorest provinces in Western China, such as Xinjiang, were only able to start developing after 2013, partly thanks to one of the main objectives of the Belt & Road Initiative: the revival of the New Silk Road, which would enhance the strategic importance of the cities in Western China and boost their economic growth. We can cautiously trust that if China achieves the same economic development in Xinjiang as they have in the cities in East China, the Uyghurs may have a much better quality of life than even we do in thirty years' time. This may seem strange, but it wouldn't be China's first miracle in creating wealth for millions of vulnerable citizens. This all sounds great, but of course does not justify why Uyghurs would have been forced to follow an extensive integration process in a confined center against their will.

NATIONAL HEROES

With a treasure house of more than 5,000 years of stories and legends, China has many more heroes than we can imagine. The Chinese grow up with historical heroes from ancient novels, including four masterpieces we can read to gain an appreciation for Chinese culture: *Journey to the West*, *Water Margin*, *Romance of the Three Kingdoms*, and *Dream of the Red Chamber*.[121] The most influential of these is *Journey to the West*, which tells a story set in the Tang dynasty (618-907) over one hundred chapters. A monkey and its master, a monk, travel through Western China—present-day Xinjiang—to India in search for Buddhist enlightenment. The monkey is funny and smart and able to skillfully get himself out of any stressful situation on his search. It's a story that reveals the complexities and paradoxes of Chinese culture: how an untrustworthy rascal mischievously goes in search of higher morals, how the three influences—Buddhism, Taoism, and Confucianism—are different paths one can take in life, how the continued loyalty of the subject and the compassion of the master is more important than any mistrust between them, and finally how life is a constant trial of danger and suffering, but also a colorful existence of amusement and magic. The heroes in these novels are also the heroes of Chinese operas that help parents teach their children about the cultural and moral values of China.

Beyond widespread awareness of Walt Disney's portrayal of Mulan, we in the West don't know the stories of General Yue Fei, the monk Ji Gong, or the orphan Han Xin. They are all brave warriors, similar to the heroes we know in the West, but they are mainly remembered as symbols of loyalty, respect, kindness, slyness, rebellion or eccentricity, altruism, tolerance, and magic. The national heroes of China are not only physically strong, but also have a mentally strong character and are highly adaptable. These stories are often about liberation. And so it is in this light that the Chinese view the modern heroes of China: Mao Zedong liberated the population from inequality, Deng Xiaoping liberated the people from poverty, and Xi Jinping liberates the Chinese from the shadow of the West. We don't see the earlier Chinese leaders as heroes, but rather as criminals who held the people back, rather than pushed them forward. The Chinese are familiar with our narratives, but they listen much less, or sometimes not at all, to the West's negative interpretations of China's story. The Communist Party and many Chinese people generally see the liberation as more important than the pain it caused. A way for us to understand this contradiction is our own behavior when we root for the hero-protagonist of a Hollywood survival movie, regardless of the havoc they're creating. *Yippee Ki Yay* and all that.[122]

There are three major types of tension between the West and China: economic, ideological, and military. Before 2015, economic tension predominated.

The world had had enough of Chinese copycat behavior, state subsidies, and disrespecting international trade agreements. Some companies, like Huawei, were accused of all three sins. Huawei had stolen the intellectual property of its American competitor Cisco and others, then received huge state subsidies to help them beat their international competitors. Meanwhile, Western telecom suppliers in China weren't being given the promised full access to the Chinese market. This was unfair competition. China, on the other hand, called Huawei the "national champion" of China, as it had conquered the world through its Chinese vigor, innovative strength, and extreme efficiency. For the Chinese, Huawei had worked its way up from an inferior Chinese distributor of foreign technology to a world leader in just twenty-five years. Against all expectations, it turned out that it was possible to break through the West's monopoly on technology. Huawei became a potent symbol. For the West, a symbol of unfair Chinese competition and nationalism; for China, a symbol of innovative modern China and patriotism.

We could have an endless discussion about how innovative Huawei's patents really were, whether they made groundbreaking inventions that changed the world, or whether Huawei would ever have become a world leader without the support of the Communist Party. But in reality, you can't become the world leader in 5G telecommunications just by copying others, can you? Doesn't the world see that Huawei's worldwide army of 90,000 engineers are a huge army driving real innovation? Would Trump have turned up the heat on Huawei quite so high if the company really wasn't a threat to American innovation? The Chinese know the answer: Huawei's rebellious history proved to be the only way it could break free from the West's control of intellectual property in China. Playing the game according to the rules (which had been set by the West) seemed fair to the industrialized West of the last century because we wanted to protect our innovations and investments, but many Chinese people felt it gave the West an unfair advantage. This is something we don't consider enough. We designed international intellectual property laws to protect developers, but the Chinese saw it as a way for the rich West to hold developing countries back. Today it is different because China itself has become innovative. The Chinese are convinced that, since 2015, China has broken the glass ceiling of innovation that the West put in place. Since then we have seen one innovation after another from China, including inventions in quantum physics, speed tunnels, or nuclear fusion. China really doesn't need to copy us anymore, and their inventions will now be used against us via the international, or rather Western, intellectual property system. If the West keeps focusing on China's copycat risks rather than China's innovative competitiveness, we are in for a surprise. This is no problem for the Chinese, as it means they can stay under the radar for years.

ONE COUNTRY, TWO SYSTEMS

While Barack Obama put China on the military radar screen, Donald Trump put the country on the ideological radar. The verbal attacks on China and the Communist Party by the United States have further fueled nationalism in China. When Trump came to power, it was no longer just about which rules to follow and getting China to comply with the international order; but about which system was the best, and who was the strongest. America's storyline since 2017 has been about changing China's system, and that was a bridge too far for China. The problem is not that China necessarily thinks it has the best system of government or doesn't want to learn from its mistakes, but that in 2018 the United States suddenly launched an attack on the country's right to exist in terms of the ideology of the Communist Party and on sovereignty in terms of the military strength of the nation. China is very sensitive to this attack because it had to fight for those rights for 2,000 years; and it was thanks to the Communist Party that China managed to break free from the hundred-year (1842-1949) oppression of the West and Japan.

This history has taught China to be vigilant about how it guards the nation's borders. If you visit the Chinese cities known for their art, you can admire beautiful buildings in many European styles as a testament to the country's semi-colonial European history—and although many in China value the fantastic heritage of the buildings in those former concessions, they are at the same time an unpleasant reminder of the past. The country still hasn't forgotten the 1937 Nanjing Massacre perpetrated by the Japanese army. The return of Hong Kong, Macao, and Taiwan to the mainland are the last three pieces of the puzzle to make China's territory complete. Only then will China have fully recovered its honor and sovereignty. From our Western perspective, we see China guarding and using the military to defend the nation at all costs. But in fact, what China really wants to do is preserve its cultural identity, and that requires boundaries. It is also in this light that we should look at the escalation around the opposing "Summit for Democracy"[123] in the fall of 2021. In this new great game, Washington is promoting the liberal model of democracy and China is counter-attacking an alternative version. China is different from European countries, where the state and the nation form a single political unit: a nation state.[124] According to China expert Martin Jacques, we should therefore see China not as a nation state, but as a civilization state.[125] I support that view. For 2,000 years, China has had a Han culture that in terms of area is almost as large as where most of the Chinese live today: East and Central China. After the last dynasty collapsed, China became a nation state only in 1912, and therefore as a nation state it is still quite young. The reason China values its sovereignty so highly has less to do with the Communist Party and political system than with China's culture and deep identity as a civilization.

In the previous chapter, I described how China doesn't have a uniform system either, but that it is constantly evolving over time.

What irritates China is less the attack on its political system than the attack on its right to self-determination. This is also the reason Hong Kong was, in agreement with the British, peacefully united with the motherland in 1997, with a promise from China's leadership that they would maintain a two-system country for fifty years. China says it doesn't want to get rid of the current democratic system, but steadily reunite the Chinese population in Hong Kong with the rest of the country. I don't know of any other country that has done this before while keeping two systems in place during the transition. South and North Korea would be the most obvious parallel if they reunite in the future, but that would not only level the socio-economic differences between these two countries, but above all greatly weaken the military and political power of the United States and Japan in the region, which doesn't seem like a real option given the emerging power of China. It is an understatement to say that in recent years this Hong Kong experiment has turned out differently than both parties believed it would. The West complains that China is not honoring the joint agreements and sees this again as proof that Beijing cannot be trusted. For China, allowing two systems, which are increasingly polarizing, to live side by side is proof of Beijing's self-control. The West mainly looks at the differences—the changes and the growing power of Beijing—while China mainly looks at the similarities—the merging of the same cultural roots and the economic future for Hong Kong within an even greater China. The West doesn't trust in a Chinese future for Hong Kong, whereas the mainland Chinese see it as a missed opportunity for Hong Kong if they don't merge more closely with the motherland, and most Chinese don't understand how the Hong Kongers can ungratefully bite the hand that feeds them, a place that benefits because China funnels its world trade through Hong Kong. The West sees the protesting Hong Kongers as pro-democracy freedom fighters; China sees them as intolerant rioters. We support the protests as an ideological struggle; China sees Hong Kong's real problem as more of a socio-economic one, which was created by the British and Hong Kong's tycoons, and not by Beijing. The Chinese view the rioters in Hong Kong as arrogant, while Hong Kongers tend to look down on the mainland Chinese. It isn't hard for us to identify with the liberal values of the residents of this British ex-colony. Since 2020, my Western friends have been asking me how we can trust China when we see how little restraint Beijing shows in its treatment of Hong Kong. Hong Kong has become another example in the West that Beijing and the CPC cannot be trusted.

But my Chinese friends ask me how the West can be so blind to the fact that Hong Kong is really just a plaything. They go on to say that the West used the rebels in a geopolitical anti-China struggle by turning the media against both the Hong Kong police and the pro-Beijing officials, showing the true face of the West. Hong Kong has become proof to the Chinese that the West cannot be trusted. They also feel that Hong Kongers are so influenced by Western values that they have even started to destroy their own city. This is why China has decided to just slowly continue to integrate Hong Kong, without further ado. China will no longer put the safety of the nation and Hong Kong at risk for the sake of an ideological struggle. Many wealthy Chinese people have built up so many economic interests in Hong Kong in recent decades that they cannot afford to let the city burn. Meanwhile, the West has largely lost and given up on the struggle for a pro-democratic Hong Kong, leaving the Hong Kongers to take care of themselves. One reason for this is that you can't win a battle when the other side is fighting a very different war. I would like to give another example, just to illustrate. We are well aware of the position of anti-vaxxers in the West. They don't trust the vaccine, the politicians, or the pharmaceutical giants behind it. Pro-vaxxers believe that this small group is a serious threat to the safety of the entire population. Pro-vaxxers and anti-vaxxers both fail to get each other to change their minds. It's tearing families apart, but the majority just don't want to get into that fight with the anti-vaxxers and aren't listening to them, because *their* fight is against the virus—not the ideology of a few skeptics. I am certainly not saying that Beijing is right, and even less that our democracy is a virus, but that the Chinese are behaving like pro-vaxxers who have full confidence in their own system, compared to a few million Hong Kongers who are behaving more like anti-vaxxers. They may one day be right, but today they are fighting a truly hopeless battle against a nation of 1.4 billion people who don't want to be put at risk, and a central government that obviously wants to avoid the anti-Beijing views of Hong Kong spreading to the north.

In 2049, the island of Macao, right next to Hong Kong and known for its casinos, will be fully reunited with the mainland after a "grace period" of fifty years. Until then, Macao also has a "one country, two systems" agreement with Beijing similar to Hong Kong. The difference with Hong Kong is that after the handover in 1999, Macao was already much closer to China culturally, politically, emotionally, and in terms of poverty. It has more easily accepted Beijing's sovereignty and has better prepared for that transition. Macao saw China as crucial to its economic growth through Chinese tourism, investment, and inclusion in the plans for the Great Bay of the Pearl River Delta. From a socio-economic point of view, Macao has also greatly improved since 1999, while this is a different story for Hong Kong. For Beijing, this is proof that the "one country, two systems" concept can work. The irony of the situation is that Beijing exerts much less control over Macao than Hong Kong, because the people of Macao demand their individual rights far less stridently than they do in Hong Kong and are also less interested in politics—like the mainland Chinese. Portugal, which leased Macao from the Chinese Empire in 1557 and ruled it as a full-fledged colony after 1887, is also much less reactionary toward Beijing than the United Kingdom when it comes to its position on integration. This makes the Chinese think that Britain's true goal is not really to help the Hong Kongers, but to help its closest ally, the United States, in their geopolitical battle with Beijing. Macao is thirty-nine times smaller than Hong Kong and as much as 1,276 times smaller than Taiwan, so it is not really comparable. Hong Kong also had a larger middle class in 1997 that, under British influence, was very keen on democratic rights and freedoms. During the protests in Hong Kong, the "I am a Hong Konger" campaign made it very clear that Hong Kongers do not identify with the mainland Chinese.

Hidden away is the answer to why China sees "one country, two systems" as workable, but Hong Kongers and many Taiwanese no longer consider it feasible. China considers all the "Chinese" from Hong Kong and Taiwan as part of its cultural heritage, and now wants to reclaim and help them in the same way it does the rest of the mainland. But many residents of Hong Kong and Taiwan see it differently. They don't see themselves as "Chinese" at all, although ethnically they are. In any case, they don't want to be "helped" by Beijing. Meanwhile, many of the Chinese from the mainland do not understand why they are so rebellious, since they (would) get more rights than the well-behaved mainlanders. The pragmatic Chinese also don't quite understand why the "Hong Kongers" don't see the support and progress that Beijing wants to give them as something positive. This has little to do with a lack of empathy, and more to do with their belief that Beijing has given them a better and safer life. It is the same dual issue of cultural (non-)involvement and economic (dis) integration that pops up in any territorial dispute between China and its neighboring countries or border regions, and that causes a lot of misunderstanding and tension. The Chinese project their own goal toward a progressively more stable, more prosperous, and improving social environment for themselves and their families as the universal values and goal of all inhabitants of Greater China. What they don't always understand so well is that some people consider values such as greater freedom of opinion or increased democratic participation as more important than China's basic fundamental values.

The question many Chinese are asking is why the West calls its own model "democratic," as the success of that system is measured on the basis of following procedures and agreements, and not really on the basis of results. If a state is economically stagnant, with its citizens falling into poverty or inequality and having little social upward mobility, what is the value of that "democracy"?[126] The mistake we make here is to assume that it is only liberal societies that can be democratic. China's model is not "liberal" but the government still considers itself "democratic" because the model is judged on the basis of progress and results for the people, not on the basis of following institutional agreements. At the end of 2021, Xi Jinping told Joe Biden, "Democracy is not mass produced with a uniform model or configuration for countries around the world. Whether a country is democratic or not should be left to its own people to decide. Dismissing forms of democracy that are different from one's own is in itself undemocratic."[127] The idea that it is only liberalism that can lead to a full-fledged democracy is one cause of ideological tension between China and the world, which are very visible in China's border regions. China has the longest land border in the world: 13,742 miles—that's half the world's circumference—and has its hands full with a lot of disputes over territory and autonomy[128]. In China itself, this is mainly in Xinjiang, Tibet, and to a lesser extent in Inner Mongolia. Along international borders, there are disputes with Northern India, Nepal, Bhutan, Laos, and Myanmar. At sea, it is with almost all countries in North and Southeast Asia, as well as China's officially rebellious province of Taiwan.

Each of these disputes has a similar double narrative, with a polarizing point of view from a China or non-China standpoint: the Western storyline of Chinese repression against a minority within China's borders and Chinese aggression with a neighboring country at the border, versus the Chinese storyline of integration into Chinese civilization within its borders and protection of China from an attacking neighboring country. In today's geopolitical atmosphere, the Western version of China as an "aggressor" or the Chinese version of China as a "defender" determines the trust someone places in China. The real crisis is that we do less in-depth journalistic research about China and as a result greatly simplify the complexity of the situation in China. The opinion of the Chinese and facts from China count less than the position we take; it is a crisis of confidence fueled by the stories of China's emerging power or sovereignty. More books will be written about this than problems will be solved. What we can reflect on in the West is why, when reading about each of these border conflicts, we keep labeling China as the bad guy. By definition, every border conflict has two sides. These reports also usually tell us about China's totalitarian regime, about human rights violations, its desire for power, or about its undemocratic character. My advice, when China's oppressions are being negatively categorized, is to also look at China's neighboring countries and their human rights situation, corruption, and regimes. This is not to downplay China's actions, but to look at things in a broader context.

Due to this one-sided coverage that rarely addresses the problems in those neighboring countries, few Chinese people believe that the West really wants to help the people in China's conflict regions or solve problems together. That may explain why the Chinese feel that the West, and mainly the United States, has a clear geopolitical agenda to intervene in China's sovereignty. Xi Jinping told Biden in late 2021 that China would be happy to talk in a mutually respectful way about human rights, but that China is not in favor of using the topic of "human rights" to intervene in the internal affairs of other countries. After all, the United States has provided China with a whole range of past examples of how it has even overthrown regimes without ever solving the local problem. You really can't blame Beijing for being cautious of the imperialism and military power of the United States.

A POWERFUL AND PROUD NATION

The harsh reality that the West now faces is that the introduction of neoliberal democratic doctrines to the rest of the world has largely failed. Typically, this introduction came after military intervention by the United States and its allies, or through an internal national revolution fueled by Western social media or interference from Western intelligence agencies. I remember clearly how on the night of January 17, 1991, the United States and its allies launched Operation Desert Storm in Iraq. Like reality TV, we could watch the advanced military organization and firepower from our own living rooms: electronic warfare, GPS-guided precision bombing, anti-missile systems, stealth jets, unmanned aerial vehicles; clearly, Saddam Hussein didn't stand a chance. The way a powerful country like Iraq was driven out of Kuwait in less than four days and how the Iraqi army—at the time, the world's fourth largest—was wiped out in forty-two days was a demonstration of the West's well-developed military strength. The Gulf War, partly due to the fall of the Soviet Union in 1991, was the green light for the West to bring chaos, unrest, and war to the Middle East for thirty years. And in doing so, it carried on the United Kingdom's nineteenth-century tradition.

In Beijing, however, alarm bells were going off, and it suddenly became very clear how the Chinese People's Liberation Army had fallen decades behind in terms of its military strategies, army structure, and weapons. China has been a nuclear power since the 1960s, but a nuclear war with China would be self-destructive and therefore highly unlikely. If in 1991 the West had invaded China, perhaps the war wouldn't have lasted much longer than it did in Iraq, even despite China's size being twenty-two times larger.[129] The national security panic was quickly funneled into a modernization program to bring China's massive military to the high standards of the powerful US Army. The size of the Chinese People's Liberation Army has been reduced by a million soldiers over the past thirty years, while the budget increased by more than ten percent annually to reach $209 billion in 2021. Today, China has the world's second largest defense budget, after the United States with $754 billion in 2021. Given that China hasn't started a single war in that thirty-year period, you could argue that a quarter of the American defense budget is just as efficient. If you think about the $6.4 trillion that America has spent on the wars in the Middle East since 2001, then you can quickly calculate that their enormous defense budget is also relative. China's current defense capabilities may not yet be completely equal to that of the United States, but we can no longer talk about a generation gap or a difference in scale.

In recent years, the world has become quite concerned about how China will use its renewed military power given that the country will become the world's largest economic power sometime this decade. We worry about how China is militarizing the islands in the South China Sea, how it's established its first-ever naval base in the Horn of Africa (Djibouti), or how China might forcibly annex its rebellious province of Taiwan. These concerns are well founded. Certainly, if we draw conclusions based on our own history: in fact, no power in history has ever become a global power without war, invasion, colonization, and bloodshed. Not one empire: except China. In addition, China is the only nation to have grown more rapidly than any power in the past, and without invading a single country since the Sino-Vietnamese border war in 1978 (which China more commonly refers to as a defensive counter-attack against Vietnam). This growth achievement without foreign offensive is unprecedented, and also underappreciated. China speaks with pride about the harmonious and peaceful rise of the country. Do we not trust China's military rise because we're now scared that China starts to look like us? We could equally deduce that China's military rise is the direct response to their national vulnerability in light of American warmongering. It is a fact that China has become a much stronger military power, but the strange fact that China has not used its new muscles—except for in its own backyard in the China Sea and the Taiwan Strait—shows some level of self-restraint, doesn't it? Our fixation on a potentially imperialist China means that we mainly see signs of hostility and warnings that we should prepare for a possible world war with China. Perhaps we can learn something from how China restrains and controls itself in times of geopolitical confrontations with Western powers?

But today, even China's patience is slowly running out. In late 2019, Chinese Foreign Minister Wang Yi had made it clear that Chinese diplomats needed to be more assertive and outspoken to defend the interests of Beijing and the Communist Party against criticism. Any country or politician who falsely accused China would now get full retaliation. All those "recipients" of United States aggression also became China's friends—from Russia to Venezuela—who strengthened this echo and shared positive information about China with the world. In the past, China has always been very sensitive to criticism about its reputation, but it now sincerely believes that in recent years the Western media has portrayed China incorrectly, in a one-sided and deliberately polarizing way. The BBC or the *New York Times* are shining examples of independent, decent journalism, but when it comes to the Chinese CGTN or the English-language Chinese newspaper the *Global Times*, it is pointed out that their reports are made up, and the Chinese media is portrayed as pure state propaganda or tabloid press. When Beijing issues tougher financial, anti-monopoly, or data privacy rules and fines its tech giants, in the Western media we read about the power struggle of an evil Communist Party or Xi Jinping against Western capitalism. When Washington or Brussels tightens corporate rules, it is described as necessary to protect consumers or banks. When Trump shouts "America first," it is seen by some as the pride of an entire nation. "Buy Chinese," on the other hand, is described as Chinese protectionism. Americans are patriots, while the Chinese are nationalistic. This fairly common double talk is what China calls the "Western double standards." After reading thousands of news articles about China, I have come to the conclusion that this double talk is so well established in our media that very few Western journalists think about how polarizing our language and perspective on China has become.[130]

While their intention to inform the world about the potential dangers of and problems with China and the Communist Party may be good, their reporting fuels nationalism in China, and because it confirms our image of a new global power, it fuels the warmongering in the West. I fear that if the United States were to invade China tomorrow, not many people in the West would protest. That's how far it's come. The more often we attack China without first looking in the mirror ourselves, the more the Chinese evolve from true patriots into the strongest of nationalists. We claim that it is the increasing power of the Communist Party that has led to this trend, but I am more concerned about the Western media encouraging this development. The English writer George Orwell, who is famous for being against totalitarianism, wrote: "By 'patriotism' I mean devotion to a particular place and a particular way of life, which one believes to be the best in the world but has no wish to force upon other people. Patriotism is of its nature defensive, both militarily and culturally. Nationalism, on the other hand, is inseparable from the desire for power. The abiding purpose of every nationalist is to secure more power and more prestige, not for himself but for the nation or other unit in which he has chosen to sink his own individuality."[131] We cannot deny that, in this context, China and the Chinese are much more patriotic than nationalistic, especially compared to the United States and the Americans. For many of the Chinese, their love for their homeland has grown even stronger in recent years. But it's too easy to see this patriotic pride as dangerous to the world or internal to China. To confirm this danger, Western commentators point, for example, to growing tensions with China's neighbors and in the South China Sea, wolf warrior diplomacy, ethnic conflicts, protectionism toward foreign companies, or the anti-Western attitude of the Chinese on social media.

Although Chinese national pride is definitely increasing, we should look beyond the purely negative connotations of nationalism, such as cultural arrogance, economic protectionism, political desire for power, or military expansionism. While increasing nationalism has become a global trend in recent years, in China it has been driven less by power or superiority and more by China's recent success and newfound confidence. Ever since I first went to China in 1991 and later having lived there for a long time, my own observation is that in the early years Chinese people looked up to the West and had more faith in the West, even than in themselves. Although Chinese culture is 5,000 years old, in those years conversations with Chinese friends were not about their glorious past, but about their promising future. Patriotism links the worthiness of citizens to that of their nation, and until 2008 China saw the West mainly as something to emulate and aim for rather than compete against. The only country that the Chinese have consistently showed negative "nationalist" behavior toward is Japan—due to the humiliation of the Chinese people during the Sino-Japanese War in 1894-95, the deeper trauma after 1937 due to the Rape of Nanjing, and the invasion during the Second World War. China still blames Japan for honoring their own war dead as heroes—including war criminals—and not apologizing for their past wrongdoings against the Chinese. This runs very deep and is also communicated in this way by the Communist Party, but even more so by parents to their children.

But beyond this Japan example, I rarely observed the Chinese feeling superior towards other nations—until China started creating its own international tech giants. The earliest example I remember of this phenomenon was when Lenovo bought out IBM's laptop business in 2005. Especially after 2008, China had more examples of successful "Made in China" brands, from Huawei to Alibaba, which were definitely no longer inferior to their Western competitors. In 2015, China announced its national ambition to become the world leader in innovation by 2030. Given the success China had experienced in growth, wealth, innovation, and governance, this goal suddenly seemed achievable. After 2015, and for the first time in China, a real connection was created between their own performance and their position in the world. This link gave the Chinese a sense that they could take on the world, which led to more national prestige—and therefore also patriotism. Since Trump's presidency, the United States in particular sees China as its biggest competitor, and that has only fueled China's confidence in itself as a strong nation. The less the West trusts China, the more self-confident China seems to become. From a Confucian mindset, China mainly wants to regain the respected status it had before 1840. Now that they are getting less respect from the West, they are mainly searching for it beyond the West—from the other six billion people on our planet. But what we really can't reverse today is that the Chinese want to use their newfound patriotism as a driver for China's further growth, regardless of the tension that this will cause in the West.

The big difference between the type of nationalism that we in the West describe as dangerous and what is happening now in China is that China's version of nationalism, or rather patriotism, wasn't born out of misery, discontent, or powerlessness, but out of the country's recent success, hope, and influence. The Chinese are therefore more patriotic than nationalistic, since they mainly want to protect their better future and ancient civilization. It is not really about them wanting to export it to other countries. They've fought and worked hard for nearly 200 years to get back to a place of dignity, so it is unlikely they will risk all that with a war beyond their borders. The only possible exception to this is Taiwan and the area in the South China Sea, areas China considers part of its national borders or territory. Almost all countries in the world and the United Nations accept that there is only "one China." In the past, Taipei and Beijing had a different idea about the legitimate owner of that "one China" label. The current government in Taipei is now also challenging the "one China" principle by rejecting the reunification, increasing tensions with Beijing. Beijing sees the island of Taiwan as part of the People's Republic of China, the last bastion of China's "nationalists" who lost the civil war to the Communist Party of China in 1949. In contrast, the older politicians of the Republic of China (ROC, Taiwan) still view the People's Republic as an illegitimate state that currently occupies the whole of mainland China and has its citizens in its grip. This is one of the many geopolitical aftershocks that took place after the Second World War, just like South and North Korea or West and East Berlin, where the same ethnic population was torn apart by the Soviet Union and American allies. Taiwan was a Japanese colony for fifty years before WWII. When Japan lost the war in 1945, the United States returned Taiwan to China, which at the time was under the leadership of Chiang Kai-shek, the leader of China's nationalist party of the "Republic of China." Legally, Taiwan was then recognized as part of the mainland under the name of "the Republic of China" (ROC). The same name later referred only to Taiwan when the territory of mainland China was renamed the "People's Republic of China" In 1949. This is why Beijing has always legally seen the government of Taiwan as an insurgent government occupying part of the national territory. In 1949, Chiang Kai-shek fled with his followers to Taiwan when they were expelled by the "Communist bandits" led by Mao Zedong. Chiang Kai-shek and his son Chiang Ching-kuo[132] were for a long time under the illusion that they would eventually recapture mainland China, restoring China to the territory it held during the Qing dynasty.

This is the background to how Taiwan has slowly become one of the most ambiguous "nations" in the world. The irony is that during the Cold War with the Soviet Union in the early 1970s, the United States wanted to attract Beijing over to their side, first by adopting the "one China" principle and later, in 1979, by accepting the People's Republic of China (Beijing) as the only legal government of that "one China." Taiwan has not been a member of the United Nations since 1971 and is today recognized by only fifteen countries, the Vatican City being the most important,[133] which have no diplomatic ties to Beijing. The island of Taiwan exists in a stalemate, with military takeover of the mainland clearly no longer an easy option. Although international support for Taiwan to fully declare its independence is getting stronger in the United States, but also in Lithuania, for example, there is not one major power making this position explicit because it could spark a direct war between Taipei and Beijing. A prolonged status quo or diplomatic reuniting under the leadership of Beijing is therefore the only peaceful way out, but the difficult reunification of Hong Kong with the mainland is now making this prospect of the latter even less attractive for most Taiwanese. Furthermore, until 2005, the Chinese People's Liberation Army simply didn't have the military capability to conquer Taiwan. Today, there is a lot of speculation that Beijing will invade the island in the next few years because it is highly unlikely that the United States will dare to use its military power against nuclear mainland China to defend Taiwan. If Beijing were to attack the island and the United States didn't intervene, then the United States would lose another ideological battle with communism, but also its credibility with its allies as defender of the world. If the United States *were* to intervene, however, it would lead to countless American, Taiwanese, and Chinese casualties in another war that cannot be won. An impossible choice. However, Beijing has never specified a timeline for this reunification; China's time horizon could be 100 years, although many believe 2049 will be a date to watch closely. Beijing has no problem living with this paradoxical situation. As long as Taiwan doesn't formally declare independence or cause a military incident, I don't think China will endanger its 1.4 billion people by rashly trying to take back the island. Xi Jinping is also certainly waiting to see the outcome of what happens between Russia and Ukraine. Given that relations between Russia and China are the best they have ever been, the outcome of a possible invasion of Ukraine could be a good prediction for China of how the world and the US in particular would respond to a Chinese invasion of Taiwan.

My prediction is that Taiwan will one day be reunited with China, but the right moment and strategy seem to depend more and more on external factors and reactions from the West. The West maintaining its "one China" position toward Taiwan buys Beijing some more time. It is no coincidence that at the end of 2021, Xi Jinping again explicitly made Biden's "one China" position China's most important bilateral issue with America. Xi himself said that if America were to support Taiwan's independence, it would be playing with fire, and that those who play with fire get burnt. Of course, an accidental military incident in the Taiwan Strait or the South China Sea cannot be ruled out. I am confident that neither Beijing nor Washington will intentionally do anything for the time being, but that doesn't mean nothing will happen. What this recent escalation does show is that Beijing is prepared to defend its homeland at all costs. What that means for all of us is that there are two mistakes that we should no longer be making if we want to stay friends with China and the Chinese: claiming that Taiwan is a separate country or nation; and showing a map of China without the nine-dash line of the Chinese territory in the South China Sea. It might be an innocent mistake, but you'll regret it if a few patriotic internet users in China spot it. In fact, these small errors could do a lot of damage to your reputation and business in China. Many of the Chinese will interpret this mistake as anti-China, or as internet users in China say, "the internet remembers"—even in China. We've been warned.

TRUST IS GOOD, CONTROL IS BETTER

This decade will be marked by a totally new era of high confidence emanating from China. Over the past four decades, the priority has been growth, growth, and more growth: the economy, infrastructure, property, digital economy, international, military, talent, security—everything has been about quantity. More of everything, and as quickly as possible. And China has been successful—with a growth per inhabitant that was fifteen times greater than for a Westerner. But this unlimited growth ambition has allowed far too many weeds to grow—abuse of power, corruption, monopolies, scams, fraud, theft, financial and mental stress, environmental pollution, decadence, social injustice, addictions, inequality; sometimes it seemed China had become an overgrown garden where you could no longer see the flowers between all the weeds. The international community living in China felt the same, as the lack of rules or constantly changing requirements made it difficult for them to find a path through the Chinese Garden of Eden. In the same breath, China was called a country without a rule of law that doesn't play fair, and a country that is protectionist, unethical, unreliable, and corrupt. We have always assumed that this was what China wanted, and that it created these conditions so it could exploit or extort Western companies. I'm not convinced; for me, we were just easier victims than the Chinese themselves. We have become addicted to cheap products from China and to the growth opportunities in the gigantic Chinese market. The global market demand and the boards of directors of Fortune 500 companies fully supported these strategies. China's highly unregulated market was the perfect place for experimenting, offered a lot of growth opportunities, and it still delivered decent quality at prices that were just too good to pass up. For access to this market our Western multinationals paid millions of dollars, shared technology, and sometimes even compromised our values.

In fact, for nearly forty years China was like a big playground for Western investors and managers. The Chinese also liked to play in their domestic market, but they weren't yet as idealistic or as addicted as we were. They understood that China's large growth market is a more of a challenge and a danger, than simply being an opportunity. They were therefore more pragmatic and less strategic—or gullible—than we were. A bird in the hand is worth two in the bush. We looked at a sky of opportunities, they collected every win, searching for every new customer, every new deal, and every new opportunity. And if you are looking for every opportunity in a country of 1.4 billion people, you'll naturally also come across a lot of weeds. As a result of all those weeds the Chinese started to trust each other even less. Of course, this refers mainly to Chinese people who don't know each other, because those who do know each other will trust each other, just like we do in the West. As the Chinese became more suspicious, they were more likely to rely on the advice of their friends and family to make purchasing decisions. With society evolving so quickly, regulations simply couldn't keep up with the speed of change. Especially after the introduction of the 3G infrastructure in 2008, China saw rapid growth in homegrown technology companies not subject to the regulations imposed on the industry in the West. Powerful monopolies such as Alibaba or Tencent emerged in this period. Far more dangerous, however, were the many dubious companies, shadow banks, and loan sharks that were making a living off the hard-earned savings of decent Chinese people. When we read the reports of fraud, or experience it ourselves, the logical conclusion is that the Chinese cannot be trusted. I would argue, however, that it's time to focus our attention on the victims rather than the perpetrators. These perpetrators often live illegally, and the government—like any government—does not want to let that go unpunished, but they acted too slow. As everywhere, the perpetrators are also the small minority of the population or government. But in such a large population base, it does mean there are a lot of crafty bad guys around.

What I do find remarkable about China is that, as a result of this crisis of confidence caused by the rapid transformation of society, Chinese people go out of their way to demonstrate or prove their authenticity, honesty, and good-heartedness. I don't know of any other people who are as keen to show how sincere and trustworthy they are as the Chinese do. We can interpret this in two ways; either the Chinese have something to hide, or they are sick of being seen as untrustworthy. I also don't know of any other nation that is so emotionally involved in the search for more authenticity—in people, companies, and brands. At the same time, China is relentless in exposing fraudsters. This could be interpreted as a display of power from Beijing, but since the people themselves are craving a more honest and fair society, I interpret measures from the government as a reaction, not action. For China and the Communist Party, nothing is more important than national security and the country's stability. You could argue that Xi Jinping's greatest fear is not the West, but social unrest arising within China. If the Chinese can no longer trust each other and the system, Beijing will have an unresolvable problem. If the West doesn't trust China anymore, that's a shared problem as long as the world remains addicted to the Chinese market and products. In this light, more internal control could be seen as less of a choice and more of a necessity.

Today, China wants to evolve from quantity to quality, from growth to sustainability, from copycat to innovator, from lavish wealth to social justice, from exclusivity to inclusivity, from production to creation, from more exports to more internal growth and consumption, from dependence on the West to greater self-determination. China is serious about wanting to create a modern socialist society. This is not so different from Europe, although the model will remain distinctly Chinese. The great advantage of China is that it doesn't have to take into account the opinions of twenty-seven Member States, each with different ideas, interests, and values. There are also a lot of different opinions in China, but the governance structure is starkly different. The European Union is a supranational and intergovernmental body where the most important decisions need a qualified majority. A few Member States can block a lot. In China, the centralized government has much more decision-making power. This allows Beijing, after internal consideration, to turn on or off the switch whenever it thinks this is necessary. We saw this happen in 2020 when the listing of Ant Group on the stock exchange was suddenly stopped. Without a clear warning, the biggest IPO in history was blocked by regulators in Beijing. Everyone in the West pointed the finger at Jack Ma, who had been a little too vocal in his criticism of China's archaic financial regulations. My reading of this event is that better regulation was urgently needed in order to not derail the whole financial sector: including newly drafted legislation to protect consumers against technology companies selling financial products without protections or bank guarantees. Despite the drama and sensational headlines, Jack Ma's popular anti-regulation speech in October 2020 did not lead to Jack Ma being permanently sidelined in China. Meanwhile, Ant Group was restructured to comply with the new fintech legislation, so the IPO was postponed, not canceled. We like to think that China wants to restrict the tech giants, but Beijing needs those companies as badly as they need Beijing and the Chinese market. They both need each other.

In 2021, the Chinese government launched an unprecedented crackdown on companies in the tech industry. The reins were tightened at fintech companies, the largest internet companies were fined billions for forming monopolies, tech companies saw their applications being blocked because they weren't following data privacy rules, the bitcoin mines were closed, the for-profit after-school online education sector was banned overnight, live streaming influencers were given a code of conduct to follow, gaming was limited for young people, and companies like Tencent lost exclusive music rights. Week after week it felt like the Communist Party was unleashing its power, control, and rules aimed at reining in capitalism. It did not seem to be a coincidence that all of this took place in the year the Communist Party turned 100. And yet I believe it was a coincidence because many the new rules and restrictions were years in the making; they just all happened to be ready in 2021. For a deeper understanding of when, how, and why all the new rules came about, we need to distinguish between the four different types of new regulations China is deploying. By doing so now, China wants to diffuse the country's four biggest "time bombs" before they explode: financial bubbles, market paralysis caused by monopolies, industry-specific addictions, and privacy and data risks.

FINANCIAL BUBBLES

Financial rules in China were already tightened in response to the financial crisis of 2008, and further strengthened since 2015 due to the explosion of peer-to-peer lending and shadow banking. New rules were created and monitored by officials at the People's Bank of China, China's national bank. At the end of 2020, the PBOC shifted its aim, with fintech companies as their new target. Fintech companies like Ant Group, which offer credit, loans, or other financial products consumers would now be required to operate like banks. For example, Chinese fintechs must have a local banking license in every province where they operate, must be able to guarantee thirty percent of their loans with their own funds, and need to comply with much higher transparency requirements.

MARKET PARALYSIS CAUSED BY MONOPOLIES

China's anti-monopoly legislation has been around since the 1990s and became full-fledged legislation, similar to that in the West, in 2008. At the end of 2020, the rules were changed to also apply to internet companies listed abroad under dubious holding structures called a VIEs (variable interest entity). This rule change allowed the State Administration of Market Regulation (SAMR) to set its lawyers loose on major monopolies: Alibaba, Tencent, ByteDance, DiDi, Meituan, and others in 2021. At the time, the government had four goals: a ban on price fixing and/or selling below the cost price, a ban on abusing a monopoly position with regard to competitors, a ban on preventing small retailers from working together with competitors, and a ban on the misuse of big data against consumers through, for example, price discrimination.

INDUSTRY-SPECIFIC ADDICTIONS

Several key ministries covering various industrial sectors in China imposed new regulations to keep their sectors healthy and to remove the harmful practices and addictions from society. The crypto mining ban imposed in June 2021 was intended to ensure the much cheaper energy prices of China's poorer provinces were a benefit to local people, and not to the bitcoin data centers. Of course, China is also not a big fan of crypto, which enables tax evasion and capital flight.

The single biggest shock to Chinese stocks listed overseas occurred in 2021 when China suddenly banned people from making money from the after-school tutoring industry. In one day, the Chinese edtech industry, which worldwide investors had pumped billions into, was simply wiped out by a new law. Beijing's rationale was that these edtech champions were fueling inequalities in China because poorer children couldn't afford the private tuition fees and therefore had less chance of passing the *gaokao* exam at age eighteen. China wanted to prevent the children of wealthy parents having more opportunities in life (like in America). In Beijing's view, this industry had been hijacked by big money and greed, with no concern for the mental stress it placed on tens of millions of Chinese children, or for the great financial pressure on their parents who, as a result of these private fees, decide not to have more than one child. All these issues represent major headaches for the government, especially given demographic trends and steady decline in working age population. China's solution was to suddenly impose draconian new measures on many industries, and that set off a lot of alarm bells in the West.

In the aftermath of these sudden policy shifts, the world's perception of a controlling China, its mistrust in the Communist Party, and the fact that all Chinese companies must comply with what the Communist Party wants, have all been reconfirmed for many foreign investors and people. But for the Chinese, these developments proved that the Communist Party *can* be trusted. The government's prioritization of people over profit was applauded by many Chinese and seen as proof that China does want to build a healthy and more balanced society. So, who is actually right? The answer is simpler than it seems. Any company operating in a sector that the government sees as a cornerstone of Chinese society and social stability should assume it will have to comply with some strict rules. You have to examine the level of state interest and Beijing's involvement in each sector: health care, education, energy, space travel, telecommunications, banking, and others are "nationally sensitive" sectors where the government will always keep a close eye on any irregularities that could disrupt society. It does this by limiting the number of players in each sector and monitoring the market share of each player, so that it can maintain competition and innovation without losing control. In other sectors such as e-commerce, logistics, retail, hospitality, and services, the government is much less involved. In all these less-strategic sectors, most of the new rules are not designed to ensure a high degree of state control, but rather to keep industry and the market healthy and protect consumers, much like in the West.

If we separate these two types of government approaches, we find reasons to remain confident in the future growth of Chinese technology companies. China's actions also show how China implements its policies. For example, we can see where the lines have been drawn under the new rules for edtech companies. Companies are completely banned from teaching the school curriculum and paying school teachers, raising money, or being listed on the stock market. Beijing is turning off the tap of external money and also access to the national educational resources for edtech companies. Outside of the regular school curriculum, which prepares children for the national university entrance exam, edtech companies are allowed to continue making money from tutoring other subjects, especially if these align with the government's objectives. Examples of what is allowed include vocational training, adult education, creative education, sports training, and learning to code. China wants to make its people even smarter, but not by fueling inequality, exhaustion, or apathy. The Communist Party's avowed goal is to turn the country into a modern socialist society, so greater inclusiveness and social upward mobility for the almost 900 million lower-income people are top priorities. Programs that align with national priorities such as Ant Group's micro-loans, rural e-commerce purchases thanks to Alibaba's Taobao, or massive employment opportunities via a delivery company like Meituan or the taxi platform DiDi are generally encouraged by the government.

PRIVACY AND DATA DANGERS

Data, privacy, and cybersecurity laws only really came into effect in China starting in 2017. China was playing catch up, but suddenly accelerated the process as Chinese experts predicted that the data economy would make up more than fifty-five percent of China's economy by 2025. The Cyberspace Administration of China (CAC) and its staff of technical experts targeted all data companies to protect this important part of China's economy. Three key laws were passed to govern three different areas in this space: cybersecurity, national security, and privacy.

—— Cybersecurity

Since 2017, cybersecurity legislation requires that companies must ensure the security of data, databases, servers, data sharing, and profit from data under strict national guidelines. China wants to secure its data against intruders and subject databases to strict rules to prevent any misuse of data, which is certainly not uncommon in China.

National security

Since September 2021, the national security law was passed, mainly to protect data in China from cyber criminals. Just like the West, China realizes that the next war (except maybe a war with Taiwan) is likely to be a cyber war. All data used in China need to be hosted on Chinese servers, and Chinese companies operating abroad, such as DiDi or ByteDance (TikTok), will not be able to use data and algorithms from China beyond the borders. The main difference with similar laws in the West is that China's data security laws have a heavy national security undertone. The West is not very restrictive on how and where organizations store and secure data, making most Western nations as a consequence more vulnerable to cyberattacks. We will have to make a much more difficult choice in the future between the level of security and the freedom of data flows.

Privacy

Since November 2021, China's privacy law is actually stricter than GDPR in Europe. In fact, European GDPR legislation was in part the inspiration for the Chinese legislation, which is known as the Personal Information Protection Law (PIPL).[134] This law has a far-reaching impact on how companies collect and use data, and in the spirit of full transparency, puts the power in the hands of the user to consent what happens to their data. This will hopefully dispel the myth that the Chinese don't care about privacy. China is taking it a step further, making it mandatory to store cross-border Chinese data in local data centers inside China. This means all data that leaves the borders must first get approval from Chinese authorities, and all data collected from Chinese people by foreign companies must abide by Chinese laws. This is the big stick that Beijing is using to increase the pressure on Chinese companies like the taxi platform DiDi, China's answer to Uber, which operates internationally.

But normal business operations from foreign companies operating in China can also quickly become the target of regulatory scrutiny if Beijing thinks a foreign entity is wrongly accusing China of, for example, the forced labor of Uyghurs in Xinjiang. This is because Beijing will not hesitate to use the stricter data laws as a political weapon against the so-called "lying" companies operating in China. This places companies between a rock and a hard place. On the other hand, US companies suspected of doing business with factories that have "questionable" working conditions in Xinjiang, for example, may have to prove the innocence of these suppliers in a US court. Companies operating in China will therefore quickly find themselves stuck between Chinese and Western regulations, forcing them to choose either the Chinese or the Western market. Few of us would have predicted that China, which used to be blamed for not having any laws, will now use those new laws as a weapon to keep the West in check.

What is certainly unique and progressive about China's approach is that they see data not only as something to be protected, like we do in Europe with GDPR, but also as something that has a huge intrinsic value for the nation, like natural resources such as oil, water, or minerals. China therefore intends to divide all its data into different "intangible goods" categories, like intellectual property, and use and protect that data with proprietary rights. In concrete terms, this means that specific data will be kept completely secret, some data will be deemed secret for certain parties, and other data will be accessible publicly for everyone. China therefore sees data primarily as a way to create added value for the country. Since data is the new oil, whichever country extracts it more efficiently will benefit more. China's aim is to become the Saudi Arabia of the twenty-first century's data economy.

What if tomorrow, data from China increases in quality and value and is cheaper than data from the West? What if tomorrow, artificial intelligence algorithms become smarter at using Chinese data than American data? If this happens, we would prefer to fill up our "data" at the Chinese station. Admittedly, a station many of us still don't trust because it could damage our economic engine. Fast forward to 2025; the West may have to choose between trusting China or getting left behind.

TRUST THE MACHINES

Today, most countries have faith in the United States as the largest economy and main protector of the current world order. As such, the USD is still the world's preferred main reserve and trading currency. However, confidence in the US is slowly fading, as internal US divisions have alienated the rest of the world, as US military interventions have led to more global instability, and as new forms of digital currencies provide an alternative to the US dollar. Will China now start to challenge the US dollar hegemony?

In 2014, the Chinese government made the very bold decision to give full banking licenses to five private Chinese companies, including the three tech giants Alibaba, Baidu, and Tencent. In doing so, the most successful online payment systems, Alipay (Alibaba) and WeChat Pay (Tencent), became successful. This decision was intended to create alternatives to the rigid Chinese state-owned banks, which preferred to give loans and support to the large state-owned companies rather than the small entrepreneurs. On the surface, this seems like a very logical decision. But for a country like China that rescued itself during the 2008 economic crisis thanks to having a high level of control over the state-owned banks, and their ability to pump billions into the economy, it was actually far from logical. Beijing realized that by handing out those five banking licenses, the key state-owned banks would suddenly lose a lot of transaction income and consumption data. Over time, the Chinese government was slowly turning off the state-run banks' access to money and data.

Examples like this show the Chinese people that Beijing is putting the people's interests and China's future above the need for control by the Communist Party. Because what followed was a tsunami of digital inclusion for the entire population. Thanks to the Chinese super apps WeChat and Alipay and the 4G infrastructure that was built in 2014, every Chinese person who could afford a cheap smartphone could suddenly become part of the new digital economy. Without the vision and courage of the Communist Party, Alibaba and Tencent would never have been able to transform the country into the world's most digital consumer economy within just a few years. In 2019, more than eighty percent of the Chinese urban population was completely cashless. In the poorer and more remote areas of China, access to the digital economy has made a world of difference for hundreds of millions of people. Before this, they didn't even have a bank account, but WeChat and Alipay suddenly gave them the flexibility to start their own small business by easily being able to instantly make and receive free payments. The first Alipay and WeChat Pay digital currencies rapidly turned China into a financially inclusive country.

Even more impressive for me is that in 2014, Beijing started designing its own digital currency system. The concept is to create one central digital currency for all of China that has the same value as paper money and coins. In addition, all Chinese people and companies in China would be required to accept it as a form of cash. Beijing intends to use the token technology behind cryptocurrencies, using crypto-technology. This was another unexpected decision from Beijing, since issuing crypto coins was banned in China.

From the advent of cryptocurrencies such as bitcoin, China has been concerned they would be used to more easily funnel illegal money out of the country. Beijing has always kept strict controls on financial flows, which is why the Chinese currency has only very gradually, and under strict conditions, been made convertible with other currencies such as the dollar, euro, or yen. The Chinese currency is not freely convertible on the global market, which to a certain degree financially isolates China from the rest of the world. But the crypto token technology was particularly interesting for China in terms of a new central digital currency. The same token technology is also used in blockchain applications. However, today's blockchain design is too slow for the speed of payment transactions required in China. To give you an idea: bitcoin can handle 7,000 transactions per second, Visa 24,000 and Alipay 500,000. The new central bank digital currency (CBDC) of China, which has been in the testing phase since 2019, does use tokens as used in blockchain, but not the slower blockchain technology itself. This new Chinese currency will be launched in 2022 after seven years of research and experience with Alipay and WeChat Pay. To me, this is the secret to Beijing's efficiency: don't rush anything, but also don't wait or hesitate when it comes to key decisions. Beijing runs marathons but is training for them every day. We are still too quick to think that Xi Jinping suddenly woke up one morning with a new plan to use the CBDC as a way to overtake the West. In reality, China is not releasing this digital currency in order to knock the dollar off its throne—as the CBDC is intended to digitize the Chinese domestic economy and to optimize the efficiency of global trade with Chinese producers and buyers. CBDC is also not intended to exert more financial control over Chinese citizens, because China's existing financial structures already give them very high levels of control over money flows. The CBDC will provide users with more privacy than Alipay or WeChat Pay ever gave them. However, many people in the world believe that the Chinese CBDC is mainly an instrument of control. This is certainly not the primary motive, but it can indirectly contribute to it.

The main reasons for Beijing to launch its new central bank digital currency are to increase social inclusion in the country, make global trade more efficient, have more transparency in production and logistics, seamlessly integrate with the Industry 4.0 world, and make the Chinese currency convertible without becoming dependent on the international (read: Western) financial SWIFT system. However, few see the true potential disruption the Chinese CBDC could bring. I fear that Western bankers have gotten too comfortable with the existing international banking system and financial structures. Today, almost all money flows in world trade are in dollars, euros, or yen. The dollar remains the reserve currency of choice, and that won't change anytime soon. But exporting or importing between, for example, China and Vietnam in dollars is expensive, slow, and not very practical. There are a hundred countries in the Southern Hemisphere that are in this situation. As the export to emerging markets represented 49.5 percent of China's total export in 2021,[135] CBDC is a natural transition and fit for China's further economic integration with Africa, Asia, and South and Central Americas.

I believe the digital central bank currency (from China and other countries) could cause a lot of disruption for the world in four areas. Firstly, the CBDC can help the 1.7 billion people in the world who don't currently have a bank account.[136] Secondly, the CBDC will become an alternative to the dollar for all countries that want to reduce their dependence on the dollar. Thirdly, the CBDC can really kick-start the new Asian century, as Asia today has the largest concentration of countries planning on issuing this kind of currency. The added value for Asian countries to issue their own CBDC, in addition to the Chinese one, is that trade will be faster, cheaper, and smoother. The fourth and final disruption is the most important: the integration with Industry 4.0. A digital currency is better suited to this new digital world. This era of machines, rather than people, paying automatically is now dawning. The Internet of Things (IoT), or internet between machines, means that we will know instantly when a shipment has arrived in a port, and payments can happen automatically and instantly. Your 5G SIM card will be your new bank account for the CBDC. Thanks to smart blockchain contracts, your package can be steered through customs in just a few minutes, without any check required. Robots in a factory can produce a product seconds after you order online. Your monthly salary will now be on your phone a minute after the end of each month.

These are just a few examples. The real disruption that the central bank digital currency creates is that society can now be completely digitized—safely, quickly, and cheaply. I would argue that China has been ahead of Western countries for at least five years now when it comes to services linked to mobile payments. But comparing mobile payment systems to an integrated CBDC economy is like comparing a horse to a car. I dare to compare this disruptive moment to the moment when Henry Ford revolutionized the car industry through mass production of cheap products together with better wages for workers. We are at the beginning of a similar revolution, but it is now a digital transaction revolution, and each country will likely design its own CBDC based on its preferences and needs, whether using blockchain or not, with tokens or without, anonymously or not, centralized or decentralized. None of that matters. What matters is that China is the first major economy to set the standard for its CBDC. Just as happened in the Henry Ford example, many countries in the Southern Hemisphere are likely to follow the Chinese CBDC standard, or at least ensure they are compatible with it. Are we ready for a new world financial order with China leading the way? The answer is no. Many central bankers in the West still want to keep hold of their strong workhorse, or even have the new car of digitalization pull it along. I don't have a crystal ball, but if the success of Alipay and WeChat Pay in China is repeated with the Chinese CBDC, then by 2025 we will be in the new digital age of automatic payments that will no longer be made by humans, but by machines.

通

tōng

Meaning: **open (up), connect, communicate, exchange, expert, coherent, common.** The ancient character is built up on a horseman entering a passage. It symbolizes looking for new places together. Trust the unknown path while together seeking commonality.

7.

Crisis of confidence. Is China building a new world order? How should we deal with an assertive and aggressive China? Is China a danger to the planet, the world, and our freedom? What is China's master plan for the New Silk Road? What does China think about international rules and agreements? Can we still decouple ourselves from China?

World and planet

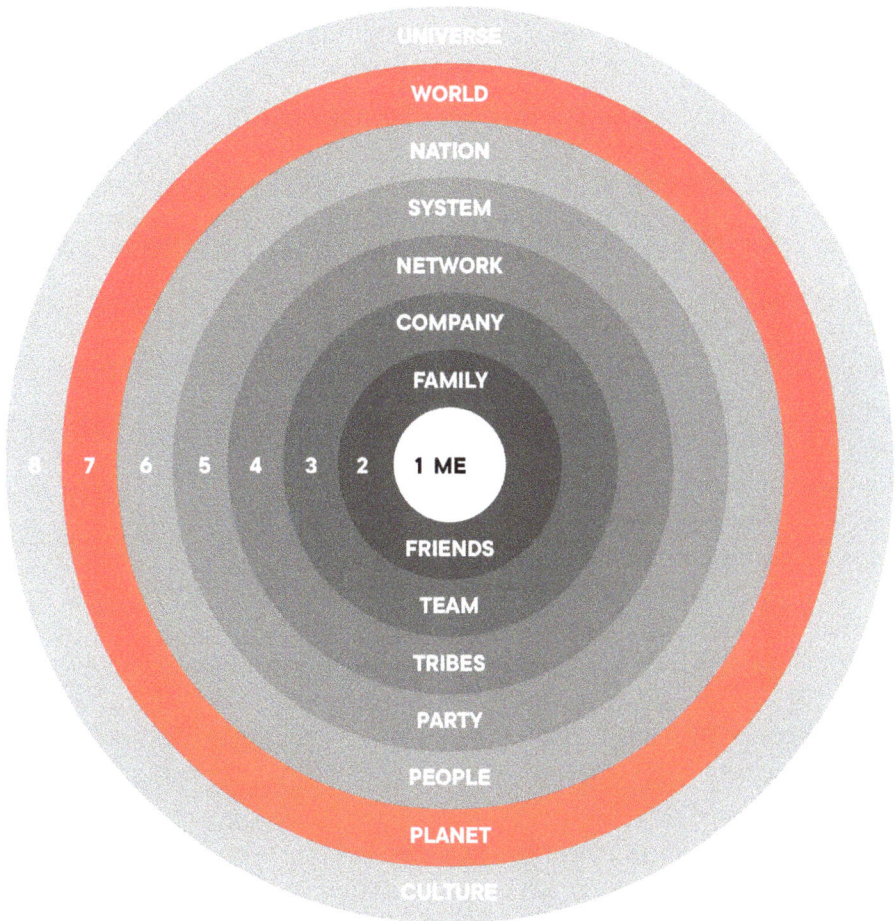

UNIVERSE
WORLD
NATION
SYSTEM
NETWORK
COMPANY
FAMILY

1 ME

FRIENDS
TEAM
TRIBES
PARTY
PEOPLE
PLANET
CULTURE

8 7 6 5 4 3 2 1 ME

LIKE A CHILD IN AN AMUSEMENT PARK

In early 1990, I took my first long-haul flight from Europe to Hong Kong. As we were descending, I looked out the window. Our plane was making its way between the hills, which were completely built up with ten-story apartment blocks. Below us, I saw a network of buildings that looked more like concrete slums. As we came in to land, we literally maneuvered between the buildings that were just a few meters below the plane's wheels. When we touched down, the pilot braked so hard he could have been an F-16 pilot landing on an aircraft carrier. This was necessary because the sea was right in front of us; the runway was far too short to land in a normal way. That was the world-famous Kai Tak airport in Kowloon Bay that closed in 1998. A good start to my China adventure.

After I'd collected my backpack, my top priority was finding an affordable place to stay. On the well-known tourist strip of Nathan Road in Tsim Sha Tsui, an Indian guy came up to me and asked if I was looking for a room. I said yes, and I followed him through a maze of side streets and an indoor market selling everything you could imagine; it was a riot of sounds, sights, and smells that I'll never forget. This place was called Chungking Mansions, known for its mix of guest house rooms, electrical stores, food stands, currency exchanges, and outlet stores. To a twenty-two-year-old, this enormous hostel-market complex with its two thousand rooms felt more like a dangerous South American prison. It was a city in itself, ready to help any backpacker like me get a Chinese visa, but you could also go there for a fake passport, drugs, and plenty of other unsavory things. I stayed there for a few days in a small room of sixty-five square feet. Some guys from Israel, Australia, and England filled the other spaces in the two bunk beds. This hostel was like the United Nations: young people from all over the world gathering in the Chungking Mansions ghetto, waiting to get their hands on a visa.

Three days and nine trips to McDonald's later, I had a ninety-day visa to China. I continued my journey heading towards Guangzhou, Shanghai, and Beijing. At Guangzhou train station, I suddenly saw a special ticket window for foreigners. That was the first time I noticed that foreigners in China were treated better than the Chinese. People providing services to us foreigners often spoke very poor English, but we would always get a seat, a welcome luxury when you'll be spending thirty-three hours on a slow train to Shanghai. At this time, for many Chinese people even a fifty-six-yuan ($9) seat on this train was unaffordable. Once on the train, I sat sandwiched between hundreds of Chinese people who kept me busy for the entire journey. Students wanted a picture with me and their parents gave me their address, asking me to visit them. Grandparents threw their grandchildren on my lap and shared their food, while the crowd of migrants looked at me for hours like I was a celebrity.

At the time, China had decided that foreigners would use a special currency not available to Chinese citizens: the foreign exchange certificate, or FEC. You could only use these FEC notes in hotels for "aliens" (i.e., foreigners) and at the only "friendship store" in every major city, which carried a higher standard of products. As China's domestic banknotes were not convertible back then, this created a parallel, convertible currency for foreign travelers. China had cleverly decided to separate foreigners from the local population. Not because they wanted our money, but because they realized we had slightly higher expectations than the average Chinese person, and also because China was ashamed of its poor people and their deprived surroundings. In the 1990s, the red carpet was rolled out for foreigners all across China. At that point in time, China trusted the world more than itself: we in the West were the shining example for China. I still remember my first business trip in the late 1990s. A professor from Beijing Polytechnic University had asked me to give a presentation about software products from the Belgian company I was representing in China. I was quite nervous because I was going to meet one of the most brilliant researchers in China, and I was just an inexperienced salesman, not an engineer with a PhD. The man was super welcoming to me. But after ten minutes of conversation in my still-poor Chinese, he took me into another room. I had expected a lab, but when the door opened, I suddenly found myself standing with him on a stage in an auditorium with 500 students and 1,000 eyes staring right at me. "Please introduce," he said, telling the audience that I was fluent in Chinese and could do the presentation in Mandarin: a baptism of fire to cure my stage fright. After my thirty-minute presentation, the applause was deafening, while I felt so ashamed that I wanted the floor to swallow me up.

In the 1990s, the Chinese looked at the Western world with the same openness, wonder, and honesty as a child in an amusement park. I felt like Santa Claus handing out candy, and I ended up selling a lot of software to that university over the next ten years. Anyone who claims that China has never trusted the West clearly didn't experience the country in the 1990s. However, China has slowly lost confidence in the West, and we bear some of the responsibility for that. For the first ten years of this century, China's faith in the Western world remained fairly constant, but then something happened that is rarely talked about. In the early twenty-first century, Chinese companies were regularly being cheated by Western business people. Foreigners boasted about how naive the Chinese were to buy unwanted or second-rate Western products, or about how they doubled the price in China and then offered fifty percent discounts. The Chinese government agencies, universities, technology companies, and the newly wealthy were so obsessive in their search for Western quality that they became an easy target for Westerners who wanted to get rich quick. Earlier, in 2003 under the leadership of then newly appointed president Hu Jintao, China started moving toward a more

Chapter 7 World and planet

scientific approach to its economic development. One result was tremendous advances in the quality of the Chinese education system, which in turn led to more and more skilled technology (STEM) graduates in China. With higher skill levels, the Chinese increasingly began to realize that Western companies weren't all equally sincere and trustworthy. At the time, as a seller of high-tech electronics from England, I noticed this growing concern from Chinese clients. In parallel, after 2008, Chinese companies started to gain a better reputation within China and worldwide. It is true to say that after the worldwide financial crisis and the Beijing Olympic Games, the Chinese gained confidence in their own country, their own politics, and the quality of their products.

After the World Expo 2010, hosted by Shanghai, larger cities in China became magnets for Westerners. It was no longer just the Western back-packers of the 1980s and 1990s, or the pioneering business people of the early 2000s, now even recent graduates saw China's big cities as a place to gain unique experiences for their resumes. These people worked as interns or English teachers or in creative sectors where China still lagged behind. At that time, I was also working in the creative industry—in event management software—and I hired dozens of young Westerners. I asked them all the same interview question: "Why are you coming to China?" And everyone gave the same answer: "China is the future." I would then ask, "Why not go to India or Africa or Vietnam?" I would say, "For Westerners arriving now in China, that ship has sailed." After digging a little deeper, it quickly became clear that they had usually not arrived because of China or the Chinese, but actually because they thought Shanghai was the next New York, a city that never sleeps and a great place to be young.

This post-2010 period gave a lot of Chinese people a whole new image of the West: as spoiled, arrogant, and lazy. This was what my Chinese neigh-bors told me after they suddenly had to share the neighborhood they'd known all their lives with newly arrived rowdy young Europeans who would whiz wildly through their streets on scooters, or even urinate in their flower pots. China's own rich kids had also suddenly become quite decadent. A Greek friend of mine had developed a nightlife app for foreigners. Wealthy Chinese twenty-somethings would show up at the door of the top nightclubs in a Ferrari or Maserati. They booked a front-row booth right by the dance floor for five to ten friends at a cost of thousands of dollars a night, includ-ing champagne and a private butler at the table. These clubs had top DJs playing every week: global music stars like Dimitri Vegas and Like Mike would easily cost them a few hundred thousand dollars in fees, but thanks to rich Chinese guests spending profligately, they still made a profit. Young Chinese didn't go to these VIP clubs at all to dance, but to give their friends and con-tacts an unforgettable evening. They were there to be seen, but only by their own social network, not by your average clubber. But a club without anyone dancing doesn't really have a good vibe. That's where my Greek friend's app came in. Any foreigner who looked hip, cool, or like a fashion model got free entry and a few drinks to specific clubs via his app. These often cash-strapped Western interns loved nothing more than to spend a night dancing to the coolest tunes between a few semi-naked models dancing suggestively from their own raised stages. Obviously, they weren't naked, because that was forbidden, but it was sometimes difficult to spot their clothes. In an instant, China was transformed from modest to decadent, at least for those who could afford it. What I found particularly striking was that rich Chinese were essentially indirectly paying the poor Westerners to dance for them, while they and their friends drank and entertained themselves lavishly in their VIP seats. I asked my Greek friend why those foreigners allowed themselves to be humiliated in front of the Chinese. His answer was that the Westerners on his app often came to the clubs to let off steam for free on the dance floor, or in search of love or lust. I can't get that image out of my head when I think about the West of tomorrow: are we becoming the actors on a stage, with the Chinese directing the play?

AN ASSERTIVE CHINA

China has become much more assertive on the global stage. We aren't really used to seeing this from Chinese politics, which previously followed the *wu-wei* principle: know when to act and when to not act. This translates into "leave the world around you largely alone," but this natural Taoist reserve and caution has become much less prominent. For years, the Chinese leadership looked so formal and characterless that we strongly suspected they had something to hide: we didn't trust their silence. Today, Chinese leaders are much more outspoken and so direct that there is no doubt about how they see the world. Our response is that now we don't trust what they say. I'm referring here to China's so-called "wolf warrior diplomacy,"[137] the confrontational attitude and language of Chinese diplomats in response to the criticism China has faced since the outbreak of the coronavirus. Because China has been known for its bland and very formal diplomats and its very cautious approach to complex geopolitical issues, we seem to have touched a Chinese nerve. China's assertive wolf warrior posture looks more like a desperate attempt by Beijing to tell the "real China story" on its own terms than a well-considered communication strategy. Chinese spokespeople discovered Twitter, so now, almost copying Trump's brash style, they could show the world a different side to China. They have not hesitated to share stories accusing America of being the real source of the coronavirus, or Australia of violating human rights in Afghanistan. The purpose was two-fold: to reveal so-called Western lies about China, and also call out our double standards. One might say that after 2,500 years with one style, China is acting out of character.

Or, perhaps China realized that in a global geopolitical climate filled with mistrust, you don't gain anything by staying silent and neutral? My own interpretation is that during the Trump era, China simply reached a breaking point and decided it could no longer maintain its silence. Perhaps we should spend less time thinking about why China has recently adopted a harsher tone, and more about what is suddenly shaking up a long Chinese tradition of stoic calm, unemotional politics, and diplomatic trustworthiness. Thinking about my own experience in China, I have only rarely seen a Chinese person lose their cool and get extremely vocal or aggressive. When anger did erupt, it was almost always due to money or a perceived injustice. We could relate the wolf warrior attitude to economic losses due to Trump's trade war, but my feeling is this has much less to do with money and everything to do with a perceived injustice—a loss of face by damaging China's new acquired reputation as a powerful nation.

In the heightened tensions of today's geopolitical climate, it is said that many Chinese resent the West because we don't want China to develop and would rather it stay poor and stupid. But from the Chinese perspective, this is about the injustices that the Chinese feel they've suffered. This is a deep cultural scar: although the Chinese generally do not like to attract public attention, every now and then on the street in China you will see someone who has simply snapped: a renter unfairly evicted, a cyclist run off the road by a Maserati, a group of elderly people who had been scammed. In the same way that the Chinese quickly adapt to collective social change, they also quickly lose their patience if they feel that they are victims of abuse of power, lies, or misconduct. This sense of injustice is collectively expressed on Chinese social media with demands for justice or calls to take the law into their own hands in what is known as cancel culture. This isn't just an online discussion or hashtag that goes viral like in the West, but a fight to protect Chinese values that can quickly destroy the careers of those responsible for the injustice. When they feel they're being played, the Chinese turn into a collective force. Such reactions explain why many Chinese openly support the wolf warrior assertiveness of their political leaders. For many Westerners that sounds illogical because to us it is the Chinese who are the liars. It is a bit too easy for the Chinese to justify their lying to foreigners as the only way for the powerless, poor, and disadvantaged China to compete against the powerful West, while the Western lies are seen more as an abuse of power. I don't agree with this, because lies are lies, but it's good to know why the Chinese find their past lies less harmful than the lies being told today by the West.

The challenge for the Chinese is that we now live in a world swirling with disinformation campaigns, conspiracy theories, viral memes, and fake news.

What is still true, and what is a lie? If China doesn't respond to a lie or double standard from the West, it confirms to the world that it's probably true. So, China has no choice but to react, which explains the new wolf warrior attitude. Previously, China would be polite, say yes, and then do what it thought best for China, not necessarily the world. The only thing that has changed now is that China has stopped nodding silently just to please the West. The Chinese will be who they want to be, not who the United States or other countries want them to be. Though at times unpleasant, this actually makes China more transparent. Every previous attempt by China to clean up its image by showing a "good-hearted" China has backfired. The 2,500-year-old formula suddenly wasn't working anymore. The consensus in the West is that China's wolf warrior diplomacy stance has made China a lot of enemies in the world. You could argue that China isn't playing the geopolitical game very well yet, or that it has misjudged the backlash from the West. Even if that's true, China's leaders can't do anything but become more assertive in their communications because the Chinese people have become much more assertive on social media as well. Chinese internet users will simply no longer stand by and watch the West dragging China's image through the mud, while the West itself continues with its double standards. Early 2022, we've seen the wolf warrior style of diplomacy weakening, especially in the run up to Beijing's Winter Olympic Games, with China apparently wanting to tell its positive stories to the whole world again—but this time in a more creative, attractive, empathetic, and effective way.

Perhaps the most revealing example of the United States' double standards is the idea "that China wants to create and control a dystopian world order." The assumption is that China is the supreme Big Brother country, will be the world's largest economic power by 2030, and will therefore probably also want to control the world order. This prospect understandably frightens the Western world. We see the build-up of China's military in the South China Sea as a proof point. We view the so-called debt trap being created in Africa and Central and South Asia around the extension of China's New Silk Road as a way for Beijing to expand its soft power. We consider China's tough talk toward Taiwan as a sign that China is no longer scared of a war with the United States. Although many of us don't always agree with what China does inside its own country, most of us can live with it to a certain extent. However, if China becomes a threat to the world and the international order, we would all have a problem with it. But the Chinese don't understand or share our fears. Instead, they look back at their history to show that China has never been expansionist; they explain that all their international actions are purely economically driven; they praise China's new naval force as proof it has regained its status and independence after 180 years; and they see the Taiwanese problem as a purely domestic issue.

The international community has become so fixated on two regions—the New Silk Road, and the chain of Chinese islands running from Taiwan deep into the South China Sea—as a sign of China's new aggression that we don't see the real transition that's happening in the world. From China's perspective, the New Silk Road is lifting the people of the Southern Hemisphere out of the West's shadow, the tensions in the South China Sea are the result of an Asian century that is happening right now, and the Taiwan question is the final act in a power struggle between China and the West that has been going on for almost 200 years. These conflicts are more about a changing world order for Europe, North America, and their "democratic" allies, who we often refer to as "the West," even though countries like New Zealand or Australia are geographically part of the East. Western allies that neighbor China, such as Japan, South Korea, or India, are firmly stuck between China and the West. Assuming they will always play the American card is like playing geopolitical poker. If we forget about these three Asian countries for a moment, it is already clear that "the West" is no longer the largest economic power, but also that it can no longer independently decide the international rules of the game, or force the rest of the world to play only a minor role. That's why I suspect that Japan, South Korea, and India will gradually distance themselves from the West in order to ensure the viability of their own position in Asia. The fact that extremely complex geopolitical and historical relationships exist between these three countries and China is delaying this logical transition.

Assuming that no new world war takes place, we can be certain that the transition to the Asian century is here to stay. This is precisely why author Graham Allison states that America and China will without a doubt fall into the Thucydides Trap. He compares the United States to the militarily strong Sparta in ancient Greece. Sparta's fear of the rising Athens (China, in this comparison) made the Peloponnesian War inevitable. Are America and China destined for war? It might seem like it. However, a head-on confrontation between America and China with the deployment of their visible conventional weaponry seems highly unlikely to me. Not only can no one really win that war, but it would put the entire world in danger and create economic chaos. From a Chinese point of view, I cannot fathom how a China that has fought and sacrificed for 180 years to restore its dignity and prosperity would now want to put everything it has gained at risk again. From a Western point of view, I cannot believe that we consider our position of power more important than the sustainability of the economic world order. So, I remain cautiously optimistic, and I do not believe there is a war coming to Asia. This said, wars are often the result of irrational minds.

Even without open warfare, I do see two major disputes arising over China's expansion, which are more of a geopolitical distraction from the real, but not so visible, conflict that's going on. The underlying conflict is due to the fact that the world is changing, and China wants to play a leading role in that change. This is why it makes less sense to analyze China's geopolitical strategic drivers than to focus on China's pragmatic, economic, and sovereign motives: the first is China's influence and expansion beyond its borders, the second China's military display of power around the Chinese islands in the South China Sea and Taiwan.

THE NEW SILK ROAD

The New Silk Road, also known as the Belt & Road Initiative (BRI), is Xi Jinping's most ambitious international project, with a long-term goal to transform Eurasian economic integration. The "Belt" was started in 2013 and refers to the revival of the old Silk Road along overland trade routes between China and Europe. The "Road" was started in 2014 and refers to the maritime routes that link China by sea to Southeast Asia, Africa, and Europe. The "Belt" route aims to connect, the "Road" to bypass future tensions at sea in Asia. By opening the China-Pakistan economic corridor, China bypasses the geostrategic Strait of Malacca in the Indian Ocean, to allow Chinese ships to now sail west from the Gwadar port in Pakistan. China is certainly not the first country to want to develop the Eurasian continent via overland connections. Europe, the United States, Japan, and South Korea were all busy with initiatives before this New Silk Road initiative was started, but the size and scope of China's version is extraordinary. Did we expect anything less of China? The New Silk Road includes six economic cooperation corridors and passageways connecting the Asian economic miracle with the European economic circle, as well as planned Chinese investments of more than one trillion dollars in infrastructure projects such as ports, maritime filling stations, railroads, bridges, industry, energy, and more. Chinese state banks and Asian investment banks are financing these megaprojects mainly by lending money to developing countries.

This is how the term "debt trap diplomacy" came about: China's approach is said to offer cheap infrastructure loans, knowing that the poorer recipient countries wouldn't really be able to repay these large debts. This would eventually allow China to take ownership of local infrastructure, such as ports, as payment from these countries for their unpaid debt. At least that is the popular myth that most of us believe is true. What is certainly true is that China took a ninety-nine-year lease on the port of Hambantota in Sri Lanka and bought a sixty-seven percent share in the port of Piraeus in Greece. What is rarely mentioned, however, is that Sri Lanka did this deal to use Chinese money, which only accounted for nine percent of its total debt, to repay international loans. And Greece saw no other way out because Europe refused to bail them out of the financial crisis. What is less widely reported is that in 2020, China either re-evaluated nearly all of its BRI loans to countries in financial distress in Africa and elsewhere for additional debt relief,[138] or wrote them off completely as a result of the impact of COVID-19.[139] However, China is still a long way from being a good Samaritan in Africa. In other words, if China made soft-power diplomacy its primary goal ahead of its economic interests, it would be less likely to act as a banker or project developer, and instead put the host country's humanitarian development above short-term gain. In the same way that the West usually uses loans or donations to force developing countries to place more impor-tance on Western liberal values such as democracy and human rights, China could equally apply conditions to its loans in order to bring about reforms more towards a Chinese authoritarian government model. Is soft power not a priority for China after all then? China certainly helps African countries with knowledge transfer, vaccines, and even $6 billion a year in development aid,[140] but com-pared to the $150 billion a year from all Western countries combined, China's development aid isn't much more than Norway's, and only twenty percent of what the United States pays. Above all, aside from the more than $207 billion in loans[141] in both Asia and Africa, China clearly remains more interested in doing business than charity. Unlike the Western powers, China wants to get involved as little as possible in the domestic policies and problems of other countries. If China could choose between loans being repaid in cash or with infrastructure, they would rather have the cash: the Chinese debt trap in Africa is a myth. In the West, we often compare the New Silk Road to the Marshall Plan, which pro-vided American money to rebuild Europe after 1948, but as a result left Europe tied to America, and we worry that China will do the same with Africa. But the New Silk Road, on the other hand, is open for the whole world to participate in and therefore doesn't have any exclusive political agenda, despite what is being written about it.

So why does China lend so much money to countries in Africa, Asia, and Eastern Europe? The New Silk Road is a solution to China's current problems for three main reasons. The first, and most strategic, is that China wants to secure its trade routes with the world by economically linking as many coun-tries as possible to China. This is much more about shared economic interests than political ones. The second reason is that the western regions of China are lagging behind the development of the cities on the eastern coast, and so China's progress is causing increasing inequality in the country. Creating an overland trade connection to Europe can help resolve this domestic geo-graphical imbalance. Finally, after more than a decade of intense construction and dramatic infrastructure expansion, China's state-owned companies now have more capacity than there is domestic demand. But this also means they have the right experience to build high-quality modern infrastructure like ports, railroads, and bridges on a large scale. All the countries that have taken out BRI loans so far were also the ones asking for this help; China didn't need to go looking for countries to loan to. These poorer countries often begged China to help them with money, implementation, and expertise. They have received aid donations and cheap loans from the West, but larger infrastructure investments in Africa, for example, haven't been as popular with Western investors and banks over recent decades. Western financial institutions and their clients simply preferred to invest in companies like Tesla, which should also make the world a better place. While on average less than twenty percent of all outstanding loans in Africa come from China, China's additional BRI financing to ten African countries has suddenly brought about a bigger debt crisis in these already vulnerable countries, overshadowing the long-term economic benefits.[142] Here, one could indeed call out a debt trap caused by the international community and China together, where the responsibility to resolve it should be shared as well. Since China already had BRI projects with sixty-eight countries in 2020, this certainly changes the way the Southern Hemisphere plans its investment.

In 1980 there were only two countries in Africa (Guinea-Bissau and Uganda) with a lower GDP per inhabitant than China. Back then, China was much poorer than Africa. Today, apart from the Seychelles Islands, there is not one African country that is richer than China in terms of GDP per inhabitant. Africa wants a slice of the Chinese dream—a dream that came true in China enabled by the construction of new infrastructure on a massive scale.[143] China had a real appetite for exporting its infrastructure building prowess but ended up biting off more than it could chew. They didn't have the experience to thoroughly evaluate these international projects, especially when it came to political or repayment risks. In fact, despite its immense scope, we should think of the New Silk Road initiative as a start-up. China has made pretty much all the mistakes a start-up makes, because they didn't have any serious experience managing complex projects in volatile regions. One big mistake was to hardly ever involve the local people in their projects. The projects were paid for with Chinese money, managed by Chinese companies, built with Chinese materials, and mostly carried out by Chinese workers, without much consideration for the local population. The Chinese always prefer to do business directly with the decision-makers and assume that those leaders will involve their own supporters and people. But the reality in many developing countries is very different. The Chinese have some understanding of this reality, but still prefer not to get involved in local politics. One of the underlying reason for China's approach is that the local populations often don't have the needed skills, creating a risk that China, ultimately responsible for delivering the projects, would rather avoid. As even qualified local people seldom were deployed by Chinese project developers, China has been widely criticized for their "space settlement" approach in Africa.

The other mistake China made was to do business with governments that, like China a few decades ago, don't always have the best policies, don't take human rights too seriously, or are simply corrupt. China is very familiar with these pitfalls from the pre-Xi Jinping era but should have stayed clear of them for the New Silk Road projects. Instead, these issues have become an open wound holding back China's efforts to build trust. As a BRI start-up, China is now learning that they need to evaluate and supervise their projects better, support better local integration, educate the local population, keep the gold diggers out, quickly learn from their mistakes, and they have to draw up new strict rules. Speaking of mistakes, there are a lot of New Silk Road projects that are failing or generating a very poor return on investment.

Even the Chinese people are not always enthusiastic about the New Silk Road. In public or government media it gets a lot of support, but behind closed doors the Chinese don't always understand why the government is investing so much money in Africa, while half of the Chinese people are still fairly poor themselves, and certainly have enough problems of their own. Just like in America, many Chinese people also want their country to first invest in their own people, and not in places, projects, and regimes they don't care about. The New Silk Road is a major prestige project that has turned into an expensive lesson for China. In the meantime, we worry too much about Chinese opportunism and not enough about the transformation that the New Silk Road is bringing about. We focus on the problems and not enough on the real opportunities being opened up in developing BRI countries. The real power of the New Silk Road for the world is not that the Chinese dragon has woken up, but that China is now beginning the process of waking up and digitally activating a few billion people living outside the West and India. In fact, China often understands the problems of poorer countries better than the West does, simply because it wasn't so long ago that China itself was extremely poor. For me, the question is not whether China has a hidden self-interested economic agenda with the New Silk Road, but rather whether China is helping these countries more than the West ever has by offering practical solutions to their long-standing problems. The answer is yes: China is simply in a better position than the West to help developing countries with 5G telecommunications, drones, software, e-commerce, smart logistics, cheap smartphones, agricultural innovations, telemedicine applications, online education, automated factories, financial inclusion, and much more.

Through the New Silk Road, China is actively upgrading countries across the Southern Hemisphere, enabling them to become more modern and resilient societies and economies that in the future will be less reliant on the West.

The West's success is also its failure: in most Western countries we don't face many problems that are a matter of life or death. We're not used to having to find really clever solutions to life's essential problems lower down on the scale of Maslow's hierarchy of needs. China has a wealth of experience in solving such practical development challenges. The pandemic and the climate crisis have partly woken us up in the West, but a little too late. The question is therefore no longer even whether we can trust China, but whether the rest of the world the West hasn't paid enough attention to will trust China more than we do in the future, and perhaps one day soon. After all, the best way to quickly gain someone's trust is to help them improve their life in a concrete way—and that's certainly what China is doing. However, we are too often distracted by self-fulfilling prophecies based on what we imagine China's geopolitical intentions are with the New Silk Road, and by the recurring role of victim that we usually assign to people in developing countries.

THE CHINESE ISLANDS

China's military presence on the islands in the South China Sea has also already caused a lot of geopolitical tension. China claims the right to the Spratly and Paracel Islands based on the argument that it was the first country to discover and settle them.[144] Although it's not exactly the same argument, China also uses history to claim Xinjiang, Tibet, and Taiwan as part of its territory. As early as the third century BC, Xinjiang (the "Western Territories") was controlled by the Han Chinese.[145] Tibet was considered part of a unified territory of the Han and Tibetans as early as the eighth century; and in the twelfth century Tibet came under the legal rule of the Han Chinese.[146] During the same century, the island known today as Taiwan also came under the jurisdiction of a Chinese prefecture.[147] Since China is the oldest and longest-running civilization in the Far East, the history books always work in China's favor, as they have extensive records describing the governance of these regions to secure trade and exchanges. This certainly doesn't mean that China has always paid the same attention to or had the same interest in these four regions, so the counter-argument that they don't belong to China is equally convincing. But the Chinese are extremely proud of their history, which they see as a strong, vibrant culture with a very influential political and social unity.

The reality of Chinese history is of course very different, with many periods of chaos and both strong and weak emperors who reigned over long periods and were not even always Han Chinese, but Mongolians or Manchus from the current North-East of China. For many Chinese people, the real turmoil that they will never forget is the chaos caused by the West and Japan in the nineteenth and twentieth centuries, which brought the two-thousand-year dynastic cycle to an end and for a century forced the country into weakness, poverty, and dependence. It is therefore understandable that China always likes to look back at its long imperial past of a united and strong China. It also makes sense that China uses its past as historical proof that the regions under its previous rule belong to today's unified China. Fortunately, China has never had colonies of its own around the world like the West. Otherwise, many more countries would now have territorial conflicts with China.

One question a lot of people ask is whether China is or could become expansionist. We can answer this question in part by looking at how China has reclaimed land on reefs and small islands in the South China Sea in recent years. China built up ports, military bases, and airstrips at lightning speed on islands it claims across the South China Sea, placing fighter planes, radars, and cruise missiles across that region. The world is concerned about China's military intentions; we are no longer in any doubt about China's military capacity, but we still wonder: what are they going to do with it? With China's military budget the second largest in the world after the United States, it already has the largest modern navy in the world in terms of the number of ships. The consensus among military strategists is that we cannot predict the outcome of a direct confrontation between China and its US allies in the South China Sea or over Taiwan. The consensus is also that a direct conflict with China, which has nuclear weapons, is unlikely given both the enormous financial and human cost. Nevertheless, a single mistake could spark a real global conflict, despite the best intentions of China and the United States. If China would suddenly take back Taiwan by force, any further escalation by the US would be too hazardous as it could lead to a nuclear war. This theory could encourage China: that if Taiwan declares independence, military action against Taiwan certainly cannot be ruled out. In other words, China could go to war with Taiwan as it is unlikely that the US would respond militarily.

By contrast, Beijing attacking the island that is not a direct response of a declaration of independence from Taiwan would cause significant damage to China in terms of image, prosperity, and stability. And so, as long as Taiwan does not declare its independence, a Chinese military action on the island seems unlikely. That could encourage the United States: that if the US would become ambiguous about their position to not recognize Taiwan as part of the People's republic of China, Beijing would likely take the bait and respond militarily on Taiwan. If China bites, most countries in the world will no longer trust China, which would help the United States maintain its position of power and hegemony in the world even longer. In fact, you could argue that a military takeover of Taiwan by China would help both the United States and China. So, the main question is who would make the first move and what the damage would be if it led to a proxy war between China and Western allies in the region. At some point in time, it is clear that America will not be able to defend Taiwan against a more powerful China, while China also can't really afford a direct military conflict against America and its allies. Despite this, we continue to see increasing military preparations and tough talk from both China and America. Both blame each other for deliberate escalation and use maintaining the safety of the South China Sea as a way to justify their military presence.

Why is this South China Sea region so important to China and to the United States? For China, the economic importance of the South China Sea is such that it has also acquired geopolitical and military importance. For the United States, the region is of such critical geopolitical and military importance that it has started impacting its economic influence in the region. America is known for using its military power geopolitically to gain economic power. Meanwhile, China is known for using its economic power to gain geopolitical power. So, they both want the same thing, but the means and the goals are reversed. The American military is a means to increase power whereas the goal of China's military is to maintain economic power. This is a small but important nuance, and it's very visible in the South China Sea. In this Asian century, China doesn't want to lose its economic power, while America wants to gain even more political influence in Asia.

When we realize that sixty percent of the world's maritime trade and sixty-five percent of all Chinese trade flows through the South China Sea, we can immediately understand why the largest exporting country in the world, which depends on this trade for thirty-five percent of its GDP, looks at the South China Sea from a largely strategic-economic perspective.[148] That's why I regard China's military parade in the South China Sea as a distraction. Both China and America are distracting the world with a military game of cat and mouse, causing us to pay less attention to the broader economic and geopolitical interests of China and America. The fear of a militarily powerful China makes us forget that we are actually witnessing a natural shift of the world's economic center of gravity from the West to the East. The nations that control the trade routes in the South China Sea are in a position to dominate a third of all world trade, as well as Asia's economy. China wants to be in this position so that it can safeguard its own future. So, the essential struggle is about control over the region. China doesn't want to lose its economic access, and America doesn't want to give up its military access. To do that, China needs a military presence, and America would rather transfer the growing economic interests in the South China Sea to China's neighboring countries in order to continue to gain military access to the region via them. The dispute between Beijing and Taipei, and between China and five other countries (Vietnam, the Philippines, Malaysia, Brunei, and Indonesia) in the region is (in addition to trade) also of crucial economic importance for each country as these waters have enormous potential in terms of gas, oil, and fishing resources. In reality, besides civil navigation, this is also about the freedom of military navigation. Chinese militarization in the region increased rapidly after Obama strengthened the presence of the US fleet in the South China Sea in 2016.[149] As a result, after twenty years of negotiations, the code of conduct for navigation in the South China Sea was suddenly scrapped. Can the United States and its allies still sail their military ships freely in the South China Sea? That depends on how territorial waters are divided, and who should give access to military ships near the Chinese islands. China itself has used its own historical facts to claim a lot of tiny bits of land in the ocean. In 2016, the Hague Tribunal rejected China's maritime claims to much of the South China Sea. China has strongly challenged this decision. It claims that the Hague has no authority over territorial disputes and that the United States is not even a signatory to the underlying "freedom of navigation" treaty. If the United States isn't playing by the international rules in the open sea, why should China in its own backyard?

China is showing no sign whatsoever of wanting to have a strong military presence outside of this "home" region; one exception is a naval base in Djibouti, in the Horn of Africa, which is there formally to keep Somalian pirates away from Chinese ships and for humanitarian and peacekeeping missions in Africa. In 2021, Xi Jinping said that China will never strive for hegemony, expansion, or a sphere of influence, and will never fight a "cold" or "real" war with any country. In China's view, Taiwan is unassociated to these promises because it is formally part of China. Of course, a clash over Taiwan would destroy any remaining trust between China and the United States. However, China seems to be in no rush to unify Taiwan, and Xi Jinping has given himself a tentative deadline of 2049. This deadline can be extended, or preferably met without ever having to fire a bullet if China can further increase its economic influence in the region.

Personally, I believe the scenario of continued political war with Taiwan, which each year for decades has become more economically dependent on the mainland, is the more likely outcome. America, on the other hand, has much less time to gain a stronger position in Asia, so it's not surprising that Biden finally withdrew US forces from Afghanistan, with the intention to pivot US attention to China's neighborhood. What strikes me as strange is that few people in the West find this development strange. Let's imagine China doing the same kind of strategic moves near US waters. Would we also think that's normal? Would we, like China, limit our reaction to tough talk, or would there be concrete military actions and economic sanctions? The question we need to ask ourselves is less whether the Chinese dragon will ever breathe fire, but how long we can continue to provoke the Chinese dragon in the South China Sea? This military game of cat and mouse between China and America, with Australia and England as its strongest allies, makes one thing clear: China is the fast mouse, and America and its allies the fat cat. We should be much more concerned that China would move our cheese (economic interest in the region) rather than suddenly turn into a big aggressive cat (military aggression in the region). The growing threat from China comes less from the country's visible military arsenal and acute threat in Taiwan or in the South China Sea than in the almost invisible technological game changers that China is targeting today—and that can be deployed militarily if necessary. The more distracted and scared we are by what we *can* see coming from China, the less attention we pay to and trust we show in what we *cannot* see coming from China.

GAME CHANGERS

It took 200,000 years of human evolution and six million years of planetary evolution for the world's population to reach one billion people, a milestone passed in 1804. Barely a hundred years later, in 1927, it reached two billion people. In 2023 there will be eight billion people, with one billion more human beings every twelve years. The previous population explosions were caused by what I will call "game changers." In the nineteenth century, the British Industrial Revolution led to fewer famines, more urbanization, better education, vaccinations, healthier lifestyles, and better living conditions. Therefore, in the nineteenth century the world order was mainly determined by England, partly due to their military superiority and expansionist colonial character. As an empire, China, which until 1820 was the largest economy in the world, was geopolitically far more protectionist than expansionist, so the European model of international relations shaped the current world order. Back then, the European powers were globally dominant, with England leading the way with its military force, close trading links, and techno-economic influence.[150]

At the turn of the nineteenth century, however, Europe became divided into two blocs, with Germany emerging as an opposing force. Over time, Germany's military and economy grew much stronger, and a series of miscalculations led Europe into the First World War. After the war, a new world order was formed with new institutions and international treaties. At the same time, new forces like the Soviet Union, the Great Depression, new technological weapons, and a humiliated Germany unleashed the Second World War. By 1945, a bi-polar world order emerged with two major nuclear powers—the Soviet Union and the United States—keeping their distance from each other during the Cold War, leaving the world largely at peace ever since. The Western world order as we have known it for nearly 100 years was strongly and single-handedly controlled by the United States.

However, this American century, defined by one country's scientific, technological, financial, and military superiority, now seems to be coming to an end. The rise of Asia is said to be the main reason, but more importantly, the United States hasn't been well-prepared to work jointly with the world's emerging economies to come up with new rules accommodating new players like China, India, and the rest of the Southern Hemisphere. Relations between Europe and the United States may also have peaked, but they still pull together when there's a critical common interest like global warming and any other global crisis related to the rise of China. Today, I believe, the future of the United States and the West hangs in the balance. The common opinion in the West is that the United States will continue to be the world's dominant superpower for a long time to come. One line of reasoning is America has spent seventy years creating the world's most sophisticated ecosystem, which isn't easy to copy. In this view, the United States has the world's most advanced applications, software, machines, manufacturing, processes, materials, centers of excellence, brands, thinkers, entrepreneurs, and financial institutions serving the global market.

Based on this, we simply assume that the next major technological breakthroughs will come from the United States or other Western countries. These breakthroughs will further strengthen America's superpower status and keep China in the rear-view mirror. While this is hypothetically possible, there are three mistakes in this logic that are blinding us to other scenarios.

The first mistake we make is underestimating the extent to which the world of technological research has become one big entity of fully communicating vessels. Researchers widely share their results, open source makes everything available, machines are used worldwide, developments are no longer just for the well-resourced Western multinationals, smart people and entrepreneurs live everywhere, the best processes are no longer a secret, financing is no longer local, and globalization has made the world into a much more uniform market. As long as the West continues to take advantage of exports from China, China will continue to take advantage of the knowledge and innovation breeding grounds of the world. As long as US companies want access to the growing Chinese market and high-quality production facilities, China will be able to close deals.

The second mistake we make is assuming that the United States is still militarily capable of protecting and keeping the world in order. After the global embarrassment of the hasty US withdraw from Afghanistan, there are fewer countries who trust that the United States is able or willing to protect them. The military focus of the Western world is also being divided: the United States now wants to concentrate its energies on the Indo-Pacific with military partners such as Australia, India, and Japan, alongside the British because of their post-colonial influence in Asia. Increasingly, the European Union realizes it will have to take care of its own defense because it is too risky to overly rely on NATO. That became obviously clear with the Russian military build-up at the border of Ukraine. If the EU were to become more independent and decisive from a military perspective, China would also treat it with more respect, attention, and caution.

The third big mistake we make is thinking that China is focused on keeping up with us, maybe because we think in an overly linear way. China doesn't want to keep up with or overtake us at all: China wants to independently set new standards. Above all, China wants to break away from its crippling dependence on the West. The motivation behind their desire to innovate is to be able to decouple from us, not necessarily to exert more power over us—although that could end up being the result. Too often we hear that China is in a technological race with the West—artificial intelligence, 5G, microchips, biotechnology, quantum, new energy, cybersecurity, etc. We look at reality through an assumption: China is always behind us, no matter how fast the country progresses. We then analyze how close China is to overtaking the West and imagine ourselves as tortoise and China as the hare from the well-known fable of the tortoise and the hare. If the hare keeps making up half the time it was behind, it will never catch up with the tortoise, even though he can run much faster. This example shows how we confuse the order of thought with the order of being. To support this flawed assumption, we give a lot of media attention to China's mistakes and problems. We read that China invests much more money than we do, but we don't believe that innovation using government money can make a big difference. That's also correct; but it is not the money that will make the real difference, but the infrastructure that is being built with that money. It is not the top-down guidance from Beijing that suddenly makes entrepreneurs and researchers innovative, but the pragmatic thinking that has already fueled thirty years of growth in China. It is that bottom-up drive for improvement in China that is creating disruptions and surprising innovations in a world of economic stability. Internal dynamics within China's hyper competitive domestic market drive a lot of the innovations taking place, not external considerations. China innovates as a response to a pull from within China, not a push from the government. As a result, China is taking an unorthodox path to innovation according to our standards and norms.

The trend that few of us want to see is that China, despite taking a very different path, is in reality now approaching its innovation plan in much the same way that the West likes to—purely to show that something is possible, even if the road to a practical goal seems difficult, improbable, or even impossible today. For example, if the Chinese company BYD launches a high-tech battery for electric cars with lithium iron phosphate that is not flammable or explosive, then that's not because they want to beat Tesla, but to set a new standard. The development process required was extremely difficult. If China tries to develop microchips by doing groundbreaking research with new materials like graphene instead of just working on silicon,[151] then they are not doing that to keep up with Taiwan's chip giant TSMC, but to overcome the limitations of Moore's law of semiconductors. It is highly unlikely that China will solve its chip gap with graphene. If China, with its ten-billion-dollar quantum computer, sets a world record with photons, the unit of light, instead of qubits, many won't see the point of it. Because photonic circuits can't currently be used to solve concrete problems, this Chinese innovation breakthrough is even being described as completely illogical.[152] But isn't that how the West made one breakthrough after another in the past? For example, the Wright brothers who made flying possible, Edison who gave us light bulbs, or Einstein who redefined light, gravity, and space. We should therefore stop claiming that China will or will not keep up with us in terms of innovation, because this is no longer a race where we have a better car and a better driver.

AN ECOLOGICAL CIVILIZATION

For thirty years after the opening of the country in 1978, the Chinese government only had one real main goal: growth. In order to lift around 850 million Chinese people out of poverty, China would take steps to become a developed nation—whatever the cost. And within thirty years, China became the largest manufacturer in the world, with its share of global exports growing from one percent in 1980 to eleven percent in 2010. In response to Western consumerism, but also China's desire to make money fast, China also quickly became the largest polluter in the world. In 2010, almost twenty percent of China's ground soil and rivers were too contaminated for agricultural use and the air was so heavily polluted that just twenty percent of the population was breathing clean air. Living in Shanghai at the time, I can attest to the fact that China didn't need environmentalists or moral persuasion to create an awareness and sense of urgency about pollution among its people.

At the turn of the century, hopes for a sustainable future for Chinese people was starting to look almost as bleak as the gray smog over Beijing, or as fiery red as the polluted water of the Zhongting River in Hebei province. More than ever before, the Chinese were aware of the environmental causes and problems, and the government started to publicly address their concerns as early as around 2003. From 2005, the phrase "lucid water and lush mountains are invaluable assets" became hugely popular in China. It was even adopted as a slogan by Xi Jinping to symbolize his personal crusade to conserve nature and save the planet. In 2007, then Chinese president, Hu Jintao, formulated the objective to make China an "ecological civilization." This goal was even written into the Party's constitution in 2012. After assuming power from President Hu in 2013, Xi Jinping put an end to the (until then common) excuse that China was a developing country with just as much right to economic development as the West—even if nature would pay the price.

China's old line of reasoning, one that is prevalent in most developing countries, is that the West shoulders the biggest responsibility for the world's

CO₂ emissions throughout history. But Xi Jinping turned this defensive rhetoric into a proactive ambition to tackle the threat to the global environmental. It would have been a real nightmare had President (maybe for life) Xi Jinping been a climate change denier like Trump. The West can describe Xi Jinping as a dictator as much as it likes, but he stands a very good chance of one day going down in history as the Chinese president who gave the planet a second chance.

In 2014, Xi Jinping presented his new vision and global commitments at the APEC gathering in Beijing, and in 2015 he delivered a historic speech at the UN Climate Change Conference in Paris.[153] Tackling climate change became a shared mission of all countries, including China, to save humanity. From then on, China would set an example for the world by committing to peak its CO₂ emissions by 2030 at the latest. They would do this by cutting the nation's carbon emissions per unit of economic output by more than sixty-five percent, and by increasing the share of renewable energy use to twenty-five percent. The challenge for China is that the country continues to grow by five to six percent annually, and therefore needs more energy every year. This is why China doesn't want to immediately reduce its CO₂ emissions in absolute numbers, but in relation to GDP. This approach has been heavily criticized. The alternative of not waiting until 2030 to cut China's overall CO₂ emissions is dire for Beijing; it would mean leaving people without heating every winter, imposing consumption restrictions on all factories, and driving up energy prices. A drastic move like that would push too many Chinese people back into poverty, cause Chinese factories to go bankrupt, and potentially even lead the world into an economic crisis.

In 2020, Xi Jinping issued another clear commitment at the United Nations General Assembly: China would be carbon neutral by 2060 at the latest. At the time, China was responsible for twenty-seven percent of the world's CO₂ emissions, making this the most ambitious promise of all countries to achieve the target of keeping global warming below 1,5°C (2.7°F) by 2100. Europe is responsible for thirteen percent of the world's CO₂ emissions, and America for twelve percent. But in 2017, Trump suddenly withdrew America from the Paris Agreement; Joe Biden then rejoined it in 2021. The world often sees China as the bad guy, but it's certainly not as inconsistent as the United States has been in its approach to CO₂ reduction. Many of us are truly impressed by the way fifteen-year-old Swedish climate activist Greta Thunberg has sparked a global movement to raise awareness among politicians about the seriousness of the climate crisis and to call for action rather than "blah blah blah." Her wake-up call has been heard around the world. What few people appreciate, however, is that China is probably really the last resort to save our planet's biodiversity, and in turn humanity. Without China's concrete efforts, it is highly unlikely that even a hundred Greta Thunbergs would be able to turn the tide.

What does it mean for our collective future when what we consider an authoritarian top-down regime is setting the rules for an ecological civilization? How should we position our bottom-up environmental approach based on the individual responsibility of citizens and businesses against China's top-down semi-forceful environmental policy? Could China's plan to save the planet also be exploited as soft power against the West? We constantly hear conflicting stories about China's incredible investments and rapid adoption of clean energy alternatives, but at the same time, China is still building coal-fired power stations and burning half of the world's coal. In fact, Coal still produces fifty-seven percent of China's total energy today. The Western media sees this as ecological deception, while the Chinese celebrate the technological progress of the more environmentally friendly coal-fired power plants. The simple answer is that China is the biggest climate champion in the world but doesn't want to make its climate plan so restrictive that it would paralyze the country through energy shortages or irreversible energy dependence on foreign countries. In reality, even more new generation coal-fired power plants will be needed to replace the dirtier and small-scale coal-burning ones: they will represent the last investments in coal in Chinese history as solar and wind energy gradually become cheaper than the price of coal-generated power.

What China needs to do now is quickly build up large-scale renewable energy sources so that it doesn't make sense to keep coal-fired power plants operational in the long run—and that is China's master plan. It's not very pretty, and perhaps not even economically justifiable, but it's a very pragmatic way of achieving big long-term results while meeting short-term needs. This is the difference in linear thinking between the West and China. In the West, we see a step backwards as a step in the wrong direction, for example the gas-fired power stations planned in Belgium. In China, they see a step backwards as a way to first find solid ground from which to then be able to jump later on. The coal-fired power plants are the solid ground, the massive infrastructure construction of wind, solar, and hydropower is the jump. This ultra-pragmatic, goal-oriented Chinese approach sometimes comes with side effects. In recent years, local governments have struggled with a lack of heating in the winter as they closed too many coal mines at once and monopolized all renewable sources to keep Beijing happy.

In 2020, fifty-five percent of households in twenty-eight major cities located in the cold northern regions of China were already using clean energy; in Beijing, it was seventy-five percent. At that time, sixteen percent of all energy in China came from renewable sources, and this should increase to over twenty-five percent by 2030. This is an impressive achievement, but at the same time it reveals a very cautious transition plan to reach the target of over eighty percent clean energy by 2060 in order to be climate neutral. Without the real threat from the United States to decouple China from the world, especially by cutting off its oil imports, China probably wouldn't be so attached to its main supply of fossil fuel—coal.

This example shows how the Chinese government is managing change. Strict targets are an ideal way to govern a vast, complex, and diverse country like China. Through a centralized system, a 2,500-year-old bureaucratic model uses clear criteria and responsibilities to decide whether to promote, demote, or fire local government officials. Until 2017, the key performance indicators (KPIs) for Chinese local governments were often directly linked to GDP growth and China's social stability. Today, environmental goals outweigh economic growth in the mix of KPIs. In the past, blind faith in data and scientists often led local governments to invest too much in short-term solutions and resort to widespread corruption to meet their targets. This was exactly what caused the environmental problem in the first place—single-minded focus on maintaining growth rates. But Xi Jinping isn't just fighting pollution, he is also attacking corruption. Through environmental campaigns, ways for citizens to report violations, unannounced inspections, crackdowns, and environmental courts, today Beijing is much better equipped to enforce environmental regulations across the country.

Setting measurable goals is a standard practice within China's regulatory management system. Keeping short-term progress on schedule to reach far-away targets is necessary to contain global warming. Of course, the use of targets is not unique to China. More than a hundred countries have signed the Paris Climate Agreement to become carbon neutral by 2050. Alongside efforts to prevent global warming, most countries are working to prevent the destruction of nature by meeting specific targets on biodiversity and pollution. The big difference in China is that it has a top-down target-setting model that has been honed into a well-oiled machine over the centuries, allowing China to often reach its targets earlier than planned. Isn't that exactly what we need in this climate crisis? There is certainly something to be said for the way in which the state, with its strict and sudden environmental campaigns and heavy-handed approach, left certain industries, factories, and farms with lower added value out in the cold.

We can also look at how China has used massive "green land grabs" in order to achieve the UN Sustainable Development Goals (SDG). Since 1990, China has planted over 193,000 square miles of new woodlands, causing its forest cover to double to twenty-three percent of the country's land mass.[154] In the same period, China has also built five of the world's ten largest hydropower dams,[155] and fifty percent more high-speed train networks than the rest of the entire world combined. These inspiring megaprojects make China much greener and more environmentally friendly. But these impressive infrastructure advances have sometimes forced many rural residents to move, some unwillingly, others lured by the opportunities in the cities. Even the large-scale planting of monoculture forests also sometimes causes the loss of biodiversity and endangered species. In some cases, mega projects have affected the cultural heritage and lifestyles of ethnic minorities and disrupted natural ecosystems by opening itself up to eco- or ethno-tourism.[156] China's preference for massive interventions does create dilemmas: how to calculate the trade-offs between protecting nature versus culture or human rights? How do we weigh up China's impressive actions in the name of environmental protection against the future risks, losses, and unintended victims?

In China, trade-off assessments are normally made by a mostly technocratic leadership in Beijing whose mindset is to re-engineer nature with copy-paste ecological policies in order to achieve China's ambitious goals. Western commentators often draw attention to China's use of ruthless authoritarian power, where the end justifies the means. While this is a very justified concern, the world is also facing a doomsday scenario because climate change could mean the end of civilization as we know it. Perhaps Chinese politicians, who think in a rather rational, logical, and analytical way, and who have more faith in science and data than in half-baked political agreements and the approval of concerned citizens, can become a model of last resort for the planet. Shouldn't all politicians be more concerned, and do more than just talk? Looking at COP26, where the political world made a spectacle of the last chance for the planet, and Biden even pointed fingers at Xi Jinping for not showing up, while he had no problem flying over with a huge army of diplomats, then I'm afraid that Greta Thunberg may be right that it's all talk, no action. The fact that the Chinese government doesn't have any popular support for its climate related actions is also a misconception: more than half of younger consumers in China see sustainability, recycling, environmental protection, CO_2 emissions, and product waste reduction as important enough that they would accept extra costs to pay for them.[157] Local authorities are also increasingly involving them in new environmental projects. But despite the rapidly growing environmental awareness of Chinese citizens, they generally see it as the government's job to protect the environment. That doesn't mean that ordinary citizens aren't concerned with the environment, but apart from buying masks and air purifiers for personal protection, their change in consumption behavior is largely driven by government initiatives, raising awareness, tax incentives, or enforced measures, for example collectively planting trees, sorting waste, buying an electric car, or bringing your own chopsticks; or for the poor, even moving to the city to make way for a dam or a national park.

This isn't so surprising when you consider that big climate protests, which are seen in the West as a driver of change, are not the most efficient way to bring about real change in China. In the West, students from around the world took part in Fridays for Future climate protests. Most protesters felt concerned, frustrated, angry, hopeless, and dissatisfied—something we can call the

"Greta effect." In China, in sharp contrast, it is mainly the government that has launched a lot of initiatives to promote sustainable production and consumption. Beijing's tone is one of hope and confidence, not of despair and mistrust, as it often is in the West. In China, the message is to create a "sustainable future" and a "harmonious society" with initiatives such as the Environmental Risk Management Initiative, the Belt & Road Initiative (BRI), sustainable economic zones, and green cities. Of course, these are political slogans, but they are extremely important. The net result is that Western young people feel much more "indebted," while Chinese youngsters feel more "empowered" to do something about the environment. In the West, it is the people giving our democratic governance a wake-up call, while in China, it is the dictatorial administration waking up the people.

We must dare to ask the controversial question: whether our planet has enough time to wait for solutions from a liberal-democratic process that is more transparent, inclusive, humane, and informative for every citizen. We think we know the answer, as it would otherwise challenge our own system and values, so we don't even ask the question. Looking at how Western countries have dealt with the COVID-19 virus, China's decisive model might prove more effective in a crisis so far, could we also extend this logic to saving the planet from an environmental crisis? But on the other hand, the West will probably prefer to go beyond solving the environmental problem, as China is doing mostly now, and really try to change the behavior of citizens and businesses so that they care more about our shared future. As we have seen with the pandemic, we could have learned a lot from countries like China, but we made a choice not to: in effect we have chosen the hard road of minimizing the impact on our personal freedom, resulting in a longer struggle against the virus that has ultimately impacted our personal freedoms even more. So far, China, with its forceful, decisive governance model combined with a collectively responsible society, has proven more effective than the West at dealing with a health crisis. Let's not delude ourselves: the environmental crisis is much bigger than COVID-19, because there is no vaccine against the destruction of our planet. At the same time, China could learn from the West's discussion-based, people-driven model to make environmental protection the ultimate responsibility of everyone, not just the government. What the West could do better is help China save the world by making the planet's sustainability dependent on a broad consensus of awareness within society.

My appeal to the West is not to focus on what China is doing wrong when it comes to climate change, but instead concentrate on how we can help China be more careful, inclusive, and consensus-oriented. We often forget that since China opened up in 1978, the country has gone from being a humble student of international rules to the role of teacher it aspires to today. For example, we see that in recent years China has become more aware of the conservation of biodiversity and wants to lead by example in this respect.[158] Since that has long been our role, we can keep trying to be the smartest in the class or instead evolve from the role of being a teacher to being a mentor for China. This means listening to China and coaching them to do better, maybe one day soon even better than us. We can make China more transparent by letting them work more closely with Western academics and anthropologists, and by involving environmental organizations in a joint (rather than our) war on climate pollution. After all, environmental management is becoming a worldwide task that we all need to tackle together before this planet becomes uninhabitable.

THE CLEAN SMART FACTORY OF THE WORLD

As this book has described, over most of the past forty years China has mainly been known as the source of cheap "Made in China" products. This outdated image is kept alive by our Western brands and sellers. Recently I bought a pair of Dr. Martens shoes in Antwerp. This English brand is known around the world for its reliable and long-lasting shoes. In 1979, at the age of eleven, I went to boarding school in Folkestone, England. That was when I discovered that Dr. Martens was a symbol of rebellion against the system. Whenever the teacher left the classroom, we would all scream out the words of the Pink Floyd song, "Hey! Teacher! Leave us kids alone!" I decided to always be a rebel; that was my calling. Forty-two years later, I found myself in a Dr. Martens shop with my rebellious childhood flashing through my mind, thinking: what have I done to really change the world? Certainly not always enough, but in recent years, often without realizing it, I've criticized the Western system just by highlighting things we can learn from China's story. Standing in that shop with my memories, I felt it was time to get back into some Dr. Martens. A $177 pair caught my eye. Right next to them was an apparently identical pair that cost $240. I really couldn't spot the difference, so I asked the salesperson. He then pointed to the sign above the rack, which indicated the more expensive pair was made in the UK. He said the cheaper pair was made in Asia, which prompted me to ask if they were made in China. No, he answered, in Asia…as if China wasn't part of Asia. He didn't know exactly where they'd been made, but this encounter reconfirmed that in the West, we still consider products from China as the most inferior one could possibly get. All Dr. Martens shoes were once made in England, but like most companies in the world they cut costs by outsourcing production to China and Thailand. And that's where the misconception is. Today, China can produce the same quality as England, but most consumers don't want to pay more, so we don't get the best, but rather the lower quality from China. Dr. Martens could also get much better quality from China, but then they wouldn't be able to explain why one pair of shoes is more expensive than the other.

A lot of Chinese smartphone factories produce the same type of device at different-quality standards and prices. They integrate different-quality parts depending on how much the end customer is willing to pay.

China's strength is not only that they can produce cheaper than we can, but that they can deliver the full range of quality, from dirt cheap to very expensive—depending on what the customer decides. I believe this manufacturing flexibility will create an invasion of sustainable "Made in China" products in our Western markets in the coming years. Take, for example, electric vehicles (EV). Global market demand for new cars continues to grow steadily every year. But with people now questioning whether or not to buy an electric, hybrid, or an internal combustion engine car one last time, we will see new car sales in the West fall. To meet environmental standards by 2030, many governments will effectively force consumers to choose an electric car.

Although electric models are much cheaper to maintain, are much more reliable, perform better, and are better for the environment, many of us plan to drive around with our non-fully electric car for as long as possible. One reason is that an electric car can quickly add an additional cost of $10,000 on the purchase price, and another is that there aren't enough stations to charge them yet. This is about a lack of capacity to produce and charge EVs. If that capacity is big enough, as it is in China, an electric car can cost even less than a diesel or petrol car. The fact that prices are going down is also the result of the Chinese government promoting electric cars very proactively with subsidies and infrastructure. In the past, China has done the same with solar panels and wind turbines. China already has more than 500 brands producing electric cars, but this isn't even half of their EV production capacity. Chinese EV companies mainly target customers who can't afford a Tesla or pay $10,000 extra for a Ford, BMW, or Renault, or target buyers unwilling to wait twelve months or longer for an EV delivery. Over time, these 500 Chinese brands will consolidate, and that will create many major large-scale Chinese EV brands that are all, like Tesla, producing their third-generation electric cars and now also delivering top quality. Compare this to the traditional European and American brands that have only recently launched their first-generation EV. Since 2021, Chinese brands have been flooding the European market with electric cars. Western manufacturers and brands are now approaching the "valley of death." Many middle-class consumers in the West will make the switch to Chinese electric cars faster because this will mean they don't have to pay the extra price for a Western brand. We saw the same thing happen with Japanese cars a long time ago. This time it will be the Chinese brands that will make the difference because the clock is ticking. Western car brands will barely be able to keep up with the fast-paced competition in terms of EV capacity, battery innovation, and EV infrastructure, because in these dimensions they can no longer leverage their existing innovation model and experience. Tesla and the Chinese EV producers have set the standard, and now it's the Western brands copying them. They will have to drastically reduce their profit margins to survive this transformation, but this late in the game, many still don't realize that.

In the West, we still have faith in our innovative strength, quality labels, and creative superiority. However, we see plenty of examples of Western consumers changing their behavior en masse when something similar comes along that is more affordable. In some places, the government can subsidize the EV transformation, as was done for solar panels, but government budgets have shrunk due to the pandemic. Consumers happy to buy products from Ikea, H&M, or Samsung, will also be happy to buy their brand-new electric car from BYD, Geely, or Hongqi. Thanks to China, the Western middle class will once again feel richer and now more environmentally conscious without having to pay a huge price premium. In my mind, this will not only be the case with EV cars, but with every product that we have to rethink because of the environment— storage batteries, heat pumps, air conditioning, heating appliances, household appliances, smart appliances, electric bicycles, CO_2 meters, building materials— extending to larger purchases by the government such as utility vehicles, high speed trains, and electric buses, which are almost all already Chinese.

Before 2030, the Chinese will flood Western markets with top-quality green innovations at affordable prices. We nearly saw the same happen with 5G technology from Huawei. In 2018, almost every telecom operator in the West planned to buy 5G from Huawei instead of Ericsson or Nokia, because it was not only cheaper but also promised better quality, faster implementation, better integration, and a good after-sales service. After Trump put a stop to Huawei's plans by accusing the Chinese of spying and calling the company a national security risk, most Western countries dutifully followed Trump's call not to buy Huawei. Within two years, Huawei had all but lost its market for 5G and smartphones in Europe and North America. This outcome resulted in extra unforeseen costs for many telecom operators. Geopolitics had won the battle against Huawei, and as many operators were dependent on the government as their largest customer or owner, they had little choice but to comply. The government was happy, but not the shareholders of the telecom companies. Will we attempt to do the same for the tens of thousands of Chinese brands and products that Western consumers want to buy? As China has become the renewable factory of the world, in the coming years all Western countries will have to make a difficult choice between the competition being flattened by China or entering into a direct trade war with every Chinese brand, like we did with Huawei. If we choose the second option, can we still achieve all our climate goals? And what if China eliminates our companies from the Chinese market in the same politically motivated way?

My prediction is that before 2030 we will be faced with a choice between reaching our climate objectives and buying from the green factory of China.

The main reason is that 6G will arrive in 2030, which will allow the entire physical world to be monitored and managed in real time using sensors. Thanks to 6G, these sensors will then become much smarter with artificial intelligence and big data, but they'll also be embedded everywhere. In other words, the entire planet can then be optimized to stay within climate standards and objectives because every object will have a cheap built-in sensor, most likely from China. This decade we will have to make the choice between trusting China by making good agreements with Beijing on cybersecurity, and the choice of not trusting China, and banning all Chinese manufacturers out of fear for our national security. We will almost have to choose between the safety of the planet or that of our country. As for the Chinese, they will continue to trust the West for much longer, so long as we continue to buy Chinese products. But if we put more obstacles in the way, China will focus more on the rest of the world, not the West. This is what we saw happen with the Huawei case. As a result, it'll take much longer for us to meet our climate objectives. It's our choice.

This partly answers the question of whether China wants to build a new world order. To a certain extent, we in the West have become addicted to our dependence on China. We really can't do without those cheaper Chinese products, and they will all soon be smarter and more personalized. China has already largely determined the way we organize our lives, without changing our world order. Everything China does with the New Silk Road, with building of the most advanced supply chains, ports, and logistics improvements, with the control of raw materials, and the supply of electric cars, is mainly aimed at safeguarding China's economic growth and keeping the West as a customer. If we think of China as a global supplier of a smarter and cleaner future, then we really should worry less about how China wants to see us as a customer and whether or not we can continue to organize our own lives. What we should be more worried about is how our companies can stay competitive without having to rely on government protection from Chinese products. I really don't believe we can afford the "Huawei ban" on everything that comes from China. So, we have little choice but to learn from the new China, but to do that we must first learn to trust China. And this is precisely the paradox because we trust China less and less.

To break through this problem, we need to let go of the fear that China wants to rebuild our world order. The best way to do that is by looking at China from their own perspective. In 2020, China partially revealed how it sees the world, and that seems like a good starting point to me. In response to the increasingly hostile and unstable Western world, China decided to revive what it calls the "dual circulation strategy." This master plan puts a greater focus on the growth of the domestic market, in other words the "internal circulation," with less reliance on exports and growth based primarily on state investment over time. We can interpret this as a country that is again shutting itself off from the world, but that is not exactly what is meant by "dual circulation." The other part of the circulation is a further opening of China to the world, the "external circulation." That might seem like a paradox, because if you focus all your attention on China, the attention on the world would seem to decrease. But that's not true. China wants to open itself up more to countries, companies, and individuals that also see its cooperation with China as a driver for China. It is certainly not the first time that Beijing has wanted to replace export growth with domestic consumption growth, but this shift has proven difficult. Internal circulation now aims to shift dependence from the world to the Chinese consumer. External circulation, however, now aims to further integrate China with the rest of the world. If China were a company, it would be as if the board of directors—Beijing—decided in 2022 to optimize "internally" by focusing on innovation, productivity, talent, and marketing (to Chinese consumers) and "externally" to improve customer focus, provide higher quality products and services, and also to further open up the Chinese market to imports and foreign direct investment. You could actually say that, with its "dual circulation strategy," China is revealing itself and saying that it definitely doesn't want to lose us as their best customer, and definitely does not want to decouple from the world.

The question we can ask is: why would China want to make things difficult for its best customer—the West—by trying to rebuild the world order that China itself benefits from? This scenario doesn't seem to fit with pragmatic China, which sees the customer as its lifeline.

Given that the world is not static and Asia is constantly becoming more important, it seems obvious that China wants to provide the existing world order with new ideas and agreements. But as long as our world order works, China's focus seems to be more about cosmetic rather than fundamental structural changes. Whether our Western world order still works is a completely different question that is less directly connected to China. Everyone has an opinion about whether or not China wants to create a new world order, but we rarely look at the reason why China is working so hard to build its own "China order" domestically into a modern socialist society. Maybe we got so accustomed to maintaining the world order we built ourselves that we can't appreciate why China would not be eager to build and manage a new world order themselves.

We can in my view be confident that as long as China is focused on building its own home, it will leave ours mostly alone. And the reality is that China still has a lot of work to do, with 700 million people who remain poor by our standards, intractable demographic challenges, a risk-filled real estate market, gigantic government debt, and a degraded environment, not to mention an uphill struggle to gain the world's trust.

梦

mèng

Meaning: **dream, hope, future.** The ancient character is built up of a **person** lying on a **bed**. It symbolizes illusions or dreams that are not real, but feel true. The dreams of a better place or future are not real but trust in them is needed to achieve them.

8.

Trust the future. Do the Chinese themselves believe the propaganda about a perfect and harmonious future for all? Will China ever catch up with the West in terms of technology? Is Xi Jinping the new all-powerful emperor of a new Chinese empire? Is Beijing redistributing the wealth of the super-rich? Do the Chinese feel superior?

Universe and culture

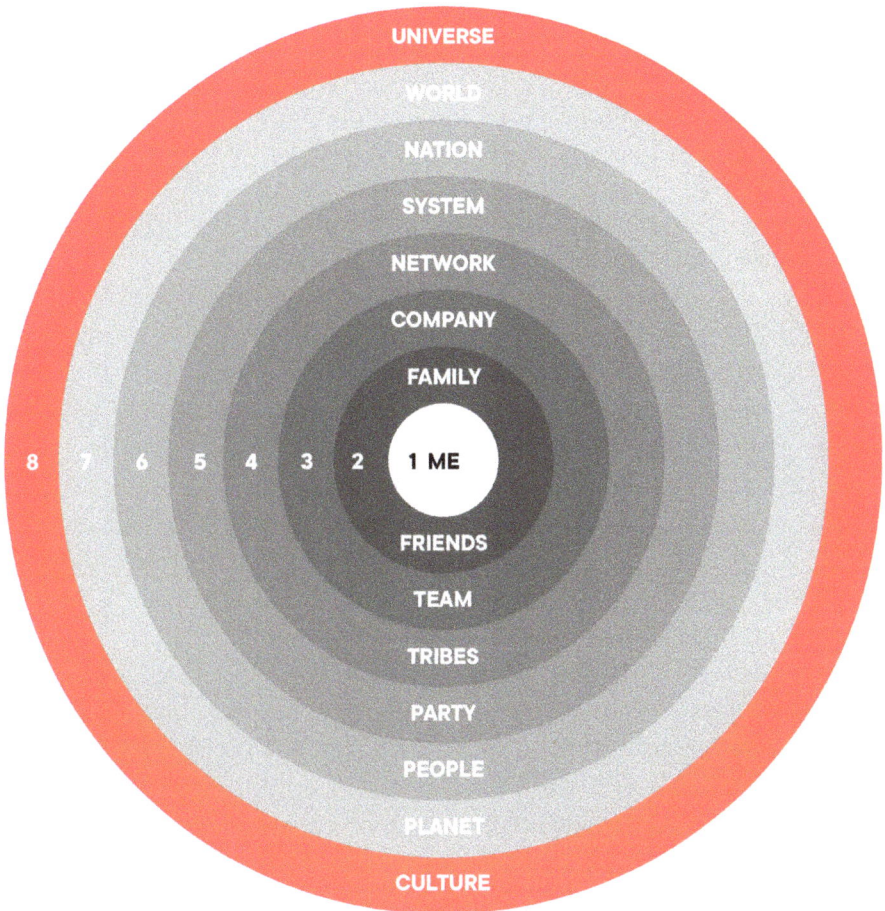

2001: A SPACE ODYSSEY

Other than China, I have two big passions: classical music and movies. As a child I grew up to the sound of J.S. Bach's BWV846-893: "The Well-Tempered Clavier." My father was a mathematics professor and an excellent amateur pianist. His life's work was dedicated to mathematically analyzing every single note of this masterpiece by Bach; he even wrote a thesis on Bach's master-piece for his PhD in musicology. From my teenage bedroom, I would hear him playing one of the forty-eight preludes or fugues every day. Not just once, but over and over, ten times or more. My father explained to me that Bach had written this piece as finger exercises. Forty years later, the cadences still echo in my head. At the age of fifty-six, my father died suddenly of a brain hemor-rhage. I was twenty-five when he passed away. Bach's music keeps my father's memory alive for me. I wrote every word of this book while listening to Bach: it creates a kind of intense hypnosis that inspires me to write. Although I mainly write about modern China and its future, when it comes to classical music I'm still very much happily stuck in the eighteenth and nineteenth centuries.

My other passion has always been movies. At the age of eighteen I started studying in the medieval city of Ghent. A cult movie theater Sphinx was just a few minutes' walk from my student room, so every week I would go and see at least three old movies, and I quickly became good friends with the owner of the theater. One day he offered me a job checking tickets at the door. The extra money was great, but the real draw for me was being able to watch movies for free. I quickly worked my way up to projectionist, and I spent eight years repairing and playing movies. This means I have seen a lot of classics, sometimes multiple times. Stanley Kubrick was my biggest hero. You've prob-ably seen one of his timeless masterpieces: *Spartacus*, *Lolita*, *Dr. Strangelove*, *The Shining*, *Full Metal Jacket*, *Eyes Wide Shut*, *A Clockwork Orange*, *Barry Lyndon*, or *2001: A Space Odyssey*. The last three films were my absolute favor-ites, partly because of the perfect use of classical music in the scores, as if the music had been written for the movies. I also love Kubrick's masterful use of tension between control, power, life progress, and the search for meaning. *2001: A Space Odyssey* is the one film that fascinates me the most. It is 142 minutes long but there is hardly any dialogue. Together, images, music, silence, and symbolism have a hypnotic effect. Kubrick's use of minimalism allows our imaginations to run wild.

In case you haven't seen *2001: A Space Odyssey*, which Kubrick made in 1968, I'll briefly explain the plot (so I can then make a comparison with China). Central to the story are the "Firstborn," who were created at the same time as the cosmos and are the caretakers of the universe. Four million years ago, they sent four monoliths to four different places in the universe to mysteriously catalyze evolution and stability. The four locations: in Africa on planet Earth, below the surface of the moon, in orbit around Jupiter, and lastly in the fifth dimension. The storyline can be divided into three parts.[159] Part one is the dawn of man. It begins in prehistoric Africa where a group of apes suddenly discovers the monolith on Earth. At first, they are scared of it, but then they realize that the bones of dead apes can be used as weapons against their enemies. The monolith gives them the insight that for a society to **progress**, there must be conflict. Part two takes place in the year 2001, when humans travel to the moon in a spaceship guided by a super-intelligent computer (HAL9000), which is both a tool and a weapon. They approach the monolith on the moon without fear or curiosity, as they feel **powerful** and in **control** of the situation. On the moon, they hear a loud noise that guides them towards the third monolith, which is orbiting Jupiter. The journey to Jupiter represents the struggle between humans and the HAL9000 machine destroying each other in order to survive. The machine becomes human, and humans become machines. On the way to Jupiter, the last survivor (Dave) manages to overpower the HAL9000 machine. In part three, Dave discovers the third monolith, which sucks him into time and space. After this teleportation to another constellation, Dave is seen on his deathbed with the fourth monolith in his room as he watches his own life flash before his eyes. He is now no longer scared and considers the **meaning** of life, experiencing his own rebirth as a star child. Everything has come full circle. He can now prepare humanity on Earth for the next step in their evolution.

CHINA'S MONOLITHS

Kubrick, who died in 1999, conceived of *2001: A Space Odyssey* as an exploration of a future time when humans would invent machines intelligent enough to guide journeys into outer space. As early as 1969 NASA reached the moon, but even today, a machine as intelligent as humans is still a long way off. As it happens, the year 2001 became perhaps the most significant moment in China's exploration of **progress**, **power**, **control**, and **meaning**. Using Kubrick's movie as an analogy, we could say that in 2001, the wealthy West sent three monoliths, or signals, to China that changed the country and its people forever. Twenty years later, China received the fourth and last monolith.

THE FIRST MONOLITH

The first "monolith" the United States unknowingly sent to China only a week after the 9/11 attacks in New York. Bush Junior's "War on Terror" statement signaled to Chinese President Jiang Zemin that the United States were suddenly on the same side as China when it came to tackling the newly defined global threat of terrorism together. China saw this as a green light to ramp up its anti-terror campaigns in Xinjiang. Interventions by the United States in Central Asia and the Middle East would show how far you could go in this war. This new type of warfare led the United States to develop completely new tools to reinforce its *position* as a global power. Because of this war, the West no longer saw China as an enemy. The Cold War against communism had ended after 1989 with the Soviet withdrawal from Afghanistan, the fall of the Berlin Wall, and a series of peaceful revolutions in Eastern Europe. It seemed that, a new democratic world order and new model for world peace had been born. In this new era, China would also *change*.

According to many in the West, it was now only a matter of time before China would evolve and eventually adopt our model, which can be seen as the second "monolith" China would get from us. Meanwhile, China's military budget[160] and efforts to develop a modern arsenal of technological weapons increased significantly. You can say it shot up, quite literally, because in 2002 China announced plans to build quite a space station (this goal was achieved in 2021). Since 2002, China has made significant strides with its space program: its first-ever manned space flight in 2003; landing on the dark side of the moon in 2019; and landing a rover on Mars in 2021.

THE SECOND MONOLITH

The second signal China received from the West came at the end of 2001, after fifteen years of long and difficult negotiations. On November 11, 2001, China was finally accepted as the 143rd member of the World Trade Organization (WTO). Shortly afterwards on December 27, 2001, it was given permanent normal trade relations (PNTR) status with the United States.[161] China had been formally admitted to the global market and trading system, but on the basis of a set of international rules that it hadn't been involved in creating. The country made firm commitments to open most of its industries to foreign investment, provide better transparency of its rules, and protect intellectual property. Years later, many in the West believe that China failed to meet its promises, didn't really liberalize, and instead abused its position within the WTO. In fact, China benefited much less from its preferential treatment in the WTO than most people think,[162] and it liberalized most industries to almost the same extent as in Western countries today. The miscalculation the West made in 2001 was to assume that, by inviting China into the Western world's economic club, it would automatically evolve into an open, free, democratic, liberal economy. Over the twenty years since its entry into the WTO, China's size, rapid growth, and economic transition have instead made Beijing one of the world's most powerful governments in terms of both internal control and external power. The sudden and poorly planned withdrawal of US forces from Afghanistan in 2021 marked the end of America's war on terror and was widely seen as a sign of weakening

America's power and influence. By making China its new number one target, Washington seems to be admitting that China is shaping the new world order. As America falters, the evolution of events allows China more freedom and confidence to continue its journey towards development and self-discovery.

THE THIRD MONOLITH

You could say China received the third signal on July 13, 2001, when the International Olympic Committee (IOC) announced that China would host the 2008 Olympic Games. In the same spirit as China's acceptance into the World Trade Organization, China's Olympic bid delegation promised that the host country would improve its openness and human rights record over the seven years leading up to the 2008 Games.[163] Beijing's bid received fifty-six votes, Toronto twenty-two, Paris eighteen, Istanbul nine, and Osaka didn't even make it to the finish line. The President of the IOC, a Belgian named Jacques Rogge said his organization's goal was to open up a country that was home to a quarter of the world's population but had never hosted the Games. The IOC saw this as a step in China's gradual social and economic reform. China saw it as such too but had a bigger objective: its first Olympics would be a long-overdue moment of recognition and glory on the world stage. After the mismanagement of the 2004 Olympic Games in Athens, which helped plunge Greece further into economic depression, the 2008 Beijing Games would be a stark and successful contrast. When the Games were held, the winning athletes stood on the podium, but so did China. In the end, China won more gold medals than the United States.

When 2,008 perfectly coordinated drummers performed in astonishing unison at the opening ceremony in Beijing's Bird's Nest stadium, China was sending a clear message to the world that it was on its way to becoming a global power. For the geopolitical experts in the West, the 2008 Games were a sign of Beijing's growing power, also the threat its authoritarian system posed to the Western way of life. Comparisons to the 1936 Berlin Games under Hitler were made in the West. For Beijing, it was important to show China in a positive light, but it was even more important to use the hosting of the Olympic Games to confirm for 1.3 billion Chinese citizens that their country, after nearly 200 years in the shadow of the West, had regained its rightful place on the world's stage. China had casually invested $42 billion dollars on the Games to ensure they would be successful. The man who made sure the Games also ran smoothly from a political point of view was none other than Xi Jinping. Nine months earlier to the opening ceremony of the Olympics, he had been promoted to Secretary of the Standing Committee of the Central Political Bureau, the highest group of leaders in China, and a few months later to Vice President of the People's Republic of China.[164] The 2008 Beijing Olympics not only put

China on the world map, but it did the same for Xi Jinping. To continue my analogy, since 2008, China has been inquisitively and courageously looking for the last monolith, something to **give meaning** and **greater cohesion** to the entire Chinese population and Chinese culture.

THE FOURTH MONOLITH

In my view, the last sign or signal came twenty years later—in 2021. This time the sign emerged not from external reflection, but internal self-reflection: this was China's moment of rebirth. The West, led mainly by the United States, confirmed to China that it was now seen as an equal. This was never stated explicitly, but our actions made it clear that China was now seen as being a key player in the new world order. China suddenly became the new enemy; and this meant China could now see itself as an equal.

For China, it could not be clearer that Canada's arrest of Huawei's CFO Meng Wanzhou, a skirmish in the growing technology war with the West, was an attempt to limit China's technological progress. Similarly, the US trade war with China driven by President Trump was clearly understood in China as an underhanded way to slow down China's economic growth. Direct allegations blaming China for the outbreak and initial poor control of the coronavirus in early 2020 were seen by China as a particularly nasty way for the West to portray China as evil and dangerous. Two years later, it appears that the alarmist allegations against the Wuhan lab were most likely false, and that Trump's trade war against China had minimal impact on China's growth and exports. In the end, even Huawei's CFO was released by Canada after acknowledging her mistakes, without pleading guilty. After three years of the West accusing or attacking China over various allegations, very few have been backed up with hard evidence. Of course, China hasn't always played nicely either. In the end, it doesn't really matter who behaved the nastiest or nicest during this cat fight: what matters is that most Chinese no longer look up to the West as a goal, example, teacher, or judge, but rather they see it as a bad loser. It seems the more control we try to exert over China, the less China will feel like engaging or playing our game. China is now finding its own path, one that we largely misunderstand. We see Beijing rolling out new laws, rules, and stricter enforcement of rules aimed at restricting the tycoons, monopolies, free market, and freedom of expression. We think: Beijing wants to strengthen Party control. This is partly because we think in terms of a deterministic world: Western thinking relies on facts, on people and their actions to determine how events will play out within the rules we know. We deduce based on details and development. But Chinese think more in terms of the relations between things and a cyclical return to an original state. We think very much in straight lines, the Chinese logic pictures concentric circles. The Chinese draw conclusions on the basis of relationships within the bigger picture, which is then reduced to the essentials. For them, you need to understand the whole before you can understand a single part.

Put simply, we in the West want to control all the essentials as much as possible, while the Chinese want to be able to let go of everything as much as possible. This is one of the basics of Taoism, which contains the philosophy of *wu wei* described earlier in chapter 4. Our interpretation is that Beijing is increasing its control over the powerful and the rich elements of society, the Chinese logic behind the government's moves is that it is precisely the controlling influence that the powerful and rich have over the poorer classes and society at large that Beijing needs to reduce or remove. In 2021, a perception of the central government in Beijing as a machine focused on control is therefore too simplistic; there is much more going on than meets the eye. Is Beijing now cleaning up excesses to gain more control over the rich and powerful as we saw during the cultural revolution, or is Beijing instead cleaning up excesses to become even richer and more powerful as a country in this new era? A subtle, but huge difference in how to read China.

China has absorbed a lot from the West over the last thirty years, which has helped the country rapidly catch up with the West. But remember that China thinks less in terms of catching up or overtaking; that's our linear way of thinking. China thinks in terms of change. As a former good student of the West, China is now busy getting its own house in order and preparing itself for a new universal (holistic) adventure toward greater unity. And to be honest: China still has a lot of work to do before its house is tidy. They need to tackle a wide range of issues: the environment, energy needs, inequality, debt, the real estate crisis, technological independence, health care, productivity. China realizes that there is no longer any country in the world that can provide the solutions it needs on the scale China represents. This means the Chinese people will have to work out the solutions and next steps for themselves. Therefore, today's China spends less and less time mirroring the West's achievements and action plans. It wants to reinvent itself on its own terms, rather than equal us.

The West is no longer the reference point. This insight extends to the cultural realm, for example China's twelve socialist values, which were established in 2012.[165] The "national values" of prosperity, democracy, civility, and harmony, then the "social values" of freedom, equality, justice, and the rule of law, and finally the "individual" values of patriotism, dedication, integrity, and friendship. If I had said these twelve values were from a European country, you might not have been surprised. What makes these words different in China, then? The biggest difference lies in China's collective mindset with its circles of trust versus our individualistic, linear, and legitimacy-based approach to trust. We all pursue the same ideals, but we're taking different paths to get there. The Chinese believe more in the individual as a member of a collective—a circle such as a family, company, or clan—that helps determine your existence and future.

As outlined earlier in this book, Chinese are less concerned about controlling others than about controlling themselves, because everyone's identity is partly determined in relation to others. Individual rights in China are part of, often subordinate to, the rights of the collective, and are not a right to self-determination if they harm others. Control in China is therefore actually more inclusive, while in the West it is more exclusive: China seeks more harmony in society; we are looking for more freedom.

We don't see China as a free country, but the majority of Chinese do see themselves as free in their national context: the pursuit of harmony. Today, the vast majority of Chinese enjoy a freedom from worry that enables them to continue their journey of self-discovery. For the entire country, this is seen as a long-term goal that could take another hundred years to achieve. This has been given a name in China: the *datong* society (or the great unity), which is scheduled to be achieved by or before 2121, for the two hundredth anniversary of the Communist Party.

THE NEXT BOUNDARIES

When I was studying Chinese at university in Beijing in 1996, we had to memorize twenty new Chinese words every day. After two months you already had a thousand new characters to remember. This reminded me of my Latin lessons as a child, but this time it was like doing military drills. Every morning, each student was called to the board at the front of the classroom for a dictation exercise. If you hadn't truly mastered yesterday's lesson, you quickly realized what loss of face means in China. Words from previous weeks could also suddenly be requested, so as a student of Chinese, learning by heart became second nature. In addition, you also have to learn the Chinese language itself. Studying English as a child, you also have to learn a lot of new words, but we only have twenty-six letters. For each Chinese word, you need to remember five things: its meaning, the specific characters, the order in which to write those characters, pronunciation, and tone. Mandarin has four tones, while the Cantonese language used in southern China has as many as nine tones. Not surprisingly then, I've never met a Chinese person who is tone deaf. You have three more things to remember for each Chinese word than you do for English.

Scientific research has shown that using the Chinese language has a very different effect on the brain. The combination of unique writing, tone, and pronunciation forces students to use both parts of the frontal lobes to learn the language, instead of using mostly the left half of the brain as we do with English.[166] The only way to remember all those thousands of characters is to rewrite them a hundred times each so that your wrist remembers them. I think I must have written out 300,000 characters while I was studying Chinese, because you need to know at least 3,000 characters to be able to read a newspaper fluently. This writing process is also supposed to help develop your motor and visual identification skills, which keep your mind sharp. It did ruin my eyes though, as I've been wearing glasses ever since. Compared to Chinese, other languages, almost all of which originally come from Mesopotamia, are fairly uniform, typically written left-to-right, and rather simplistic. Learning Chinese is simply more difficult than English, but as a side effect it increases the neural activity of motor and thinking abilities, as well as the spatial memory of the brain. This doesn't make the Chinese any smarter, but it does possibly give them an advantage when it comes to understanding mathematical concepts. In any case, those intense Chinese language lessons in Beijing felt like a daily overdose of gymnastics for the brain.

What I remember best are moments when our teacher suddenly transformed from being a drill sergeant into a superbly passionate teacher. This happened when she started talking about China in superlatives: China had the longest wall, the oldest surviving culture, the largest imperial palace, the highest mountain, the lowest spot of land on Earth, the furthest point from the sea, the largest population, the biggest army, the longest trade route in the world, and so on. She couldn't get enough of it; she knew every number by heart, right down to the last digit. And yes, we were also tested on these facts the next day. This was when I first realized that the Chinese really are obsessed with numbers and superlatives. Whatever the cost, they would set targets to build the largest dam in the world, the tallest skyscrapers, the biggest high-speed network, the longest bridge, the largest airport, the most windmills and solar panels, the largest ultra-high-voltage grid, and the long list goes on. We often hear that China can "think big" because it thinks much further ahead in time than the West. China has impressive and detailed five-year plans, ambitious innovation goals to be achieved by 2030, a comprehensive social welfare system to be created by 2049, and dreams that reach as far forward as 2121. We also often wrongly conclude that the Chinese simply have more time than our politicians, who have to be re-elected every four years, or business leaders, who have to make quarterly reports and annual dividend targets for their shareholders. For me, these explanations don't fit with the enormous impatience the Chinese can show, or the extremely rapid speed of execution that sometimes affects quality in China. In my mind, the Chinese don't think further ahead because they have more time, or because they are less accountable for their decisions; they think further ahead because they have a greater understanding of change.

The power of their overambitious planning is rooted in the *I Ching* (Yi jīng 易经), or *Book of Changes*. This is the oldest book in the world—again a superlative—written in 1300 BC. These ancient Chinese texts are based on the psychology of the process of individuation; outlining a system of continuous self-reflection through character training and development of the psyche. The concepts in the *I Ching* formed the cradle of Chinese culture and thought; especially the two main philosophical traditions: the ever-changing natural world (as opposed to organized society) of Taoism and the Confucian philosophy of social organization. The *I Ching* explains that in the perceptible part of our existence nothing remains without movement, or without change. Every single thing comes into being, develops, perishes, or disappears. But there is also a paradox contained in the character for the word "change" (yì 易), which is made up of a sun (rì 日) and a moon (yuè 月): implying both change and stability are always present, but not always visible.

The *I Ching* embodies three fundamental principles regarding change:
- The first constant is that everything changes.
- The second principle is that change can be understood through simplification, relationships, and unity.
- The third principle is that although things change, things cannot change.

Writing about the *I Ching*, Carl Jung commented that every process is completely or partly disrupted by chance, so that under natural conditions a state of affairs that completely conforms to certain fixed laws is an exception. The implication is that Chinese thinking is not based on the Western science-based belief in causality, but rather on patterns that cause random events. Implicit ambiguity makes the *I Ching* the best guide for dealing with uncertainty and for understanding the Chinese approach to life. If we greatly simplify the differences between Western and Chinese thinking through the lens of the *I Ching*, three things stand out:
- Chinese leaders work towards a *long-term vision*, because they assume everything is always changing: good can become bad, and vice versa; loss can become gain, and vice versa; crisis can mean an opportunity, and vice versa.
- The Chinese are more comfortable with *ambiguity*. We recognize this in the symbol of yin and yang. The acceptance of direct opposites and contradictions clashes with our Western binary thinking.
- Chinese individuals and organizations think less analytically and causally, and much more in terms of *relationships* and *networks*. The holistic Chinese way of thinking sees an entity as a relationship of the parts, not a combination of the parts.

In a country like China, where the only constant is change, committing yourself to one direction is a bad strategy. You might end up where you wanted to, but the world around you will have already changed. The Chinese start by first setting a clear goal, but they don't decide on the direction. The main goal for China, within all circles of trust, is harmony and stability. Next come the steps of vision and implementation. In China, vision is often expressed by a leading figure as a collective quest. The path toward the goal isn't linear, but pursued by constantly scanning the way ahead, like a radar looking for signals. The Chinese are less likely to focus on the specific facts or the immediate changes, but rather pay attention to the reactions to changes. They are less obsessed by a specific strategy or choice and are more attuned to the underlying cycles, or sequences of events that repeat themselves. Implementation is next, and this is where the great strength of China's pragmatism comes to the surface. In this game, the speed is constantly changing: sometimes speeding up; sometimes slowing down; sometimes even stopping; now and again, jumping. It's like crossing a fast-flowing river using the stones hidden just under the surface of the water. The goal is to safely reach the other side of the river—without falling in the water. This demands a lot of self-control, agility, attention, self-reflection, and quick research. While making the crossing, you are allowed to make mistakes, as long as everyone learns from them quickly. This river crossing analogy can help us better understand China's and Chinese people's unique mix of self-control and risk-taking. Today, after centuries of experience in how to deal with change on a massive scale, modern China is able to start and properly manage its many mega-projects. In my mind, these mega-projects therefore symbolize China's deep cultural appetite for change, and they are not the result of hubris, as is sometimes claimed.

The Chinese really love their symbolism, which has ancient origins. We see this with numbers; Chinese numerology is still deeply rooted in the superstitions or taboos of modern Chinese culture. Numbers like four should be avoided, while eight is considered very lucky. This is based on the pronunciation of the characters, where four (sì, 死) sounds like "death" (sǐ 死), and eight (bā 八) sounds like (fā, 发)—prosperity or something being started. The sound of number combinations is also used to indicate things, expectations, or symbolism.

We therefore shouldn't underestimate the deep symbolism behind any of China's master plans. They reveal more how China is steadily moving ahead than how great China is. If we look more at China's international mega-investments from this symbolic perspective, maybe we will also be able to trust China more. However, we often do exactly the opposite because our Western perspective has taught us that international relations are always strategic, or always conducted in a country's own selfish interests. Of course, China also pursues its own interests, but there is often more emphasis on the word "own" than "interest." There is a significant difference between our Western *inside-out* thinking vs. the Chinese approach of thinking from *outside-in*. The Chinese approach is much more contextual, or thinking in circles. In many situations, China's main aim isn't to exercise its **power** on the world, but rather to strengthen its **own** position in **relation** to the world powers.

China's leaders explicitly state their desire to give their 1.4 billion people confidence that China is on a steady path to restore its former glory. Keystone projects and world-first achievements are seen as symbolic milestones towards restored greatness. Chinese explorers reaching the bottom of the ocean at a depth of 10,000 meters creates a milestone. The significance of Chinese space missions being the first to land spacecraft on the dark side of the moon is another step. Clearly overambitious plans for the New Silk Road, which already connects more than 180 countries to China by land and sea, fall in the same category, as does the more questionable groundbreaking dream of a new maritime route from China to Europe across the North Pole. There are many other examples of this zeal: the Chinese Beidou GPS satellite system and the Chinese space station are both in operational orbit today; by 2035, China wants to activate an orbiting solar power plant so that rays from the sun that don't reach the Earth can still shine on China. China already has its own rover on Mars and plans to land the first humans on the red planet by 2033. In contrast, many Western institutions have severely delayed or even canceled many of their mega-project ideas, because they are unprofitable or too likely to fail.

For Chinese people, the symbolism of these "moon shot" programs is clear. Since the next boundaries of exploration are in these remote places, China's aspirations and progress not only have symbolic meaning for China, but they also send a strong signal to the West that China is positioning itself to win the race for the future. Needless to say, the unexplored places in the oceans, under the ice, in Earth orbit, and the universe have potential value for scientific advancement and economic exploitation. China is extending a hand to the international community to work together on many of these projects, but far too little attention is being paid to this. We don't trust China's intentions because we realize that this groundbreaking research (from our own experience) could also achieve economic, geopolitical, and military objectives. We instinctively think in terms of conflict and competition, not in terms of harmony. With our confrontational posture, we may be forcing China to enter into increasingly direct competition with the West. The question is whether we should try to hold China back, and whether we still can even achieve this? Wouldn't we be better off exploring the unknown together with an overambitious country? In its lofty aspirations, China is mainly seeking change and improvement. Don't we have the same goals? Do we realize that our growing distrust of China strengthens not only China's self-confidence, but also that of all other countries that the West distrusts? Despite Xi Jinping's calls to join forces to build a global community with a shared future for humanity and a better world for everyone, the West may very well limit its chances for a better future by shunning China as a potential partner.

The most recent example of this pattern is the Beijing Winter Olympics in February 2022. In 2021 there were worldwide calls for a boycott of the Winter Games because of China's violation of human rights. The International Olympic Committee pointed out that, according to the Olympic charter, the Olympic Games are an apolitical event that aims to bring the whole world together. Despite this, Joe Biden decided to boycott the Winter Games by not sending any US diplomatic representation to Beijing. Other countries followed suit: Canada, Australia, United Kingdom, India, Lithuania, Estonia, Kosovo, Denmark, and Belgium. The intention to put this pressure on Beijing, however, backfired and only increased the pressure on the West. With an absence of prominent Western leaders, all of Xi Jinping's attention and China's spotlight focused on one person: Vladimir Putin.

At that point, Russia had as many as 100,000 soldiers at the border of Ukraine, ready for possible military action in the country. Putin had already been warned by America and the EU that an invasion of Ukraine would end up costing him and his country in the form of a Western boycott and sanctions for Russia. Putin kept claiming that he had no intention of invading the country, but he demanded a guarantee that Ukraine would never become part of NATO; a guarantee he didn't get. Xi had a very good understanding of Putin's position, because China shares concerns about the military presence of America and some close United States allies at its own borders under one of these names: Five Eyes, QUAD, or AUKUS. China and Russia have a very different past, mindset, and priorities, but they are both concerned about Western world hegemony. In some ways, the absence of Western politicians at the Winter Games and our distrust of China brought Putin and Xi Jinping closer together. China and Russia are now aligned in opposing any attempts to expand Western troops along their borders. They also signed a massive trade deal, which sees Russia giving more energy security to China, and China giving much more economic security to Russia—especially in the event of an economic boycott. A win-win for them. The reason we keep making these mistakes is that we think from our own perspective and self-interest, and don't quickly enough make that mental shift to understand the concerns and mindset of countries like China or Russia. If it were to come to a real war in Ukraine, we will have lost the opportunity to go back and restore trust.

PUBLIC AND PRIVATE

Under Mao, all of China's companies were nationalized. Under Deng Xiaoping, the exact opposite happened, meaning most companies were privatized. Today, ninety percent of all companies in China are private companies that contribute fifty percent of tax revenues, sixty percent of the GDP, seventy percent of

R&D investment, and create eighty percent of national employment. In parallel, state-owned companies built the infrastructure and financed the growth that enabled China's economic miracle and trade.[167] Of the 135 Chinese companies that were part of the Fortune 500 global ranking in 2021, eighty-two are state-owned, including forty-nine centrally owned and thirty-three local companies.[168] Another eleven firms could also be added to that list, such as the state-owned banks and the Chinese postal service. State-owned companies play an important role in the Chinese economy, for example, containing the financial crisis of 2008, eradicating extreme poverty, or helping to control the coronavirus in 2020. Xi Jinping calls these companies the economic and political foundations of China's socialist system. Today, he intends to make them even stronger, bigger, and better, with an emphasis on making them better managed and more competitive. This has been a challenge for years, with one reform being introduced after another. The focus today is on more cross-fertilization with the private sector, combined with restructuring. Tencent invested in the state telecoms company China Unicom, Geely in China Railway, and Alibaba in China's Broadcasting Network. ByteDance has already sold one percent of its shares to the state, which now has a seat on the board of directors.

The trend is clear: private technology companies will increasingly work closely with state-owned companies to raise their standards and improve their innovation to globally competitive levels. The idea that Beijing wants to limit private tech companies like Alibaba or Tencent in order to return the economy to a pure communist model where the state controls production (which would no doubt limit innovation) is our Western misinterpretation of the situation. In reality, Beijing desperately needs its successful tech giants to help upgrade its state-owned enterprises in new and innovative ways and achieve prosperity for China. The goal of common prosperity (gòngtóng fùyù 共同富裕) doesn't mean we're returning to the communist period of Mao's communes, but that 600 million poorer people are to be uplifted into China's middle class. In the United States, the capitalist model creates the country's vast wealth. But the fair distribution of that wealth to the wider population is made extremely difficult by a self-sustaining wealthier elite and often powerless government, so the gap in wealth and opportunities between people of different socio-economic backgrounds widens. This growing inequality has all kinds of dangerous consequences, including a rise in crime and increasing public health problems. Professor Richard Wilkinson[169] predicts that this trend of greater inequality will put extreme pressure on the overall social model in the US over time.

The Chinese economic miracle caused inequality to grow rapidly until 2008 as productivity soared; but since 2008, productivity growth has slowed.[170] China really needs productivity growth to become a high-income country, but not at the cost of more inequality in the country. Beijing doesn't want to risk the system falling apart due to a hyper-competitive and ultra-capitalist model where growth and profits become the only real driver for Chinese companies, to the detriment of Chinese social stability. China has consciously embedded capitalist elements into its economic engine with visible results: global leadership positions in trade, finance, stock markets, entrepreneurship, the wealthy, technology companies, innovations, and much more. China wants to create even more wealth using these capitalist elements, but it also wants to guarantee access to opportunities for the lowest layers of society. In China, anyone can become rich, as in the United States, but in China that wealth must be achieved *thanks* to the people, and not at the expense of the wider population. In China, money will always be controlled by politics, while in the United States it is the other way round. Beijing is like a strict father who wants to give his children every opportunity, so long as there are some solid agreements in place. Washington is more like a successful father who wants to set an example for his children but is too busy to watch them grow up.

Because the Communist Party is that father figure, we easily assume that Beijing is more interested in controlling and holding its children back than giving them the right direction and opportunities. The old image of a "Marxist-Leninist" Chinese government still closes down even the most open minds in our Western society. If we read that Beijing is encouraging private companies to invest in state-owned companies, or that someone from the Party is suddenly made a mandatory employee of every company, we naturally assume that Beijing is increasing its control for some sinister reason. The question is whether China taking steps to increase its control is all that unreasonable. When a Chinese private company, such as the giant property developer Evergrande, with its constant "capitalist" hunger for more growth, pushes the entire Chinese economy into crisis and leads millions of citizens and subcontractors to the brink of bankruptcy, then Xi Jinping's strategy to make the Party and the state-owned enterprises once again a stabilizing foundation of China's dynamic economy doesn't seem so preposterous. Beijing does intend to limit or nationalize "greedy" companies that made too many risky investments and expanded too fast with too few controls, but on a selective basis. As I described in my book *China's New Normal*, a very excessive growth model (I call it the N curve) encourages Chinese start-ups to make too many investments too quickly, while large companies build up enormous debt with Chinese state-owned banks in order to substantially increase both assets and liabilities on the balance sheet. The systemic problem is that many Chinese companies have done this across dozens of sectors, and that if some of them were to fail, this might create a sudden panic among investors, which in turn could shake a company, sector, or even the entire country. This became painfully visible with China's real estate crisis in 2021 when the upward trend over years and decades (as with Evergrande) suddenly came crashing down.

Direct government bailouts like the West made after the 2008 financial crisis are no longer an option in China. If a private company gets itself into serious trouble, Beijing will not hesitate to restructure and even nationalize its business activities. This decade, therefore, we can expect further nationalization of private Chinese companies. In fact, we have already seen this happen with HNA Group, Anbang Insurance, and most recently Evergrande. The government's litmus test is a simple one: if a business model enriches private individuals at the expense of the state (which is usually the largest creditor), the state will split those companies up or sell their assets to provide enough liquidity; with the remainder then being nationalized. Finally, the owners may be prosecuted for misconduct, and possibly face prison sentences. For foreign investors in China this is a real risk to consider. Should their Chinese business partner face serious government scrutiny over misconduct, they might suddenly find themselves dealing with a state-owned company as a new business partner. And the reason this is annoying is because projects in the West based on government involvement often have a different level of sensitivity. You can find that overnight your partner, who was a private Chinese investor, is now the Chinese state; a whole new ball game. So, we cannot be sure that Chinese private companies will always remain private, but we can be confident that Chinese state-owned companies will increasingly resemble Chinese private companies, and become more efficient, competitive, and international. When it comes to partnerships with the Chinese in sensitive sectors for the state, it is therefore important to carefully screen all investors and their backgrounds before entering into business deals. A lot of misunderstandings between the West and China come about because we evaluate public and private companies differently, while China sees them as two sides of the same coin.

THE GOOD EMPEROR

More than 3,000 years ago, King Wen of the Zhou dynasty (1046-256 BC) became the first Chinese ruler to claim that his authority came straight from heaven.[171] "Heaven" was the embodiment of a universal divine power that gave a particular individual the power to rule the Earth in its name. The belief that kings and later the emperors were the "sons of heaven" had its roots in the even more ancient Chinese tradition of the worshiping ancestors who ascended to serve in the court of heaven. Under this belief system, the power to rule was only legitimate if the "son of heaven" upheld his moral obligation to be a good ruler for his people, otherwise the country would experience terrible tragedies. During his peaceful reign, King Wen became a symbol of good and charitable government. Around 300 BC, the philosopher Mencius (the second-biggest influence on Chinese thinking after Confucius) wrote that the universe had not created humans for the monarch, but rather the monarch for humans. Of course, not all Chinese emperors were good in practice, but they all used the concept of the mandate of heaven as justification for their power. The misery some emperors caused and even natural disasters that occurred during their reigns were blamed on their personal moral misconduct, which meant the mandate of heaven was withdrawn, thereby giving the population the right to overthrow the ruler. Throughout China's history, rebels and revolutionaries have risen up to overthrow immoral emperors who have lost the mandate of heaven. In recent history, it is mainly the 1911 and 1949 revolutions that are fixed in the memory of every Chinese person. The student uprising of 1989 on Tiananmen Square, while it didn't go down in the history books as a real revolution, remains etched into the memory of the entire world.

The 1911 revolution finally ended more than twenty centuries of dynastic rule in China. This was led by the Nationalist Party of China, which, under the presidency of Sun Yat-sen, founded the Republic of China (ROC), the name still used today for the island of Taiwan. In fact, the Republic of China still officially uses 1911 as the year zero of their calendar, instead of the Gregorian calendar most of the world uses. The Communist Party of China considers the 1911 revolution, in which Mao himself served as a soldier in a local regiment, as a great event overthrowing the dynastic rule, but not as a victory in terms of stopping the landowners and semi colonialism that had created an elitist, privileged class.

Given that overthrowing weak emperors and immoral rulers is justifiable in China's culture, it is not surprising that most Chinese approve of an extremely strong leader like Xi Jinping, and also that the Party should keep a very close eye on any form of mass unrest or demonstrations that could endanger the system. The fear of a bottom-up revolution that will throw China into chaos is real and should definitely not be underestimated. In the West, we place our trust in the opposite idea: that protests and demonstrations in fact keep the system in balance. We activate the masses as a counterweight to indifferent or passive politicians, while in some way the slightly more passive and politically indifferent Chinese population motivates their active politicians to take even more action.

As long as the Chinese emperor is not only about talk, but even more about action, the people will have confidence in the path towards the future. In today's China, the biggest decision maker (some say the emperor) guiding all that action is Xi Jinping. To the extent few in the West appreciate; he therefore enjoys a high level of recognition, trust, and respect among the vast majority of the Chinese people. A thousand years ago, China's Confucian thinkers claimed that the emperor not only had a mandate from heaven to serve and improve the lives of the people, but also that, as a civil servant, it was his role to maintain the natural order of the world, or what the Chinese call "everything under heaven." Therefore, when Xi Jinping uses the phrases such as "global harmony," "prosperity for all," "contribution to civilization," or "progress of mankind" in his speeches, in some respects this is less about propaganda uttered by the General Secretary of the Communist Party of China as it is confirmation of his traditional Chinese leadership role general secretary of the universe. It's best to look at the "universe" (Everything under Heaven - tiānxià 天下) in the historical Chinese context here, and certainly not as if Xi Jinping were an ambassador or mouthpiece of a higher force; let's not forget that the CPC is officially atheist. However, what we perceive as the empty rhetoric of China's top leader has for millennia served as a signal of the ruler's moral responsibility to keep the natural order of China, Chinese culture, the world, the entire planet, and the universe in balance. This means in the eyes of most Chinese people, the near-absolute power taken by and granted to Xi Jinping is appropriate for the enormous task he has been given. The new emperor, as Xi Jinping is often called in the West, reminds us of historical dictators with nearly unlimited power who haven't really made the world a better place but rather led people into disasters. Few in the West believe that Xi Jinping was, is, or will remain a "good emperor," but this is what most Chinese people do believe. Not only because according to Chinese publications, Xi has an almost flawless track record as a civil servant, leader, and individual. But mainly because, building on the work of his predecessors Deng Xiaoping, Jiang Zemin, and Hu Jintao, he has steered half of China's population out of poverty and into the middle class and the other half out of extreme poverty.

All former leaders of the modern People's Republic of China since Deng have had to make tough decisions during times of crisis—the Tiananmen uprising, SARS, the 2008 financial crisis, etc., but Xi Jinping's handling of the coronavirus pandemic will surely be remembered by the entire population for how he kept the country safe with his clear communication and timely measures. The proof of this is the hundreds of millions of Chinese people who complied with the sudden drastic lockdowns, and the 500,000 volunteers who threw themselves into the fight. The unprecedented scale of the solidarity across the country became the real success of China's zero-COVID-19 policy. After Chinese people watched the pandemic news reports from the West, full of endless talk and doubts about the seriousness of the pandemic, together with delays and ambiguity of decisions, China's direct and effective steps to control the pandemic were seen as ultimate proof of the expertise and competence of its leaders. We assume this obedience is due to China's totalitarian regime, which takes an authoritarian approach because it doesn't have the trust of the people. Perhaps this is a reflection of our own experience, because it is citizens of the West and not the Chinese who are losing their faith in politics, science, experts, and the pharmaceutical industry. If we want to understand China, we need to stop projecting onto Chinese our distrust of our own system.

Consider one example: the spontaneous riots that broke out across Europe at the end of 2021 because people no longer wanted to follow the coronavirus restrictions, and the police crackdowns that followed. Viewed from China, the West seems increasingly chaotic, and sometimes even totalitarian in how it acts. Throughout the pandemic, China had less need for similar action to contain the people, despite the fact that the initial outbreak in Wuhan did create an explosive situation. Tremendous anger was unleashed on Chinese social media in early January 2020, directed towards the local Wuhan government, up to and after the death of Dr. Li Wenliang a month later. Mass uprisings could have erupted across the country given the impatient, pragmatic nature of Chinese people. Forcing the Chinese to stay home and stop their business or stop working for a while is as difficult as telling an American he is no longer allowed to keep guns in the house; this is about the right to exist. In fact, spontaneous local protests against cases of fraud or immoral behavior are happening all the time all over China. The Chinese police usually move swiftly to get these riots under control before they are too big to resolve locally. Given the depth of dissatisfaction with the mismanagement and mistakes made in Wuhan at the start of the pandemic, the lack of protests was especially surprising. Had a hundred million Chinese people across the country reacted as many people in the West did, Beijing wouldn't have been able to contain the masses. But they didn't need to.

Xi Jinping's strong leadership, clear communication, and warnings to any local leaders who broke the rules quickly made it clear that the war against the virus should be fought by all Chinese people together, not between each other, like in the West. The Chinese people proved that when they work together in a selfless way, they are mentally and operationally much stronger than other countries. We either ignore or underestimate the enormous boost in self-confidence that their victory for two full years over the coronavirus has given the Chinese. For many, this is the first time in almost 200 years that the Chinese people and government have visibly stepped out of the shadow of the West. In my view, China's key advantage in the war against the virus has not been top-down control from Beijing, but above all bottom-up discipline—the power of the people. Without their trust in Xi Jinping, it is now believed that many millions of Chinese people might have died. As China's top leader, he personally took responsibility for handling the COVID-19 crisis. As a result, almost all Chinese people now have confidence in him as "the people's leader"—an honorific title given by the CPC politburo that has only ever been used by Mao Zedong and Xi in modern Chinese history. In some ways, it is also a logical name for the leader of a country that calls itself "the People's Republic of China." Clearly, the word "people" is central to China's thinking.

Because we in the West are reading so much about human rights violations in China and China's totalitarian regime, it seems unlikely that the CPC or Xi Jinping genuinely care a lot about their people. But the Chinese certainly

think they do; in fact, many Chinese believe Xi Jinping is more concerned about their welfare than most leaders in the West are about their own citizens. How can that be? The answer lies mainly in China's idea of inclusivity.

INCLUSIVITY

Another reason China's top leader—Xi Jinping—is considered a good leader is because he prioritizes inclusivity over exclusivity. His ten-year fight against corruption is a good example of this. Since 2012, Xi Jinping has been determined to arrest, try, and when found guilty imprison anyone, regardless of their position, who got rich through an abuse of power or pure corruption. This "good emperor" wants to restore and reinforce the moral integrity of the Party members, the government, and the business leaders. This is certainly no easy task, because sometimes those same people were the ones who put him in power. Corrupt politicians who stood in Xi Jinping's way naturally became prime targets. And to complicate matters, it is a fact that most Chinese people who got rich at the end of the last century did so in a context where corruption and abuse of power were very much the norm. You could almost say that the logical path to wealth that suddenly opened up after the death of Mao Zedong was paved with backdoor politics and insider deals.

The expression **zǒu hòu mén** (走后门), meaning "go in through the back door," was popular in the 1990s and early this century. In my experience it was more the rule than the exception among Chinese companies and government officials. Using private, backdoor channels and doing side deals or special arrangements was how China worked in those early days. It's not surprising that many wealthy Chinese people who had been given apartments, shares in businesses, or large sums of cash through political influence were eager to get a Canadian or Australian passport for themselves and their families, and to move their money abroad. Their motivation was simple: not because they didn't trust China but because their wealth wasn't legally obtained. China has even established a worldwide manhunt to bring corrupt people back to the country for trial. Separately, Xi Jinping now wants even those who have become rich through legitimate means to share their wealth more equitably with fellow citizens who are not yet benefiting from the advantages of China's middle class. This "prosperity for all" or "common prosperity" policy may eventually take the form of higher direct taxes, or commitments to donations or social investments. This is particularly true for large companies such as Alibaba or Tencent that have grown enormously powerful and wealthy thanks to China, but do not proportionally share their profits made in China. China will be happy to maintain a quasi-capitalist economic model as long as profits created are mainly reinvested or spent in China, but we can expect the country to take a stricter approach to international stock market listings going forward. You either belong or you don't.

This is the other meaning of Chinese inclusivity, which is also closer to the way we use this term in the West. Within China, there are people who do not want to be included or be fully integrated into the Chinese system: many Hong Kongers and Taiwanese, but also (to a lesser extent) Tibetans and Uyghurs. For cultural, religious, or other reasons, they don't need or want the opportunities, wealth, or advantages China can bring them. From the Chinese point of view, this response is difficult to understand. This is partly because China typically portrays minorities as happily part of China. The conventional reaction in China is then a "mandatory integration" process in some form, which has taken very difficult or even violent forms. China cannot send these people back to the countries they came from, like we do in Europe, because they were born in China and are a source of pride as part of China's ethnicity. The problem of integration in China is more about form of governance, and much less a discussion about religion, culture, or ethnic origin as in the West. China has the huge advantage—but also the big disadvantage—of being officially atheist. The advantage is that the CPC sees different religions as less threatening to its own values, but also mean it pays much less attention to them. China mainly integrates these religious and ethnic groups within its own progressive economic and social framework, not on the basis of their religious belief systems. As long as religious people and organizations don't interfere in Chinese politics or the power of the CPC, then generally speaking they can continue to worship and grow under the supervision of the state. But this is where things get difficult because believers have to accept Beijing's oversight of and at times interference in their religious communities. There are many fascinating examples of this practice. When China builds an expensive new bridge to connect a minority community of perhaps several hundred people deep in the mountains of the southwest, it is obvious this project is completely unjustifiable from a purely economic point of view. Similarly, when China builds an incredibly expensive high-speed train line to connect Lhasa, Tibet, with the rest of the country, it seems like a waste of money. When the thirty-four-mile bridge and highway system linking Hong Kong, Zhuhai, and Macao opened in 2018, China knew that this $130-billion investment would never be repaid with the toll revenue. These are all real examples; the reason China continues to carry out projects like this all over the country is precisely because it wants to promote inclusivity among its people. China sees itself figuratively (and literally) as a builder of bridges to the many minorities and disadvantaged people in the country, while perceiving that the West only (figuratively) wants to blow up the bridges that China builds in these more backward regions. The fact that local communities don't always ask for bridges to be built is difficult to reconcile with Beijing's proactive inclusion policy.

Example: To the Greatness of Small

This basic idea of Chinese inclusivity can also be seen in business examples. Take mobile payments, for example. The whole world started offering this service through expensive devices—iPhones and payment terminals—which made it more of a gimmick for an exclusive group of elite consumers. China, on the other hand, focused on QR codes, which anyone could print and which even the cheapest smartphone could scan. By using QR code-based payment systems, every Chinese person could earn extra money and make transactions without paying any additional charges to the banks or technology companies. People who have not visited China to see this phenomenon in person usually underestimate the impact of this, but it has given hundreds of millions of Chinese people who didn't have bank accounts the opportunity to earn extra money or make cheap purchases. This is how Ant Financial, the financial arm of Alibaba, has provided inclusive financial services to hundreds of millions of Chinese citizens and literally millions of small businesses. Unlike companies like Apple or Tesla, almost all Chinese technology companies are launching applications that are very simple, cheap, and highly accessible to everyone, not just the privileged. This basic idea of serving the poor, the middle class, and sometimes also the rich means that their offerings are mainly aimed at the ordinary citizen, not the pioneer users. Alibaba calls this "The Greatness of Small."

Given China's track record, it therefore shouldn't surprise us that most Chinese people really believe in the feasibility of Xi Jinping's "common prosperity" strategy. Inclusivity as a goal is simply more in the DNA of the average Chinese. Providing "charity" to those who cannot help themselves is one of the core values of Confucianism. In the West, we claim to pay so much attention to inclusivity in the context of diversity, gender equality, religion, opinion, and organization, while accusing China of repression of minorities and nonconformists. To claim that China is more inclusive in some respects than the West seems very naive, but it's true. The difference lies in the starting point being the collective vs. being the individual. China is more inclusive from a collective point of view; while the West focuses almost entirely on an individualistic point of view. But to achieve "common prosperity" for all Chinese people in the near term, China's collective approach to inclusion is simply more effective as every Chinese person will be included within their own network of relations in the greater common goal. This is the effect we saw at work during the handling of the pandemic—one for all, all for one.

SUPERIOR CHINESE

You could argue that China today again sees itself as the "Middle Kingdom"—the literal translation of the word "China" (**zhōngguó** 中国). This word is over 2,000 years old but wasn't really used to describe the country until recently. Over its long history, the name of each succeeding dynasty was used as the country name. The name "China" was only officially used in an international context during the last dynasty in the nineteenth century. In fact, China has never really been a nation-state as we're familiar with this concept in the West. For two millennia, the Chinese Empire usually acted as a universe of its own, seldom building any lasting ties to countries outside the Empire. At this point, "China" referred to the dynasty or the various realms in the center of China. It indicated the civilized part of the country within the natural boundaries between the sea to the east, the frozen and barren lands of present-day Mongolia and Russia in the north, the mountains of Tibet to the west, and the jungles of Thailand and Vietnam in the southwest. Everything beyond these regions was the land of the barbarians, which contrasted with sophisticated China. Over such a long history, the extent of China's territory was in constant flux, expanding and contracting depending on the strength of a given emperor or dynasty. Everyone who lived under the Chinese heaven belonged to the Empire, whether they were Han Chinese or ethnic minorities. And all these different Chinese peoples under heaven called themselves **huàrén** (华人) or *hua* people. *Hua*, which means "magnificent" or "radiant," was one of the ancient names for China. So the sense of identity and even superiority of the Chinese is less driven by ethnicity, and more by a sense of place.

Sinocentrism, which refers to the worldview or ideology that China is the center of the world, is not really comparable to Eurocentrism. It's not about Han Chinese versus Uyghurs or Tibetans, nor is it about China's great empires of the past compared to the British or Roman empires. What sinocentrism means is a sense of being unique in the world and having a kind of inherent cultural advantage over the primitive world of the barbarians they were faced with throughout history. The real power of China lies in its 5,000 year-old culture or civilization. China expert Martin Jacques makes a clear distinction: "China is a civilization society, not a nation society."[172] In this book I have highlighted many aspects of Chinese civilization, which I hope can lead us to the conclusion that China truly is unique, with a very different identity and a different set of values. That uniqueness is the result of the oldest continuous civilization in the world, one that still exists and continues to evolve. What reinforces this continuity is the enormous population, which in Chinese history has also been a source of its power. Even when different tribes of barbarians from the north conquered China, the invaders always underwent a rapid cultural "sinification" that made them even more Chinese than the Chinese. China acted as a cultural magnet, absorbing those who wanted to rule the country: that says a lot about China. The country is so immense, complex, and diverse that it is nearly impossible to run it centrally from the top down. The relationship and trust between the state and the people are determined more by culture than by legal principles or the law, as in Western democracies. The state, the Party, or the good emperor enjoy legitimacy because of their role in protecting Chinese culture. We are proud to protect our countries; China seeks to protect its culture. I believe that Westerners often underestimate this difference. We see the state as separate from culture, or historically, from the church. We see our rulers as outsiders who must be independent in order to govern well and enforce laws impartially. This is precisely why our citizens do not trust governments or politicians easily: they are not an involved party. Often, our politicians behave as if they are superior, and don't understand us. The Chinese see the emperor, the state, and today the Party as an intimate part of the Chinese family that must maintain and defend Chinese culture and values. In that context, Xi Jinping is the benevolent father of all Chinese people.

Since Chinese culture has been a unifying force for over 2,000 years, most Chinese people who are ethnically non-Han still feel as connected to the country as the majority group of Han Chinese. Temperance Shen (Meng) is one of my best Chinese friends and was also the first person to read the draft of this book. She is from the Manchu minority group from the far cold lands in the northeast of China but feels 100 percent Chinese. In fact, the ethnicity or origin group of people in China matters less and less when it comes to feeling Chinese. This is because China has been working on integration for centuries. What gives legitimacy to the good emperor is above all his inescapable political task of preserving the coherence and integrity of Chinese culture. No matter how many times we shout that the Chinese Communist Party is a control state and Xi Jinping is a dangerous dictator or a danger to the world, the Chinese themselves only have one standard—their culture. This means the more we attack Chinese values, the stronger we make China and the CPC. Since Mao Zedong came to power in 1949, the West has usually looked down at China as an enormously disadvantaged country compared to the West in terms of technology, infrastructure, sophistication, governance, communications, and more. Old attitudes and habits die hard. Our habitual arrogance and profound ignorance of China and the Chinese people have led us to misjudge and underestimate the immense cultural power of China. And now as the second decade of the twenty-first century opens, we are confused. We really cannot understand how the Chinese model with different values and priorities is challenging even America, the most powerful country in the world, in the very domains it has proudly claimed it is most successful at: governance, execution, wealth, innovation, entrepreneurship, influence, integration, etc.

How is this possible? I think the answer is simple: China is not a model, but the oldest culture and form of social organization in the world. All of the 1.4 billion Chinese see their values, which are over 2,000 years old, as the basic foundation of their identity and moral authority. In that context, the Chinese do sometimes feel superior: culturally superior. This may seem especially absurd to Western Europeans and countries around the world which have a European cultural heritage, who generally consider themselves more cultured than anyone else. It is true that China has admired the West for what we have achieved on a cultural, artistic, and technological level, and for our economic success. But morally and spiritually, the Chinese today increasingly see Westerners as self-righteous, arrogant, decadent, unfaithful, unpredictable, ignorant, and fickle. One could say that this feeling has been growing ever since the British crushed the Chinese in the Opium War, but in 2016 the most powerful leader in the Western world, Donald Trump, managed to personify all these negative characteristics in an almost caricature form, reconfirming China's assumptions. Today, the result is that China has developed a sense of moral correctness and even superiority versus the West. This has led in China to increasingly well-substantiated criticism of the West. Many Chinese sense their country is undergoing a historic renaissance, returning to its traditional role as Middle Kingdom, the largest empire in the world, while the West is inexorably falling into moral decline. China feels superior partly because too often the West behaves in a morally inferior way. The problem is not that we are immoral and China is moral. The problem is that most of us in the West are totally convinced that values are universal, and that these universal values are our Western values. First, we impose our values, and then we disregard and trample all over those values.

The Chinese see their 2,500-year-old values as equivalent to, if not superior to, Western values. Traditional Chinese values such as modesty, tolerance, patience, respect, faithfulness, frugality, tradition, piety, goodness, solidarity, self-sacrifice, temperance, diligence, inquisitiveness, flexibility, honor, friendship, gratitude, objectivity, caution, care, and wisdom combine to ensure harmony and continuity in Chinese society. Our Western values, on the other hand, are much more oriented towards how we treat others rather than on how we ourselves should act or behave. We place most of our focus on human rights, inclusivity, justice, diversity, and individual self-expression. However, values and norms are largely determined by culture, and for that reason they are not truly universal. Ironically, the more we in the West are convinced that our values are universal, implicitly rejecting Chinese values, the more the Chinese will feel culturally and morally superior.

福

fú

Meaning: **blessing, happiness, good luck, good fortune.** The ancient character is built up of a **person** carrying a **wine jug** next to an **altar**. It symbolizes the praying and offering to a higher power to achieve a better life for yourself. You can believe and trust that fortune will follow.

Conclusion

Trust China. In this book I have explored a range of extremely sensitive topics, cultural differences, personal stories, and both Western and Chinese perceptions. In doing this, my intent has been to raise as many issues as possible in order to build up an overall picture of China. In this concluding chapter, I would like to bring it all together by reducing the relationships between the eight circles of trust to their essence. This holistic thought process is a Chinese style of inductive reasoning. Therefore, the end of this book is not just a summary, but in fact critical content for gaining an alternative perspective of a country in transition. I realize this might be a bit challenging near the end of the book, but I would like us to explore this conclusion together.

EIGHT CIRCLES OF TRUST

In reading this book you've traveled through eight universal circles of trust. These eight relational and systemic structures give meaning not only to our existence, thinking, and actions, but also determine the trust we place in others. How we see our own circle often determines how we trust others, who in turn have a different understanding of their circle. I believe the key to trusting people is not to reflect on how others fit into our circles of trust, but how we can understand and possibly accept their circle of trust. You could call this an exercise in empathy. This also explains why we are much more likely to trust people who are culturally, ideologically, relationally, and physically closer to us than people who are different or distant from us. In the Netherlands and Flanders in Belgium we speak the same language, Dutch, but many of us don't fully trust our neighbors across the border. Allow me to illustrate my argument using differences between the Dutch and the Flemish; not to reinforce prejudices, but to demonstrate diversity from a broader perspective, and how differences can be bridged. Close neighbors: we have more similarities than differences, but we communicate differently, build friendships differently, don't have the same self-assurance, and do business in very different ways.

The stereotype the Flemish have of their northern neighbors is that the Dutch are quite arrogant, stingy, and aren't afraid to cheat you. The traditional image the Dutch have of the Flemish is that they are naive, stuck in the past, and not always very smart. That's why we don't easily trust each other.

The stark cultural differences between two neighboring European countries who speak the same language demonstrates that the problem of trust is not about who is right or wrong, but the reality that people from the same nation or culture trust each other more easily within their own context. This is why we have to look beyond the stereotypes at the specific context of why the Flemish, Dutch, Chinese, or any other people trust "someone" or "something," and "how" that trust is earned. In my model, the circles of trust start from the innermost circle, the individual, and widen to the largest circle, the universe. Let's walk through the framework of eight concentric circles to understand the eight most important "anchors" and "drivers" of trust in China.

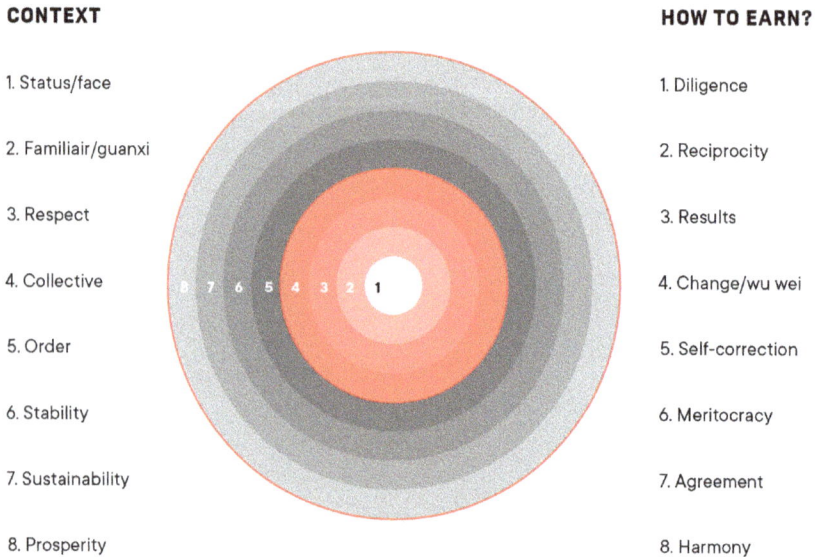

CONTEXT		HOW TO EARN?
1. Status/face		1. Diligence
2. Familiair/guanxi		2. Reciprocity
3. Respect		3. Results
4. Collective		4. Change/wu wei
5. Order		5. Self-correction
6. Stability		6. Meritocracy
7. Sustainability		7. Agreement
8. Prosperity		8. Harmony

Figure 4 / The context of trust in China and how to earn trust

1.   INDIVIDUAL

The individual is the core element for Chinese to find self-confidence by gaining "**face**," which inspires confidence in the individual's environment to give the individual **status**. The level of respect that the group or society gives to someone determines the position of that individual in their societal environ-ment. One could say this is a universal principle, but in China it works based on a finely honed interpersonal calculus, a mechanism with established rules and rituals. If we want to trust the Chinese, we have to take steps to give them face and develop relationships with people who already gained a lot of respect. The Chinese do respect people who have gained status by working **diligently** more than those who didn't have to work for it. In China, someone who becomes successful through corruption or abuse of power can get rich quick, but just as quickly see their status and confidence come crashing down.

2.   FAMILY AND FRIENDS

The strongest circle of trust in China is the family. Blood relatives come first, but close friends also belong to the extended Chinese definition of family. "Affective trust" is very strong in China because the glue binding family bonds was created over a period of 2,500 years by Confucian values. The mechanism at play here is what the Chinese call *guanxi*, an idea which has no direct English translation. *Guanxi* or "close relationships" are built through **reciprocity**. True friends help each other out without thinking about what they might get out of the relationship (but with the unspoken assumption that if they ever need help, their friends will help them). If we want to make and stay friends with the Chinese, we need to learn to help them in the way people who are already real friends would help each other—proactively and without question. Not only with deals, investments, gifts, or nice dinners, but with sincere affective and personal gestures. For example, at the highest political level, Angela Merkel was clearly Xi Jinping's best friend in Europe. Not for what she did to support German-China relations, but for how she did it. She saw relations between the countries as balanced and understood the reality of China better than many of her peers. Above all, she was genuinely interested in the country and its people. If we want to reduce the distance between us and the Chinese, this internal familial circle is the best place to start. It is practically free, but very valuable. Think about what would make your best friend happy, and then do that for your new Chinese friends.

3. COMPANY AND TEAM

Your place of work or company is where you will spend most of your life outside of the family. Your job shapes you as a person and it also shapes your future. Most parents see good education, followed by a good job as the ideal life path of their children. Your choice of work determines whether you have taken the best path to a better future. **Respect** for your leaders and delivering **results** are what should lead to success. In China, leaders and mentors themselves gain trust mostly through their practical achievements. In short, we can say that Chinese companies trust their employees, suppliers, and partners mainly when they produce results or success: a very pragmatic scorecard. And vice versa: it is mainly the companies and business leaders that achieve results that are trusted and respected.

4. NETWORK AND TRIBES

This fourth circle is a transition circle to the top/outer four circles. Here, trust is experienced as a **collective** event. The Chinese perceive themselves in this circle as individuals who strengthen the group. This is the foundation of the collective mindset of the Chinese—everyone together moving in the same direction toward a common, better future. The Chinese implicitly trust that their participation can make a real difference, but not by everyone raising their voices at once like we do in the West. There is a French proverb that says: "*C'est le ton qui* *fait la musique*": It's the tone that makes the music. When we demand **change**, we like to make a lot of noise; the Chinese prefer to make a lot of music, which is also music to the ears of Chinese leaders. The Taoist paradox of *wu wei* is key to understanding this dynamic. It can be freely translated as "action without effort," where movement occurs because everyone in the group is at peace with themselves, and despite apparent passivity, everyone is moving in the same direction. To trust China, we have to learn to understand these "non-actions" by the Chinese as representing not passivity, but their trust in natural processes shaping the direction of rapid change. This is the most difficult circle for Westerners to accept because it is about letting go of total control and having confidence in the natural course of things. One reason we keep relying on all our systems, even when they are outdated, is that we are less confident that the natural course of events can lead to as many positive outcomes.

5. SYSTEM AND THE CPC

This fifth circle is a transition circle to the lower/inner four circles. The socio-political system and the Party empower the Chinese system by maintaining the basic **order** of the inner four circles. The reason that most Chinese people have confidence in their political and social system is that China has remained stable despite rapid change over recent decades. As China is a country in fluid state of continuous rapid change, the system also has to adapt constantly. This is where it gets confusing for Westerners. When we see sudden changes happening in China, we attribute it to top-down decisions made by the leaders of the next circle, the nation, and not to the self-regulation of these actors within this system circle. It is true that the Communist Party and its pervasive institutions are the enabler of these changes to society or to the inner four circles. These institutions include massive state-owned companies down to local neighborhood organizations in every single community across the country. They serve as the senses and limbs of Beijing, rather than as independent referees protecting a liberal system like in the West. China has become very adept at reading "signals" coming back up from this system and making timely adjustments when needed. We distrust China's highly vertical and authoritarian model, where the state is always above the power of money, because we don't really trust the **self-correcting** function of a powerful political elite. To better appreciate China's system, we need to understand its surprisingly flexible, step-by-step, meritocratic, experimental, and pragmatic nature.

6. NATION AND PEOPLE

With a deep fear of chaos, the Chinese trust the leaders who can maintain the **stability** of the country. Throughout history, China has experienced long periods of peace and prosperity under the leadership of strong emperors who held the country together, interspersed by transitional periods of chaos and violence. Even today, the top priority for China's leaders is to ensure that the inner four circles remain stable by preventing risks from erupting into chaos. For Hong Kong, the Uyghurs, or political dissidents and nonconformists, from Beijing's point of view this means: "trust is good, but control is much better." Surveys point to Chinese people becoming more and more patriotic today, not just thanks to the stability of the country, but even more because of the progress most of the 1.4 billion Chinese have achieved under the current leadership. Within China, this largest national circle is more focused on the future than the past. Sometimes, we in the West don't trust China and its leaders because we think China wants to go back to the period of Mao, the Cultural Revolution, or the dynastic empire of the emperors. But no one in China wants to go back to the past, except through reviving Chinese culture and civilization. Widespread confidence in China's leaders is based on real progress achieved so far, and collective dreams of greater prosperity and social inclusion in the future. "Controlling the population is good, trust from the people even better." China's **meritocracy** based political system rewards leaders who help China achieve tangible progress, and mostly filters out incompetence. Because China is a very cyclical country, there are clearly defined moments of more control and moments of letting go. Like anywhere, the best leaders know how to dance to the beat of the music. Our own level of confidence in China's leadership and intentions is largely a factor of our trust or distrust in our own future. The less we trust our own future, the more we tend to see China as a control state and power-hungry threat. The more confident we are in a better world, the easier it is to see China as the positive catalyst of the future.

7. WORLD AND PLANET

Throughout its long and rich history, China didn't have to spend a lot of time thinking about the outside world or the planet. This changed during the Opium War of 1840 when the Western powers and internal decline pushed the country into what is now called "a hundred years of humiliation." Thanks to Mao Zedong's revolution, China regained its independence and the Chinese people regained their self-esteem. Thirty years later, Deng Xiaoping released the dynamic energy of the Chinese people and opened the country to the world, creating hope and growing prosperity. Today's leader Xi Jinping is building on his predecessor's achievements and restoring China on the world map as a proud, powerful nation, the position it held for centuries before 1840. The stability of the world and **sustainability** of the planet is certainly no less important for China than it is for us. However, China doesn't believe in the Pax Americana model that holds the world in the powerful grip of one country to enforce peace and stability. China believes that every country should be able to maintain its sovereignty in order to find its own path to a safer and better future. China's way to accelerate this trend globally is by adopting a constructive rather than a heavy-handed approach. For centuries, China has believed that if you want to follow a road to prosperity, you first have to build that road (or canal, or bridge, or tunnel): the New Silk Road is the most ambitious plan for achieving that. The Western world doesn't trust this megaproject because we usually view China's actions from a perspective of soft power. It's hard for us to take a very different perspective from the one we've had for 400 years. We also don't completely trust Beijing's promises that China will be carbon neutral by 2060, although Beijing is taking more action today than most Western countries combined. If we want to trust and work with China on a global scale, we must look for common goals to reach more **agreements**. Today, we have found those mainly in the protection of the environment and climate change. But the West is being shortsighted to believe that cooperation is less needed in health, scientific research, education, nutrition, energy, security, and furthermore that we can continue to independently make rules and achieve progress despite China's huge scale and rising capabilities. Although China signals that it is looking to cooperate with the world to solve urgent common problems, we prefer to push China into a position of direct competition with the West. The question is whether we should take the easiest or the best way. If together China and its like-minded partner countries solve the problems of the world that we're busy avoiding, then we will be the ones paying the price later on.

8. UNIVERSE AND CULTURE

China has a dream, and we don't trust it. That dream is for **prosperity**, **harmony**, and a **good quality of life** for all Chinese, and hopefully the whole world. For inspiration, China looks back at its 2,500-year-old culture as a source of meaning for the future. China represents the oldest civilization, philosophy, and language still in use in the world today. Over the past twenty years, thanks to learning from the West and the unstoppable energy of its huge, hard-working population, China has been able to renovate its ancient house and equip it for the future.

China is now at the stage of development where it is wondering how it wants to live in this new house, who the neighbors are, and what there is to discover beyond it. Since China's own future lies in the unknown, and it doesn't want to be a copy of the West, the country is now looking to push the boundaries in highly symbolic ways: far into space, deep into the oceans, via groundbreaking home-grown innovation, and socially inclusive technology and systems. China no longer sees the West as the only point of reference, and this new reality makes us anxious. If we don't want China's dream to become our nightmare, we'll have to learn to accept that new normal and work with China in constructive ways. We can do that with a lot of mistrust, as we do today, or we can do it according to the Taoist *wu wei* principle by using China's power for our own benefit and common future. The question or challenge is whether we can think "universally" enough to be able to share in China's search for more harmony and prosperity. We don't have to abandon our own values, principles, or rules to achieve it, but instead first accept that not everything the West believes or comes up with is truly universal. China's last circle of trust is more about the process of using introspection to develop alternatives to the existing world, while in the West our energies are devoted to making the rest of the world more like us. What will the future look like? Will it be the 2,000 year-old Chinese magic mirror[173]—which both reflects and broadcasts an image—potentially leading to a new period of enlightenment for humanity, or will it be the Western prism—which weakens and displaces the image of China—that will bring the rest of humanity toward our version of Western enlightenment?

FOUR INNER AND OUTER CIRCLES

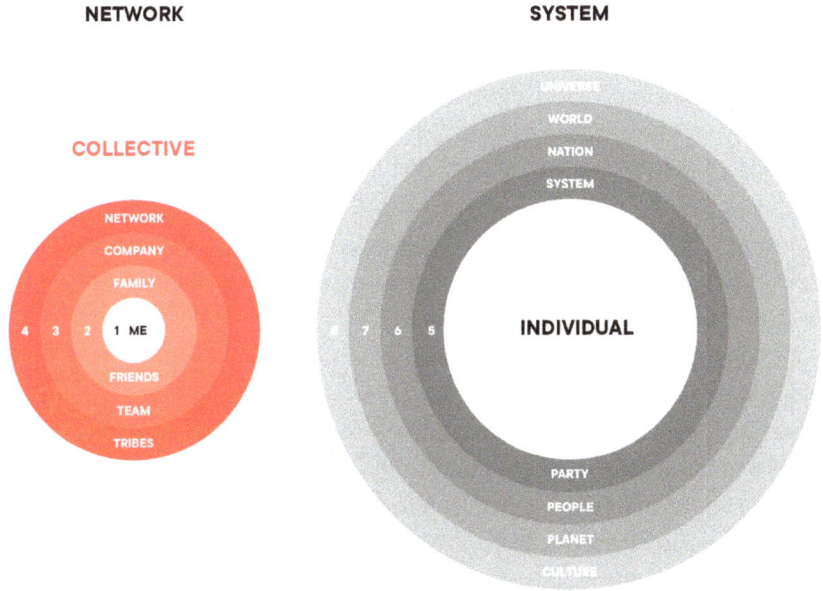

Figure 5 / The Chinese inner and outer circles of trust

The linear construction of the eight circles of trust starts from China's rich past and the traditions that determine individual and family values. The two smallest circles—"individual" and "family and friends"—are the strong magnetic force that keeps the Chinese true to their culture and traditions. Cultural values such as "face" and *guanxi* are also seen in the next two inner circles—"company and team" and "network and tribes." In these direct living, learning, and working environments of the Chinese people, "respect" and the "collective" are key to being trusted within organizations and networks.

These four inner **network circles** are characterized by the security, bonding, and relationships (including the balance of power) of the Chinese within society. Having trust in relationships and in the collective is like a safety blanket offering protection during the rapid changes that the Chinese are experiencing. Therefore, trust in the Chinese context is first and foremost about individual people. If we want to trust the Chinese, we should look not at the abstract level of the entire population, all company executives, or the political leadership in Beijing, but at the specific and unique worker in a factory, the passionate and inspired entrepreneur behind "the company executive," or "the political leader" who is also someone's father or mother, and child, and so on. To trust China, we must therefore make the effort to move and create relationships within these internal Chinese circles. Everyone outside those circles is almost automatically less trusted than the people inside them. This is the meaning of the collective in China. The close-knit network circles symbolize the Chinese idea of the **collective**.

The first two outer circles—"system and the Party" and "nation and the population"—are much less determined by interpersonal and cultural traits, and more mechanical and systemic. The Chinese trust their leaders to improve the nation and the lives of all citizens without discarding their ancient culture. The two largest outer circles—"world and planet" and "universe and culture"—represent the search for the balance between dream and reality. The Chinese dreams and beliefs in these outer worlds act like a thick atmospheric layer that both "protects" the Chinese (culture and future) and is necessary for its "well-being" (world and planet). The biggest circle, and ultimate goal, is China's *datong* dream: to become one with the universe and Chinese culture. The last circle also brings us right back to the first—the rebirth of man, the individual.

The four outer **system circles** pertain to improvement, well-being, and change and transition in China, ultimately for the benefit of the Chinese individual. If we want to trust China, we should make an effort to combine our dreams with their dreams and find some middle ground where we can all stand. You might say that both dreams are common to the whole world, but that we have different political and social systems to achieve those dreams. The only way to trust each other is to see those dreams and goals as part of a bigger picture. By doing this we can bring together the pieces of the puzzle, look for the similarities in our dreams, and then work together on solutions, each with our own system and our own priorities.

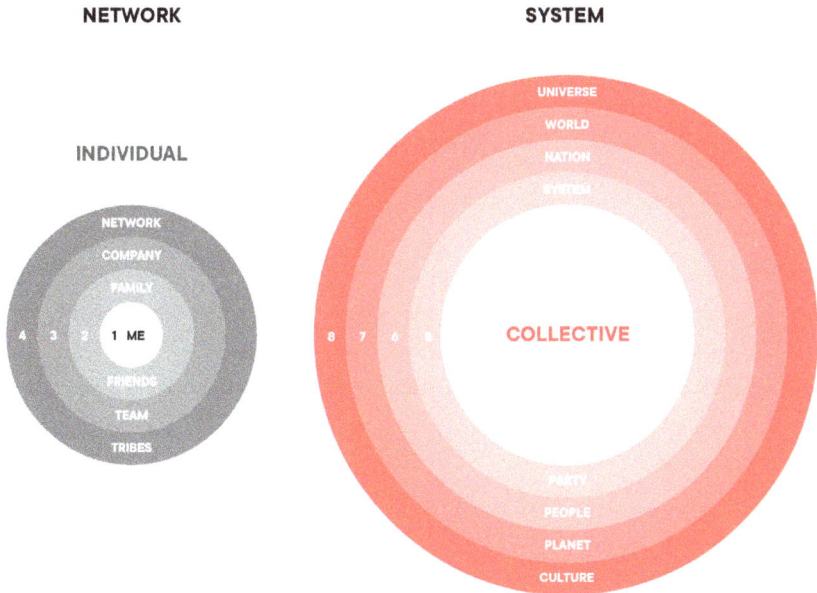

NETWORK

SYSTEM

INDIVIDUAL

NETWORK
COMPANY
FAMILY
4 3 2 1 ME
FRIENDS
TEAM
TRIBES

UNIVERSE
WORLD
NATION
SYSTEM
8 7 6 5
COLLECTIVE
PARTY
PEOPLE
PLANET
CULTURE

Figure 6 / The Western inner and outer circles of trust

Despite having largely similar dreams, our relationships to our own circles of trust are the biggest mental barrier to trusting China. The circles of trust have the same labels in the West, but we have completely opposite expectations from the Chinese. The four inner **network circles** of trust in Western societies more so determine the search for improvement, well-being, and transition. This is certainly the case in the more individualistic Western societies; as individuals we seek improvement, strive for happiness, and try to outdo ourselves. Our network circles of trust are built almost exclusively around the individual, based on the **inside-out aspiration** that we embrace as the starting point for a meaningful life. This is why we place so much importance on family, organizations, and networks to be happy, pursue our passions, and hopefully find that elusive goal: a good work-life balance. We don't rely on the system, country, or culture to achieve our personal goals, as we believe it is ultimately up to each of us.

The Chinese expectation is quite different: they do expect the system to help them make progress. Therefore, the human experience in China is primarily defined by the **outside-in aspiration**. They just assume that they will have to fit into the system if they want to take full advantage of opportunities for improvement, well-being, and success. This doesn't mean that they blindly follow the Party in every respect, but that they give it the benefit of the doubt and generally have more confidence in it. We believe it to be the individual's role and right to determine their future, rather than the role of a bigger system. Our contrasting approaches to climate change are a vivid illustration of this difference. The Chinese believe it is the government's role to solve large-scale problems. Our approach is to first set an example by changing our personal practices and behaviors and then, if necessary, taking to the streets to force our governments to make climate change a priority. Put very simply, you could say that we trust ourselves more than our system, while the Chinese trust their system more than themselves.

The four Western outer **system circles** of trust determine our system's role in taking care of society, security, relationships, and the balance of power. Western countries want to maintain their prosperity as the first priority. Our system circles are first and foremost based on the **collective**. For this, we rely on the stability, optimization, and power of the system. This is the **outside-in role** of power and the system.

ANOTHER PERSPECTIVE OF A COUNTRY IN TRANSITION

As per Chinese cultural tradition, the Chinese, like good Confucian fathers, keep this role within the family and organizations that guide how people live and work. The stability of China can only be guaranteed if each smaller circle of relationships remains stable through clarity in the agreements and the balance of power between father and child, teacher and student, boss and employee, citizen and state. This is the **inside-out role** of power and the system. Based on this mindset, the Chinese government doesn't hesitate to interfere in the private lives of citizens and families, including regulating divorces, marriages, treating addictions, shaping education, and many more dimensions. The stated aim is not to control people, but to help all the people live more harmoniously. We would see this as unwanted interference, and a violation of our freedoms and privacy. Given this, Western countries rely less on family members, relationships, and local communities to ensure the stability of the country. The Chinese expect these foundations of their network circles to provide security, stability, and preserve the status quo. Perhaps the Chinese are much more in tune with their culture, and more comfortable relying on the advice of their family and immediate networks, or even the government if necessary. This doesn't imply that they blindly follow their parents, teachers, or bosses, but they generally approach superiors with a lot more respect than we do. Possibly because of our obsession with youth, we have lost our sense of deference and respect for the wise and elderly. We expect the system to lay out all the rules and then try to catch us when we don't follow them.

Even today, most Chinese feel responsible for their parents, often living together with them and supporting them in their old age. And Chinese employees are in general incredibly dedicated, willing to work hard for a teacher or boss they respect. In the West, it has become normal to move our elderly parents into a retirement home, and we see working ourselves to the bone for a boss or teacher as unjust, or even as an abuse of power by the superior. At the risk of oversimplifying, we have more faith in preserving our system while the Chinese have more faith in preserving their network.

In the four inner **network circles**, the Chinese look for more security, collectivity, relationships, and power, while in the West we do exactly the same in the four outer **system circles**. In the four outer **system circles**, the Chinese look for progress, prosperity, and meaning, while we do that more in the inner network circles. We all look for the same thing, but the Chinese find stability in their networks and we look for change within our networks. We have the same dream, but the Chinese dream about personal improvement via the system and we dream about stability via our system. One key reason why it's difficult for us to trust the Chinese system (its leaders, its global impact, and its dreams) is that we understand the outer **system circles** as China's way of gaining more stability through greater global control, while China would trust it aims for change by finding more harmony with the world. China's dream is to change China, and not change the world. In response, we want to change China in order not to change the world.

I believe the only viable way out of this impasse is to strive for common goals. Today, the most important common goals relate to the climate and the environment. It is clear we can't save the planet without China. The planetary crisis forces us to work together because we have a simple, existential goal in common: to save nature, the planet, and humanity. If we want to overcome the barriers to cooperation, we must first understand China's main objectives. To do this, we need to set aside our deeply ingrained Western perspectives and dated stereotypes of China seeking world domination, new cultural revolutions, or a dystopian totalitarian world state. Viewed from a Chinese perspective, the new China under Xi Jinping has three major goals: more independence, people focus, and leadership.

1.   INDEPENDENCE

China is striving for more independence from the West, in order to continue on its growth path with much greater self-sufficiency. This goal is not a return to a closed society. Quite the contrary, China wants to open up further to the world, but believes it cannot do this without first stepping out of the "shadow" of the West. This doesn't necessarily mean China wants to switch places and put us in its shadow, although there is a risk we might crawl into a shadow by ourselves if we close ourselves off from China's rapid development. China calls its future development model the "dual circulation strategy" as I explained in chapter 7. In essence, China wants to have more control of the future, generate more economic growth more sustainably within the country, and remain strongly engaged with the rest of the world, but less as an export market as a motor of its economic growth and more as an additional source of energy to fuel its innovation. The West could adopt a similar approach, to view China as an additional energy source for high-quality talent and innovation rather than just a giant market for sales or purchases. More than ever before, China can help us more in the domains of innovation, financing, infrastructure, talent, creativity, global standards, and common prosperity.

2. PEOPLE FOCUS

Chinese leaders often say that they are a people-centric society, but we don't see how that can be true because China isn't a liberal democracy. Chinese leaders say they serve the people, and China calls itself the People's Republic of China, and leaders are promoted on the basis of their practical service to the Chinese people. China exists as a country and leadership for its people. China understands "democracy" as meaning more inclusivity, less inequality, more responsibility and accountability, with increased common prosperity. This goal certainly doesn't mean a return to the rigid form of communism under Mao, but to a nation of equal opportunity for all Chinese people. And China is making gradual progress in removing excesses and abuses from its excesses in society as well as implementing new rules and regulations to protect all citizens. According to Confucian tradition, leaders are expected to put ethics above profit. We have a different view, because we don't really trust politicians anywhere to truly act for the benefit of the people. China has already become the world's largest laboratory, where new technologies, models, standards, and rules are being launched and continuously improved on a large scale. I strongly believe the West could learn a lot from this massive Chinese "laboratory," especially Europe, where we have similar social and environmental goals. For some reason we prefer not to look to China as an example. Out of ignorance? Or fear? Are we missing real open-minded leadership and a willingness to learn from other societies?

3. LEADERSHIP

China clearly wants to take on a bigger leadership role in the world. This ambition is partly opportunistic, coming at a time when the Western liberal international order is under pressure. But with a bigger leadership role comes greater responsibilities. China is conflicted. It is not eager to replace the existing world order with its own world view, because it recognizes that the existing liberal order has given China many more advantages than disadvantages. Also, China has seen how playing this role has really weakened America over the past several decades.

At the same time, as the world's second largest economy, Beijing is very aware that it has to defend and promote its interests, as well as those of countries friendly with China. The West now faces a stark choice: either welcome China's participation, and over time China's leadership, in the Western sphere of influence, or shut the door to China. The latter approach will only further widen the gap between the West and the rest of the world, especially in the Southern Hemisphere and the world's growing Muslim communities.

HOW TO TRUST CHINA?

What if we did decide to trust China? How would we do that, and what would it look like? Everyone has a different answer as we all have different information, experiences, and insights about China. I can only speak from my own perspective, as I have done throughout this book. For me, trusting the Chinese people can be likened to the trust that exists between brothers and sisters. Let's take my own brother Christophe, who is two years younger than me. We are very different people. Christophe has been working as a truck driver for Coca-Cola in Belgium for thirty years. My brother has a lot of qualities: he is a perfectionist who has renovated two of his own houses, a great father to his children, easily suspicious of what he doesn't know, very practical and handy, highly structured, fairly materialistic, and he has always had a lot of determination. After reading this book, it might sound like I'm describing a Chinese person who works for a state-owned company, but he's Flemish born and bred. I, on the other hand, am an entrepreneur at heart, rather prefer starting things to finishing them, have friends with extremely diverse backgrounds, am very absent-minded, impatient, deeply regret not really seeing my daughter grow up, and I realize that I am an idealist and dreamer. To be honest, I probably wouldn't be friends with my brother if he weren't my brother. As children we argued a lot. He was a mama's boy; I got more of my father's support. But if my brother needs help, I drop everything to help him, and he does the same for me. He has a heart of gold. I respect his choices and slightly different values, and I trust him blindly, and I know he feels the same about me. We have a bond of trust, and that's all that matters to me. When I make friends with a Chinese person, I also want to be like a brother to them. I like to be called **xiōngdì** 兄弟 (sibling—brother) or **dàgē** 大哥 (older brother) by my Chinese friends. I will consciously and proactively help them whenever I can, which means I am usually quick to gain their trust and respect. Personally, I would rather put more time into cultivating a few good Chinese friends who I trust than having a large "database" of Chinese contacts. In order to get through into the four innermost **network circles** of China and create mutual trust, my personal advice is to first start with the intention to be like a brother or sister to your new friends.

To start to trust the larger Chinese system and the four **system circles**, I don't think about my brother, but instead draw a parallel with my father. I remember him as a fairly strict, but very involved father. As a mathematics professor, he relied mainly on facts to convince, not on stories. He supported me in all the choices I made in life, but he couldn't stand the fact that I didn't get things finished or wanted to rush through everything. I found this very difficult because I'm very inquisitive and easily distracted by nature. But he was my greatest role model and I had an enormous amount of respect for his intellect, determination, and perseverance. He worked to pay the bills, but every other minute of his life he dedicated to a hobby that had gotten out of control. Every year he would hide away in the Swiss mountains for a few weeks and write a book about chess, or music. I clearly inherited his genes. As a child, I always wanted to prove myself to him. I started studying Chinese at university because that was what I was interested in, but to prove to my father that I was also scientifically grounded, I paused my studies of Chinese, and I began studying business engineering. This was a difficult choice for me because I didn't have a good knowledge of mathematics. My father would spend hours helping me with hundreds of questions to prepare me for my exams. When he died so suddenly and so young, I immediately stopped studying engineering and went back to my real passion: China. My father always showed me the direction, set the example, and provided his support, but he also set the rules tight enough so that I would achieve. He always found great ways to reward me, too.

My own experience is the prism through which I understand the Chinese leadership approach and governance system. In China, I see the image of a strict father who wants the best for his 1.4 billion children but is quite demanding of himself too; I see an intelligent father who knows how to frame the ambitions, capacities, and realities of the country and its situation; finally, I see a brave father who remains an idealist, entrepreneur, and dreamer. As a child, I certainly didn't always agree with my father, and I often said that what he wanted for me was not what I wanted at all. For me, China is no different. Now that my father is gone, I see that he was more often right than wrong, and based on my experiences in their country, I believe that most of the Chinese feel the same way about their leaders and system. To trust China, or the four outer **system circles**, we can more easily understand the decisions and attitude emanating from Beijing from the perspective of a child who wants to obey and please their big-hearted but strict father.

If we view the eight Chinese circles of trust as the Chinese do in the form of concentric contextual circles, then we should start with the outer **system circles** and work our way toward the inner **network circles**. We start with the goal of achieving a shared "prosperity" or a shared "well-being" for all humankind. That goal, in the Taoist sense, is not a strategy but a dream, utopia, or ambition. This is China's concept of a *datong* society that was conceived 2,000 years ago. Of course, that dream disappears when the previous circle (the world) comes under too much pressure from war or climate change or other crises. Therefore, it is the task of the circle just below—"nation and people"—to preserve the sustainability of the penultimate circle—"world and planet." According to China, this objective can only be achieved through cooperation with the world. And here we encounter a mutually reinforcing loop: progress towards greater cooperation is blocked; because the West no longer trusts China it declines opportunities to work closer together, and this behavior leads China to trust the West less and less. But we all know that it is only through greater cooperation that the world can become more stable, secure, and prosperous. The next circle—"system and Party"—is the basis for really making and keeping the country healthy. This is the machine that connects the inner **network circles** to the outer **system circles**.

The Chinese socio-political system—whether we call it communism, state capitalism, or a meritocracy—tries to connect that Chinese dream with reality. Reality here doesn't refer to China's economy or politics, but to the moral standards that the Chinese have carried in their culture for 2,500 years. The key word or concept in this culture comes from the second circle—"family and friends": the *guanxi* between the Chinese, which determines whether you deserve "respect" in the third circle—"work," and are included in the fourth circle of everyone's "network." The group doesn't trust individuals whose moral compass is broken; and especially not if they harm the well-being of the collective. In China, these "untrustworthy" people were traditionally reprimanded not by the system, law, or imperial palace, but by the network. Within the third circle of "company and team," respect is therefore so important that it becomes proof of your trust status. For example, teachers, bosses, and politicians are highly respected. Less because they are successful or popular, as is often the case in the West, but because their network backs them. This is the real reason the second circle of friends and family is so important. Because only your closest friends and family really know if you can be trusted. And so we come to the smallest circle of each "individual" where how much "face" you've built up during your life determines your trust status.

CAN WE TRUST CHINA?

In March 2019 I gave a presentation to 600 people in Belgium. I started my keynote with the question: "Who in this room trusts Huawei as a 5G supplier for Belgium?" Less than twenty people put their hand up. The answer was almost unanimous: we don't trust China, and we don't trust the Chinese. I then briefly explained to the audience how we didn't trust Japan fifty years ago, either. At that time, Japan had been a democracy for thirty years, so the reason wasn't the Japanese socio-political system. Many people saw the Japanese are not transparent. They lived in inaccessible, closed, and very tight relational communities, and they had an almost inhumane work ethic. They shamelessly copied our Western innovations. Isn't this similar to what we think about China today? But nobody today is still asking if we can trust the Japanese or Japan. We've gotten over our mistrust of Japan and developed a balanced respect for the hard-working, innovative, and honest Japanese people and system. The main reason we trust Japan today is because Toyota, Sony, Honda, Nintendo, and many other brands have disproved our original stereotypical association of Japan with poor quality. Japanese minimalist design, flower arranging, tea ceremonies, the samurai code of honor, anime movies, and many other positive things have changed our understanding and attitude towards Japanese culture. We have also experienced the same change in perception toward South Korea. So why are we so convinced that we won't trust China in time? Given that Japan and South Korea themselves absorbed many cultural traditions, symbols, and values, and even language and technologies from China throughout their history, shouldn't we give China the benefit of the doubt?

In the same presentation session, I then asked the audience who was on Facebook or WhatsApp. Almost everyone put their hand up. The question I then rhetorically asked was why almost all of us trust Facebook with our personal data and not Huawei? Facebook was clearly guilty of giving personal data to the consulting firm Cambridge Analytica, which caused a scandal when it was revealed to have influenced the US elections and Brexit. By contrast, there was very little hard evidence that Huawei had misused or spied on our data. Thanks to James Bond movies, we all believe the UK has one of the best national intelligence services in the world: their very best people checked the code and design of Huawei's products but found no direct evidence of any danger to national security. So why do we trust "friends" like Facebook who really can't be trusted more than "enemies" like Huawei who, when we take a closer look, cannot objectively be considered as an untrusted party? No one in the audience could answer that one.

After my presentation, a woman approached me during the reception to congratulate me on my speech. But then she asked me the question: "Do you personally trust China?" It was my turn to be quiet. "Yes and no," I said. I didn't know what to say and started talking about Huawei's rapid evolution from copycat to innovator. It was as if my brain had suddenly frozen. Then another person came up to us and asked if I thought Europe could still keep up with China. I was saved by the Chinese gong, as this was much easier to answer! For weeks afterwards, I thought about the woman's question: Did I personally trust China? In hindsight, I could have kicked myself for not immediately answering that I trust my good Chinese friends blindly, that if the Chinese can trust each other, their companies, and their government, then we should be able to as well. I would have gone on to tell her that China is as diverse as the European Union, and that it also finds it difficult to get all of its "Member States" on the same page. Also that China is constantly evolving and that the Chinese of yes- terday are not the Chinese of tomorrow, that China itself is doing everything it can to solve the trust problem with rules that are in many cases even stricter than in Europe, and that China is now using blockchain technology, and so on…

I could have told a hundred stories about China to explain why I trust China just as much as Belgium, and the Chinese people just as much as the Belgian people. It's just that the context and our perspectives are different. To be honest, that's also why I wrote this book, I wrote it for her: I hope that one day the woman whose name I've forgotten will read it. And I want to con- clude this book with a clear and confident answer for her. You already know my answer: yes, I trust China and I trust the Chinese people. Not blindly, but certainly no less than I trust my own homeland Belgium or my fellow Belgians. I hope this book has provided a lot of non-binary answers to the many questions we all have about China that so often lead to doubts and mistrust. My intent is not to convince you that we can now trust China blindly. In fact, quite the opposite: I believe we can only really learn to trust China by staying very criti- cal about everything that happens there. But being extremely critical doesn't just mean expressing an unending stream of criticism, but also being truly open to different perspectives about China. If we can open our thinking about today's China, it will also lead to more clarity about the China of tomorrow. If we can't open our thinking, we're simply increasing our blind spot about the incredible and admirable things that this ancient, rapidly modernizing country and its 1.4 billion people can give us. Deeper understanding may lead to us being even more critical of China in some respects, which is healthy, as long as we also dare to look more critically at ourselves and our societies. I do believe our current posture of automatically not trusting China will mean that we miss out on the many opportunities that China's transition offers us. In other words, our current distrusting, mildly or strongly anti-China position could become self-destructive.

The aim of this book, which highlights the many misunderstandings and tensions between China and the West, certainly wasn't to defend China or attack the West, but in fact to provide more explanation and nuance; and to reflect on stereotypes and assumptions about China. I sincerely hope that it will be read as a positive contribution to better understanding and won't stir up even more disputes and unrest. I hope that this book can bring us closer to "the Chinese" as individuals and as a people in a unique moment in their history with ambitions, passions, and dreams. As China rises, it is natural that the Chinese will also increasingly expect us to see, respect, and understand them as equals. It's up to each of us to decide whether to accept that out-stretched hand and start building true trust-based relationships. To trust China, we will need to think more with our hearts than with our brains. It is our senses that usually mislead us today under a barrage of images and negative associations, while the emotional world of the Chinese has actually never been closer to ours. The world is slowly waking up to China's innovative capabil-ity, its political and military power, as well as the country's cultural strengths. I believe our biggest surprise will come sometime before 2030. Many in the West will be left speechless when we suddenly wake up and realize that China no longer wants to copy or learn from us. This moment is coming: when the West is no longer an example for China, and China looks inwards to take its own path to more meaning, depth, and refinement. We have time to open our minds and learn. If we don't learn to trust China sometime soon, then one day—like a magnet—China will attract the trust of the new world, which will gradually repel our old Western world..

ENDNOTES

1   https://documents1.worldbank.org/curated/en/833041539871513644/122290272_201811348
    034146/additional/131020-WP-P163620-WorldBankGlobalReport-PUBLIC.pdf

2   https://www.modernatx.com/modernas-work-potential-vaccine-against-covid-19

3   https://www.amazon.com/When-Cultures-Collide-3rd-Leading/dp/1904838022

4   https://www.indexmundi.com/china/religions.html

5   https://foreignpolicy.com/2019/10/16/china-intellectual-property-theft-progress/

6   https://money.cnn.com/2017/08/14/news/economy/trump-china-trade-intellectual-
    property/index.html

7   https://www.huffpost.com/entry/where-are-the-chinese-nob_b_759749?
    guccounter=1&guce_referrer=aHR0cHM6Ly93d3cuZ29vZ2xlLmNvbS88&guce_
    referrer_sig=AQAAAEG1xV6edNZCxBkULoGOQrK5jo1oruSnlGmtVD3FfIyPfM0v
    GlgknRpDi6c4TYTZBNlfblUGhhwfXX6oWnQ0w4auhln-Flu7lK4kG7pzYizZ

8   https://www.telegraph.co.uk/technology/2020/08/08/silicon-valley-turned-
    imitation-insincere-form-flattery/

9   https://op.europa.eu/en/publication-detail/-/publication/0edda84b-5137-11ea-aece-
    01aa75ed71a1

10 https://itif.org/publications/2015/09/17/false-promises-yawning-gap-between-china%
    E2%80%99s-wto-commitments-and-practices

11 https://world101.cfr.org/global-era-issues/trade/what-happened-when-china-
    joined-wto#:~:text=Chinawantedtojointhe,tableinaglobalizingworld

12 The hundred-year marathon, Michael Pillsbury (2016), Griffin Publishing

13 https://news.cgtn.com/news/2020-08-30/How-China-s-ancient-tributary-system-
    has-been-misunderstood-TntznvZDNu/index.html

14 https://www.nature.com/articles/d41586-020-01984-4

15 http://chinascope.org/archives/25046

16 https://www.comparitech.com/vpn-privacy/the-worlds-most-surveilled-cities/

17 https://www.infoplease.com/world/diplomacy/communist-countries-past-and-present

18 https://www.scmp.com/news/china/diplomacy/article/3094467/
    us-secretary-state-urges-chinas-citizens-help-change-behaviour

19 https://carnegieendowment.org/2021/11/22/who-s-in-and-who-s-out-from-
    biden-s-democracy-summit-pub-85822

20 https://www.scmp.com/news/china/politics/article/3101986/
    china-claims-vocational-training-given-nearly-13-million-people

21 https://news.cgtn.com/news/2020-06-19/CGTN-Exclusive-Memories-of-fighting-
    terrorism-in-Xinjiang-RqHhw388WA/index.html

22 http://be.chineseembassy.org/eng/zt/xinjiangEN1/202103/t20210310_10165109.
    htm#:~:text=InOctober2019thetrainees,andtrainingcenterinXinjiang

23 https://www.globaltimes.cn/page/202101/1211945.shtml

24 https://www.mckinsey.com/business-functions/marketing-and-sales/our-insights/
    survey-chinese-consumer-sentiment-during-the-coronavirus-crisis

25 Data obtained in 2019 during a company visit presentation at JD.com headquarters in Beijing.

26 https://jdcorporateblog.com/in-depth-report-how-jd-tackles-counterfeits/
    https://jdcorporateblog.com/in-depth-report-how-jd-tackles-counterfeits-2/

27 https://merics.org/en/opinion/chinas-social-credit-score-untangling-myth-reality

28 https://en.pingwest.com/a/7770

29 https://www.ncbi.nlm.nih.gov/pmc/articles/PMC2975357/

30 http://cesi.econ.cuhk.edu.hk/wp-content/uploads/Wu_Lingwei_The-Invisible-Wound_The-Long-Term-Impact-of-Chinas-Cultural-revolution-on-Trust.pdf

31 https://www.nzherald.co.nz/business/chinese-teen-who-sold-kidney-for-iphone-now-bedridden-for-life/TADQKKJF2YTITTXDXWJQLCNLPU/

32 https://asiasociety.org/education/women-traditional-china

33 https://www.thinkchina.sg/no-bride-price-no-marriage-china

34 https://www.newswise.com/articles/entrepreneurship-in-china-the-rise-of-female-billionaires

35 https://sweden-science-innovation.blog/beijing/are-chinese-women-holding-half-of-the-sky-in-china-part-1/

36 https://chinapower.csis.org/china-gender-inequality/

37 https://digitalcommons.iwu.edu/cgi/viewcontent.cgi?article=1054&context=constructing

38 https://www.wsj.com/articles/SB100014240529702037353045771666520002366514?mod=article_inline

39 https://www.unicef.org/executiveboard/media/2901/file/2021-PL1-China_CPD-EN-ODS.pdf

40 https://borgenproject.org/left-behind-children/

41 https://www.wsj.com/articles/china-migration-rural-return-xi-economy-11605652518

42 http://www.xinhuanet.com/english/2021-02/03/c_139717966.htm

43 https://www.forbes.com/sites/johnkoetsier/2020/10/21/44-of-global-ecommerce-is-owned-by-4-chinese-companies/

44 https://www.oliverwyman.com/content/dam/oliver-wyman/v2/publications/2019/November/china-retail-digital-transformation.pdf

45 https://global.chinadaily.com.cn/a/202009/21/WS5f68007fa31024ad0ba7aad7.html

46 https://www.usnews.com/news/best-countries/articles/2019-10-28/obesity-rates-in-china-have-tripled-over-the-past-10-years

47 https://www.economist.com/china/2019/12/12/as-china-puts-on-weight-type-2-diabetes-is-soaring

48 Book China's evolving consumers, 8 intimate portraits by Tom Nunlist. Earnshaw Books.

49 https://www.chinaskinny.com/blog/china-elderly-online-infographic/

50 https://www.scmp.com/abacus/culture/article/3029400/forget-millennials-chinas-newest-internet-stars-are-senior-citizens

51 https://technode.com/2021/02/22/chinas-digital-accessibility-push-for-the-elderly/

52 https://medium.com/hackernoon/the-chinese-social-network-bb282204af9c

53 https://daxueconsulting.com/wechat-mini-programs-2020-report/

54 https://uxspot.com/insights/why-and-when-users-like-using-wechat-mini-programs

55 https://technode.com/2019/03/15/what-facebook-needs-to-learn-from-wechats-group-chat-pains/

56 https://www.cjr.org/tow_center/wechat-misinformation-china.php

57 https://www.poynter.org/fact-checking/2018/on-wechat-rogue-fact-checkers-are-tackling-the-apps-fake-news-problem/

58 https://techcrunch.com/2021/03/17/pinduoduo-surpasses-alibaba/

59 https://www.china-briefing.com/news/chinas-city-tier-classification-defined/

60 https://blog.lengow.com/c2m-consumer-to-manufacturer/

61 https://edition.cnn.com/2019/04/15/business/jack-ma-996-china/index.html

62 https://clb.org.hk/content/food-delivery-workers-need-trade-union-push-real-change

63 https://dergipark.org.tr/en/download/article-file/145951

64 https://media.haworth.com/asset/82857/a-shifting-landscape_chinese-millennials-in-the-workplace.pdf

65 https://www.frontiersin.org/articles/10.3389/fpsyg.2020.01758/full

66 https://jefftowson.com/2019/10/huawei-is-going-to-beat-trump-with-human-resources-not-technology-pt-1-of-3/

67 Haier's leadership model is better known outside China through a quite similar model described by the Brazilian author Ricardo Semler in his book Maverick, The success story behind the world's most unusual workshop, 1993, Warner Books

68 https://asiatimes.com/2019/07/average-monthly-salary-for-shanghai-young-adults-more-than-us1000/ and https://www.shine.cn/education/2001200177/

69 https://www.forbes.com/sites/nazbeheshti/2019/10/16/hi-tech-still-isnt-getting-genderdiversity-rightbut-we-can-learn-from-their-mistakes/

70 https://www.cnbc.com/2020/08/04/bookingcom-is-laying-off-up-to-25percent-of-its-workforce-due-to-coronavirus-downturn.html

71 https://nypost.com/2018/02/17/chinese-millennials-are-about-to-kick-us-millennials-butts/

72 https://www.entrepreneur.com/article/370364

73 https://www.bbc.com/news/world-asia-china-57348406

74 https://jingdaily.com/china-genz-millenial-brand-collaborations-adidas-heytea/

75 https://sloanreview.mit.edu/article/how-culture-gives-the-us-an-innovation-edge-over-china/

76 https://mronline.org/2006/09/21/did-mao-really-kill-millions-in-the-great-leap-forward/

77 https://www.jstor.org/stable/25790563?seq=1

78 https://www.ncbi.nlm.nih.gov/pmc/articles/PMC5486276/#:~:text=The2008 WenchuanEarthquakemeasured,injuriesand17923missingpeople.&text=Sichuan oneofthewestern,QiangYiandTibetan

79 https://minorityrights.org/trends2019/united-states/

80 https://history.state.gov/milestones/1830-1860/china-1#:~:text=TheTreatyofWangxia (Wang,FirstOpiumWarin1842

81 https://www.npr.org/2018/08/04/635654200/ai-wei-weis-beijing-studio-destroyed-by-chinese-authorities

82   https://news.artnet.com/art-world/ai-weiwei-slams-us-canada-china-1452409

83   https://medium.com/world-economic-forum/from-male-colonel-to-female-ballet-dancer-the-extraordinary-story-of-jin-xing-b010dbd972bd

84   https://www.nytimes.com/2012/11/17/world/asia/peng-liyuan-first-lady-of-china-dimmed-her-star.html

85   https://www.youtube.com/watch?v=oP4I9LKANew and https://www.weforum.org/events/world-economic-forum-annual-meeting-2020/sessions/an-insight-an-idea-with-jin-xing-4e24e8770a

86   https://www.globaltimes.cn/page/202105/1223668.shtml

87   https://www.parklu.com/guochao-chinese-consumer-culture/

88   https://jingdaily.com/kols-impact-e-commerce/

89   https://medium.com/@aliciateolixia/where-content-meets-commerce-%E5%B0%8F%E7%BA%A2%E4%B9%A6-little-red-book-4bffa17f39f1

90   https://www.ted.com/talks/tasha_eurich_increase_your_self_awareness_with_one_simple_fix?language=en

91   https://www.telegraph.co.uk/travel/comment/rise-of-the-chinese-tourist/

92   GDPR = General Data Protection Regulation, a regulation in EU law on data protection and privacy in the European Union (EU) and the European Economic Area (EEA)

93   https://hbr.org/2021/05/chinas-new-innovation-advantage

94   https://www.scmp.com/news/china/society/article/3047753/chinese-premier-li-keqiang-arrives-wuhan-lead-coronavirus-fight

95   https://www.theregreview.org/2018/03/15/horsley-china-implements-participatory-rulemaking/

96   https://www.cfr.org/in-brief/social-media-and-online-speech-how-should-countries-regulate-tech-giants

97   https://techcrunch.com/2019/02/12/tencent-reddit-nononono/

98   https://theprint.in/india/shocked-by-bjp-membership-numbers-chinas-communist-party-wants-to-know-about-its-rise/289705/

99   https://www.aljazeera.com/news/2021/9/10/infographic-us-military-presence-around-the-world-interactive and https://www.esquire.com/news-politics/a38223198/united-states-veterans-day-at-war-afghanistan/

100 https://www.uscc.gov/sites/default/files/3.10.11Kaufman.pdf

101 https://www.eiu.com/n/campaigns/democracy-index-2020/

102 https://globalriskinsights.com/2016/12/china-not-a-walking-contradiction/

103 https://www.jerrymichalski.com/ and https://www.youtube.com/watch?v=BKmtBWYkERO

104 https://www.ips-journal.eu/in-focus/the-politics-of-memory/70-per-cent-good-30-per-cent-bad-2216/

105 https://www.britannica.com/topic/Liji

106 https://www.jstor.org/stable/j.ctvk3gng9.12?seq=2#metadata_info_tab_contents

107 Women's Federation – Fùlián 妇联

108 http://www.stats.gov.cn/tjsj/Ndsj/2011/html/D0305e.htm

109 neighbourhood committee – 居委会 jū wěi huì

110 https://www.chinadaily.com.cn/a/201911/15/WS5dce6bc4a310cf3e35577b6e.html

111 https://www.scmp.com/news/china/politics/article/3123174/xi-jinping-declares-extreme-poverty-has-been-wiped-out-china

112 https://www.scmp.com/economy/china-economy/article/3086678/china-rich-or-poor-nations-wealth-debate-muddied-conflicting

113 https://www.brookings.edu/blog/future-development/2021/01/25/deep-sixing-poverty-in-china/

114 https://www.statista.com/statistics/234578/share-of-migrant-workers-in-china-by-age/

115 https://onlinelibrary.wiley.com/doi/epdf/10.1002/psp.2008

116 The Gini coefficient is not perfect. For farmers, the income does not include, for example, production for their own maintenance. Capital does not include the right to work a piece of land. As a result, the coefficient is disproportionately high for a country with a lot of farmers, such as China.

117 人挪活 树挪死 Rén nuó huó shù nuó sǐ – Jin Xing speech weforum.

118 https://www.pascalcoppens.com/my-china-story/chinatrip91-93

119 https://oxfordre.com/asianhistory/oso/viewentry/10.1093$002facrefore$002f9780190277727.001.0001$002facrefore-9780190277727-e-13;jsessionid=250AE1E3680CC66D449C5B96E5F0E252

120 http://be.chineseembassy.org/eng/zt/xinjiangEN1/t1872293.htm

121 https://theculturetrip.com/asia/china/articles/the-canonical-works-the-four-classic-novels-of-chinese-literature/

122 Reference to Bruce Willis as John McClane in Die Hard.

123 https://www.state.gov/summit-for-democracy/

124 https://www.britannica.com/topic/nation-state

125 https://www.bbc.com/news/magazine-19929620

126 Democracy (from the Greek μ/dèmos, "people," and /kraine, "rule," so literally "popular rule") is a form of government in which the will of the people is the source of the legitimate exercise of power.

127 http://www.news.cn/english/2021-11/18/c_1310318394.htm

128 https://theprint.in/theprint-essential/not-just-india-tibet-china-has-17-territorial-disputes-with-its-neighbours-on-land-sea/461115/

129 https://www.usni.org/magazines/proceedings/2021/march/chinas-desert-storm-education

130 https://www.globaltimes.cn/page/202103/1217099.shtml

131 https://www.orwellfoundation.com/the-orwell-foundation/orwell/essays-and-other-works/notes-on-nationalism/

132 https://www.britannica.com/biography/Chiang-Kai-shek; and https://www.britannica.com/biography/Chiang-Ching-kuo

133 https://worldpopulationreview.com/country-rankings/countries-that-recognize-taiwan

134 https://www.scmp.com/tech/tech-war/article/3146523/chinas-privacy-law-borrows-page-europes-gdpr-it-goes-further-beijing

Endnotes

135 http://english.www.gov.cn/news/pressbriefings/202112/30/content_
     WS61cd9dcbc6d09c94e48a2f06.html

136 https://www.cashmatters.org/blog/globally-17-billion-people-did-not-have-bank-
     accounts-in-2017-world-bank-2018

137 The term comes from Chinese blockbuster movies (2015, 2017) called Wolf Warrior,
     which were patriotic, Rambo-style macho action movies. A strange combination of an
     individualistic, military Hollywood plot and the noble approach of Maoist socialism.

138 https://www.scmp.com/news/china/diplomacy/article/3122496/
     debt-trap-diplomacy-myth-no-evidence-china-pushes-poor-nations

139 https://www.scmp.com/news/world/africa/article/3089492/china-forgive-interest-
     free-loans-africa-are-coming-due-xi?module=inline&pgtype=article

140 https://www.cmi.no/publications/7750-chinese-aid-a-blessing-for-africa-and-a-
     challenge-to-western-donors

141 https://www.voanews.com/a/china-s-belt-and-road-initiative-is-about-profit-
     not-development-study-finds/6252992.html

142 https://www.scmp.com/news/china/diplomacy/article/3122496/
     debt-trap-diplomacy-myth-no-evidence-china-pushes-poor-nations

143 ttps://data.worldbank.org/indicator/NY.GNP.PCAP.CD?locations=ZG

144 https://scholarlycommons.law.case.edu/cgi/viewcontent.cgi?article=1644&context=jil

145 https://www.mfa.gov.cn/ce/cegv/eng/zywjyjh/t1683694.htm

146 https://www.mfa.gov.cn/ce/cebw//eng/xwdt/t541816.htm

147 http://english.www.gov.cn/archive/202007/28/content_
     WS5f1f8c45c6d029c1c2636d06.html

148 https://santandertrade.com/en/portal/analyse-markets/china/
     foreign-trade-in-figures?url_de_la_page=enportal
     analyse-marketschinaforeign-trade-in-figures

149 https://thediplomat.com/2016/11/a-chinese-perspective-on-obamas-asia-policy/

150 https://hal-hprints.archives-ouvertes.fr/hprints-01794264/document

151 https://inf.news/en/science/7283712b912c40e71152e6454685aac1.html

152 https://www.nature.com/articles/d41586-020-03434-7

153 https://www.chinadaily.com.cn/world/XiattendsParisclimateconference/2015-12/01/
     content_22592469.htm

154 https://www.rapidtransition.org/stories/how-china-brought-its-forests-back-to-
     life-in-a-decade/

155 https://www.bloomberg.com/news/articles/2020-07-03/china-s-era-of-mega-dams-
     is-ending-as-solar-and-wind-power-rise

156 Book *China Goes Green* by Yifei Li en Judith Shapiro, Polity Books, 2020

157 https://daxueconsulting.com/sustainable-consumption-china/

158 http://english.scio.gov.cn/pressroom/node_8026519.htm

159 https://medium.com/rreview/2001-a-space-odyssey-explained-228c2d551cbf

160 https://www.macrotrends.net/countries/CHN/china/military-spending-defense-budget

161 https://georgewbush-whitehouse.archives.gov/news/releases/2001/12/20011227-2.html

162 https://theconversation.com/myth-busted-chinas-status-as-a-developing-country-gives-it-few-benefits-in-the-world-trade-organisation-124602

163 https://www.nytimes.com/2001/07/14/sports/olympics-beijing-wins-bid-for-2008-olympic-games.html

164 http://www.china.org.cn/china/2012-12/24/content_27495894_2.htm

165 https://en.m.wikipedia.org/wiki/Core_Socialist_Values

166 https://asiasociety.org/china-learning-initiatives/learning-chinese-pays-dividends-characters-and-cognition

167 https://www.pwccn.com/en/research-and-insights/china-economic-quarterly-q1-2020-hot-topic.pdf

168 http://en.sasac.gov.cn/2021/08/03/c_7528.htm

169 https://www.ted.com/speakers/richard_wilkinson

170 https://www.lowyinstitute.org/the-interpreter/china-low-productivity-superpower

171 https://www.worldhistory.org/Mandate_of_Heaven/

172 http://www.martinjacques.com/articles/civilization-state-versus-nation-state-2/

Endnotes

www.ingramcontent.com/pod-product-compliance
Lightning Source LLC
Chambersburg PA
CBHW052015030426
42335CB00026B/3150